"We have been growing crops unsustainably on the land for at least one hundred years. Now we are making the same mistakes with agriculture in our oceans. The criminal multinational fishing corporations and their complicit politicians are actively harming the marine environment and pushing their toxic product to unaware consumers. After reading *Salmon Wars*, I doubt you will choose to eat net pen farmed salmon again."

—**Yvon Chouinard, founder of Patagonia**

"This excellent book is buoyed by deft portraits of the important players on either side of the nets—poignantly so in regard to some honest scientists whose careers were derailed by industry attacks—and its final chapters describe some hopeful initiatives now in progress." —*The Wall Street Journal*

"Leaping and struggling against the current, dodging hungry bears, mature salmon spawn where they themselves hatched, and then they die. That's the scene hungry shoppers imagine when they buy slabs of glowing pink fish at the local supermarket. But the reality of how that fish actually reached the table contradicts raw nature." —*Booklist*

"Impressively researched and absorbingly written, *Salmon Wars* will compel you to think again about the fish you love to eat so often for dinner."

—**Martin Baron, former editor of *The Washington Post***

"*Salmon Wars* is a deep dive into the damage caused by current fish-farming methods to ocean environments, wild fish and their habitats, and the farmed fish themselves. It is also an account of the dismal failure of governments to stop such practices. Salmon farming needs reform. Until it gets it, read this book, and you will never eat farmed salmon again."

—**Marion Nestle, author of *What to Eat***

"Absorbing . . . A compelling investigation that will leave consumers reevaluating their food choices." —*Kirkus Reviews* (starred review)

"In this impeccably researched dive into salmon farming, the authors . . . provide a searing account of toxic industrial practices, health risks and blatant disinformation. Their portrait of chemical-fed, pathogen-ravaged fish caged in pens (usually marketed as 'organic,' 'sustainable' and 'naturally raised') is convincing and devastating." —*Maclean's* **(Canada)**

"From cigarettes being tossed in a salmon pen to dark murky waters filled with litter, this is how America's favorite fish are being 'cared for.' *Salmon Wars* will open your eyes to cruelty that parallels puppy mills and all the things we, as Americans, stand against." —**Allen Ricca, coauthor of** ***Catching Hell: The Insider Story of Seafood from Ocean to Plate***

"*Salmon Wars* will change the way people look at the supermarket seafood counter. Frantz and Collins pierce the pastoral facade of Big Salmon and show what's really happening under the water." —**Bill Taylor, president, Atlantic Salmon Federation**

SALMON WARS

The Dark Underbelly of Our Favorite Fish

DOUGLAS FRANTZ

and

CATHERINE COLLINS

A HOLT PAPERBACK

HENRY HOLT AND COMPANY

NEW YORK

Holt Paperbacks
Henry Holt and Company
Publishers since 1866
120 Broadway
New York, New York 10271
www.henryholt.com

A Holt Paperback® and 🅗® are registered trademarks of Macmillan
Publishing Group, LLC.

The Library of Congress has cataloged the hardcover edition as follows:

Names: Frantz, Douglas, author. | Collins, Catherine, author.
Title: Salmon wars : the dark underbelly of our favorite fish / Douglas Frantz
    and Catherine Collins.
Description: First edition. | New York : Henry Holt and Company, 2022. |
    Includes bibliographical references and index.
Identifiers: LCCN 2022002894 (print) | LCCN 2022002895 (ebook) |
    ISBN 9781250800305 (hardcover) | ISBN 9781250800312 (ebook)
Subjects: LCSH: Salmon industry. | Fish as food.
Classification: LCC HD9469.S22 F73 2022 (print) | LCC HD9469.S22 (ebook) |
    DDC 338.3/713756—dc23/eng/20220128
LC record available at https://lccn.loc.gov/2022002894
LC ebook record available at https://lccn.loc.gov/2022002895

ISBN: 9781250871503 (trade paperback)

Our books may be purchased in bulk for promotional, educational, or
business use. Please contact your local bookseller or the Macmillan Corporate
and Premium Sales Department at (800) 221-7945, extension 5442,
or by email at MacmillanSpecialMarkets@macmillan.com.

Originally published in hardcover in 2022 by Henry Holt and Company

First Holt Paperbacks Edition 2023

Designed by Omar Chapa

Printed in the United States of America

1   3   5   7   9   10   8   6   4   2

In memory of Paul Collins, a dedicated fly fisherman

CONTENTS

Contents

SALMON WARS

INTRODUCTION

Every trip to the grocery store presents a dilemma. Which cereal do you buy? Are the chickens that laid the eggs really cage-free? What about trying that new plant-based meat? A hidden problem awaits at the seafood counter, though, when considering salmon.

This might seem surprising. Consumers have been told that salmon is a healthy and environmentally friendly food. Doctors recommend eating salmon for protein, nutrients, and heart-healthy omega-3 fatty acids. The U.S. Department of Agriculture suggests two servings of fish a week. The salmon's packaging may show a fish leaping upstream in pristine rivers and boast that it is a certified-natural product: "organic," "sustainable," "naturally raised." Sure, there are many salmon choices and little information to help consumers choose from among them, but shouldn't any fillet you buy be just fine? What's the problem?

To start with, in almost every case, the salmon in front of you spent its life in a cage and the marketer's claims are false. "Organic?" There is no USDA-approved definition of organic salmon, so that term is misleading at best. "Sustainable?" When farmed, salmon are carnivores raised on a diet heavy in small wild fish ground into meal and oil, which makes salmon inherently unsustainable. "Naturally raised?" Nothing is natural about feed laced with chemicals and antibiotics or fish swimming in crowded, parasite-plagued cages for two years or longer. Outside the alternative reality of marketing, the slabs of reddish flesh at the seafood counter have nothing to do with pristine waters or muscular salmon navigating upstream and everything to do with the industrialization of food in today's world.

Now, few Atlantic salmon remain in the wild anywhere. Rivers that once saw tens of thousands of returning fish currently count returns in double or single digits, even though groups like the Atlantic Salmon Federation and the North Atlantic Salmon Conservation Organization are working against heavy odds to restore salmon and their rivers. Look at the fine print on the label of the Atlantic salmon in your local market and you may see that it is farmed—if you are able even to find a label that identifies the origin of the fish. In fact, 90 percent of the salmon consumed by North Americans is farmed Atlantic salmon, raised in feedlots floating on the ocean and flown in from Canada, Scotland, Norway, and Chile; the remaining 10 percent is mostly wild-caught Pacific salmon from Alaska, one of the few places where wild salmon are still fished commercially.

We didn't always eat farmed salmon; we used to have a choice. There was a time when wild Atlantic salmon was known as the "king of fish." Ice Age humans painted images of salmon on cave walls in Dordogne, France. Caesar's legions brought the taste for salmon back to Roman markets. In North America, salmon was a principal food and cultural icon for Indigenous people, and it sustained early settlers from Europe. For millennia, millions of Atlantic salmon migrated three thousand miles from the freshwater rivers of what is now the northeastern United States and eastern Canada to the western coast of Greenland, where they fed and matured for years before following Earth's magnetic fields, their own genetic coding, and a strong sense of smell to return to their precise river of origin to spawn and create new generations. Variations on this journey were repeated across Europe, Scandinavia, and Russia, creating a sustainable food source and an enduring wonder of nature.

So, what went wrong? Why do we find ourselves eating unsustainably farmed salmon?

There are many culprits in the king's demise. Beginning during the Industrial Revolution in the late 1700s, waste was dumped directly into rivers and streams, and the seemingly inexhaustible stocks of salmon began to decline across Europe. By the mid-1800s, numbers were reduced further by commercial fishing and the construction of dams and mills that destroyed habitats and blocked salmon rivers. Within another century, and because of these continued activities, salmon that once numbered in the millions were nearly extinct in Europe and parts of Scandinavia—foreshadowing the disappearance that has left the rivers and streams of New England and Atlantic Canada nearly empty of salmon today. In recent decades, the climate crisis has warmed the oceans and rivers, industrial and municipal pollution has poisoned waterways, deforestation and chemicals like DDT have spoiled habitats, and intensive overfishing has decimated wild populations. And in the past forty years, a new threat emerged in the form of industrial-scale salmon farms in fragile coastal regions along salmon migration routes. The primary means of farming salmon is in large cages suspended in the ocean, known as open-net farms. Once seen as a means of taking pressure off overfished wild salmon, these farms turned out to pose a new, man-made danger.

As wild Atlantic salmon disappear, these floating feedlots have made salmon one of the world's most popular and inexpensive fish and have created a twenty-billion-dollar global industry. In Asia, North America, the United Kingdom, and Europe, what was once a luxury in restaurants or reserved for special occasions at home is eaten at millions of meals a day; a decade ago, salmon replaced tuna as the most popular fish in the American diet, second only to shrimp in seafood consumption.

But availability and cheapness come at great cost. What you consume today is not your parents' salmon; instead, it is bred to grow fast, raised in crowded pens, and fed a diet of dried pellets made from smaller fish and grains and laced with chemicals. Industrial-scale farms in coves and bays off the coasts of Norway, Scotland, Chile, and Canada harbor millions of salmon in cages. The only barrier between the cages and the environment is a net that allows the ocean to flush the pens. Excess feed, chemical residue, and fecal matter form a layer of slime on the seabed below the farms, smothering marine life and plants. Parasites and pathogens proliferate in the crowded cages and spread disease to wild fish. Hundreds of thousands of farmed fish escape each year, competing with wild salmon for habitat and food and interbreeding to produce hybrid fish too weak to survive.

Quite simply, the rise of salmon farms demonstrates the hubris in, and the price to be paid for, transforming a natural biological process into an industrial operation. And so, your choice at the seafood counter may be much more fraught than you thought—and it definitely matters.

A few years ago, and like most people, we regularly bought farmed salmon without giving much thought to its origins. We had read about the health benefits of salmon and other oily fish. Catherine had grown up eating Atlantic salmon caught by her father in eastern Canada. We knew that what we purchased at Costco or Whole Foods was not the same fish brought home by Catherine's father, but it was what was available and, surely, it must be fairly healthy, we thought. There was no way to question where that fish came from or to test its healthiness, was there? When we moved to Paris, we were fascinated by the fishmongers who noted the origin of each fish and the way it had been caught or harvested. We saw that there was a more informed way to put fish on our plates. Could we do that in North America? What were we doing instead? We didn't linger on these questions long.

Then, on a Sunday afternoon in January 2020 in Mahone Bay, Nova Scotia, a small coastal community a few minutes from our home, we went to a public meeting. A neighbor had sent us a notice that a group called the Twin Bays Coalition was holding a session to discuss plans by two multinational companies to locate more than twenty large open-net salmon farms along the coast of Nova Scotia. Nearly thirty years earlier, we had seen a single small salmon farm create a dead zone on the seabed in front of Catherine's parents' home on Nova Scotia's South Shore. The prospect of more farms was worrisome, and the warnings we heard in the crowded hall from environmentalists, lobster fishers, and ordinary folks reinforced our concerns.

We decided to do some research. We are curious, persistent, and skeptical, characteristics developed through many years as newspaper reporters, investigators for the U.S. government and law firms, and authors. But it did not take long for us to discover that the threat from the proposed salmon farms was bigger than we imagined, that the province's picturesque coastal waters would be at risk, and that the area's valuable lobster industry and dwindling number of wild salmon would be endangered. The idea for this book began to sink in.

We found scientific studies showing that, for all its promotion as a healthy source of protein and fatty acids, farmed salmon contains residues of pesticides and other chemicals that pose risks to humans, particularly fetuses and young children. What we learned about untreated waste was just plain gross. According to a study in 2003 by a coalition of advocacy groups known as the Pure Salmon Campaign, a salmon farm containing around 200,000 fish produces fecal matter roughly equivalent to a city of 65,000 people. Today's salmon farms hold up to a million fish. A 1989 study of Norwegian salmon farms estimated that the organic waste in the fjords that is generated by the production of 150,000 tons of fish equaled 60 percent of the waste generated by Norway's total population of 4.7 million people; today, Norway produces more than six times as much farmed salmon, and a lot more waste. Sewage and other waste cause far-reaching damage to the environment, contaminating the seabed and nearby marine life. A city must treat its sewage, but the farms dump the excrement and excess feed on the seabed. Waste beneath farms turns the ocean floor toxic, consuming oxygen needed by marine life and dispersing contaminants through the water. A 2014 study in Scotland found a reduction in biodiversity up to two hundred yards away from salmon cages; other studies described wider impacts on marine life and wild salmon. A single photograph on the internet sealed our commitment to this project: a yardstick plunged into the seabed beneath a salmon farm showed an accumulation of feces and excess feed reaching the thirty-two-inch mark.

For the next two years, we worked to understand the impact of open-net salmon farms on the health of the planet and its people and to delve into the inner workings of the oligopoly that controls the market and the quality of what ends up on our dinner tables. What we found was a new Wild West created by globe-straddling salmon-farming companies that operate outside meaningful regulation. The more we dug, the more the salmon-farming industry began to seem like a combination of Big Tobacco and Big Agribusiness. Just as cigarette manufacturers spent decades discrediting critics and concealing research, Big Fish employs counter-science and public relations campaigns to undermine scientists and environmentalists who challenge its practices and products. Just as agribusiness turned to hyperintensive farming of cattle, chickens, and pigs on land, salmon farming exploded from small operations to industrial-scale feedlots on water. This unchecked expansion occurred because regulation remains weak and because governments tend to promote salmon farming at the expense of the environment and the health of consumers.

Humans aren't the only ones being harmed by the status quo. Farmed salmon face their own staggering health risks from disease, parasites, and predators. In Norway, the government reported that 52 million fish died before harvest in 2020; the previous year, the figure was 53 million. In Scotland, the mortality rate for farmed salmon quadrupled between 2002 and 2019, according to government figures. In 2019 in Newfoundland, more salmon died in cages than were harvested. Norway and Scotland are the only salmon-farming countries that release mortality statistics, but estimates are that between 15 and 20 percent of all farmed salmon worldwide die each year before they can be harvested. By comparison, the U.S. National Chicken Council reports that its average mortality rate is 5 percent, and cattle feedlots average 3.3 percent.

Getting farmed salmon to the world's tables does not have to be this way. We found innovators raising Atlantic salmon in land-based, closed-containment facilities where chemicals and antibiotics are unnecessary and where there is no threat to wild salmon. Studies show that consumers are willing to pay a premium for products raised or manufactured without damaging the environment or endangering their health. Land-based salmon farmers are trying to leverage that sentiment into a market for a more environmentally friendly and healthier product. Challenges remain for this disruptive new technology, but it offers hope for the future of the industry—perhaps the only hope. But just as the auto industry fought mandatory safety innovations like seat belts and air bags, Big Fish resists the logical transition from ocean-based farms to cleaner and safer land-based operations.

This book is about what happened when the king of fish was dethroned and an industrial usurper took its place, degrading the environment and risking our health. The narrative takes readers from the origins of modern open-ocean salmon farming in the fjords of Norway to the shiny tanks in a pioneering land-based plant in southern Florida, from the industry's marketing hype to the dystopian vision of salmon farms below the waterline. We show how the collapse of a single farm in Puget Sound led to a ban on salmon farms in Washington State. We take readers to the rocky coast of Newfoundland, where three million caged salmon died in a single incident. We travel to the front lines in the battle between the open-net industry and a colorful resistance movement, describing an international struggle that has profound economic, regulatory, environmental, and health implications. Finally, our book charts the way forward toward a salmon industry with the capacity to feed the world responsibly—because the technology and the innovative solutions are out there.

Millions of people rely on fish for protein. The salmon they eat needs to be safe. For too long, the salmon-farming industry has wrapped itself in a cloak of virtue, asserting that it is feeding the world and putting healthy food on our tables while discrediting the science that paints a contrasting picture—and resisting the only viable way forward. This book shows what is happening and what you are actually eating—and how both could be much better. We hope the stories and hard data in these pages will inspire a movement toward a better way of producing healthy, sustainable salmon.

PART I

BIG FISH EAT LITTLE FISH

CHAPTER 1

CONSOLIDATING THE FORCES

Every summer, Gulfstreams, Boeings, and Bombardiers crowd the tarmac of the single-runway airport in Alta, a town on the northern coast of Norway. The private jets bring business tycoons, celebrities, and royalty to the Land of the Midnight Sun so they can cast a fly into the fabled Alta River, regarded by aficionados as one of the best remaining salmon rivers in the world. People wealthy enough to own hundred-million-dollar airplanes think nothing of paying ten thousand dollars a day for the chance to catch and release a twenty-pound wild Atlantic salmon. Mere mortals take their chances in a lottery for day licenses that cost around four hundred dollars.

For three days in July 2007, a private helicopter was parked alongside the jets. It belonged to billionaire John Fredriksen, the sixty-three-year-old son of a welder who grew up near the port in Oslo, left school at sixteen, and came to own the world's largest fleet of oil tankers. Over the decades, Fredriksen had built a ten-billion-dollar empire in oil tankers and global shipping. His holdings made him Norway's richest man—except that by 2007, he was no longer Norwegian. A year earlier, Fredriksen had relinquished his citizenship to become a subject of Cyprus, where taxes were far lower. Still, he returned regularly to cast his fly in the waters of the Alta in search of salmon befitting a master of the universe.

After three days on the river with his buddies, Fredriksen was contemplative as he prepared to board his helicopter. Rune Ostlyngen, a reporter for the local newspaper *Altaposten*, buttonholed him at the airport and asked about the contradiction of fly-fishing for wild salmon while owning salmon farms contributing to their demise. Fredriksen's response was surprising: "I am worried about the future of wild salmon. Fish farming should not be allowed in fjords where wild salmon are present in local rivers. What is happening here in fjords is not good."

Fredriksen's words resounded through the industry and among conservationists. A year earlier, he had acquired control of Marine Harvest, the largest salmon farmer in a fragmented industry. The company, which was later renamed Mowi, operated open-net salmon farms in countries ranging from Norway and Scotland to Canada and the United States. Many of those farms were along the migratory paths of wild salmon and adjacent to sensitive breeding grounds for lobster, crab, and other marine life. The spread of disease and escaped farmed salmon pose serious threats to the declining population of wild salmon on the Alta River and every other place where farms are located near migration paths.

Fredriksen could not have predicted the response to his spontaneous expression of support for moving salmon farms away from salmon rivers. A wave of hope spread through the passionate corps of people desperate to save the world's wild salmon. Conservationists, environmentalists, and anglers alike greeted his comment with unbridled optimism. Thirty-three conservation groups from six countries wrote a letter praising Fredriksen for what they interpreted as a promise to move his farms out of sensitive waters. Politicians and fishing associations in the United States, Canada, Scotland, and Norway heaped accolades on him. "Mr. Fredriksen's call to move salmon farms hopefully comes just in time to save wild Atlantic salmon populations in the whole of Norway," said Sven-Helge Pedersen, a wild salmon advocate from a region of Norway where the fish were disappearing from every river.

They should have saved their breaths.

Historians trace the first fish farms to China as early as 3000 BC, when carp were trapped and kept in ponds. Around 475 BC, a Chinese historian named Fan Lai wrote an instructional book called *The Classic of Fish Culture*, the first written record of aquaculture practices. The history of modern salmon farming, however, is relatively brief. In 1733, a German fish farmer successfully fertilized fish eggs to cultivate fish, the beginning of modern aquaculture. For the next two centuries, fishermen in Northern Europe and Scotland maintained small salmon pens for local markets. But the practice of raising just a few hundred salmon in a pen would be extinguished by the industrialization of food production.

Conflicting stories are told about how commercial salmon farming got its start. The consensus is that Norwegians were at the forefront, but exactly which Norwegians is debated. There is general agreement that Jay Laurence Lush, an American animal geneticist regarded as the father of livestock breeding, provided the road map that led to the faster-growing, domesticated version of salmon that is now the industry standard. In 1963, Lush was teaching at Iowa State University when he met a young graduate student from Norway named Trygve Gjedrem. Captivated by Lush's theory, the Norwegian returned home and applied Lush's breeding principles to fish farming in 1971.

At about the same time, Thor Mowinckel was floating rudimentary salmon pens in the sea along Norway's western coast. His first attempt was a total loss when a storm wiped out the pens and the salmon escaped. He moved the pens to a protected inlet about a mile away and started over. In 1971, Mowinckel harvested sixty metric tons of salmon, enough that most industry historians credit him with officially starting the commercial salmon-farming business.

Mowinckel named his company Mowi. In the years that followed, Mowi produced half of all the farmed salmon in Norway. After a merger, the company was renamed Hydro Seafood, and it shifted its headquarters to Bergen, the closest big city. Surrounded by mountains and fjords, Bergen would emerge as the home of salmon farming, as companies based there came to dominate the growing global market.

In those early years, Hydro Seafood and its competitors located their salmon pens in hundreds of deep, cold inlets along Norway's southwestern coast. As the numbers of salmon in individual pens increased, the farmers found that the inlets did not provide enough water flow to keep the crowded cages clean and the fish free of parasites. The turning point came in 1987.

Hydro Seafood's pens had attracted infestations of sea lice, tiny oval crustaceans that attach themselves to salmon and feed off the mucous, blood, and thin skin of the fish. Though smaller than a fingernail, these parasites can literally eat a fish alive. Sea lice occur naturally in the wild but pose a limited danger. Wild salmon are constantly moving, and the rush of water knocks off most lice. Also, wild salmon weakened by lice become easy prey for predators, which minimizes the spread of lice to other fish and keeps the numbers of lice low.

What Hydro Seafood discovered was that thousands of salmon jammed into cages attracted high concentrations of sea lice. Swarms of parasites attacked farmed salmon, and the sickened fish died and sank to the bottom of the cages, steadily increasing the concentration of lice. Hydro Seafood, and eventually other big farmers, tried to solve the problem by moving their cages farther from the shore. The hope was that the stronger tides would sweep away the parasites, or at least reduce their numbers to a manageable size. It did not work, and as the industry has grown, so has the damage inflicted by sea lice.

When Fredriksen arrived on the scene, twenty or so medium-size companies were producing most of the world's farmed Atlantic salmon, and consolidation was just getting underway. Small farmers still existed, but they were struggling. As Fredriksen acquired more companies, he changed the industry forever, accelerating consolidation, paving the way for a small number of multinational companies to control salmon farming and, ultimately, creating greater environmental problems.

Dissecting the early deals can be dizzying, but think of big fish eating little fish. In a series of multimillion-dollar transactions, Fredriksen gained control of Marine Harvest, a collection of companies that included the successor to Thor Mowinckel's Mowi. Fredriksen had no experience in aquaculture, but he understood the value of concentrating production and power. With the acquisition of Marine Harvest in 2006, he was poised to become the major player in salmon farming. At the time, the company was based in the Netherlands, and the Norwegian press greeted Fredriksen as a national hero when he brought the headquarters home to Bergen. Norway dominated salmon farming. Its biggest advantage was geographic: the natural conditions that exist along its more than fifty thousand miles of coastline provided deep, cold waters. Another factor, however, was the cooperation among the government, scientists, and industry in providing support that turned salmon into Norway's second-largest export (after oil) and a point of national pride.

One of Fredriksen's rare setbacks occurred in 2013. Eager to solidify Marine Harvest's dominance, he launched an unsolicited bid for Cermaq, a salmon-farming company controlled by the Norwegian government and ranked third in size behind Marine Harvest and another Norwegian company, Leroy Seafood Group. Fredriksen was determined to control the market for farmed salmon the way he had for oil tankers. Cermaq was a good fit because it had significant operations in Chile, a place where Marine Harvest had no presence.

The government rejected the offer as too low, and the Oslo stock market reacted by sending Cermaq's stock higher. Fredriksen had put Cermaq in play, but he eventually lost out to Mitsubishi Corporation, part of the giant Tokyo-based Mitsubishi Group. Mitsubishi already dominated the global tuna-fishing industry, and with farmed salmon rising in popularity in Japan and elsewhere, its executives saw Cermaq as a means of expanding its holdings in Chile and gaining a foothold in Canada, where Cermaq also operated salmon farms.

Fredriksen's star was also dimming among environmentalists, who eventually understood that he had no intention of protecting wild salmon in Norway or anywhere else. He'd said that salmon farms shouldn't be allowed near wild salmon, but given that it was allowed, you did not need a crystal ball to know that the voracious tycoon was not going to put fish welfare ahead of profits. Today, Mowi, the successor to Marine Harvest, owns farms everywhere wild salmon struggle to survive. The number and size of the farms have grown, the number of salmon crammed into each pen has risen, and concerns about the impact on the environment, the well-being of the fish, and the health risks of eating farmed salmon have increased, too.

Rather than opening the door to a new way of doing business by protecting wild salmon and the environment, the consolidation sparked by Fredriksen changed everything. Open-net salmon farming might have had minimal impact on the environment and the fate of wild salmon if it had continued at a small scale. But the big companies bought up the little operations and turned them into industrial-scale feedlots. Fredriksen did not start the trend, but he accelerated the mutation of a noble fish into a domesticated commodity no different from the oil carried by his fleet of tankers. Open-net salmon farms spread from the major producers, such as Norway, Chile, Scotland, and Canada, to include smaller operations in Ireland, the Faroe Islands, Iceland, New Zealand, and Tasmania.

Growing at a breakneck pace, salmon farming became a high-yield, high-profit part of the global industrial food chain. While consumers saw the price of salmon in restaurants and markets going down, the biggest beneficiaries were the industry's biggest owners. Buoyed by the low cost of starting farms, and supported by handouts from governments eager for jobs, the big salmon companies were earning huge sums providing a product widely accepted as sustainable and healthy.

The result of consolidation is a dystopian vision. Like factory farms invented in the 1960s for beef, chickens, and pigs, today's salmon farms are designed to raise fish quickly, cheaply, and with minimal capital investment. Overcrowded pens and overused antibiotics and chemicals in beef and pig feedlots have led to reforms. Similar concerns about global salmon farming have been largely ignored by the industry, government regulators, and people who eat farmed salmon. The main reason for the difference is that the manure and muck of a feedlot for cattle and pigs are easily visible, but the crowded cages and environmental degradation caused by salmon farms are unseen, below the waterline.

Today, aquaculture is the world's fastest-growing food-production system. At its most basic, the practice involves raising fish, shrimp, and mussels in cages, ponds, streams, and pens on the ocean. In the last thirty years or so, aquaculture has contributed to the rise in human consumption of fish and has developed a range of species that can be farmed efficiently and sustainably because their diet consists of plants and grains.

Still, there are downsides, ranging from pollution to the overuse of antibiotics and chemicals that often find their way into the human food chain. When it comes to farming salmon, the negatives are greater than the positives. Salmon are carnivores; feeding them smaller fish contributes to pillaging the oceans and deprives people in lower-income countries of food essential to their survival. Salmon farms also spread diseases to wild fish and pollute waters with excess feed and waste.

Think of a salmon farm as an iceberg: you can see only about 10 percent of it on the surface. Unlike the majestic beauty of an iceberg, though, an open-net salmon farm is ugly on the surface and worse below the waterline, where fish are confined in mesh cages that are often choked with mussels, seaweed, and other growth. Below these pens, the seafloor is fetid with feces, chemical residue, and parasites. It is a study in environmental degradation.

Nine out of ten Atlantic salmon are produced in these open-net pens floating in bays and coves along coastlines. A single salmon farm generally contains ten to twelve cages, also called pens or net pens. The cages are spread across an area slightly wider and longer than a football field. Each cage can contain up to one hundred thousand fish, meaning a farm can have a million salmon. The cages are arrayed side by side and suspended by floatation devices. A small barge attached to the farm contains a generator to keep the lights on at night and to power the automated feeding machines. Nets are made of nylon mesh arranged in a tight grid pattern designed to keep the fish inside and keep out predators like tuna, sharks, and whales. The nets are anchored to the seabed by mooring cables. In addition, mesh nets cover the pens to keep birds away when the salmon are young. Cages can be square or rectangular, but most are circular, roughly ninety-five feet in diameter and thirty-three feet deep. Below the surface, the mooring lines must be long enough to allow the cages to move with the current and tides, extending the boundaries of the farm. Buoys mark the outer perimeter of the farm, which can cover as much as one hundred acres, and fishing boats and other craft are prohibited from entry.

After the eggs are fertilized and the young salmon are raised in hatcheries on land, they move to the ocean pens and spend two years or longer maturing in cages. Automated arms feed the fish a diet of a fish meal made from wild-caught fish and grains ground into pellets often laced with antibiotics and chemicals. No barrier exists to prevent the discharge of waste, excess feed, parasites, or chemicals into the surrounding water. Farms are usually clustered within a few hundred yards of shore, in sheltered coves to protect them from stormy seas and to allow workers easy access by boat. Ideally, these locations are designed to take advantage of ocean currents that flow through the open nets, providing oxygen and dispersing waste from excess feed, excrement, and chemicals. But they are more like sewers. The water tends to be shallow, with weaker currents and lower rates of water exchange, allowing waste and effluent to build up along wild salmon migration routes and near sensitive breeding and feeding grounds for sea creatures like lobsters, crabs, and scallops.

Tucked along the fjords of Norway or the coves of Puget Sound, the farms appear benign from the surface. Salmon can be seen swimming in circles, occasionally leaping out of the water. Beneath the waterline is a different story. Scuba divers who maintain the pens say that the nets can become clogged by mussels and other marine life, making them almost impenetrable. In videos, the clogging—known as biofouling—is so dense that the nets essentially become walls, impeding the flow of water and leaving pens murky with excrement, food waste, and decaying fish. Sharks and tuna sometimes breach the netting in search of food, only to be killed by divers with handmade spears or workers on the rigs with shotguns. Those carcasses are dumped into the ocean, often in violation of government regulations.

The ability to discharge freely into the water allows salmon farmers to avoid costly waste treatment. Those savings are part of the allure of open-net salmon farming for investors. Initial investments and operating costs for ocean-based facilities are low. Profit margins can exceed 50 percent. But those corporations are freeloaders. The real costs, paid by society, are much higher. Leases for public land (that is, the ocean floor below the farms itself) are inexpensive. In many places, taxpayer-financed government subsidies encourage expansion and, when things go wrong, cushion the industry from losses. The world supply of Atlantic salmon has increased nearly 500 percent since 1995, reaching nearly 2.6 million metric tons in 2020. (One metric ton is equal to 2,204 pounds.) Demand has remained strong because the fish seems cheap and because experts praise its health benefits. From a business perspective, salmon farming has surpassed all predictions.

The allure is simple, and simply wrong. Salmon farming is part of an industrial food chain with enormous hidden costs that range from damaging the environment and threatening wild salmon to saturating the market with fish whose flesh contains higher concentrations of toxins and cancer-causing polychlorinated biphenyls (PCBs) than that of wild salmon. The industry's growth has led to overfishing of sardines, herring, anchovies, and other small fish used in feed, taking marine resources away from subsistence fishers in low-income countries along the coast of West Africa and diminishing the staples of local diets. The salmon-farming industry has made limited progress in replacing fish meal and fish oil with alternative protein sources like plants and insects, but rising demand for salmon has maintained pressure on the fish down the food chain. People who eat farmed salmon are literally taking food from the mouths of the less fortunate.

As global demand for salmon grew and industry consolidation continued, farms became larger and more crowded. The jammed cages reflected the industry's axiom: The more fish you grow, the more money you make. The common industry response to criticism about overcrowding is that salmon like to congregate. Marine biologists, however, say wild salmon swim in large schools only to ward off predators by appearing to be a single, larger fish.

Greater density in cages translated into greater parasite problems, creating what has been called "sea lice soup." Salmon have been found with hundreds of these parasites eating away skin and flesh. One biologist counted 747 lice on a single fish. The lice can be so numerous that at some fish-processing plants, workers use Shop-Vacs to remove them from incoming salmon. Large numbers of lice on a salmon cause loss of fins, scarring, open lesions, secondary infections, and, in some cases, death. Badly scarred fish are less marketable, though some show up in stores. A wide-ranging analysis of the costs of salmon farming by Just Economics, a research organization in London, estimated that the ten largest companies have spent between $3.5 billion and $4 billion combating sea lice since 2013 and that lice caused 30 percent of farmed-salmon mortalities.

For the companies, dead salmon are a cost of doing business, tallied in antiseptic terms like *biomass*. From a humane perspective, the numbers are staggering. An average of 15 to 20 percent of farmed salmon die every year before harvest—about 150,000 dead salmon at each farm every year, roughly 100 million worldwide. Catastrophic losses have become so common that the industry has a name for them: "mortality events." In 2019, a die-off at ten farms owned by a subsidiary of Mowi in Newfoundland, Canada, killed as many as 3 million salmon and littered beaches with rotting fish for miles. Similar die-offs occur regularly at salmon farms worldwide.

The danger of sea lice concentrations extends beyond the cages, threatening wild salmon and other sea life in the vicinity. The most vulnerable are migratory juvenile wild salmon, called smolts. Salmon are born in rivers, where they live for one to three years. From late spring until early summer, the smolts migrate to salt water and the ocean. The smolts are still small when they begin their journey, three to six inches long, and their scales and skin are soft. On the way to the ocean, the smolts often must pass by farmed-salmon cages. The timing is bad because sea lice are shedding larvae in the same months, creating a gauntlet of millions of microscopic lice for the smolts to navigate. Even a few lice can prove fatal to a young smolt.

The dramatic expansion of salmon farming has led to another problem: escapees. Countless studies have shown that escaped farmed salmon pose a major threat to the declining population of wild salmon. They compete for food and interbreed to produce hybrids that are less able to survive in the wild. The twin threats of sea lice and interbreeding are why conservationists were momentarily buoyed by Fredriksen's comments in the summer of 2007 and let down when it became apparent that he had no intention of moving his farms.

The salmon-farming practices that have come with consolidation and skyrocketing growth impose a high cost not just to the environment, but also to the world economy. The 2021 analysis by Just Economics, called *Dead Loss: The High Cost of Poor Salmon Farming Practices*, concluded that, since 2013, poor salmon-farming practices have cost the global economy $47 billion in damage to marine ecosystems through pollution, the spread of disease and parasites, and the high mortality rates of fish in cages. Focusing on the four major salmon-farming countries of Canada, Chile, Norway, and Scotland, the assessment found that fish mortality had increased dramatically and so had the cost of treating salmon for sea lice and other diseases. According to Just Economics, Mowi alone lost fifty million salmon between 2010 and 2019, at a cost of $1.7 billion.

Despite those losses, the industry remains highly profitable. The *Dead Loss* study estimated its value at $20 billion a year, a figure that a spokesperson for Mowi seized on to applaud the study: "We are pleased that the report finds that, when considering the full range of benefits and impacts, the business of salmon farming demonstrates overall positive benefits. We agree that there are opportunities for continued improvements for our business."

No one has personally profited from and promoted the benefits of salmon farming more than Glenn Cooke. With only a high school education, he transformed a small family operation in Canada into the world's largest independent salmon-farming company. It's time we met him.

CHAPTER 2

CONQUERING CANADA

Glenn Cooke, a stocky, damp-looking man with wispy hair and a fleshy face, sat silently while a makeup artist glued a sparse goatee to his chin, fit a dark wig on his large head, and carefully placed rimless eyeglasses on his face. His disguise complete, Cooke walked down the stairs to the foyer of his home. His two young children and his wife, Pamela, greeted him with giggles. His parents looked on silently.

Cooke is confident, someone who follows his passions without glancing in the rearview mirror. That day, he was preparing for his starring role in an episode of *Undercover Boss Canada*, a reality show in which high-level executives assume fake identities for candid looks inside their own companies. Cooke's weeklong star turn would take him to four locations of his business, where he would pose as a forestry expert working on a documentary about aquaculture.

"You think people will know who I am?" he joked as he headed out the door to start his undercover adventure.

There was a time when few people would have recognized Glenn Cooke. That was before he turned a small fish farm in his hometown into the world's largest privately owned salmon-farming company; before he acquired more than one hundred million fish in farms and hatcheries in four countries; before he boasted sales topping $2.4 billion a year in seventy countries; before he owned most of the salmon farms in the United States; before his partnership with food maven Martha Stewart; and before Canada's largest newspaper dubbed him "business royalty."

Cooke loves to tell the story of his humble beginnings. He grew up in the tiny town of Blacks Harbour, New Brunswick, on the western shore of Canada's Bay of Fundy, a vast inlet of the Atlantic Ocean between the provinces of New Brunswick and Nova Scotia that touches Maine. The bay extends ninety-four miles inland and is thirty-two miles wide at its entrance. Among the hundreds of islands in the bay, the most famous is Campobello, where President Franklin D. Roosevelt spent his summers. The bay is famous for boasting the world's highest tides (with a range as high as seventy feet), which constantly flush and churn nutrients into the salt water to support a rich marine ecosystem. Twelve species of whales spend summers in the bay, feeding on the krill, squid, and herring there. Grey seals, porpoises, and white-sided dolphins are attracted by the herring, pollock, and mackerel. The occasional wild salmon traverses these waters to reach its spawning grounds in the freshwater rivers that empty into the bay.

When Cooke was a boy in the 1970s, Blacks Harbour was the quintessential "company town," dominated by a sardine producer called Connors Bros. The company owned the houses, streets, and surrounding land. It paid the police and fire departments and operated the generator that supplied the town's electricity. If you lived there, you rented from Connors Bros. If you wanted a job, you went to work for Connors Bros. Cooke grew up in a house rented from Connors Bros., just as his grandparents had. His father worked as a marine mechanic for the company. It was a class system that persisted for generations, and the Cooke family lived well below the top rung.

When he graduated from high school in 1983, Cooke was determined to be his own man. He turned to the only business he knew: fish. "I just had this aching to get into business," he told the Toronto *Globe and Mail*. "The first business I was involved in was a failure. I bought and sold seafood around the world. You're 18 years old and think you have the world by the tail but it's not possible." He turned to farming mussels and to a few other sideline businesses. Those failed, too. "I didn't have the knowledge or experience to do what I was doing," Cooke conceded.

After two years of failures, Cooke tackled one last venture. He convinced his father to provide a nest egg and partnered with his brother, Michael, to start Kelly Cove Salmon Farm. They started small, with two cages in the Bay of Fundy and five thousand salmon. Cooke would later say that he took care of the business, Michael managed the operations, and their father kept them on track.

"As a young fellow you dream big dreams and I've always had big dreams," he told the newspaper. "We struggled through. At the time there were about 35 players in the aquaculture industry in New Brunswick. As people failed or wanted out, we kept acquiring and building. We are big believers, maybe it's from Scottish background, in reinventing our business."

Cooke's timing could not have been better. Atlantic Canada's commercial fishing industry, long a mainstay of its economy, began a sharp decline in the early 1970s. For four hundred years, the Georges Bank, an oval submerged shelf larger than Massachusetts that sits off the coasts of Cape Cod and Nova Scotia, had been one of the world's richest fisheries, home to cod, halibut, and herring. In the 1960s and '70s, fleets of Soviet, European, and Japanese factory ships began trawling the bottom of the bank, scooping up cod and other fish before they could reproduce. Herring were virtually wiped out; cod and other fish were devastated. The United States and Canada both extended their territorial boundaries to two hundred miles offshore and signed a bilateral treaty in 1979 to protect their fisheries, but the damage had been done. When wild Atlantic salmon began to disappear about the same time, the Canadians were determined to find a way to take the pressure off salmon fisheries and preserve the remaining fish. They turned to aquaculture.

Across the Atlantic in Norway and Scotland, salmon farming was becoming a good business, creating jobs and exports. With 25 percent of the world's coastlines and countless bays and coves, Canada seemed like a natural location for the promising new enterprise. In 1979, a Canadian team of marine biologists went to Norway to learn. They returned with big plans, and the first Atlantic salmon cages were put in the Bay of Fundy late that year. The cages were near the Department of Fisheries and Oceans' biological station at St. Andrews, New Brunswick, where the biologists could monitor them. The location seemed to make sense: strong currents and high tides in the bay offered a healthy environment for the fish. At least as important, the farms would be close to Maine, a transit point for quick access to the big markets in Boston and the entire Eastern Seaboard. Even the Atlantic Salmon Federation, an international organization founded in 1948 to conserve and restore wild Atlantic salmon, supported the concept, and it worked with the fledgling industry in Canada to get the ball rolling.

In the pioneering days, salmon farming was the province of small operators in the bays and coves of eastern Canada. The momentum changed in 1985, when the government imposed a moratorium on commercial salmon fishing in response to dramatic declines in the wild population. Shutting down the commercial fishing industry increased pressure to develop a bigger salmon-farming industry. The government responded by pouring millions of dollars into research and subsidies to expand the fledgling industry in the sparsely populated coastal provinces of New Brunswick and Nova Scotia. From a government perspective, salmon farming offered increased tax revenue, jobs in rural areas, and a means of protecting the remaining wild salmon.

Inka Milewski was there at the beginning. The young marine biologist arrived in St. Andrews in 1983 to take a job at the federal biological station there. "I witnessed the emergence of aquaculture in Atlantic Canada," said Milewski, now a researcher at Dalhousie University in Halifax, Nova Scotia. "This is where it started, and hopes were so high." Milewski spent seven years working in St. Andrews. The industry grew steadily, but so did the problems. Everywhere that open-net salmon farms were located, the same set of challenges arose. Caged salmon were attracting parasites and diseases in numbers never seen in the wild. Farmers responded by pumping larger and larger amounts of antibiotics, pesticides, and other chemicals into the feed and water.

In addition, for an industry marketed as sustainable and healthy, the ratio of feed to farmed salmon was off the charts in the wrong direction. Salmon are carnivores, and they were fed pellets made largely from smaller fish ground into meal, fish oil, and grains. In the early years, farms often required 3 or more pounds of feed to produce a single pound of salmon. In the last decade, improvements in feed reduced the ratio to less than 1.5 pounds of feed to produce a pound of salmon. The feed conversion ratio for salmon is slightly better than that for chickens and roughly four times more efficient than that for cattle. There is, however, a key difference: chickens and cattle eat grains, a plentiful and recurring resource, while farmed salmon eat smaller fish, a diminishing and hard-to-restore resource worldwide. As the industry has grown, demand for salmon feed has depleted the smaller fish that are staples of the diets of millions of people in lower-income countries.

The existential question for government regulators is how to balance the scales between economic growth and protecting the environment. In the short term, economic development translates into jobs for people and revenue for governments. Yet the overuse of natural resources to drive development creates risks of long-term damage to the environment, which in the case of salmon farming leads to the destruction of other marine-based businesses and job losses. Policy makers and regulators in salmon-farming countries have tilted heavily toward promoting the industry at the expense of the environment, wild salmon, and other marine life.

Nowhere was this trend more evident than in Canada with the push in the 1980s to encourage salmon farming to ease pressure on wild salmon and provide jobs for coastal communities desperate for economic development. Between 1985 and 1996, the Canadian government's business-promotion agency pumped $75 million into the industry, and the federal Department of Fisheries and Oceans financed research into how to grow fish faster in cages. The department, known by its initials DFO, has a dual, inherently conflicting role: promoting aquaculture and protecting the oceans. Like their counterparts in Norway, DFO officials placed their bet on salmon farming and were determined to make it work. Protecting the oceans took a back seat.

"The industry is the child of the federal government," Milewski said. "That is important because the government has facilitated, through its regulations and policies, the growth of the industry but resisted acknowledging the harm. The government has spent too much to back away." As often happens when humans tinker with nature, the law of unintended consequences turned plans for a new industry into a threat to both the environment and the survival of wild salmon.

Some early supporters began to sour on salmon farming as the harm became more evident. Milewski turned into a fierce critic, eventually producing a groundbreaking study showing the damage done to lobsters and their breeding grounds by pollution from a single salmon farm in a small bay on Nova Scotia's South Shore. The Atlantic Salmon Federation changed its position, too, advocating tighter regulations and a prohibition on new farms where wild Atlantic salmon were present because of the increasing threat of disease and genetic contamination of wild fish.

Don Ivany joined the federation, known by its initials ASF, just as its views were shifting. He said the ASF's early thinking that farmed salmon could meet consumer demand and ease the pressure on wild salmon had been proven wrong. "ASF got involved on the research side, but once the industry really started up, we realized the side effects," said Ivany, who has headed ASF's office in Corner Brook, Newfoundland, for thirty years. "It was an experiment that went wrong, and we recognized it as such."

Across the border in the United States, salmon farms began appearing in Maine and Washington State, where they would introduce the same problems as their counterparts in Norway, Scotland, and Canada.

Glenn Cooke rode the salmon-farming wave. Like his family, dozens of people living around the Bay of Fundy had obtained licenses and leases for a few hundred dollars from the government and set up small salmon farms. At one point, there were roughly a hundred operations around the bay. As was happening in Norway, however, the industry began to consolidate. Some farmers failed because they were not good managers, and others did not have the capital to reach the scale demanded by the increasingly global market. By 1998, the number of farmers was down in New Brunswick, and Cooke was the largest.

Cooke Aquaculture, as the company was known by then, went on a buying spree. Between 1989 and 2004, the company bought twelve competitors in the Atlantic Canadian provinces of New Brunswick, Nova Scotia, and Prince Edward Island, and in Maine. The first purchase was a bankrupt fish hatchery, and the second was a fish-processing plant in receivership. Those acquisitions integrated its business, allowing Cooke to grow its own salmon from eggs and process the mature fish for the commercial market under its own brand, True North Salmon.

Glenn Cooke, not yet forty years old and the company's chief executive officer, was just getting started. In 2005, Weston Foods, a public company and a giant in Canada's food service and distribution industry, was bleeding money at its Heritage Salmon subsidiary. The Toronto-based company blamed the losses on an oversupply of farmed salmon that was driving prices down, outbreaks of disease among salmon stocks, and recent news reports suggesting that farm-raised salmon contained PCBs and other toxins. The potential existence of toxins in farmed salmon was especially sensitive because Weston owned one of Canada's largest supermarket chains, a far more lucrative part of its portfolio. When Weston put Heritage on the block in early 2005, Cooke bought its salmon farms in New Brunswick and Maine. With this biggest acquisition to date, Cooke doubled the size of his company and removed a major competitor overnight. Suddenly, he was the dominant salmon farmer in North America.

Cooke's relentless growth mirrored the consolidation occurring in the industry globally. The drive to capture market share led to more farms and more fish squeezed into cages. The crowded pens meant bigger profits, but they also increased the threat from sea lice. As the parasites developed resistance to some chemicals, salmon farmers resorted to more powerful pesticides. Many of those chemicals can be fatal to nearby marine life, including lobsters. This did not stop Glenn Cooke.

CHAPTER 3

POISONING YOUR OWN BACKYARD

For hundreds of years, the Bay of Fundy has shaped the lives of generations who live along its shores and on its islands. The first residents were Indigenous people from the Mi'kmaq, the Algonquin, the Atikamekw, the Nipissing, the Ottawa, and the Ojibwa tribes. They were eventually joined (and largely displaced) by European settlers. Bryant Green has spent more than half a century on the bay, hauling lobsters up from the bottom and eventually bringing his son, Derek, into the business.

Shortly after dawn on a chilly December morning, Bryant and Derek pulled out of the harbor at Deer Island on their forty-foot lobster boat. They were headed for a sheltered cove nearby where they stored their lobsters in a mostly submerged pen known as a "car." The Greens kept their lobsters in the car until they had enough to take them to a wholesaler. The trip to the holding cage was routine, something Bryant and Derek did every couple of weeks in the three-month lobster season. But there was nothing routine about what Green and his son found that morning.

The 2009 winter lobster season was coming to an end. It had been a tough year: prices were low, and every lobster counted. The Greens figured they had about seven hundred to eight hundred pounds of lobster stored in crates stacked inside the car, worth between three thousand and four thousand dollars. As they began to haul the crates out of the water, Bryant noticed something amiss. Normally, the lobsters would have been scrabbling and aggressively waving their claws as they emerged. "The minute you saw them, you could tell something was wrong," he recalled years later, the memory still vivid. "They couldn't move. All of them seemed like they were nearly dead or dying."

The Greens were shocked as they loaded the lobster carcasses onto the boat and took them to the wharf. The wholesaler was puzzled about what had happened, too. Clearly the lobsters could not be sold, so the Greens got nothing for a month of hard work. Bryant Green was angry, about both the lost money and the senseless death of the lobsters. Determined to find the cause, he notified the federal Department of Fisheries and Oceans. They instructed him to put some of the lobsters on ice for later examination. DFO passed the information on to the regional office of Environment Canada, the federal agency in charge of maintaining the country's waterways.

What the Greens did not know was that four similar incidents had occurred in other locations around the bay two weeks earlier. In mid-November, four commercial fishers had discovered dead lobsters in traps set in four separate locations near Grand Manan Island, about fifty miles from Deer Island. A sample of those lobsters had been taken to the local fishermen's association, which had put them on ice and notified Environment Canada. No one was certain what was killing the lobsters, but the prime suspects were the dozens of open-net salmon farms scattered along the bay's miles and miles of coastline.

The reconstruction of the government's investigation of Cooke Aquaculture here is based on official documents and interviews with people involved in the case. The only publicly available record was an "Agreed Statement of Facts," which was submitted to the court by the prosecution and defense at the close of the criminal case. The statement listed fifteen Cooke farms where the insecticide cypermethrin had been detected by inspectors over several months, describing its impact on lobsters. Extensive additional records were obtained from people associated with the investigation, including a forty-nine-page affidavit for the search warrant of Cooke offices that provided a detailed chronology of the investigation and the conclusions of the investigators.

The dead lobsters from the first four incidents had been delivered to Robert Robichaud, the senior enforcement investigator at Environment Canada's regional office in Moncton, New Brunswick. He sent them to the agency's regional laboratory for testing. He suspected that they might have been killed by cypermethrin, a pesticide banned for marine use in Canada because of the threat it poses to lobsters, shrimp, and other crustaceans. There was long-standing evidence that salmon farmers in the Bay of Fundy were using the pesticide illegally to fight infections of sea lice in the pens. But there had never been a formal investigation. Robichaud, an aggressive investigator who would later become regional head of enforcement, decided to dig into the incidents near Grand Manan.

On December 4, Robichaud was out on the bay collecting samples at salmon farms near the four sites where the dead lobsters had been found in November when he got a call from the office in Moncton. He was told that a couple hundred dead lobsters had been reported to the DFO. Robichaud recognized the potential significance of the much larger incident. He telephoned Bryant Green immediately and drove to meet the lobsterman. Green explained precisely where and when he and his son had discovered the carcasses. He handed Robichaud five dead lobsters, and the investigator returned to Moncton and delivered the second batch to the laboratory, which was already examining the previous mortalities.

Tensions had existed for years between the salmon farmers and the lobster fishers over competition for fishing grounds. Some of Cooke Aquaculture's farms in the bay had been vandalized; at one point, fifty thousand salmon escaped after a net at a farm was cut. As word about the lobster deaths spread among the fishing associations along the bay, fingers were pointed at the salmon farms and the array of chemicals they used. The associations and conservation groups called on the government to investigate the incidents. Concerns also came in from lobster fishers in nearby Maine, where Cooke was the largest salmon farm operator.

In late December and January, test results confirmed that concentrations of cypermethrin had been found in the dead lobsters from all five locations. The pesticide was also found in some of the salmon samples that Robichaud had collected from salmon farms in the vicinity of the kills, indicating that the banned pesticide was likely used at those farms. Water can carry harmful chemicals long distances, but the distance between the two kills indicated that there were at least two sources of the pesticide. Robichaud opened the first formal criminal investigation into the use of the banned pesticide in the Bay of Fundy.

Cypermethrin is used to control insects in homes and agricultural fields, but only under strict guidelines. It is classified as a neurotoxin, and scientific studies show that cypermethrin crosses the blood-brain barrier and attacks the central nervous system, inducing a loss of motor control and death. For lobsters, exposure to even small concentrations has been shown to cause significant mortalities in adults and damage to the eggs of female lobsters in breeding grounds. The chemical also kills shrimp and other crustaceans. Cypermethrin is "amongst the most toxic insecticides known[,] and marine crustaceans are generally more sensitive to cypermethrin than marine finfish," according to the Agreed Statement of Facts. The U.S. Environmental Protection Agency says cypermethrin is a possible human carcinogen and has strict guidelines for its use.

In 1998, Canada banned cypermethrin for use in marine environments because of the danger to aquatic life, especially lobster and shrimp. But the pesticide was commonly used to combat sea lice infestations in Norway, Chile, and the United States, including across the border from the Bay of Fundy in Maine. Perhaps the pesticide had been carried by currents into Canadian waters from Maine. Robichaud suspected, however, that the source was closer to home. In both instances, the dead lobsters were found close to salmon farms owned by a single company, Kelly Cove Salmon Ltd., a subsidiary of Cooke Aquaculture.

In February 2010, Environment Canada inspected every salmon farm operating in the Bay of Fundy. Samples were collected at each farm and submitted for testing at the laboratory in Moncton. The results confirmed the presence of cypermethrin in "significant concentration levels" in samples from fifteen farms owned and operated by Kelly Cove Salmon in six different parts of the bay, according to court documents. Concentrations of cypermethrin were also found at other Cooke farms months after the investigation began, according to the Agreed Statement of Facts.

The investigators found evidence that cypermethrin use by salmon farms in the bay had been widespread for years. The local aquaculture industry association had even distributed a manual with instructions on how to avoid detection when using the pesticide. A government research scientist provided Robichaud's team with that pamphlet. The pamphlet described how to apply pesticides containing cypermethrin "discreetly, so it would be unnoticed by regulatory officials, other fishermen and environmentalists."

The instructions on deception coincided with a July 10, 1996, incident in which tens of thousands of live lobsters stored in a pound in Back Bay, New Brunswick, were killed. Stewart Lamont, the managing director of Tangier Lobster, which owned the pound, said roughly 110,000 pounds of lobsters worth millions of dollars had died after nearby salmon farms dumped several liters of cypermethrin into their cages. Cypermethrin was detected in the lobsters by a government laboratory, but the source of the contamination was never found.

There are no records of any previous investigations or prosecutions for using cypermethrin, but federal and provincial authorities were well aware of its widespread use. A list provided to Robichaud's team showed cypermethrin use had been detected at twenty-eight sites in the Bay of Fundy between October 1997 and October 2004. Four of those locations were operated by Cooke's Kelly Cove Salmon.

Salmon farmers in the bay had turned to powerful cypermethrin-based pesticides after sea lice developed resistance to a premixed feed additive called SLICE, which had been used for the previous decade. Like other chemicals used in salmon farms, SLICE was applied widely internationally, although studies show that its active ingredient, emamectin benzoate, is toxic to mammals, birds, marine plants, and lobster. When severe sea lice infestations occurred at farms in the southwestern portion of the bay in late 2009, Cooke tapped cypermethrin as a way around the resistance to SLICE.

Robichaud and his team got a break in June when Luke Little, a former worker at a salmon farm, told them cypermethrin had been purchased in Maine and brought to Canadian salmon farms concealed in gasoline cans. Little said the cans were easily hidden from regulators among cans filled with other material. Cypermethrin is not banned in the United States, and records showed that Maine officials had given Cooke permission to apply cypermethrin on one occasion at five of its salmon farms in the state in 2010. The question was, had the company used it in the bay, knowingly flouting Canadian law?

To confirm that the pesticide had been brought from Maine to Canada, the Environment Canada investigators turned to the U.S. Environmental Protection Agency. The American investigators canvassed suppliers in Maine and discovered that a Kelly Cove regional manager had bought seventy-two gallons of cypermethrin on ten or eleven different occasions from a pet and feed store in Calais, just across the border. Canadian investigators were told by the EPA that the powerful pesticide was apparently smuggled from Maine to New Brunswick aboard two of Cooke's vessels.

In the fall of 2010, another piece of the puzzle fell into place. Bryant Green telephoned Robichaud and told him that Cooke Aquaculture had given him three thousand dollars' worth of fish bait in compensation for the 2009 lobster kill. The information was potentially significant enough that another investigator, Fernand Comeau, went to interview Green in person. The lobsterman told Comeau that he had repeatedly telephoned Michael Cooke demanding that the company reimburse him for the loss of his lobsters. Michael Cooke had cofounded the company with his brother, and he oversaw operations. Finally, in April 2010, Michael Cooke had agreed to make good on the loss. A few days later, Green told the investigator, he picked up one and a half pallets of frozen herring at Cooke Aquaculture's feed plant in St. George, New Brunswick. The herring would be bait, but to the investigators, the transaction was more like a catch: it constituted what they viewed as an acknowledgment by the company of responsibility for the lobster deaths.

Green's call was one of the final pieces of the puzzle. The investigators felt they had gathered sufficient evidence of widespread use of cypermethrin at Cooke Aquaculture salmon farms to take the final steps toward bringing criminal charges. The key findings were that a Cooke employee had smuggled the pesticide into Canada from Maine, and that traces of it had been found at fifteen Cooke farms. The evidence, and explanations of its significance, was laid out in Robichaud's forty-nine-page affidavit seeking court approval to search Cooke facilities. The judge approved the request.

On November 18, 2010, Robichaud led a team of agents in simultaneous raids on eight Cooke offices, including its headquarters in Blacks Harbour, New Brunswick. The search warrant authorized the agents to confiscate computers and related storage devices, work manuals and other business material, and all records related to the possible purchase of cypermethrin between January 2008 and September 2010. The raids surprised company workers and executives.

The volume of material was extensive, and required months to examine and weave together into criminal charges. A year after the raids, in November 2011, Environment Canada filed eleven criminal charges for violations of the federal Fisheries Act against Cooke Aquaculture; its chief executive, Glenn Cooke; and two other executives. Robichaud said at the time that each count was punishable by three years in prison and a million-dollar fine. A few months later, eight more counts were added to each defendant's charges after additional offenses were discovered. Prosecutors determined that Cooke Aquaculture had used the banned substance to fight major infestations of sea lice at fifteen farms in the bay.

Charging three individuals with crimes in an environmental case was highly unusual. More often, corporations are charged, and executives escape being shamed publicly. Legal experts said charging Cooke and his colleagues was an aggressive move by Environment Canada. Robichaud, a veteran investigator with a reputation for not pulling any punches, had been among those arguing for sending a strong message. The company took a beating in the press from conservationists and neighbors as people pondered why the company would have poisoned waters in its own backyard. Its spokeswoman, Nell Halse, fought back, criticizing the media and proclaiming that Cooke served as "custodians of the marine environment."

After months of negotiations, the company struck a sweetheart deal that kept its CEO and the two other executives from going to trial and possibly winding up with criminal records. On April 26, 2013, Kelly Cove Salmon pleaded guilty to two new counts of using cypermethrin at fifteen of its salmon farms and agreed to pay a $500,000 fine, one of the largest ever levied in Canada in an environmental case, but only a fraction of the $19 million in potential penalties it faced. As part of the plea bargain, the criminal charges against Glenn Cooke and his colleagues were withdrawn.

Court records confirmed that the company had used cypermethrin at its farms in six separate parts of the Bay of Fundy between October 2009 and November 2010 "in an effort to control sea lice infestation and associated losses to the company." In an illustration of its disregard for the damage it caused, according to court records, the company continued to use cypermethrin months after the start of the criminal investigation and Michael Cooke's payment to Bryant Green.

The guilty pleas were entered in a small courtroom in St. Stephen, New Brunswick, just across the border from Calais, Maine. No one had notified the press, and neither Cooke nor the other two executives were in court. So, they did not hear the criticism from Judge Julian Dickson of New Brunswick Provincial Court. Dickson said the banned pesticide represented an "extremely high risk" to lobsters. He said its use by Kelly Cove was not the result of "accident or negligence." Rather, the judge said, the company had "failed miserably" to meet legal standards and had "willfully ignored" the ban on cypermethrin.

The only person who ended up with a criminal conviction was Clyde Eldridge, the sixty-five-year-old owner of the feed and pet store in Calais who had sold the cypermethrin to the Cooke employee. He was fined five thousand dollars and placed on probation for a year after pleading guilty to lying to American investigators about the sales.

For Glenn Cooke, the half-million-dollar fine was just the cost of doing business. In a statement posted on the company's website, the CEO did not acknowledge any mistake and offered no apology for ignoring the ban on cypermethrin and jeopardizing lobsters and other marine life in the bay where he grew up. He said nothing about the Greens or the others whose lobsters had been killed by his use of a banned pesticide. Instead, Cooke contradicted facts contained in the Agreed Statement of Facts approved by his own defense attorneys. "We made the difficult decision not to fight these charges even though we question the allegations," he said. "Our main reason for this decision was to relieve our people, our company and our customers from a lengthy and public court battle. We want to resolve this matter today and move on." Cooke said the company had invested millions of dollars in other treatments for sea lice and that it was committed to improving its internal protocols. "Fish health is at the core of our business as farmers, as is the sustainability and health of our farms and the marine environment on which we depend," Cooke said.

The statement added a thinly veiled threat. Cooke said the company would now "limit stocking" of its salmon farms. "We cannot stock these farms until the industry has access to a full suite of pest treatment and management tools," he said. "Unfortunately, this will have negative consequences for jobs and for the local economy."

In his own public statement, Robert Robichaud said the five-hundred-thousand-dollar fine was "in the top three fines in Canada. We feel that it will definitely send a strong message, not only to the aquaculture sector, but to other marine users, that the illegal use of pesticides is simply not tolerable." Privately, Robichaud told a colleague that he was deeply disappointed the charges had been dropped against Cooke and the two managers.

The guilty pleas ended the criminal case. Next door in Nova Scotia, Cooke Aquaculture was confronting a new problem from a virus called infectious salmon anemia, or ISA.

Seawater teems with invisible viruses. Scientific studies have found two hundred thousand different viral species in a sample of ocean water and one hundred billion virus particles in a liter of seawater. Viruses adapt to attack vulnerable organisms, sometimes causing massive mortalities and mutating along the way. In the natural world, ISA is a nuisance that does not kill in large numbers because wild salmon are spread out and predators pick off ailing fish before they can infect others. It is a different story in pens jammed with tens of thousands of salmon, which become petri dishes for growing the virus. An outbreak of ISA can wipe out an entire cage, and then a farm, and then even spread to nearby facilities.

Like any animals that live in close quarters, farmed salmon are vulnerable to infectious diseases. Once it shows up in a farm, ISA spreads quickly and kills Atlantic salmon at alarming rates. Ridding a farm of ISA can require slaughtering large numbers of fish and upsetting people who live in the area. ISA-infected salmon suffer hemorrhages, bloated abdomens, bulging eyes, and, ultimately, death. The U.S. Department of Agriculture warns that the disease can also develop without the infected fish showing any external signs. They keep eating and then suddenly die. By the time the virus is detected, it is usually too late. The USDA says there is no cure for ISA. The only solution is getting the fish out of the water before the infection spreads.

The first outbreaks of ISA were recorded in Norway in 1984. Since then, scientists have reported infections in every country where farmed salmon is raised in open-net pens on the ocean, including the United States and Canada. In 1998, a quarter of the farms in New Brunswick were shut down to stop the spread of ISA. In 2007, an ISA outbreak in Chile killed millions of fish and caused two billion dollars in losses. Like sea lice, ISA is a relentless enemy that continues to kill millions of salmon every year. And it spreads to wild fish.

Nova Scotia had been spared the disease until early 2012, when a Cooke Aquaculture salmon farm in Shelburne Bay sustained what the federal government identified as the first case of ISA in the province.

Shelburne is a small town in southwestern Nova Scotia with a natural port on the Atlantic Ocean. From the 1700s to late in the twentieth century, Shelburne was a bustling seaport. Today, however, fewer than two thousand people live there, many of them descendants of the original settlers. Most who remain earn their living from the sea or, more recently, from tourism.

Before dawn on February 17, 2012, two trailer trucks drove away from the wharf at Shelburne Harbour. The trucks contained thousands of dead salmon from two cages at Cooke's farm in the harbor. As reports of the predawn departure circulated, local environmentalists, never fans of the farms, suggested that the fish had been killed by ISA. Eventually, the rumors reached the Canadian Food Inspection Agency, and inspectors turned up. As a precaution, they immediately quarantined Cooke's operations in the harbor and sent samples from remaining salmon to the federal laboratory in Moncton, New Brunswick, for testing. The company issued a statement confirming that it had "humanely euthanized two cages of fish in Nova Scotia after routine testing raised suspicion of the Infectious Salmon Anemia virus." The statement said the company had used the same strategy employed by salmon farmers around the world for dealing with the virus. Cooke declined to provide the number of fish harvested early or killed because of the virus.

Two weeks later, the Food Inspection Agency confirmed that a strain of ISA was responsible for the deaths of tens of thousands of salmon at Cooke's farm in Shelburne. The quarantine remained in place for several months as the farm was cleared and cleaned. There were suspicions that the virus had arrived in juvenile salmon brought to Shelburne from a Cooke hatchery in New Brunswick, but this was never confirmed. Despite the presence of the virus, the Canadian Food Inspection Agency said the diseased fish posed no risk to humans, and it allowed Cooke to market 2.5 million pounds of salmon from the quarantined farm. Sobeys, the second-largest food retailer in Canada, said it would refuse to sell any of the infected salmon.

Two aspects of the ISA incident remained a secret for nearly two years. First, CBC News, Canada's national broadcaster, filed an Access to Information request for documents related to the ISA outbreak in Shelburne. The records, released in January 2014, showed that the infections had forced Cooke to slaughter a million salmon. The documents also showed that the federal government had paid Cooke $13 million in compensation for the salmon it had slaughtered. The company refused to confirm the amount of the payment, but a spokesperson compared the deal to compensation that land farmers receive for damaged crops. It was, the spokesperson said, just like a $2.3 million package offered by the government to strawberry farmers after a virus destroyed their crops.

Cooke was not the only salmon farmer to benefit from the government compensation program. The same year, the federal government paid $4 million in compensation to two Norwegian companies, Cermaq and Grieg, to cover losses due to exposure to another virus, infectious hematopoietic necrosis, in British Columbia. The payments to Cooke and the two Norwegian firms were part of a huge bailout of the industry financed by Canadian taxpayers. The Atlantic Salmon Federation found that between 1996 and 2012, the federal government paid more than $100 million in compensation to salmon farms in Canada's three eastern provinces (Nova Scotia, New Brunswick, and Prince Edward Island) for destroying diseased fish.

The Nova Scotia government certainly held no grudge against Cooke Aquaculture. In June 2012, while its farm in Shelburne was still under quarantine, Cooke received $25 million in grants and loans from the provincial government to expand operations in Shelburne and two other locations in the province. The lure of jobs and greater tax revenue trumped complaints from the public and conservationists about the impact of the farms on the environment. "This is an industry with great potential in our province," Darrell Dexter, Nova Scotia's premier, told a local newspaper at the time. Even the mayor of Shelburne embraced the promise of economic development.

The same month the loan package was approved, Cooke suffered a second ISA outbreak. This one was about thirty-five miles up the Atlantic Coast, at its farm near Liverpool. Again, the federal government quarantined the site, which contained about four hundred thousand salmon in fourteen cages near the aptly named Coffin Island.

The second incident of ISA infections touched off a round of complaints from people living in Nova Scotia's coastal communities and from conservation and environmental groups. Faced with growing public criticism, the provincial government in Halifax imposed a moratorium on new salmon farms in May 2013. The government promised to develop new regulations to bring better controls to the industry before the moratorium was lifted.

Using a neurotoxin in his home waters and slaughtering a million salmon because of an infectious disease was not part of the story when Cooke appeared in disguise on *Undercover Boss Canada* on January 3, 2014. The carefully scripted reality show presented its star as a humble man who treated employees like family and worked to keep them safe, not someone who had spread poison through the waters from which he made his living or who had brought the first case of ISA to Nova Scotia.

"It's an incredible journey we've made," he says in the opening segment of the show. "Family means the most of all to me."

In his Everyman's flannel shirt, wig, and goatee, Cooke visits several of the company's operations in eastern Canada. He says his name is "Bruce" and explains that the video crew trailing him is working on a documentary about aquaculture. At a hatchery in Newfoundland, he works a shift alongside a woman named Jean, who hefts and empties twenty-five-pound bags of magnesium and calcium into tanks containing juvenile salmon. After lifting the bags himself, Cooke says he is worried about the risk of injury. Jean agrees that it is a strain, but she says her biggest concern is keeping the water cool enough to avoid damaging the young fish as they are flushed out of tanks through hoses to trucks waiting to transfer them to the ocean pens where they will spend the next two years.

At a salmon farm on the Newfoundland coast, Cooke talks with James, the chief mechanic, who maintains fifty-five vessels in four different harbors. James says he has worked in the job for five years but does not have a mechanic's license, despite multiple requests to his boss for support in obtaining one. He is thinking about quitting and says low wages are making it hard to keep good people at Cooke.

In southern Nova Scotia, Cooke meets Chris, who is responsible for monitoring feed going into twelve net pens at one of the farms. When Cooke nearly slips on the feed boat, Chris says he has been asking fruitlessly for safety rails to be installed. Using an underwater drone, he shows Cooke how he tries to avoid feeding the salmon too much. Excess feed falls through the mesh to the seabed below, a financial cost for the company and a threat to the environment because of the contaminants it contains.

Later in the show, Cooke looks at the camera earnestly and says, "We have to be sustainable. We live in that area, so we can't go and damage the environment."

In the concluding segment, each worker featured in the show is flown by private plane to Cooke's hunting lodge in New Brunswick. He reveals his identity, tells each of them they will receive a gift, and promises to fix the problems they've raised—Jean will get a machine to lift the bags and chillers to cool the tanks, James will get his mechanic's license, and rails will be installed on the company's feed boats for Chris.

As portrayed on television, Cooke Aquaculture sounded like a good steward of the environment and a heartwarming business success. Ask people who live around its open-net farms or who work for Cooke, however, and the stories are quite different. They talk about environmental dead zones around Cooke farms created by feces, uneaten salmon feed, and contaminants. They describe working long hours in difficult conditions. They recount gruesome stories of turning salmon deformed and rotting from disease into fillets. They talk about having to treat fish brutally. These are folks who do not see Glenn Cooke, disguised or not, or his company as a champion of sustainability or a clean environment. These folks don't appear on TV or call the shots in Canada's agencies.

Soon, however, the company would confront a well-organized opposition and a less forgiving government.

CHAPTER 4

THE RESISTANCE

Resistance movements are generated by people who refuse to accept the world as they find it and who are willing take personal risks to make it better.

Alexandra Morton is the godmother of a passionate corps of environmental activists across North America and Europe fighting to protect the oceans and the creatures that live in them from the damage caused by industrial salmon farming. Morton and her cohorts are the heart of the resistance, driven by a common concern and a deep commitment. Like Morton, many are marine biologists; others are nutritionists and physicians alarmed by studies showing the health risks associated with eating farmed salmon. A vocal contingent comprises lobster fishers who fear their traditional livelihoods suffer collateral damage from the salmon farms. Still others are animal rights activists outraged by the caging of these magnificent migratory fish in the best of times and their slaughter in the worst.

In her midsixties, Morton has a round face, an impish smile, and long gray hair. For most of her adult life she has fought salmon farming and the government agencies she is convinced conspire with corporate interests to despoil waters off the western coast of Canada, the home for eons to a wealth of marine life and seabirds. Her journey mirrors the path taken by many members of the resistance, though few have been as dedicated or as polarizing. Morton told her story in her 2021 memoir, *Not on My Watch*.

Her father, Earl Wade Hubbard, a painter and futurist who thought humanity was doomed, instilled a sense of moral urgency in Morton while she was growing up in northwestern Connecticut. After graduating from American

University in Washington, DC, in 1977, Morton worked with John C. Lilly, a controversial polymath in California who was trying to teach dolphins to speak English. Lilly was part of a generation of counterculture scientists and thinkers that included Werner Erhard and Timothy Leary, both frequent visitors at his home. The conventional scientific community was skeptical of Lilly's research, but Morton was inspired by it. She believed that killer whales, also known as orcas, were as intelligent as dolphins, and she began taping the sounds the whales made in the ocean and studying their behavior, which mimicked that of humans in many ways. Convinced she needed to study the whales in the wild, she moved north to Vancouver Island, off the coast of British Columbia, in 1979.

A few months after arriving, she was camping on a beach when she met Robin Morton, a Canadian filmmaker who specialized in killer whales. She recalled watching him walking out of the water in a dive suit, stripping it off, and standing on the beach naked, except for a killer whale tattoo on his shoulder. "I was married, pregnant and living on a boat with him within a year," she said.

The young couple towed a small floating house into Echo Bay, in the Broughton Archipelago, a wilderness of islands and inlets along the central coast of British Columbia, near Vancouver Island. Echo Bay had no roads, electricity, or telephones. Eventually there was a small school, a post office that received mail by seaplane, and a tight-knit group of about two hundred residents who lived in floating houses and worked primarily in the forest and fishing industries. For Robin and Alex, it was an idyllic environment for pursuing their shared passion for whales.

The idyll ended abruptly in 1986. Robin, Alex, and their four-year-old son, Jarret, were out in their Zodiac, a lightweight, inflatable boat. Robin was underwater filming killer whales while Alex and Jarret waited on the boat. To avoid antagonizing the whales with the bubbles and noise of regular scuba tanks, Robin was using a rebreather. Unlike scuba equipment, which allows divers to breathe compressed air and exhale into the water, a rebreather is a closed-circuit breathing device in which the exhaled air is scrubbed of carbon dioxide by a chemical absorbent canister and recirculated. The diving world is divided on the dangers of rebreathers because malfunctions can permit a slow buildup of carbon dioxide that goes unnoticed until it is too late.

As time passed and Robin failed to surface, Alex grew anxious. She remembered Robin's dictum—"Do not wreck the shot"—so she waited and watched. Finally, fear won out. Leaving Jarret on the boat, Morton tied a rope to herself and dove in. She found Robin lying on the sea bottom. He had lost consciousness from a spike in carbon dioxide in his blood and drowned. She could see where the camera had rolled into deeper water.

A widow at twenty-nine years old, with a young son in a remote community, Morton could have packed up and headed back to civilization. But science and mothering got her through those difficult days. The whales she had come to study were still there, and so was her small community. Yet, all this was about to change, too, sending Morton in a new direction with equal passion and commitment.

In 1987, a year after the accident, the first salmon cages were towed into the Broughton Archipelago. The farm was owned by Marine Harvest, the Norwegian company that would later be bought by John Fredriksen and renamed Mowi. Morton welcomed the new industry, trusting the provincial government, which predicted that salmon farming would create jobs and assured the fishers in the region that the Atlantic salmon in the farms would not pose a threat to the native Pacific salmon. "The government said this will be good for you," Morton said. "I had a son in the school, and I thought there would be more kids. I wanted to talk to the women to tell them what a fabulous way of life this was."

Morton soon learned she had been naïve. Instead of helping to expand Echo Bay, government officials actively tried to drive off residents to clear the way for salmon farm workers. People who had built good lives in the small communities around the archipelago were told their floating houses suddenly did not meet standards. Residents began to move away. Morton refused to budge, even as more troubles emerged.

The number of salmon farms increased, and the killer whale population dropped. The research that had sustained Morton was getting harder to carry out as whales disappeared. She suspected a connection to the farms, but provincial officials told her there was no link. Morton estimated that she wrote thousands of letters to federal and provincial agencies from 1987 to 1997 on her own behalf and that of her remaining neighbors, asking for an assessment of the impact of the farms. She said she never received a serious response.

In the late 1990s, a Scottish tourist staying at a small fishing lodge in Echo Bay struck up a conversation with Morton. When the topic turned to the salmon farms, he asked, "Do you have the scourge of sea lice yet?" Morton asked what he meant, and the visitor explained that after salmon farms came to Scotland a decade earlier, the locals began to see parasites attached to large numbers of wild salmon. He said he had seen the same tiny sea lice on Pacific salmon he had caught a few days earlier in the archipelago's waters. The next day, Morton took a net and pulled dozens of juvenile wild pink salmon out of the water. Many were covered with sea lice and bleeding from the eyeballs and the base of their fins. She had encountered a problem plaguing salmon farming and jeopardizing wild salmon everywhere salmon were farmed.

The parasites were also being found in Clayoquot Sound, not far from Morton's home. For thousands of years, Clayoquot Sound had provided passage for wild salmon returning from the Pacific Ocean to the rivers and streams of British Columbia to spawn and for the return migration by young salmon. Before the industrial farming of Atlantic salmon, an exotic species on the Pacific Coast, sea lice were not a serious threat to wild salmon. But the proliferation of fish farms and the accompanying infestations of sea lice in the pens broke what biologists refer to as "a natural cycle of protection."

The closed environment of the cages at salmon farms are like petri dishes where sea lice flourish. The wounds they inflict are often fatal and cost salmon farmers tens of millions of dollars every year. Defenders of salmon farms blame wild salmon for spreading sea lice, saying the tiny parasites occur naturally in the ocean. This much is true: adult wild salmon can be infected naturally with sea lice in the ocean. But the numbers of lice in the wild are minuscule compared with the concentrations in cages. Further, when wild salmon migrate from salt water and swim upriver to spawn, the freshwater kills the lice.

As we've seen, the biggest danger to wild salmon comes in the spring, when juvenile salmon, called smolts, begin their migration out of the rivers and streams and to the ocean. They start their journey lice-free, but as the smolts pass the salmon farms, they are forced to swim through vast plumes of sea lice. As the immature salmon pass by the farms, huge numbers of lice attach themselves easily to their delicate skin. Vast numbers of the juvenile salmon either die from the lice or are weakened to a point where they are easy prey for larger predators awaiting them along their journey.

Morton believed the threat posed to wild salmon by sea lice in her archipelago and in Clayoquot Sound was linked to the disappearance of killer whales in the waters around Vancouver Island. Killer whales depend on salmon, eating more than fifty pounds of fish a day. She began researching a possible connection. Her study eventually broke new ground by establishing that the salmon farms along the migration routes were spreading sea lice that were killing young wild salmon. Applying science and rational thought, Morton had found a classic example of a food chain being disrupted in three distinct phases. In the first phase, the sea lice weakened and killed juvenile wild salmon, reducing the number of young fish that made it to the ocean to mature. In the second phase, fewer adult wild salmon returned to the rivers to spawn. The data on this was clear. In 2002, government scientists predicted that 3.6 million pink salmon would return to the Broughton Archipelago from their ocean migration—the actual number was less than 150,000. The dramatic decline led directly to the third phase: killer whales did not have enough salmon to eat, so they left to find food elsewhere.

Several years earlier, Morton had founded a nonprofit group called Raincoast Research Society, a collaborative effort with other scientists and activists to study threats to marine life. In what she calls "partnered science," she worked regularly with experts from academic institutions. The academics would develop the research plans, and Morton would conduct the fieldwork. Both sides benefited: the academics found a first-class field scientist, and Morton blunted criticism from the industry about her lack of an advanced degree. Together, they began publishing papers in scientific journals and speaking out at public hearings about the systemic threat to wild salmon and other marine life posed by salmon farms.

The new focus became so consuming that she turned her house into a research station. She also found a patron in Sarah Haney, a retired nurse and environmental campaigner whose fortune came from an ex-husband who was one of the inventors of the game Trivial Pursuit. Morton's floating house officially became the Salmon Coast Field Station, and Haney provided the money to buy several houses and build a small laboratory nearby. Professors at the University of Victoria, Simon Fraser University, and other institutions sent graduate students to live in the houses and study the impact of sea lice on wild salmon. Three years later, Morton was looking for a new partner to expand her research from Broughton to Clayoquot Sound and turned to a nongovernmental organization (NGO) in Washington State called the Wild Fish Conservancy, which was building a reputation for smart science and tough courtroom tactics. A new alliance in the resistance movement was about to be formed.

In the summer of 1989, near the Cascade mountain range in Washington State, thirty people huddled in the back room of a Chinese restaurant in Ellensburg, a small city best known for its annual rodeo. They would not have called themselves a resistance movement; "aging hippies" might have been more appropriate. They had been brought together by Kurt Beardslee, a Washington State native who had grown up fly-fishing with his father in the days when salmon and trout were plentiful. In the early 1970s, Beardslee worked for an advertising agency in Seattle, where his main client was the National Science Foundation. He soon tired of the advertising business, but the connection with the foundation had sparked a lifelong interest in science that, combined with his passion for the outdoors, made him a natural resistance leader.

Like many Baby Boomers, Beardslee had yearned for a simpler life. When he quit the advertising business, he and his artist wife, Candace, moved to Duvall, half an hour northeast of Seattle. He helped found an organization dedicated to controlled growth, and one of his early victories was blocking construction of a regional airport. When salmon and trout began disappearing from the region's streams and rivers, Beardslee did not think existing organizations were paying enough attention. The danger was usually relegated to a brief discussion in the last five minutes of a meeting about urban sprawl or logging. In response, he tapped into a network of scientists, biologists, and lawyers united by a common love of fly-fishing and a growing concern over the plight of the region's wild fish. They gathered at the Palace restaurant in Ellensburg to start a new organization to tackle the problem.

The goal was to establish a science-based organization devoted to reversing the decline of wild fish. There was a sense of urgency and frustration with the government's weak efforts to identify and solve the problems. A few days after the initial meeting, representatives of two existing organizations, Oregon Trout and California Trout, met with the group to describe how they were set up to pursue the shared mission of changing what Beardslee called "the misguided workings of their respective state management agencies."

Washington Trout was created. The group rented space in a commercial building Beardslee owned in Duvall, and he was named executive director. It was slow going in the beginning. "Simply speaking, we were overwhelmed with the scale of the problems and our obligation to fix what was broken," Beardslee said. "There was no manual to follow, no map. But we were hopeful that, if we always used science as our compass, worked smart and extremely hard, and kept our eye on the prize, we would prevail."

Beardslee recruited staff and raised money to finance scientific research and a raft of lawsuits aimed at forcing the government to protect fish and their habitats. Despite a small budget, the work expanded from trout and salmon to protecting whales and other endangered species south to the California coast and north to British Columbia. In 2006, the group filed two lawsuits aimed at holding the federal government accountable for restoring a trout run called Icicle Creek under the Clean Water Act, which was created by Congress in 1972 to regulate discharges of pollutants into the waters of the United States. The suits led to negotiated settlements in which the U.S. Environmental Protection Agency and the Fish and Wildlife Service agreed to reduce permissible discharges into the creek and to remove obstacles in order to open up miles of habitat for fish.

The same year, Washington Trout joined a regional coalition of conservation groups suing the federal government under the Endangered Species Act, which protects habitats where threatened and endangered plants and animals are found. The suit contended that weak management of fishing in Puget Sound was jeopardizing efforts to restore the population of Chinook salmon, which was on the Endangered Species List. The successful suit was a milestone that shifted the group's focus beyond trout and salmon to the wider deterioration of the Puget Sound ecosystem.

Puget Sound was formed by receding glaciers about fourteen thousand years ago at the confluence of the North Pacific Ocean and hundreds of rivers and streams that flow from the Cascade and Olympic mountains. The result was a nutrient-rich estuary that became home to a huge variety of marine life, from killer whales and Pacific salmon to octopuses and Pacific cod. Its winding coast is lined by old-growth forests, fishing wharves, and deepwater ports and by cities and businesses that are the backbone of the state's economy. For the four million people in the region, Puget Sound is a cultural icon and an economic engine. So are the endangered Pacific salmon, which are far older than the sound itself.

Atlantic salmon and Pacific salmon share a common ancestry. Genetic science says a single species of salmon divided about twenty million years ago when the cooling of the Arctic Ocean isolated the Atlantic and Pacific oceans. A single species of Atlantic salmon emerged, along with five species of Pacific salmon: Chinook, coho, chum, pink, and sockeye. Atlantic salmon are silvery, with large black spots on their backs; their Pacific cousins are each distinctive in appearance. For instance, the sockeye is also known as red salmon because of its bright red color. Both Atlantic and Pacific salmon species are "anadromous," which means that they live in freshwater and salt water. They are born in freshwater and can spend as much as a year in their natal waters before migrating to the ocean, where they spend two or more years to mature before returning to spawn in the river of their birth. The females make nests, each called a redd, in gravel or small rocks at the bottom of a stream or river and lay their eggs, which are later fertilized by males. Atlantic salmon can survive spawning and repeat the cycle. Pacific salmon are one-timers and die after spawning, leaving behind an infusion of nutrients that sustain a diverse, independent ecosystem. As befits their names, Atlantic salmon are native to the Atlantic Ocean and the rivers and streams of North America and Europe. Pacific salmon live in Pacific waters and surrounding freshwater. Another key difference is that the depletion of Atlantic salmon stocks led to a ban on commercial fishing, but Pacific salmon are still fished commercially in the Pacific Northwest, Alaska, and British Columbia—under tight limits.

For Pacific salmon, Puget Sound is a key passage from the ocean to the fish's spawning grounds in Washington State and British Columbia. Like their Atlantic cousins, they face a variety of threats. Studies have found damage to more than half of Puget Sound's salt marshes, salmon runs, and habitats. Rising sea levels and other climate-related issues have contributed to the area's problems, as have everyday human activities, ranging from the release of industrial waste to faulty septic systems to changing water chemistry caused by the absorption of carbon dioxide from fossil fuels and deforestation. Marine biologists point to another culprit: the increasing number of salmon farms in Puget Sound. According to the Puget Sound Institute and the University of Washington, the number rose from a handful of small farms two decades ago to 130 farms by 2018.

In February 2007, Washington Trout changed its name to the Wild Fish Conservancy to reflect its recognition that the ecosystems on which the wild fish, whales, and other marine animals depend are inseparable and borderless. At the time, the organization employed nearly twenty full-time marine biologists, ecologists, water quality experts, and other specialists, and it carried on work across the region. By the time Alexandra Morton asked Kurt Beardslee for help in 2009, the Wild Fish Conservancy had built a reputation for effective, science-based activism.

Morton wanted the Conservancy to start a research project in Clayoquot Sound, on the western side of Vancouver Island, in British Columbia. The region was a long-standing hotbed of environmental activism over damage caused by the logging industry. This time the threat was the spread of sea lice from dozens of salmon farms. Over sixteen months, the Wild Fish Conservancy's biologists collected more than twelve thousand juvenile chum and Chinook salmon. Each fish was scrutinized for sea lice in each fjord of Clayoquot Sound. The results showed that juvenile salmon migrating to the ocean through fjords where salmon farms were located had significantly higher rates of lice infections than those passing through waters with few or no farms. This was not anecdotal or visual—it was hard data that confirmed Morton's long-held suspicions.

With Morton's increasing prominence came increasing criticism. Industry representatives and industry-related publications attacked her credentials and credibility. Despite working with leading academic scientists, Morton was dismissed because she lacked an advanced degree. She was accused of lying, and her ethics were challenged. "She selectively highlights information that, taken out of context, appears to support her predetermined point of view," said Mary Ellen Walling, executive director of the BC Salmon Farmers Association.

The industry tried to shut up Morton by taking her to court. In 2016, Marine Harvest filed a lawsuit charging her with trespassing at three of its salmon farms. Morton had spent the summer monitoring salmon farms aboard the RV *Martin Sheen*, a research vessel operated by the Sea Shepherd Conservation Society and named in honor of the American actor and supporter of the organization. As part of the nonprofit conservation group's Operation Virus Hunter, they were collecting waste from the farms in a search for evidence of viruses. Marine Harvest claimed that Morton and others tampered with equipment and violated biosecurity procedures by scooping excrement off buoys marking the farm boundaries. The suit also accused Morton and her accomplices of flying a drone over and diving at one facility and ignoring the company's demand that they leave.

The suit was ultimately dismissed, but it was just a small part of the long-running legal and psychological battle between Morton and the industry. In 2008, she had filed a lawsuit claiming that the British Columbia government was ineffective at regulating salmon farming in its waters. Authority for regulations lies with Canada's provinces, but Morton won, and the federal government took aquaculture licensing out of the hands of the province. Later, Morton joined First Nations groups in suing Marine Harvest for introducing a virus to Puget Sound.

The industry retaliated with acts that Morton considered harassment. In one example, she was again on the *Martin Sheen* with colleagues, checking on salmon farms in the summer of 2018, when two large aluminum speedboats with blacked-out windows appeared in her vessel's wake. The menacing boats followed the activists for days as they sampled the waters near Marine Harvest farms. Computers on the boat began to fail, new icons showed up on screens, and cell phones registered unusual data usage—all signs that Morton and her colleagues had been hacked and were being monitored. The incident took a weird turn when a local reporter published an article saying the company that had leased the two speedboats following the *Martin Sheen* was called Black Cube Strategies. The name was nearly the same as that for an Israeli private intelligence firm known for controversial tactics. In the end, there was no proven connection, but the similarity in names added an ominous element to the encounter. The article caused a spokesman for Marine

Harvest to acknowledge hiring the local company, but he denied any connection to the Israeli firm.

After years of run-ins with the salmon industry in general and Marine Harvest in particular, Morton was becoming press savvy. She understood that controversy and criticism raised her profile and drew attention to what she saw as the damage caused by aquaculture. "The problem with this whole issue is if nobody sees it, nothing happens," she once told a *New York Times* reporter. Because most farmed salmon harvested in British Columbia ends up in California markets, she said, "It can't be just the Canadian public. It has to be the American public."

Don Staniford, a British marine biologist and critic of salmon farming, said, "Alexandra Morton is to salmon like Dian Fossey was to gorillas and Jane Goodall is to chimpanzees. She is spearheading a salmon revolution not just in B.C. but around the globe."

Staniford's role in the movement is different from Morton's or Beardslee's. From outposts in England, Scotland, Canada, and Norway, he has devoted more than twenty years to fighting the salmon-farming industry through a provocative combination of science and theatrics. "One of my favorite people growing up was John Sweeney," said Staniford, who was born in Liverpool, England, in 1971. "He was an investigative journalist for the *Observer* newspaper and BBC. One of his quotes stuck in my mind when I was an undergraduate and beyond. He said, 'The job of the investigative reporter is to poke powerful people with sharp sticks and then stand back and see what happens.'" It turned into a job description for Staniford.

After graduating with a degree in environmental ecological science in 1993, he enrolled in a doctoral program at the University of East Anglia and spent four years studying marine biology and working on a thesis about the privatization of fish from a cultural perspective. He left before finishing, Sweeney's words ringing in his head. "Instead of finishing the PhD, I became a campaigner," he said. "I have a passion for digging dirt. If I didn't have salmon farming, I would have done genetically engineered food or bottled water. But the salmon-farming issue is so exciting. Salmon is a migratory species, and caging them is cruel. It is like farming eagles. Cramming the king of fish into a container is like force-feeding lentils to a lion." Almost by accident, Staniford found an early home with Friends of the Earth, the environmental organization founded in 1969 by David Brower.

A few months after leaving university, Staniford contacted the Friends of the Earth chapter in Scotland and asked why they were not campaigning against the growing number of salmon farms on the Scottish coast. "Why don't you do it?" was the response—and with nothing more than a desk and a telephone, he soon found himself working as a volunteer in Inverness, on the northeast coast of Scotland. But Staniford had a platform, and he did not waste any time.

In 2000, he spoke at a public meeting in Scotland alongside a representative of Marine Harvest. Staniford accused salmon farmers of using toxic chemicals illegally to fight diseases at their facilities, polluting Scotland's waters and endangering other marine life. The accusation prompted an outcry from industry supporters in the audience. Staniford shrugged off the criticism, which would become a pattern for him. When he got back to his office, he found another sort of response.

Jackie MacKenzie had heard Staniford's talk and telephoned him. While working at one of Scotland's salmon farms on the northwest coast, MacKenzie said he had been told by his bosses to buy and use a product called Deosect to combat infestations of sea lice in the cages. Deosect contains high concentrations of cypermethrin, the same neurotoxin Cooke Aquaculture would later be caught using illegally in Canada's Bay of Fundy. In Scotland, cypermethrin was approved for killing parasites on horses and sheep, but it was banned for use with fish because it kills lobsters, crabs, and other marine life.

Remembering his youthful idol, *Observer* reporter John Sweeney, Staniford contacted a reporter for the paper, Anthony Barnett, and described what he had been told. Barnett flew to Inverness and interviewed MacKenzie, who signed a statement attesting to his claims. The following Sunday, the newspaper ran MacKenzie's story under the headline "'Illegal Poison' Used on Salmon." MacKenzie was quoted as saying he had bought the Deosect from a farm supplier, using a false name and paying in cash so he could not be traced. An anonymous veterinarian quoted in the story said of Deosect, "As far as marine life goes, it is about as toxic as you can get."

It was the first of many clashes between the salmon-farming industry and Staniford, who has an uncanny knack for getting under the skin of his opponents and drawing a constant stream of vitriol from them. Norway's state broadcaster, NRK, described him as a "hair in the soup of the global salmon farming industry"; *Intrafish*, an industry newsletter, labeled him salmon farming's "No. 1 enemy." There was also praise. In 2002, Staniford received the top prize at a British environment and media awards ceremony. Three years later, he shared a prize as one of six coauthors of *A Stain Upon the Sea*, a book about salmon farming on the west coast of Canada. One of his coauthors was Alex Morton. By then, Staniford had shifted his base from Scotland to British Columbia, following the Norwegian salmon-farming giants to Canada and setting the stage for a bit of guerrilla theater.

In March 2011, salmon-farming giant Cermaq filed a defamation suit against Staniford and his organization, the Global Alliance Against Industrial Aquaculture. Cermaq operated twenty-seven salmon farms around Vancouver Island, and the suit claimed the company had been defamed by mock cigarette packages Staniford had sent to the media and posted on his website. The packages, which resembled red-and-white Marlboros, were emblazoned with the warnings "Salmon Farming Kills," "Salmon Farming Is Toxic," and "Salmon Farming Seriously Damages Health." On the day Staniford was scheduled to testify, a police officer and an officer from the Canada Border Services Agency appeared in the back of the courtroom. When he finished explaining to the judge why he believed farmed salmon were dangerous, the officers served Staniford with deportation papers; he had overstayed his visa. It was an unusual public provocation, but Staniford was not intimidated.

After the trial but before the judge had issued her verdict, Staniford arrived at Vancouver International Airport for his flight home. He wore rubber chains and an orange jumpsuit like those worn by prisoners at Guantánamo Bay. Holding up the rubber chains around his wrists for the press, he was led off by immigration officials. After spending a few days back in Liverpool, he headed for a new job working with a conservation group in Norway.

In September 2011, Justice Elaine Adair of the BC Supreme Court issued her decision in Cermaq's suit. She dismissed the defamation suit, but it was not exactly an endorsement of Staniford. The judge said his statements were defamatory and that he was motivated by malice. She called him a "zealot" and challenged his credibility. Despite the harsh words, Adair said that

Staniford honestly believed what he said and that animosity was not his dominant motive. As a result, she ruled, his claim of fair comment required dismissing the suit.

A few months later, the British Columbia Court of Appeal ruled against Staniford, and he was ordered to pay $75,000 in damages and not to repeat his claims. Cermaq, part of a multinational giant, called Staniford a cyberbully. Staniford has never paid the $75,000, which he calculates has by now reached close to $500,000 in court costs and interest. "I'm not blasé about it, but I'm not looking over my shoulder," he said as he continued to campaign against the salmon-farming industry, particularly in Norway and Scotland. He said he has occasionally returned to Canada for holidays without incident.

The salmon-farming industry's attacks on individuals like Morton and Staniford are part of its playbook for trying to discredit science and critics, a pattern first seen a few years earlier.

CHAPTER 5

ATTACK, COUNTERATTACK

On January 9, 2004, the prestigious journal *Science* published a study that changed the conversation about farmed salmon. Before then, concerns about contamination and health risks in farmed salmon had been overwhelmed by the slick marketing campaigns of the industry, with the collaboration of experts who championed the attributes of eating fish. The *Science* study was designed to raise a bright red flag about the health risks, and it worked.

The study was carried out by scholars from Cornell University and Indiana University and scientists at public-interest organizations. It was financed by the Pew Charitable Trusts, an independent nonprofit based in Philadelphia. At that time, it was the largest study to examine contaminants in salmon. The authors adopted an investigative strategy, starting with the purchase of 594 individual wild and farmed salmon from wholesalers in the major salmon-farming areas, including Scotland, Norway, British Columbia, Chile, Maine, and Washington State, and of 144 wild and farmed-salmon fillets from supermarkets. The samples were tested in laboratories for fourteen contaminants. Four of the toxins (PCBs, dioxin, toxaphene, and dieldrin) were found to be "consistently and significantly more concentrated in the farmed salmon as a group than in the wild salmon." The headline grabber was the high level of PCBs, a probable carcinogen. Farmed salmon contained levels of PCBs seven times higher than that in wild salmon.

The dangers from PCBs, or polychlorinated biphenyls, had been well documented before the study was published. PCBs are man-made chemicals that, for fifty years, were used extensively in electrical transformers, pesticides, and appliances like TVs and refrigerators. PCBs were even sprayed on dirt roads to keep the dust down. Estimates are that 1.5 billion pounds of PCBs were used in the United States before the federal government banned the compound in 1979. The ban came after independent studies uncovered evidence of links to cancer in humans and other health risks like damage to immune systems, brain development, and endocrine systems.

Despite the ban by the United States, and eventually other countries, PCBs remain present in large quantities in the environment all over the world. Estimates are that 10 percent of all PCBs manufactured remain in the environment today because the chemicals biodegrade slowly and linger in air, water, and soil.

Within the marine environment, PCBs enter the food chain when plankton absorbs the chemicals before being eaten by small fish. When the small fish are caught and ground into fish meal and fish oil for salmon feed, the PCBs are concentrated in the feed pellets. Eating contaminated salmon poses a long-term health risk because PCBs "bioaccumulate" in fat, leading to higher concentrations in fatty fish like salmon and the small fish on which they feed—and ultimately in the humans who eat the fish. Wild salmon also contain PCBs, but the *Science* study found concentrations were much higher in farmed salmon because they are fattier and because their diet is more restricted.

The *Science* study also found high levels of two banned pesticides, toxaphene and dieldrin. Toxaphene is a combination of hundreds of chemicals once used as a pesticide on cotton, for tick control on livestock, and to kill unwanted fish in lakes. The U.S. Environmental Protection Agency banned its use in 1990, after it was linked to convulsive seizures in livestock. Dieldrin was produced as an insecticide for corn, cotton, and citrus crops and for mothproofing clothes and carpets. The U.S. Department of Agriculture banned dieldrin in 1970, and the EPA followed suit in 1987. The presence of these toxins and PCBs in salmon long after the substances were banned demonstrates how long they remain in the environment and how long they continue to threaten human health.

The concentrations of toxins varied according to where the salmon were purchased. Farmed fish from Chile and Washington State had lower levels of overall contamination than those from Europe. The differences likely stemmed from variations in feed for the farmed salmon.

Fish oils and fish meal used in salmon feed are derived from drying and pressing small fish, such as herring, sardines, and anchovies. Contaminants in the small fish are concentrated during the processing of the feed. The *Science* authors acknowledged that the individual contaminant levels did not exceed U.S. Food and Drug Administration standards, but they said the FDA levels were not based strictly on health risks. Instead, the study relied on guidelines developed by the EPA, which take a broader view of risks from multiple contaminants that accumulate over time in the body. Using the EPA standard, the study concluded that farmed salmon contained up to ten times as much cancer-causing chemicals as their wild counterparts.

The authors took care to acknowledge the health benefits of eating salmon. But they concluded that most farm-raised Atlantic salmon should be eaten at one meal or less per month. Eating farmed salmon more often, the study said, "may pose risks that detract from the beneficial effects of fish consumption." The authors recommended that farmed salmon be labeled according to its country of origin, that contaminants in feed be reduced, and that the EPA and FDA develop a single standard for evaluating contaminant levels in seafood to provide consistent advice for consumers.

The findings echoed a similar, less-noticed analysis conducted in 2003 by the Environmental Working Group, a nonprofit advocacy organization based in Washington, DC. According to laboratory tests, seven out of ten farmed salmon purchased by the group at grocery stores in Washington, DC, San Francisco, and Portland, Oregon, were contaminated with PCBs "at levels that raise health concerns." The analysis found the level of PCBs in farmed salmon averaged 16 times higher than PCBs in wild salmon and 3.4 times the level in other types of seafood.

The 2003 analysis was smaller, and it was not published in a scientific journal, so it did not attract the attention of the later study. The stature of *Science* as a respected journal, published by the American Association for the Advancement of Science, the largest federation of scientists in the world, and the scale of its analysis propelled its warnings onto front pages around the world. The *New York Times* published a lengthy article recounting the findings and followed with an editorial raising the specter of "mad cow disease" in farmed salmon. The paper called for greater transparency to "help consumers make wise choices and put pressure on the dirtier parts of the fish farming industry to clean up." CNN broadcast a graphic drawn from the data under the headline, "Farm-Raised Salmon Is More Toxic." Down-market, the *New York Post* ran a front-page headline: "Salmon-Slammin' Study Says Farmed Fish Are Foul." The *Scotsman*, one of Scotland's quality newspapers, ran an article under the headline "Eating Farm Salmon 'Raises Risk of Cancer.'"

The industry responded swiftly with a sophisticated public relations campaign to discredit the findings on two fronts. The first strategy was to ignore the data and attack the methodology of the study by claiming the authors had not used the best standards. Critical articles from experts and government officials began to appear in the days after the study's publication. Many of the criticisms came from experts aligned with the salmon industry— like John Webster, an adviser to Scottish Quality Salmon, who called the study's conclusions "scaremongering" and said, "If we were to take that sort of advice, we'd have nothing on the menu at all."

Dr. Walter Willett, a professor at Harvard University's School of Public Health, was stronger in condemning the *Science* paper. In an article in the *American Journal of Preventive Medicine*, Willett wrote, "That publication was particularly troublesome, perhaps even irresponsible, because the implied health consequences were based on hypothetical calculations and very small lifetime risks." Astoundingly, he claimed the report "almost certainly contributed to a reduction in fish consumption that likely caused substantial numbers of premature deaths."

The Harvard professor's accusation about premature deaths drew a sharp response from the paper's authors. In a formal reply published in *Science*, they called Willett's comments defamatory, inaccurate, and scurrilous. One of the authors, Dr. Ronald Hites of Indiana University, later pointed out that Willett's research was financed by the U.S. Tuna Foundation and the National Fisheries Institute, both major lobbying organizations for the fishing industry. The financing was not disclosed by Willett, unlike the *Science* study's disclosure that it was financed by Pew.

The second line of attack targeted the study's funder, Pew Charitable Trusts. Industry-backed nutritionists and representatives had long attacked Pew and other philanthropies for promoting "sustainable seafood" campaigns. In this case, one commentator called the authors "pawns of the environmentalists," and the industry claimed Pew had "a position against salmon farming." The Scottish salmon-farming industry asserted wildly that it was the victim of a global conspiracy. "This was a deliberately engineered food scare orchestrated to attack the salmon farming industry in Scotland," said Brian Simpson, chief executive of Scottish Quality Salmon. The *Observer* in London said Pew was the "research body with an anti-pollution agenda."

So, one might ask, who has a *pro*-pollution agenda?

As part of the campaign, Scottish Quality Salmon hired a London public relations firm to counter the *Science* article with a global campaign of counterinformation. The PR firm analyzed supposed inaccuracies in the article and prepared an initial media statement that went to 600 UK media contacts, various elected officials, civil servants, and 22,500 international media outlets. A second statement followed, focused on scientific condemnation of the study, much of it from industry-backed experts and emphasizing the health benefits of eating salmon.

As the public relations counterattack gained ground, American and international scientists defended the *Science* study. "It is based on sound science, and the results are undeniable," said George Lucier, a former director of the U.S. Department of Health and Human Services national toxicological program, who had written more than two hundred studies on toxic chemicals. Others pointed out that Pew's financing of the study was transparent, a sharp contrast with the tactics employed by the industry. "We did get a bit of heat, but not too much," Hites recalled. "We were certainly never asked to retract the paper by anyone. In fact, no one ever criticized the data at all that I know about."

The full extent of the salmon industry's campaign to discredit the criticism remained hidden until 2007. David Miller, a professor of political sociology and cofounder of Public Interest Investigations, a British nonprofit organization, published a lengthy scholarly article called "Spinning Farmed Salmon." As recounted by Miller, the main pro-salmon-farming association in the United States, Salmon of the Americas, set up fake websites to drive traffic to captive sites that described the health value of farmed salmon. One example was www.pcbsalmon, which assured visitors that they should not worry about toxins in farmed salmon. "PCBs and similar compounds are so widespread in the environment that they are in the air we breathe, the water we drink and swim in, and the foods we eat," said the site. Nowhere did the fake sites indicate that they were run by the salmon industry, which Miller called "a classic deceptive PR technique."

The salmon-farming industry had learned its lessons from Big Tobacco, which deflected legitimate science and health concerns for decades by attacking critics, trying to discredit scientific findings, and financing efforts to dispute the risks of smoking. More recently, oil companies like ExxonMobil have tried to shift the blame for the climate crisis away from fossil fuels by portraying themselves as essential to economic development and responsive to consumer demand. Naomi Oreskes, a professor at Harvard University, said ExxonMobil depicts itself as reasonable and inevitable "not by outright lies, but by misrepresentation, by misleading claims, and by misdirection." In the same way, salmon farmers and aquaculture in general promote themselves as the best solution for feeding the global population while downplaying the health and environmental risks of their business.

The goal of the industries is to exploit the uncertainty that often accompanies scientific findings. In a paper with the catchy title "Scientific Certainty Argumentation Methods" (acronym SCAMs), the late sociologist William Freudenburg said the outcome of scientific controversies "may depend less on which side has the 'best science' than on which side enjoys the benefit of the doubt in the face of scientific ambiguity."

The media often abet the ambiguity by giving equal relevance to both sides of a debate, leaving consumers with doubts that can be exploited by industry. Professor Hites said he did not pay much attention to the campaign against his study by the salmon-farming industry, but he recognized the role of the press in the fight to inform the public. A presentation for his classes at Indiana University contains a section on dealing with the press. Hites cautions his students that reporters often have not done their homework and that they sometimes lack the expertise to understand important facts. And he offers specific advice for scientists when talking to reporters for publications linked to businesses: "Be careful talking to 'special interest flacks.'" He concludes by saying, "Be helpful—after all, the press is trying to bridge the gap between science and the public."

The 2004 study by Hites and his colleagues grabbed the attention of the press, the public, and the industry. The findings moved the dial on awareness of the health risks in eating farmed salmon, sparking an ongoing debate and an onslaught of contradictory advice for consumers. Making a wise choice depends on a full grasp of the benefits and risks and an understanding of where the salmon you are eating originated.

The question is whether enough accurate information is available to enable consumers to make smart and healthy choices about farmed salmon, a product that has divided medical experts and nutritionists.

CHAPTER 6

HEALTH MATTERS

The debate over the health benefits and risks of eating farmed salmon have divided government agencies, the industry, and medical experts. For consumers, the absence of clear guidance creates confusion and dangers, particularly for certain population groups.

Dr. Leonardo Trasande of New York University has a much broader view of health issues than most physicians or scientists. He is a medical doctor with advanced degrees in environmental science and public health policy, all from Harvard University. His work at "the intersection of environmental science, medicine, and policy," as he describes it, has made him an internationally renowned leader in the study of the impact on children of toxins, pesticides, and other contaminants. Despite his expertise, Trasande acknowledges that he is puzzled when shopping for salmon near his home in New York City.

"It is confusing, and I suspect there is willful confusion out there," said Trasande, who published *Sicker, Fatter, Poorer*, a book about the urgent health threat from chemicals in food and the environment. "We know that every fish is a tradeoff between omega-3 content and toxic content like PCBs. From the perspective of salmon in general, the balance favors consumption of that fish. Now the challenge here is that I can't tell which salmon is farmed the right way or the wrong way."

From Trasande's perspective, the wrong way to farm salmon involves a diet heavy in fish meal and fish oil, which increases the level of PCBs, and the use of pesticides and other chemicals, which leaves residues in the salmon flesh that is harmful to humans. His concerns persist despite a decline in PCB levels in the general environment and in farmed salmon. Even small amounts of residual PCBs pose a risk because flushing PCBs out of the human body is difficult. The same inertness that made the compound effective in industrial applications like flame retardants makes it hard for human enzymes to eliminate it from the body. As a result, someone who consumes food contaminated by PCBs as a teenager will still have some of the compound in their body when they die.

Trasande's biggest worry is that prenatal exposure to PCBs impairs brain development in fetuses and young children. Scientific proof of this link has been around since the late 1990s, when a series of studies reported brain impairment in Michigan children exposed to PCBs because their mothers ate contaminated fish. Sandra and Joseph Jacobson, professors at Wayne State University in Detroit, studied children born to mothers who ate contaminated fish from Lake Michigan for more than a decade. The children, known as the "Jacobson cohort," showed persistent neurological effects from birth to eleven years of age. The most highly exposed children were three times as likely to have low-to-average IQs and to be at least two years behind in reading level.

Since the groundbreaking study by the Jacobsons was completed, science has evolved to show that when it comes to these contaminants, little things matter. "We used to think that dosage was the thing that made a poison," Trasande explained. "With lead, PCBs, and pesticides, we now realize that low-level exposures can be especially harmful regardless of doses. There is a danger based on minimum levels." The risk increases over prolonged exposure because PCBs and other toxins accumulate in both fish and humans. This means that eating farmed salmon just a few times a month could still lead to unhealthy accumulations of toxins.

Beyond these dangers, there is a glaring lack of transparency and accountability when it comes to knowing where and how the farmed salmon at your local market was raised and what that means for your health. The baseline disclosure should specify whether the salmon was caught in the wild or raised in an open-net farm on the ocean or on land. If it was farmed, as most salmon is these days, the label should specify where the farm is located and disclose what additives and chemical treatments were given to the salmon. The process is easier than it sounds. QR codes, the small black-and-white squares that are ubiquitous on all sorts of products, could be scanned by a smartphone to disclose where a salmon was raised, what it was fed, which chemicals and antibiotics were used, and a range of other information. This kind of transparency could help consumers make smart choices and build trust in farmed salmon and other seafood. The information would also be valuable for food safety inspectors tracing food-borne illnesses and potential violations of U.S. laws governing contaminants in seafood.

As things stand now, Trasande said, neither the FDA nor companies provide enough data to allow consumers to make an informed choice. "You need transparency, and for transparency you need data," he said. "You need better lay language to advise people about the health benefits of fish consumption. There is no clear-cut signaling mechanism here. We have to level with the consumer." Until that happens, Trasande recommends eating a balance of diverse types of seafood, ranging from shrimp and scallops to wild salmon, but eating only those farmed salmon raised without chemicals.

Trasande's solution is realistic and within the power of governments: environmental and nutritional data on labels and in written statements on company websites would take the guesswork out of buying farmed salmon for consumers looking for fish that is healthy and easy on the environment. Given the industry's history of marketing hype, the information would need verification by independent scientists and nutritionists. Several organizations offer endorsements of a product's sustainability, impact on the environment, and health benefits. Not all findings are created equal. The most trusted sources are independent, third-party certifications that rely on scientific data. Far less trustworthy are self-declarations from salmon-farming companies and the judgments of industry-financed certification programs. Because there are no established government standards for or oversight of labeling, these examples of self-regulation are often vague and vary in rigor, scope, and accuracy.

The most popular guide for consumers interested in the environmental impact of their food is probably Seafood Watch, which is operated by the Monterey Bay Aquarium, a nonprofit in California dedicated to ocean conservation. Seafood Watch uses a color scale like a traffic light to rank farmed salmon and other seafood. Green means the seafood is on the "Best Choices" list—that is, it is caught or farmed in ways that cause little harm to other wildlife or habitats and that use minimal chemicals. Yellow is for "Good Alternatives," indicating, buy it, but be aware of concerns about how the seafood is caught or farmed. Red means "Avoid"—don't buy. The red badge is reserved for seafood that is overfished or caught or farmed in ways that harm other marine life or the environment and for aquaculture facilities that use too many chemicals.

Industry has pushed back against Seafood Watch's recommendations, arguing that the guide is overly broad and does not consider economic factors. On the other side of the coin, environmentalists and nutrition experts complain that Seafood Watch and similar guides for consumers are simplistic and do not provide enough information about the health risks of farmed salmon. The result, these critics argue, is a false sense of security for consumers who think they are buying safe, sustainable salmon when the reality is more complex. Still, absent full disclosures by companies on their labels, the broad rankings of Seafood Watch provide a useful, if incomplete, guide. The organization's credibility is assured, too, because Seafood Watch does not rely on the industry for financing. It receives roughly half its funding from the Monterey Bay Aquarium, with most of the remainder coming from independent foundations.

In the case of farmed salmon, trustworthy rankings can help people avoid fish raised in the least environmentally conscious manner and that are more likely to contain harmful contaminants. But these recommendations shift the choice, and the guilt, to individual consumers rather than holding an industry accountable or requiring government agencies to protect public health and the environment. The transparency required to instill trust in consumers will not occur until governments require full and accurate disclosures for salmon just as they do for other processed food.

Some stores label salmon as farmed, though identifying the country of origin is rare, and data about PCBs and other potential contaminants is absent. Others simply market the fish as "fresh Atlantic salmon," without reference to its origins on a farm. Just because it is called Atlantic salmon does not mean the fish has ever seen the Atlantic Ocean. Even when the salmon is labeled, the information is not always accurate. A survey by Oceana, a nonprofit conservation organization, found that 43 percent of salmon samples it tested were mislabeled. The most common form of misrepresentation was selling farmed Atlantic salmon as wild salmon.

Another major health concern is the content of the dry pellets of feed given to farmed salmon. In the 1980s, the major salmon-farming nations began to use antibiotics to fight diseases like furunculosis, a highly contagious bacterial infection that can kill salmon. Antibiotics to combat the disease were mixed into the feed with little understanding of the long-term effects. As more diseases occurred, more antibiotics were used. Norway, the world's largest producer of farmed salmon, used fifty metric tons of antibiotics in 1987. Farmers soon discovered that overuse of antibiotics causes resistance in salmon, leading to the need for larger quantities and more powerful drugs. The effects do not stop with salmon. Epidemiological studies have found that antibiotic-resistant genes in farmed salmon can make their way into the human food chain and possibly contribute to antibiotic resistance in people.

This persistent overuse of antibiotics creates microbes that evade the natural immune defenses and are resistant to drugs used to treat diseases in humans. Researchers at Arizona State University also found increases in drug-resistant strains of antibiotics in farmed seafood over the past three decades. While the study found that the seafood complied with FDA regulations on antibiotic levels, the researchers said subregulatory amounts can lead to resistance. Antibiotics like amoxicillin and ampicillin are used both in aquaculture and in treating humans, posing an additional potential risk that requires monitoring, the researchers said.

The World Health Organization has called antibiotic resistance one of the biggest threats to global health and safe food production because the overuse in humans and animals is accelerating the natural resistance process worldwide and across the food and drug spectrum. "Antibiotic resistance leads to longer hospital stays, higher medical costs and increased mortality," said the World Health Organization. "The world urgently needs to change the way it prescribes and uses antibiotics." Health officials in the United States have long acknowledged the dangers of overusing antibiotics in animal feed and agriculture. The biggest fear is that excessive use causes dangerous pathogens to mutate. The U.S. Centers for Disease Control and Prevention estimates that drug-resistant infections kill more than thirty-five thousand Americans each year.

The origin of farmed Atlantic salmon matters, as Trasande pointed out. In the late 1980s, the Norwegian Veterinary Institute developed a vaccine to reduce the need for antibiotics in feed. The vaccine is injected into the abdomen of salmon at an early stage in their development through an automated process. Within a decade, Norway's salmon farmers switched to the vaccine, and their use of antibiotics declined sharply. Since then, vaccines have been developed for many of the diseases commonly found in farmed salmon, including infectious salmon anemia, the most common and costly disease in the industry.

Yet, because vaccines can be expensive and cumbersome to administer, some salmon farmers and some countries continue to add large quantities of antibiotics to feed. Chile, the second-largest producer of farmed salmon behind Norway and the largest salmon exporter to the United States, used more than 933,000 pounds of antibiotics in 2013, according to a report by Chile's National Fisheries and Aquaculture Service. The same year, Norwegian salmon farmers used only 2,100 pounds. Chilean salmon farmers have begun to reduce the use of antibiotics, but they are far from reaching their goal of cutting it in half by 2025. Seafood Watch placed 50 percent of Chile's farmed salmon on the "Avoid" list in 2021 because of the high volume of antibiotics and pesticides used to control diseases and sea lice.

The rapid growth of Atlantic salmon farming in Chile since the early 1980s turned salmon into one of the country's leading exports. The growth has been accompanied by large-scale outbreaks of bacterial and viral diseases. In 2007, an outbreak of the infectious salmon anemia virus at a farm in Chile owned by Norway's Marine Harvest spread through southern Chile, where most of the salmon farms are in cages along the Pacific coast. The Chilean industry sustained two billion dollars in losses, and more than twenty-five thousand workers were laid off.

Fred Kibenge's lab, at the University of Prince Edward Island in Canada, traced the outbreak in Chile to a strain of ISA first identified in a 1996 outbreak in Norway. In an email to the International Society for Infectious Diseases, Kibenge said the virus was introduced from Norway several years before the outbreak and had probably circulated undetected for more than a decade. Cermaq, which was controlled by the Norwegian government at the time, eventually acknowledged that salmon eggs it had shipped to Chile were likely responsible for the outbreak. Kibenge's pioneering work on ISA would later come back to haunt him.

Environmentalists claimed that the ISA virus was so devastating in Chile in part because the pens were so overcrowded. The Chilean government tried to institute structural reforms, but outbreaks continued to plague the industry, and high levels of antibiotics are still being used in Chile. Authorities there say their salmon is safe to eat and that the antibiotics they use have been approved by U.S. food and drug regulators. But the concerns led Costco to reduce imports of Chilean salmon in 2015, from 90 percent to 40 percent of total purchases, with Norwegian salmon making up the remaining 60 percent.

Salmon farmers have reduced the level of contaminants and chemicals in their fish, but as Trasande and other scientists have found, even small amounts accumulate over time and pose a danger to consumers. Trasande explained that assessing the risks of pesticides to humans changed radically when researchers discovered that effects could be seen at low levels. The lower levels were first found to disrupt brain growth in animals. Alarm increased when studies showed that the lower levels of exposure that damaged animals corresponded roughly to the levels found commonly in humans. The studies were in animals, but the findings undermined the basis for assuming that low-level pesticide exposure might be safe in humans. "It turned this scientific field of study upside down," said Trasande.

Invisible contaminants are found in many aspects of everyday life. Humans are exposed to pesticides through food, skin, and inhalation. The National Marine Fisheries Service suggested placing restrictions on aerial spraying to reduce runoff in rivers and streams that pose a danger to salmon and other fish. One of the most dangerous contaminants is chlorpyrifos, which is widely used to protect crops from insects. The U.S. government's top fisheries experts found that chlorpyrifos is one of three widely used pesticides threatening the survival of wild salmon and the orcas that feed on them. In recent years, scientists have found evidence that exposure to chlorpyrifos residue can harm the developing brains of small children, leading to tremors, poor motor skills, and autism. A 2019 academic study found that feeds given to farmed salmon can contain trace amounts of chlorpyrifos and other agricultural pesticides. An attempt by government scientists to ban the chemical in 2018 was blocked by the Trump administration, but in 2021 the Biden administration prohibited use of the pesticide.

Despite these concerns, farmed salmon can be part of a healthy diet. The primary benefit comes from salmon's omega-3 fatty acids. Omega-3 reduces the risk of coronary heart disease, helps lower blood pressure, and can improve neurological functioning and reduce inflammation. But a study published in 2016 in *Nature*, the British science journal, found that omega-3s had fallen by about 50 percent in farmed salmon because farms were substituting plant-based sources like soybeans and corn for fish meal. The diet has been changing in part to reduce levels of PCBs in fish meal and in part because overfishing has sent the price of small fish soaring, necessitating cheaper substitutes. The switch to more grains like genetically modified soy and corn in salmon feed has increased levels of omega-6 fatty acids. The American Heart Association cites numerous studies supporting the heart benefits of omega-6 fats. Concerns arise, however, when the ratio between the two types of fatty acids is out of balance. Omega-3 helps blood flow, reducing the risk of heart problems, but omega-6 helps blood clot. Omega-3 fights inflammation, but omega-6 contributes to it. Most people in developed countries already consume more omega-6 than is considered healthy, and excessive levels may be linked to obesity, bowel diseases, and inflammatory diseases like rheumatoid arthritis and Alzheimer's.

Scientists and nutritionists differ on the health risks posed by the organic pollutants and chemicals in farmed salmon. When you eat salmon, you are consuming all the pollutants and additives to which the fish has been exposed, which are stored in its fat. Farmed salmon are much fattier than their wild counterparts, leading to higher concentrations of dioxins like PCBs. These same chemicals are found in wild salmon, but research indicates that farmed salmon contain higher concentrations of dioxins and dioxin-like substances. Studies have linked these contaminants to Type 2 diabetes, an increased risk of strokes in women, and infertility in men. Sharp differences have arisen among scientists and physicians over who should eat farmed salmon and how much is safe to consume.

What is considered settled science is that PCBs pose health risks. A paper produced by the U.S. Public Health Service and the EPA in 2015 found that elevated PCB levels in humans have "compelling implications," particularly for a broad category of susceptible populations like the elderly, fetuses, nursing infants, children, and pregnant women. Scientists have been most worried about the impact of PCBs on rapidly developing bodies of children in the womb and soon after birth. The paper suggested that exposures can have serious and lifelong consequences. It described behavioral problems and developmental deficits in newborns exposed before birth to PCBs that continue through school-age children. An earlier study by researchers at the U.S. National Institutes of Health linked high levels of PCBs and similar environmental pollutants to difficulties in becoming pregnant.

In 2013, a dispute broke out in Norway when two hospital clinicians said that children, teenagers, and pregnant women should limit their consumption of farmed salmon. Dr. Anne-Lise Bjorke-Monsen, a pediatrician, and Bjorn Bolann, a professor of medicine at Haukeland University Hospital in Bergen, said PCBs and contaminants could disrupt developing brains and might be linked to autism. The Norwegian government responded by advising children and pregnant women to restrict their consumption to just two portions a week, matching standards in place in the United Kingdom. The industry-backed National Institute of Nutrition and Seafood Research claimed the research was based on outdated data and that there was no reason to restrict consumption of farmed salmon. Pamela Lein, a developmental neurobiologist at the University of California, Davis, said PCB exposure is unlikely to cause autism, though she cautioned that it might increase the likelihood of autism in children predisposed to it through genetic makeup.

The salmon-farming industry objects to criticism of the health benefits of its product. Studies financed by the industry have countered findings by independent scientists that have shown risks from pesticides, PCBs, dioxins, antibiotics, and the red dye that gives farmed salmon the illusion of health. Salmon of the Americas, which represents salmon farmers across North and South America, boasts about the nutritional value of salmon on its website. "Ocean-farmed salmon is a high-protein meal that is rich in Omega-3 fatty acids, which are important for kids and adults alike," it says. "Evidence strongly suggests that increasing Omega-3 fatty acids in the diet helps prevent heart disease and, in increased consumption levels, may dramatically cut the mortality rate in heart attack survivors."

Some websites and publications that dispute the health risks of farmed salmon are tied to the industry, though it can take a couple of extra clicks on the computer to figure that out. For instance, the website Healthy Fish promotes eating farmed fish and debunks the so-called "myths" about contaminants. The fine print includes the words "By Regal Springs," and a couple taps on the keypad reveal that the website is sponsored by one of the world's largest producers of farmed tilapia, with facilities in Honduras, Indonesia, and Mexico. A host of other publications and websites advocating for the industry have financial ties to aquaculture that are often obscured by phrases like "a grassroots organization."

Consumers can be excused for being confused. For instance, the Mayo Clinic, recognized as one of the world's leading centers for medical care and research, offers conflicting advice on eating salmon. In a July 2019 paper, the clinic staff praised salmon for its omega-3 content and said it is low in saturated fat and cholesterol, making it a good source of protein. The paper suggested that pregnant women follow federal guidelines and eat eight to twelve ounces of seafood a week. Under the heading "What's Safe to Eat?" the clinic listed salmon as one of the beneficial seafoods. But the staff did not differentiate between wild-caught salmon and farmed salmon, the latter of which has more PCBs, saturated fats, and omega-6.

In another paper a year later, Jennifer Nelson, a professor at the Mayo Clinic's College of Medicine, cautioned that PCBs pose serious health risks to people who frequently eat contaminated fish. "They can be transferred from a mother to her unborn baby, increasing the risk of preterm delivery and low birth weight," said Nelson. "They may also be transferred from mother to baby through breast milk, and exposure has been associated with learning defects." In this case, the paper differentiated between wild and farmed salmon, pointing out that farmed salmon are higher in PCBs. "Farmed salmon that are fed ground-up fish have been found to be higher in PCBs, compared with wild-caught salmon," Nelson wrote, suggesting that consumers follow recommendations from the FDA and EPA: trim away fatty areas of farmed salmon, remove the skin before cooking to allow the fat to drain off, and do not fry or deep-fry the fish, because doing so seals the chemical pollutants in its fat.

Some recommendations are stricter, depending on personal health. For instance, a recent Harvard Medical School publication suggested that omega-3s might tip the balance in favor of farmed salmon for older people who have a greater risk of heart disease. But, Harvard cautioned, if you are pregnant, the risks from PCBs are larger, and you might want to reduce salmon in your diet. For people who have a personal or family history of cancer, the Harvard paper suggested eating only one or two servings of farmed salmon a month.

Two other groups, Physicians for Social Responsibility and the Association of Reproductive Health Professionals, recommend limiting your intake of salmon and other fish with high levels of PCBs.

To follow these and other guidelines, it is important to understand where the salmon originated, which requires that its origin be accurately declared on the label. Surveys have found that farmed salmon is often misidentified as wild-caught salmon. Some regions produce farmed salmon higher in contaminants, including antibiotic residue and PCBs.

A simple way to think about all the health concerns surrounding salmon is to parse the common saying "You are what you eat." The axiom does not go far enough, because you are also *what was eaten* by what you eat. When it comes to farmed Atlantic salmon, it can be difficult to figure out what the fish you are eating ate. And the industry's marketing practices rarely contribute to clarity.

CHAPTER 7

WHOM CAN YOU TRUST?

Given all the contradictory medical advice and evidence of misrepresentation in labeling and marketing farmed salmon, the question to ask as you stand in front of the fish counter is: Whom can you trust? Civil lawsuits filed in American courts and ongoing regulatory actions indicate that the world's biggest salmon producer is probably not the answer.

Three lawsuits filed against two subsidiaries of Mowi, the world's dominant farmed-salmon player and a presence in every country where salmon is farmed, accused the subsidiaries of deceptive marketing and false advertising for selling smoked Atlantic salmon as "all natural" and "sustainably sourced" fish "from the coast of Maine." The accusations against Mowi USA and Mowi Ducktrap were made initially in two lawsuits filed in 2020, one in Superior Court in Washington, DC, on behalf of the Organic Consumers Association, and the other in federal court in Maine on behalf of an individual. The third was a class-action suit nearly identical to the Maine case, filed in federal court in New York City.

Court documents in the suits challenged virtually all Mowi's marketing claims about its Ducktrap smoked salmon. For example, the packaging boasted that the fish was "the finest naturally smoked seafood from the coast of Maine." The fish-smoking facility is in Belfast, Maine, but the suits allege that the salmon came from Mowi's industrial farms in Canada, Chile, Norway, and Scotland. Mowi said its Ducktrap smoked salmon was "all natural" and "100% natural." But the company's own audit documents showed that farms providing salmon to Ducktrap used pesticides, antibiotics, and other chemicals to treat their fish.

The lawsuits said Mowi intended for consumers to rely on its "sustainably sourced" representation and that "reasonable consumers" did in fact rely on this representation. By deceiving consumers about the nature and sourcing of its products, Mowi was able to sell more smoked salmon at higher prices and thus take away market share from competitors, according to the lawsuits. All three suits said that Mowi's claims of sustainability violated warnings from the Federal Trade Commission about misusing terms such as *sustainability* and *eco-friendly*. The FTC, which protects consumers from fraud, says that general claims like "sustainable" convey to consumers that the product has no negative impact on the environment. The FTC has warned companies not to use this type of unqualified claim because it is highly unlikely that all reasonable interpretations can be substantiated.

In the case of Mowi's claims about its smoked salmon, the lawsuits said conditions on the farms where the salmon was raised were not sustainable and that the sites posed grave risks to the environment, animal welfare, and public health. "At industrial salmon farms, salmon are confined in overcrowded and unsanitary marine pens that can contain more than 70,000 fishes at a time," said the Maine lawsuit. "These high-density conditions not only inflict extreme stress on the salmon, but also lead to the development of ecologically dangerous diseases and parasitic infestations. Because the marine pens are connected directly to the ocean environment, outbreaks can endanger surrounding ecosystems. These crowded and disease-ridden conditions cause industrial salmon farms to use large amounts of pesticides and antibiotics. This can contribute to the emergence of antimicrobial resistance in bacteria that may be transferred to humans." The complaint cited the CDC's warning that thirty-five thousand Americans die every year from antibiotic-resistant infections and the World Health Organization's description of antibiotic resistance as "one of the most urgent health risks of our time" and as an "invisible pandemic."

The suits said consumers had been paying higher prices for Ducktrap salmon because they had been tricked into thinking it was natural, healthy, and would not harm the environment. The complaints all said that consumers are particularly vulnerable to these misleading claims because they are unable to disprove them. "Most consumers choosing a smoked Atlantic salmon product with the words 'All Natural' on the package would be surprised to learn that that salmon was raised in a crowded pen where it was treated with artificial chemicals including pesticides and medically important antibiotics," said Ronnie Cummins, director of the nonprofit Organic Consumers Association.

Cummins's nonprofit group brought the first of the three lawsuits against Mowi, the one in DC Superior Court. The association was represented by Richman Law and Policy, the New York firm that a year earlier filed a lawsuit against another big salmon farmer, Cooke Aquaculture, over the brutal conditions for salmon at that company's hatchery in Bingham, Maine.

In a press statement in response to the lawsuit filed in Maine, Mowi said, "All Mowi farm-raised Atlantic salmon products in the U.S. are certified as sustainably and responsibly sourced by independent third parties. Following a rigorous certification process, Mowi has been recognized to abide by industry best practices for sustainable agriculture."

Mowi's assertions raised several questions. Chief among them was the veracity of the third-party certifications cited by the company. Most Mowi salmon farms are located in regions on the Seafood Watch "Avoid" list because of heavy use of chemicals and sustainability concerns. "Atlantic salmon farmed in Canada's Atlantic, Chile, Norway and Scotland (except the Orkney Islands) are on the 'Avoid' list," said Seafood Watch at the time the lawsuits were filed. "The overuse of chemicals is a critical concern in Chile and a high concern for the other sources. In Norway and Scotland, escapes of farmed salmon are a major risk to the genetic composition and fitness of wild, native salmon populations." Except for Chile, where there are no wild salmon, Seafood Watch said the impact of disease on wild fish in the other countries was a grave concern.

Mowi and its subsidiaries have experienced problems in many places. In early 2019, antitrust regulators raided salmon farms in Scotland owned by Mowi and four other big Norwegian companies as part of an inquiry into whether they were working together as a cartel to fix prices on the international salmon market. Norway is not a European Union member, and the government blocked attempts by EU investigators to raid the head offices of the Norwegian companies. The companies were identified as Mowi, Cermaq, Grieg, Leroy, and SalMar, and together they control about 80 percent of the world's salmon market. In the United States, the U.S. Department of Justice opened a similar antitrust investigation into the same companies, and five salmon wholesalers filed a class-action civil suit accusing the Norwegian companies of coordinating sales prices and exchanging sensitive market information to reduce competition. The companies have denied any wrongdoing.

Mowi was also among several salmon farmers accused by the Scottish government of overusing chemicals like hydrogen peroxide to fight sea lice infestations and of polluting waterways with formaldehyde, a toxic pesticide used by salmon farms to control fungus, parasites, and disease. Formaldehyde, a colorless, flammable chemical, has been linked to cancer in humans. Scottish government documents showed that Mowi dumped nineteen metric tons of formaldehyde into Scotland's lochs and inlets over nine months in 2019. In its use of both hydrogen peroxide and formaldehyde, the company denied wrongdoing.

Mowi has a history of problems in Scotland, which is the third-largest producer of farmed salmon after Norway and Chile. In 2017, data from the Scottish Environment Protection Agency showed that forty-five lochs in western Scotland had been contaminated by toxic pesticides and other chemicals from seventy salmon farms in 2017. Among the companies identified in the records as responsible was Marine Harvest, the Norwegian farming giant now known as Mowi. Seafood Watch rates salmon from open-net farms in some parts of Scotland as "yellow," meaning it is a "good alternative." But large swaths of Scotland's farms are ranked in the "red" zone and should be avoided, according to the group.

When it comes to fish health and welfare, Mowi says it is "second to none," a claim contradicted by other recent incidents. As we will see in chapter 19, in the summer and fall of 2019, roughly 3 million salmon died at ten farms off the southern coast of Newfoundland owned by a Mowi subsidiary, Northern Harvest Sea Farms. The company blamed the mass deaths on warm weather, but according to biologists and a government-authorized review, other factors were involved. Mowi lost more fish than it harvested that year in Newfoundland. On the other side of the Atlantic, 737,000 salmon were killed by algae blooms, poor health, and disease at twelve Mowi farms in Scotland in 2019, and 1.5 million juvenile salmon died in a single episode in early 2020 at a new Mowi hatchery in Norway.

The claims in the lawsuits about false advertising challenge the entire salmon-farming industry, which employs similar language in much of its marketing. The potential for an industry-wide black eye brought aquaculture's leading certification organization, the Global Aquaculture Alliance, into court in Washington, DC. The alliance, which is financed by the industry, filed an amicus brief in support of Mowi's argument that the company and its subsidiaries complied with the group's "Best Aquaculture Practices," or BAP, which set standards for sustainability, treatment of fish, and impact on the environment. "A reasonable consumer would understand references to 'sustainably sourced' seafood to refer to seafood sourced from practices certified to comply with industry-leading standards, such as BAP," the group maintained in its filing, a piece of circular logic that translated into "trust us."

Six months after the class-action suit was filed in New York City, the protests from Mowi and the Global Aquaculture Alliance collapsed. The company agreed to pay $1.3 million to settle the lawsuit. As part of the settlement, Mowi agreed to stop using the phrases "sustainably sourced," "all natural," and "naturally smoked salmon from Maine" on any Ducktrap product for two years. In the weeks that followed, Mowi's Ducktrap subsidiary removed marketing material that described its products as "sustainably" or "naturally" raised and eliminated the claim that the salmon came from the coast of Maine. Instead, the company reverted to phrases like "smoked in Maine" and "inspired from the natural beauty of the Kendall Brook River that flows into the Ducktrap River of Maine." The $1.3 million was no more than a rounding error for Mowi, but for the company and the industry, the case was a warning to companies to substantiate all labeling claims. For consumers, the result of the lawsuit is a reminder to be wary of claims like "sustainable" and "natural" for salmon raised in open-net pens.

Instead of relying on companies with financial interests in certifications, laws should require that truly independent organizations provide accurate, verifiable information about how and where farmed salmon is raised. The extent of pesticides and other chemicals used at the farms should be disclosed, and the percentage of fish meal and fish oil contained in the diet should be clearly stated. Consumers should also be told if the feed includes genetically modified grains like soybeans and corn. The industry should no longer be permitted to slap on labels like "sustainable" or "all natural."

Pick up almost any packaged food or beverage and you will see a detailed list of ingredients and nutritional values on the label, which is required by the Food and Drug Administration. Even when it comes to what we feed our pets, the FDA mandates a list of ingredients and the manufacturer's name and address on labels. Some U.S. states go further and require nutrition and calorie statements even for pet food. Technology is beginning to embrace transparency on labels. Apple now requires software developers selling apps through its App Store to provide scannable "privacy labels," which list the types of data being collected by the app. If tech companies can make data security easier for consumers to understand when we're deciding how to use our smartphones, salmon farmers can provide clear and understandable information about the origin and content of their farmed salmon when we are deciding what to eat. Scannable labels on farmed salmon and other aquaculture products would allow consumers to access the full range of health and environmental data needed to make informed decisions at seafood counters.

If you can't trust the label, can you trust your eyes? Next time you're at the store, take a close look at the farmed salmon sitting on the crushed ice, assuming it is labeled properly as farmed. The deep pink color is appealing, conjuring images of wild salmon and rushing rivers, right?

In the wild, salmon range in color from pink to red because of their diet of algae and crustaceans like krill and shrimp. Color differences occur in wild salmon, and after they spawn, their flesh turns gray. A farmed salmon's diet of ground-up small fish, poultry by-products, wheat, and corn and soybeans, which are often genetically modified, produces gray meat. But studies have found that gray salmon does not appeal to shoppers, who are willing to pay more for fish that is red or pink. Salmon farmers responded by adding dye to their feed to make the fish appear rich in color like their prespawning wild counterparts. The most common additive is astaxanthin, an organic pigment that the FDA says is safe for humans. The industry even developed "Salmofan," a color chart like those found in paint stores, and instructs farmers on how much astaxanthin to add to the feed to produce the desired shade of pink, red, or orange.

Industry representatives bristle at the word *dye*, and reject the notion that color is added to farmed salmon. They prefer a rather elastic definition of "natural" in defending the practice. "It sounds like someone is injecting color into the fish, but the fish is actually 'colored' naturally from the feed we give the salmon," said Egil Sundheim, U.S. director of the Norwegian Seafood

Council. "We replicate all of the food and nutrients that salmon eat in the wild, including astaxanthin, an antioxidant found in the wild."

Given the conflicting advice on how healthy it is to eat farmed salmon and the widespread doubts about the industry's claims of sustainability and naturally raised salmon, the logical question is: What role does government play in ensuring the safety of this increasingly popular food, one that is often recommended for children and pregnant women? The answer is: Not much.

So, whom can you trust when you're browsing for salmon at your local store? Right now, nobody.

CHAPTER 8

OUT OF SIGHT, OUT OF MIND

The United States is the world's largest importer of seafood. The U.S. government estimates that about 90 percent of the seafood consumed in the country comes from outside its borders. Shrimp comes from Mexico and Vietnam; tilapia from China and Chile; salmon from Canada, Chile, Norway, and Scotland. Most of this seafood is produced through aquaculture, the practice of farming fish and shrimp in cages, ponds, streams, and open-net pens on the ocean. As a food-producing sector, aquaculture surpasses both wild fisheries and livestock. The industry's adherents are fond of proclaiming that they are feeding the world.

The global shift to aquaculture was dubbed the "Blue Revolution," reflecting the expanded role of the oceans in feeding the world. A 2003 editorial in the *Economist* praised the potential of new technologies and new breeds of fish to provide protein for rich and poor people. But it warned about the dangers, saying, "If fish farming starts to become a big business in international waters, it could become a big, hard-to-regulate and polluting industry; in other words, a tragedy of the commons."

Fast-forward two decades: some of the promise has been fulfilled, and so have most of the fears. Aquaculture today delivers cheap, vacuum-packed salmon, shrimp, tilapia, and other seafood to grocery freezers and millions of dinner tables every day. Simultaneously, the industry has far outstripped the ability of governments to regulate its practices, from polluting the oceans and producing contaminated products to contributing to illegal fishing and to food shortages in lower-income countries.

As we have seen so far, the risks to our environment and our health have increased at a worrisome pace alongside the industry's expansion. When it comes to farmed salmon, scientists, scholars, and physicians have found clear evidence that contaminants from chemicals and antibiotics are a danger to consumers, particularly pregnant women and young children. Pesticides and other chemicals have been found in Atlantic salmon raised in farms around the world. Often residue from these contaminants makes its way into the fish sold at grocery stores and restaurants.

Against this backdrop, governments have a clear role to play in protecting consumers from the health risks associated with aquaculture in general and farmed salmon in particular. The evidence suggests they are not playing that role well.

In the United States, the Food and Drug Administration is responsible for ensuring that fish and other aquaculture products imported into the country are safe and accurately labeled. The FDA has a broad and demanding mandate, with responsibility for supervising food safety, tobacco products, dietary supplements, prescription and over-the-counter drugs, vaccines, and a host of related products. Before the all-consuming demands of the COVID-19 pandemic, the agency was criticized for paying too little attention to imported seafood even as Americans were eating more of it. Imported foods come into the United States from dozens of countries where standards may differ, may be ignored, or may not exist at all. In many countries, the emphasis of government and producers is more likely to be on promoting exports than on protecting consumers. Yet the FDA pays little attention to what arrives at U.S. borders. In particular, the agency has never demonstrated any enthusiasm for inspecting farmed salmon or other imported seafood. Its budget is strained, and imported salmon and other aquaculture products have not been a pressing matter for Congress or any recent administration. A single statistic tells the tale: in 2017, congressional investigators said the FDA inspected 86 samples from 379,000 tons of imported farmed salmon in 2015, an infinitesimal fraction of the total.

Comparing the standards and frequency of inspections for domestic livestock and imported seafood in the United States demonstrates a stark contrast. A dairy farmer can see from an FDA-approved label that a drug can be used safely on cows producing milk. Domestic food manufacturers and farmers know that their facilities are likely to be inspected at any time, and their products are sampled regularly by the FDA or the Department of Agriculture, which is responsible for the safety of domestic meat, poultry, and eggs. The USDA employs more than 7,000 inspectors to monitor 6,400 domestic food-production facilities. Slaughterhouses for beef and chickens are required to have a USDA inspector present to operate, and meat processors are inspected at every shift.

The situation for imported seafood is completely different. More than 170 countries export seafood to the United States that is worth $27 billion annually. Studies show that consumers consider imported seafood riskier than domestic products, but those concerns are not reflected in the FDA's actions. Determining precisely how effective the agency is can be difficult because information is not easily available and overall inspections are low. For instance, figures obtained through the Freedom of Information Act show that in 2020 the FDA had about 700 food inspectors for more than 80,000 food facilities. Inspectors do not visit fish farms or commercial fishing vessels, restricting their rare in-person examinations to food-processing facilities. When it comes to regulating seafood, the adage proves true: Out of sight, out of mind.

Numerous research papers and news articles have over the years raised questions about how effectively the FDA is protecting Americans from risks posed by imported seafood. The most thorough inquiries have been conducted by the General Accountability Office, the respected, independent congressional watchdog agency. In a series of four reports dating back more than a decade, GAO investigators determined that the FDA has consistently lacked follow-through on potential violations of U.S. law and has relied too heavily on foreign processors and U.S. importers to verify the safety of imported farmed salmon and other products. In a 2021 review of FDA actions, the GAO found that the agency "did not consistently follow key procedures or meet key goals" and that it had failed to conduct follow-up investigations even after issuing formal warning letters to importers.

GAO reports present an alarming case study in failed regulation and a cautionary tale for consumers, particularly when you start with the fact that only a fraction of imported seafood is even inspected by the FDA. Despite the GAO's sharp criticism and specific recommendations for improvements in the first report, the investigative agency's latest report again criticized the FDA for failing to follow its own procedures or meet key goals to reduce the public health risk from imported seafood. For example, the FDA set a goal of conducting follow-up investigations within six months of issuing a warning letter after finding significant food safety violations in seafood. When investigators examined 167 warnings issued for risks from imported seafood between January 1, 2014, and March 11, 2019, they found that 125 warnings reflected serious violations of health and safety laws. Yet the GAO found that the FDA met its goal of conducting follow-up investigations within six months in only 14 of the 125 cases. It took an average of two years to follow up with inspections at 62 of the companies and allowed the remaining 49 violators to resume operations without an inspection.

There are plenty of reasons to inspect imported seafood thoroughly and regularly. A snapshot of violations discovered in recent FDA inspections disclosed a host of health hazards in imported seafood: residues of antibiotics and pesticides, illegal dyes, and decomposed insects and rodents. Also present were salmonella and *E. coli* bacteria, food-borne pathogens that can cause infections in humans ranging from mild diarrhea to life-threatening illness. FDA guidelines say violations should lead the agency to issue "import alerts," which can block products and place importers on a blacklist to stop further exports to the United States. Getting off the blacklist and resuming exports is supposed to be contingent upon a further inspection by the FDA.

But the GAO found that the Food and Drug Administration routinely failed to follow its own guidelines on violations. In a review of cases over a seven-year period, the GAO said the FDA had issued 274 decisions to block the importation of specific seafood products to the United States. For a foreign company to resume exports to the United States after a blocking order, the company can submit laboratory results showing that their products are not contaminated. The results come from private laboratories hired by the companies themselves. FDA internal guidelines require the agency to double-check the work of the private labs before clearing the company to resume imports. But when the GAO reviewed 274 cases in which the FDA accepted the results of the private labs, it found that the agency had checked the work of the labs in only 14 cases. Ninety-five percent of the time, the FDA took the word of the companies themselves that they were complying with health laws.

The most serious violations of oversight rules occur when entire seafood-processing plants, rather than individual shipments, are flagged for potential public health violations. In these cases, its guidelines require that the FDA conduct physical inspections of the foreign seafood-processing facilities before resuming importation, to ensure that practices have changed and health concerns have been resolved. Between 2011 and 2018, the FDA identified thirty-two violations deemed serious enough to require physical inspections. Yet the GAO found that the FDA conducted only one inspection, allowing other plants to resume operations without inspections.

Ryan Talbott, an attorney at the Center for Food Safety, a nonprofit advocacy group, said the GAO's findings were shocking. "That's a big problem and a red flag," he told the Counter, a nonprofit news organization focused on food safety. "FDA is not following through on their obligation to ensure that our food is protected. If you're eating fish, and it doesn't look any different, it doesn't smell any different, but it is infected with a pathogen, it's potentially a deadly problem."

Contaminated seafood continues to flow into the United States and onto shelves in grocery stores and tables in restaurants. We just don't know how often or how much, exactly where it's coming from, or what the specific threats are. Performing proper inspections would require more money to hire more inspectors and enlisting government laboratories to carry out the follow-up analysis. A decade ago, Congress passed legislation expanding the FDA's oversight on the supply chain and authorized the agency to undertake more preventative steps to ensure the safety of all imported food, but the budget to discharge these duties remains woefully inadequate.

The GAO recommended that the FDA establish a process to monitor whether the agency was meeting its goals for sampling and inspecting seafood imports and to develop measures to improve its safety program for imported food. The FDA accepted the recommendations and indicated that new steps would be undertaken to ensure that imported food met the same health standards as food produced domestically. The FDA did not respond to our specific questions but repeated that it has worked to improve its inspection process in the United States and with partners overseas. Yet gaps still exist. Senior FDA officials have acknowledged publicly that it is impossible to stop all unsafe food products before they reach U.S. markets. That admission means that whether as much as 90 percent of the seafood Americans consume is safe to eat is determined by foreign governments and companies that often have different health standards and financial interests than the United States when it comes to food safety.

Numerous studies have recommended increasing resources for the FDA and other agencies overseeing food safety and health; improving their ability to trace the origins of seafood and its route through the supply chain; and obtaining better, more accessible government data to identify the greatest risks and to ease consumer fears about products proven to be safe. The blueprint for doing a better job has been mapped, but it will require political will and public pressure to follow it.

One of the few nongovernmental watchdogs keeping an eye on the FDA is Food and Water Watch, a Washington, DC–based organization that tries to protect food and water from what it sees as corporate exploitation. Zach Corrigan, the organization's senior staff attorney, said an overhaul of the FDA food-inspection system is overdue. Reforms should start with a clear, public list of priorities for inspections. Food and Water Watch also recommends additional money for more inspectors. The absence of on-site inspections and weak enforcement send a signal to importers and exporters that they are unlikely to get caught breaking regulations. "We import a lot of seafood in the United States with few safeguards in place," said Corrigan. "Enhanced, targeted inspections would have a deterrent effect. It doesn't have to be ninety-nine percent, but it can't be one percent. That change could happen overnight, with the political will."

Even when governments try to get answers to questions about the environmental harm caused by salmon farms and the risks to human health, the effort rarely seems to make much difference, as Canadians found when their government tried to save wild salmon in British Columbia.

CHAPTER 9

NO SMOKING GUN

For more than a century, industrialized countries have intervened extensively in agricultural markets to protect their farmers and to promote positive trade balances through tariffs, subsidies, and controls over imports and exports. In recent years, new actors have appeared on the scene to advocate for issues like food safety, environmental concerns, and the climate crisis, which often conflict with existing policies. Despite those new concerns, government policies too often put politics and economics ahead of public health and the environment.

Canada, a major supplier of farmed salmon to the United States, presents a case study in misplaced priorities and conflicting missions. The Canadian government's role has changed little since it played midwife to the country's salmon-farming industry in the late 1970s. Back then, the government saw farmed Atlantic salmon as a replacement for the declining cod fishery and as a way to protect wild salmon. The government envisioned jobs for sparsely populated coastal regions and tax revenue from exports. Even as it became apparent that farmed salmon would not be a savior for their wild brethren, the regulators chose to ignore the emerging risks.

Regulation of aquaculture in Canada is divided between the federal and provincial governments. Primary responsibility lies with the federal Department of Fisheries and Oceans, or DFO, and with Environment Canada. Licensing and day-to-day oversight rests with the provincial governments, except in British Columbia. Thanks to Alexandra Morton and her lawsuit, which we saw in chapter 4, responsibility for regulating salmon farms there rested solely with the federal government.

But the damage in British Columbia had been done. The province's lax regulation and generous subsidies had attracted the big Norwegian salmon farmers in the early days of the industry in Canada. Marine Harvest, the industry's biggest player, arrived in British Columbia in the late 1980s, followed by two other big Norwegian companies, Cermaq and Grieg Seafood. In December 1990, Jon Lilletun, a member of Norway's parliament, the Storting, explained the influx of Norwegian companies to a Canadian parliamentary committee in Ottawa this way: "We are very strict about the quality and the environment questions. Therefore, some of the fish farmers went to Canada. They said we want bigger fish farms; we can do as we like. That is a very hot subject, I think."

Canadian officials ignored Lilletun's frank assessment. Policy and economic considerations outweighed evidence that salmon farms were contributing to the decline of wild salmon on the country's Pacific and Atlantic coasts and damaging other fisheries. Licenses for salmon farms in British Columbia and New Brunswick, the provinces where most of the farms were located, remained cheap while taxpayer-funded subsidies to install farms and open processing plants were plentiful. Not only did the government provide initial support, but it covered the salmon farmers for losses from disease and other causes. The combination of generous financial incentives and the policy of promotion worked. By the late 2000s, Canada was exporting more than five hundred million dollars' worth of farmed Atlantic salmon annually, most of it to the United States. The country ranked fourth among producing nations, behind Norway, Chile, and Scotland. But the consequences confounded expectations.

The concentration of farms was highest in British Columbia, and that was where the first problems arose by the late 1980s. Chief among the concerns was the spread of parasites and disease from farmed Atlantic salmon to the native wild Pacific salmon, which are considered a keystone species, crucial to the ecosystems, economies, and cultures along the U.S. and Canadian Pacific coasts. Canadian government auditors criticized the DFO for failing to protect the health and habitat of wild salmon. Efforts by independent biologists and other scientists to call attention to threats to native Pacific salmon encountered opposition from the industry and even the DFO. For its part, the industry continued to deny that its farms were endangering wild salmon or damaging the environment. All the while, the numbers of salmon returning to the rivers and streams of British Columbia were dropping.

Fisheries experts use various methods to count returning salmon. The simplest way is to monitor rivers and count salmon as they swim by. Other times, fish are counted as they climb fish ladders or stop behind a low dam on a river known as a weir. More sophisticated operations involve using sonar equipment to monitor the fish or estimating the numbers from aircraft flying above rivers. By 2009, the Canadian government could no longer ignore the dwindling numbers of wild salmon. That year, ten million sockeye salmon were expected to return to the Fraser River, the longest river in British Columbia and once a source of abundant salmon for First Nations and other people up and down the coast of the Pacific Northwest. But after declining steadily for nearly two decades, the bottom fell out in 2009. Instead of ten million salmon, only one million returned, the sharpest drop since 1913, when the counting began. Fishing rights for both First Nations tribes and nontribal fishers were suspended in Washington State and British Columbia, creating political pressure on the Canadian government to identify a cause or, more accurately, causes.

Climate change, logging, and urbanization contributed to the decline. But critics pointed the biggest finger at a new factor: the proliferation of commercial salmon feedlots located in the coastal waters that are essential to migrating sockeyes and other wild salmon. As currents pass through a farm's cages, parasites and pathogens are dispersed into the water outside the cages and directly into the paths of the wild salmon, effectively killing them off. It was not a new insight. A decade earlier, Morton noticed that salmon were dying as they arrived at their spawning grounds in the Fraser River. When she cut them open, she found thousands of unlaid eggs. Morton suspected the farms were spreading disease to the returning salmon, and they were dying before they could breed the next generation. Other conservationists found that the spread of sea lice from salmon farms to wild fish was a particular threat for young salmon leaving freshwater for the ocean. The salmon farms were killing wild salmon both coming and going.

A scientist working at a Department of Fisheries and Oceans laboratory in Nanaimo, British Columbia, had been searching for the reasons behind the crashing numbers of salmon for years. Kristi Miller-Saunders has a doctorate in biological science and has been head of molecular genetics at the DFO lab in Nanaimo since 2004, where she has a staff of twenty-two, including two research scientists, three biologists, and sixteen technicians. Her lab examined genetic data stored in salmon immune systems, searching for tiny changes at the cellular level that are clues to fish health.

Starting in 2006, she and her team began examining dead salmon native to the Fraser River. In wild Pacific salmon, they found genetic markers for immune system decay and types of disease more commonly associated with farmed Atlantic salmon. The anomalies appeared to explain, at least in part, why large numbers of wild salmon were dying. To determine whether the infectious diseases had spread from farmed salmon to wild salmon, Miller-Saunders needed to test farmed salmon. But no farm would provide salmon to test, and the DFO refused to require the farms to cooperate with the request from its own laboratory. Important scientific questions were left unanswered because of the industry's role in financing government and academic research into aquaculture.

In response to the dramatic 90 percent drop in sockeye returns to the Fraser River, in November 2009 the Canadian government created the Cohen Commission. It took its name from Bruce I. Cohen, the British Columbia Supreme Court justice chosen to lead the investigation. The commission's assignment was to determine the cause for the salmon decline in the Fraser River and to provide recommendations to the DFO for restoring the salmon. Cohen had a reputation for rigor and fairness, and he spent months establishing the parameters for the inquiry, assembling a small staff and lining up witnesses from industry, government, and conservation groups.

The proceedings opened officially in October 2010 in the federal courthouse in Vancouver. Witnesses testified under oath and were cross-examined by attorneys associated with the commission and by Cohen. Experts came from the federal and provincial governments, industry associations, academia, conservation groups, and First Nations tribes. At the end of 133 days of testimony over many months, 179 witnesses had provided evidence resulting in 14,166 pages of transcripts and 2,145 scientific papers and other documents. As part of the inquiry, Cohen and his staff made 14 visits to salmon farms, hatcheries, and First Nations fishing locations.

Not surprisingly, scientists and other experts disagreed sharply. In a prime example, a panel of four scientists differed on the extent of the threat posed to the sockeye by sea lice. The diverging opinions, especially on a problem already regarded as a major threat to both wild salmon and farmed salmon in Norway and Scotland, reflected one of Judge Cohen's major challenges: Testimony and papers that could help him reach a verdict were often based on limited studies, often financed by the industry. The government and its scientists did not know enough to draw conclusions about the causes for the declines in salmon. For its part, the DFO had clearly paid little attention to scientific examinations of the threats to sockeye salmon and other wild fish. In fact, Cohen was told that the government had blocked what might have been groundbreaking research. The government scientists who testified assumed a common position, pleading scientific uncertainty as justification for doing nothing and allowing salmon farms to continue harming wild salmon.

The hearings took an illuminating turn in late August 2011. Dr. Kristi Miller-Saunders testified about her research and the government response to it. In January 2011, she had published a paper in the respected journal *Science* describing her laboratory's discovery of genomic evidence that a viral infection was causing Fraser River sockeye salmon to die in large numbers. The virus, a variant of the piscine orthoreovirus (PRV), had never been found before in fish in British Columbia, and its discovery was considered groundbreaking, possibly a major reason for the dramatic decline in the salmon.

The editors at *Science* had recognized the significance and the potential impact of the evidence. Seventeen years earlier, an article in the same journal about PCBs and other contaminants in farmed salmon had opened the door to questions about the health risks of eating such fish. The editors sent notifications of the forthcoming article to more than seven thousand journalists worldwide and told Miller-Saunders to expect her article to spark widespread interest. She asked the Department of Fisheries and Oceans for permission to do media interviews after the article was published. It was a routine request, and the DFO initially seemed fine with the publicity. It even wrote a joint press release, with the University of British Columbia touting the findings.

The first sign that this rollout was not going to be routine came shortly before the *Science* article was posted online. After some internal review at higher levels, the DFO decided to remove its name from the joint press release. The department also delayed giving Miller-Saunders permission to speak to the press. As the journal's editors had forecast, posting the article online led to a rush of calls from journalists to Miller-Saunders's office. Without her agency's approval to speak with the press, she was forced to refer the callers to her two coauthors from the university, Scott Hinch and Anthony Farrell. After several days of confusion and some personal embarrassment, Miller-Saunders was told that she would not be given approval to speak to the press because her article was considered a bad-news story.

Miller-Saunders assumed the decision had come from her department. She was wrong. In another example of the suppression of negative news, information surfaced later that her muzzling was not routine and that the decision had not been made within the DFO. Margaret Munro, a reporter for the Canadian news agency Postmedia News, wrote an article a few weeks later describing the behind-the-scenes maneuvering that led to the last-minute decision to gag Miller-Saunders. Emails and other material Munro obtained showed that the decision had been made by senior government officials in the Privy Council Office in Ottawa, which provides administrative help and advice to the prime minister, much the same way senior staff aid the president in the United States. In this case, the prime minister was Stephen Harper, a member of the Conservative Party. Munro's documents showed that the top bureaucrats in the capital killed the DFO press release, saying it "was not very good, focused on salmon dying and not on the new science aspect," and then blocked Miller-Saunders from giving interviews.

In early October 2011, Cohen thought the testimony phase of his inquiry was over, and he settled in to evaluate the evidence, resolve the discrepancies where he could, and write his final report to the DFO. A few days later, his plans were upended when Alexandra Morton and Rick Routledge, a professor at Simon Fraser University in Vancouver, held a press conference. Working with Routledge's team from the university, Morton had collected forty-eight juvenile sockeye salmon from a small inlet on the central coast of British Columbia. Routledge had sent the samples for testing to Fred Kibenge, the Canadian scientist who had earlier found infectious salmon anemia in Chile and who operated one of only two labs certified by the World Organisation for Animal Health, to test for the infectious salmon anemia virus. In evaluating the British Columbia samples from Morton and Routledge, Kibenge's lab found positive results for ISA in two of the forty-eight fish. Morton and Routledge had also sent samples to Dr. Are Nylund at the University of Bergen in Norway, and he reported finding evidence of ISA.

At the press conference, Routledge explained that this was the first-known instance of ISA in the Pacific Northwest. While ISA was not considered dangerous for human consumption, he said the highly infectious virus could spread through farms throughout the region and reach south along the Pacific Coast to Washington State, Oregon, and California and north to Alaska, where wild salmon were a major commercial industry. He said the source of the virus had to be identified and shut down as soon as possible. The presence of any ISA was reason for alarm. Morton explained that finding any sick fish established the presence of a significant threat. "If we test five million fish and found two sick, okay," she said. "But two of forty-eight in the middle of nowhere?" She warned that the same strain of ISA had devasted the salmon-farming industry in Chile in 2007. She used the discovery to bolster her argument that aquaculture should move to land-based methods of raising salmon.

The stakes were high for the Canadian salmon-farming industry and the government. Regulations in the United States prohibited importing salmon exposed to ISA. On the U.S. side, Senator Maria Cantwell of Washington State also saw the potential harm. "We need to act now to protect the Pacific Northwest's coastal economy and jobs," she said after the press conference. "Infectious salmon anemia could pose a serious threat to Pacific Northwest wild salmon and the thousands of Washington State jobs that depend on them." Indeed, the claim by Morton and Routledge threatened to cause major damage to the biggest market for Canada's farmed salmon.

The DFO and the Canadian Food Inspection Agency, known as CFIA, responded by retesting Kibenge's samples at the government's diagnostic lab in Moncton, New Brunswick. In early November, a month after the Morton-

Routledge press conference, the government announced that its laboratory had found no evidence of ISA in the samples. The findings were described in a telephone conference call with reporters by Dr. Con Kiley, the director of animal health at the CFIA. He said emphatically that tests on the same samples used by Kibenge found no confirmed case of ISA in British Columbia. Kiley said Kibenge's test results were wrong, but that the government would monitor the issue through an expanded surveillance plan anyway. One journalist who participated in the call said he was appalled at the lengths to which the government officials would go to try to discredit Kibenge's results and downplay the threat of ISA. The government officials later boasted in internal emails about how they had "won" the public relations war. Government officials in British Columbia downplayed the findings. "Well, we've got another example of spinning media headlines and fearmongering from the opposition," said Don McRae, the province's agriculture minister.

Concerns about the potential impact of the ISA disclosure on the U.S. market persisted despite the Canadian government's best efforts to dismiss them. On December 12, 2011, in a conference call, the DFO and CFIA provided an update to Canada's Department of Foreign Affairs and International Trade. In an indication of the seriousness of the issue, four officials from the Department of Foreign Affairs participated, along with representatives from Canada's consulates in Los Angeles, San Francisco, Seattle, and Anchorage. "DFO Science noted they have been seized with this issue for the past two months, and speaking with media and other interested parties," according to a draft summary of the call.

Alarmed by the new information from Morton-Routledge and by competing claims from the CFIA, Judge Cohen took the unusual step of reopening his inquiry for three days of additional testimony in December. One of the initial witnesses, Dr. Kim Klotins, a senior manager from CFIA, offered a surprisingly candid assessment of how the government saw the stakes involved in the discovery of ISA. "Let's say we do find ISA in B.C. and markets are closed, then there will be no trade," she said. What she meant but didn't explicitly say was that the CFIA therefore couldn't afford to find ISA in British Columbia. Her admission demonstrated the triumph of economics and politics over protecting the environment in the federal government. The same government priorities were evident when the Cohen Commission learned about a suppressed draft research paper in which two DFO scientists reported that they had detected segments of the ISA genetic sequence in farmed and wild salmon in British Columbia in 2002 and 2003. The paper, which had not been disclosed to the commission by the government despite a request for all relevant documents, surfaced only after Morton learned of its existence from a colleague.

Kibenge was called to testify, and described a surprise review of his lab a few weeks earlier by government officials. He said he suspected they were trying to discredit his ISA findings. Gregory McDade, a lawyer for two conservation groups, suggested to Kibenge that he would not have come under scrutiny if he had not found evidence of ISA in the salmon. "I agree, yeah," Kibenge replied. "Negative findings are very easy to deal with . . . it's the positive findings that are difficult to accept." When McDade finished questioning DFO and CFIA officials, he offered a dire prediction about Fred Kibenge's future. "I suggest to you that the federal government is going to try and take away his . . . certification as punishment for this," he said. "I predict within the next 12 months Canada will go after his credibility."

Sitting beside Kibenge was Dr. Nelle Gange, the head of the DFO diagnostic lab in New Brunswick that agency officials said had reported finding no evidence of ISA in the forty-eight samples. Her testimony diverged from the government's claim that her lab had found no evidence of ISA. Instead of no evidence of ISA, she had found that the samples were too degraded to determine whether the virus was present, which meant the lab results were inconclusive. It was a significant contradiction of the earlier statements by government officials in their attempt to dismiss the findings, but Kiley and others who had claimed there was no evidence were not called to clarify their earlier statements.

Kibenge was not the only scientist to have found evidence of ISA in wild salmon in British Columbia's waters. His wife, Molly Kibenge, detected the virus in fish sampled in 2002 and 2003, while she was doing postdoctoral work in British Columbia. Morton and Routledge were unaware of her findings because they were never published. It was a draft of her paper that was leaked to the Cohen Commission during the reopened inquiry.

Judge Cohen spent another year analyzing the record and producing an exhaustive three-volume report, parts of it written in the first person. The final report was released on October 31, 2012, with a lengthy statement from Cohen. "Some, I suspect, hoped that our work would find the 'smoking

gun'—a single cause that explained the two-decade decline in productivity—
but finding that a single event or stressor is responsible is improbable," Cohen
wrote. Instead of a single cause, Cohen wrote that the inquiry had uncovered
many factors behind the decline of the Fraser River sockeye, ranging from
habitat loss and warming waters due to the climate crisis to the potential
spread of disease from commercial fish farms. Given the absence of a single
cause, Cohen made seventy-five recommendations to protect wild salmon in
the Fraser River and up and down the Pacific coast of North America.

One of the most far-reaching recommendations called for shutting down
the nineteen salmon farms in the vicinity of the Discovery Islands archipelago by September 30, 2020, unless the DFO found scientific proof that the
farms posed only a "minimum risk of serious harm to the health of migrating
Fraser River salmon." The Discovery Islands are a cluster of ten islands in an
expanse of narrow passages and inlets between Vancouver Island and mainland British Columbia. For centuries, the waters around the islands have been
an important source of salmon for the First Nations. For migrating salmon,
the islands are a bottleneck that forces them to pass near the salmon farms
during their migration.

For critics of the industry, the recommendation offered the chance of a
better future for the sockeye and all wild Pacific salmon. Despite the absence
of a ban, opponents of salmon farming saw the recommendations as a road
map for eventually eliminating open-net salmon farming in British Columbia.

For the industry, Cohen's recommendation that the farms in the Discovery Islands be shut down was a recipe for its decline. The nineteen salmon
farms were owned by Norway's big three: Marine Harvest/Mowi, Cermaq, and
Grieg. Shutting them down threatened to create a domino effect across the
province and beyond. Some in the industry were relieved Cohen did not recommend immediately shutting down the salmon farms around the islands.
"We're very happy with Justice Cohen's praise of the quality and quantity of
our data," said Stewart Hawthorn, a member of the board of the BC Salmon
Farmers Association. "He didn't ask us to stop farming, just to do more
research, which we are happy to do." Still, the lobbying began to ensure that
Judge Cohen's most hot-button recommendation was never carried out.

Judge Cohen's two chief recommendations were rejected by the government. The DFO refused to relinquish its conflicting responsibilities for promoting salmon farming and protecting wild salmon, and in the fall of 2020,

the department said its scientists had determined that the salmon farms in the Discovery Islands caused no discernible harm to sockeye salmon and refused to ban them. The nineteen salmon farms in the Discovery Islands archipelago would continue to operate. Industry had won that battle.

Sockeye salmon continued to disappear from the Fraser River and other parts of the Pacific Northwest. Only about 650,000 sockeye salmon returned to their spawning grounds in 2019, a far cry from the 10 million expected in the Fraser a decade earlier.

After the Cohen Commission Report was issued, the government did take decisive action on one front. As Gregory McDade had predicted, Fred Kibenge paid a price for finding positive results for ISA. The Canadian Food Inspection Agency returned to Kibenge's lab at University of Prince Edward Island in late December 2011 and, after an audit, asked the World Organisation for Animal Health to strip the lab of its certification. The Paris-based organization agreed after its own review, saying the lab's practices "fell well short of acceptable quality standards." The lab lost its certification, leaving Kibenge damaged and dumbfounded.

When contacted about an interview for this book, Kibenge, who remains at the university and continues to carry out other related work, replied with the following: "Thank you for your email. The material you wish to interview me about has cost me and my wife Molly emotionally, financially, and professionally, and we are both still trying to recover. I respectfully decline your request to be interviewed."

The Kibenges were not the only people whose careers were damaged when they got in the way of the salmon-farming industry.

CHAPTER 10

MOTHER NORWAY

Norway has the world's largest population of wild Atlantic salmon, a distinction that should carry a global responsibility to protect these noble fish by safeguarding the country's rivers and streams. At the same time, Norwegian multinational companies dominate the global market for farmed salmon, producing more fish than all other countries combined. The result is the need to balance environmental and economic concerns.

The regulatory regime in Norway is generally harmonized with that of the European Union and is considered more stringent than the more relaxed government oversight in Canada, Chile, Scotland, the United States, and other countries where salmon are farmed in ocean pens. In a positive step, Norway instituted a pioneering regulatory system in 2017 that linked levels of salmon production to ocean conditions. Norway also charges the world's highest prices for licenses to raise fish in the ocean and has developed vaccines that allow its salmon farmers to reduce the use of chemicals when combating the many diseases that affect salmon in the net pen farming model. Those are the pluses. The big negative is that the tighter restrictions and high-price licenses have motivated Norway's big salmon-farming companies, Mowi, Cermaq, and Grieg, to seek more pliant regulators in foreign waters.

Even in Norway, however, the balance between protection and promotion tips in favor of the industry. Salmon farming represents annual exports of more than eight billion dollars in Norway, second only to oil, at times leading the government to promote the industry at the expense of the environment and public health. Some government agencies have dual and sometimes conflicting mandates to protect the health of consumers and to promote the sale of salmon. For instance, in 2014, as some Norwegian scientists were raising concerns about the health effects of farmed salmon, particularly on children and pregnant women, the Norwegian Scientific Committee on Food and the Environment recommended nearly doubling salmon consumption for any healthy diet.

When it comes to protecting its wild salmon, Norway's record is mixed. Despite tighter restrictions on salmon farms, its wild salmon population has dropped by half in the last twenty years to an estimated 530,000 fish today, a sign that more needs to be done. The climate crisis and other habitat changes have contributed to the sharp drop, but scientists and environmentalists include the salmon farms lining the country's fjords among the chief culprits for two reasons.

First, hundreds of thousands of farmed salmon escape from their cages each year, spreading disease, damaging spawning areas, competing for food, and diluting the gene pool of wild salmon species. A survey found that seven out of ten rivers in Norway contain a new breed of salmon, the direct result of interbreeding between the wild fish and escaped fish. The Norwegian Directorate of Fisheries reported that more than 2.1 million salmon escaped from the country's farms from 2010 to 2020, roughly four times the number of wild salmon remaining in its rivers and streams. Researchers say the actual number is likely higher because of underreporting by the industry.

Second, infestations of sea lice originating on farms kill young wild salmon in large numbers. Crowded pens are prime breeding grounds for sea lice, and their concentrations can kill tens of thousands of fish in cages. But the sea lice also pose a risk to wild salmon, a danger that is highest for juveniles during migration to the ocean. Warming waters caused by the climate crisis are increasing the threat from these parasites. In 2016, lice infestations drove Norway's salmon production down 5 percent and cost the industry an estimated four hundred million dollars. Outside Norway, the damage was worse. Nearly 10 percent of the world's farmed salmon were killed by sea lice that year, leading to a shortage of fish that drove prices higher for consumers and cost the industry hundreds of millions of dollars.

In the beginning, the industry in Norway and worldwide responded with chemical warfare. Scottish salmon farms have been accused by the government of polluting coastal waters by overusing chemicals and pharmaceuticals to combat lice. Salmon farms in Atlantic Canada and Chile have been put on "Do Not Eat" lists by consumer groups because of chemical use in the pens. Even the strongest chemicals, like the neurotoxin cypermethrin, become ineffective because the lice develop a resistance to them, which leads to the use of new and stronger chemicals.

Alternatives come with their own baggage. Norway was a pioneer in the use of "cleaner fish" (the name describing their function rather than their essence) to eat the sea lice. Lumpsuckers, ballan wrasse, and other members of the wrasse fish family keep the lice numbers down, but animal welfare advocates estimate that 150,000 cleaner fish die every day in Norway because they cannot survive in salmon cages.

Mechanical methods can be effective at combating sea lice, but at the cost of damaging the health of the fish. The ideal in salmon farming is never to touch the fish until it is harvested, to minimize stress. A technique known as a thermolicer clears away lice by pumping salmon from cages into a water bath at temperatures between eighty-two and ninety-three degrees Fahrenheit. Manufacturers say the process is an environmentally friendly alternative to chemicals that damage the environment. Academic studies, however, raise concerns about the impact of these hot-water baths on the salmon. A study in the journal *Veterinary and Animal Science* concluded that thermal delousing damages the gills, eyes, brains, and possibly other organs of the fish. The scientists saw fish exhibiting pain and flight behavior when exposed to the hot water. The findings echoed a 2018 study in a Norwegian veterinary journal that found "the present use and technical solutions for thermal delousing are inadequate and likely to cause serious lesions in treated fish." Mowi disclosed that it lost 115,283 salmon in one year because of a thermolicer treatment.

Hydrolicers, another mechanical method, pump the fish from cages through a system of tubes and train a low-pressure jet of water on them to dislodge the lice. Hydrolicers appear to cause less damage than thermolicers, though a survey of farmers found evidence of scale loss, gill bleeding, and wounds that led to increased mortalities. Both techniques have spread beyond Norway, to Scotland, Canada, and Chile. Calls to ban thermolicers have also spread, with groups like the Royal Society for the Prevention of Cruelty to Animals in the United Kingdom and conservation groups in North America seeking to end the practice. The Norwegian Food Safety Authority concluded that salmon suffer pain from the hot-water machines and called for phasing out the process unless the technique could be improved.

After the record losses in 2016, the Norwegian government's new regulatory structure to try to fight the scourge of sea lice consisted of restricting salmon production in areas where infestations were out of control. The regime is known as a "traffic light system" not all that different from the one Seafood Watch uses to guide consumers. The coastline was split up into thirteen production zones. Those with lower numbers of sea lice than in the previous year were identified as "green," and allowed to increase production by 6 percent. Zones where levels remained unchanged were "yellow," which required farms to freeze production at existing levels. "Red" zones, where sea lice levels had risen, had to reduce production by 6 percent. In the most recent determination in 2020, nine areas were defined as green, two as yellow, and two as red. The objective was to increase salmon production and decrease sea lice infestations by rewarding good actors and punishing those who did not control the parasites.

The government also made it more expensive to expand salmon production in open-net pens along the coastline. Open-net farmers must buy additional capacity at a government auction every two years, and costs run into the millions of dollars even for small increases in capacity. For example, in August 2020, salmon farmers paid $670 million to produce 27,000 metric tons more salmon, a steep price for a production increase of about 1.2 percent. By contrast, salmon farmers in the United States, Canada, and Chile pay almost nothing for licenses, and production is virtually unlimited. The high price tag is part of Norway's effort to encourage salmon farmers to move to land-based systems. The Norwegian Seafood Council exists to defend and expand the country's fishing and aquaculture products, chiefly farmed salmon. In an unusual arrangement, the seafood industry finances the council, but it is owned by the Ministry of Trade, Industry and Fisheries. The council has local offices in thirteen countries and describes its purpose as developing markets for Norwegian seafood and reputational risk management. In recent years, managing the reputation of farmed salmon has taken on greater importance because of high fish mortalities caused by sea lice and the threat to wild salmon from escaped farm salmon.

Anette Grottland Zimowski, a spokeswoman for the council, said the organization works with the government to ensure that growth is contingent on fish health and environmental conditions. She praised the traffic light system as an example of how production can be reduced quickly if the numbers of sea lice exceed maximum limits. Zimowski said nonchemical methods of combating sea lice have also improved the situation.

While acknowledging that escaped salmon pose a risk to wild salmon, Zimowski said a national monitoring system to track escapes and improved practices at farms have reduced the threat. "The decline of wild salmon stocks has not been witnessed in Norway alone, indicating that other reasons for the decline should be looked at," she said.

Norway has been careful not to go too far in regulating salmon farming. When a 40 percent tax on salmon farm rents was under discussion in the Storting, Norway's parliament, the industry backlash forced the withdrawal of the proposal. From the start of commercial salmon farming in the early 1970s, government policies have benefited the industry, often at the expense of wild salmon and the health of people who eat Norwegian farmed salmon.

"In India, it's the holy cow," said Ola Braanaas, a small-scale salmon farmer in Norway. "In Norway, it's the sacred salmon."

While Norway's tighter restrictions have failed to fully protect its wild salmon population or eliminate the plague of sea lice, the lesson for other countries is that the damage could have been even worse without these efforts.

Claudette Bethune crashed into Norway's sacred salmon culture after starting work as a senior scientist at a Norwegian government institute in 2003. Her case, among others, demonstrates what happens when public health concerns collide with concerns about a profitable salmon market.

An American scientist with a doctorate in pharmacokinetics and metabolism, Bethune was developing new medicines in California when she met and fell in love with a Norwegian man on a holiday in 2001. Following her heart, she left California and took a job at the National Institute of Nutrition and Seafood Research, known as NIFES. The institute, which is affiliated with the Norwegian Ministry of Trade, Industry and Fisheries, was located in a historic building on the harbor in Bergen. The lab had a reputation as a center for excellence, one of the top facilities in Europe.

Bethune joined a team analyzing contaminants in seafood to provide risk assessments for the government's food safety authority, which worked to coordinate Norway's standards with the European Union. Her academic and work experiences fit well with the job, but Bethune felt like an outsider from the start. The analysis of seafood was not as well funded or respected as other work at the institute. Still, she found the research stimulating. The goal was to identify new toxic contaminants, develop methods for quantifying them, and provide risk assessments on the levels to meet EU market standards. Because it was Norway, her work focused primarily on farmed salmon. "I took a pay cut when I moved to Norway because I thought it was important work," she said. "From a health perspective, I thought prevention was the best medicine and [that] if we knew the types and levels of contaminants, we could then work toward providing this information so that regulatory bodies could phase out these toxins from their source, such as brominated flame retardants in consumer goods. I was happy. It was a joyous time for me personally and professionally."

Not long into the job, Bethune discovered that the institute was not independent from the salmon industry, and she began to have questions about the scientific integrity of the work performed by some of her colleagues. She learned that salmon farming started in the late 1960s and early '70s as a government-supported activity to help rural fishing communities facing depressed economies from declining wild fisheries. As the business consolidated and grew, government policies and scientific research were coordinated closely with the industry. She also saw that top government officials sometimes came from the ranks of the salmon-farming business. Eventually, Bethune concluded that the industry, not science, was the most influential factor in determining the guidelines developed at institutes that had been established to protect the health of people consuming Norwegian farmed salmon.

She soon learned how the relationship played out in the day-to-day operations at her lab. Her research, mandated by the Norwegian Food Safety Authority, found that Norway's farmed salmon contained consistently higher levels of contaminants than wild salmon, including PCBs, pesticides, and man-made chemicals used in flame retardants. A wide variety of common household products contained brominated flame retardants to make them less flammable. Like PCBs, the chemicals in the retardants enter the food chain by contaminating air, soil, and water. Some forms do not break down easily and, instead, accumulate in the fat of fish and other animals. The highest levels are generally found higher up the food chain. In the late 1970s, the United States and the European Union banned or restricted most chemicals in flame retardants after they were linked to developmental problems in children, but the chemicals remain in the environment. Studies have shown that flame retardants migrate out of consumer goods, accumulate in dust, and end up in people's bodies, where they can cause a range of health problems, including thyroid disease, infertility, decreased IQ, and cancer. Bethune found them in farmed salmon.

Bethune believed that some of the contaminants, such as dioxins and PCBs, represented a serious health threat to people who ate even the recommended portions of farmed salmon. She was not alone; her findings tracked research elsewhere, including in the groundbreaking article in *Science* published in early 2004 that we discussed in chapter 5. The problem for Bethune was that her results contradicted the well-tuned image of Norwegian farmed salmon as the world's healthiest fish. By December 2005, Bethune suspected some contaminants came from salmon feed. When she raised the issue with colleagues, she was surprised to find that they recognized the level of contaminants but did not share her concern. Instead, her supervisors and colleagues chose to ignore the results or to use other models to support the orchestrated response from Norwegian food safety officials and the salmon-farming and feed companies to discredit the *Science* article. Avoiding sanctions in the European Union, their biggest market, took precedence over investigating evidence of health risks to consumers.

In mid-December 2005, news articles were published warning that Russia had discovered high cadmium levels in imported Norwegian salmon and was considering a ban. U.S. government officials in Stockholm, Sweden, sent alerts saying the safety of Norwegian salmon was being challenged again, citing the 2004 *Science* article. Cadmium is a toxic chemical element that can lead to kidney, liver, and heart problems. Norwegian authorities rejected the Russian assertion, but Bethune decided to investigate the Russian claims by evaluating the levels of the chemical the Norwegian Food Safety Authority had reported in salmon feed with the estimated time of salmon exposure to the contaminated feed. Her analysis quickly turned up plausible metabolic and tissue-specific scenarios for the elevated levels of cadmium found by the Russians. She also found that, in 2005, Norway had successfully persuaded the European Union to raise the limit of allowable cadmium in salmon.

In late December, Bethune took her findings to her supervisor and the institute director. They scoffed at her conclusions. They told her to find six academic papers that supported her concerns about the level of cadmium in feed that could accumulate in salmon. She readily found six papers published between 1992 and 2005 on the ability of salmon to accumulate cadmium from feeds. The most recent report had been conducted by professors at Cornell University and recommended that, because of contamination, people limit consumption of farmed fish from Norway, Scotland, and eastern Canada to three times a year. When Bethune presented the information and references to her supervisors, the lab leaders made clear, as they had previously with other contaminants, that they had no intention of allowing negative information about toxins in farmed salmon to become known to the Norwegian public. Bethune was shunned by her bosses and some colleagues.

On January 1, 2006, Russia halted imports of all fresh Norwegian salmon, citing unsafe levels of cadmium. Blocked from raising a red flag on what she regarded as a potentially serious health issue, and ostracized within the institute, Bethune considered her next steps, including the option of going to the press. First, she sought advice about going public from the union representing Norwegian scientists. Her union representative at the institute was sympathetic, but she was not optimistic about saving Bethune's job if she spoke out. In a written response, the union said, "We believe that your supervisors [are] allowed to censor your work against the public. If you handle as a private person—and go public without your employer knowing about it and not [being] given a chance to do something—you may cross the limit to what is expected of you as a loyal employee."

Bethune weighed her responsibilities to her employer and her happiness in Norway against what she felt was a genuine public health threat. She decided to go to the press and take her chances. In mid-January, she spoke to several reporters in Norway and explained that her research showed that the levels of cadmium the Russians had found were plausible given the amounts of the chemical in the feed she had analyzed. She also told reporters about her earlier concerns that the levels of dioxins and PCBs in the recommended serving size of the salmon exceeded the daily intake specified by the World Health Organization. She said the risk was particularly serious for children and pregnant women. The first newspaper articles, published on January 17, 2006, ignited a firestorm of anger from the industry, industry-supported institutes, and the Norwegian government. Russian complaints could be shrugged off as political, but a warning from a scientist inside a Norwegian government institute upped the ante.

Still shaken by reverberations from the *Science* article two years earlier, the multibillion-dollar Norwegian salmon-farming industry was not about to allow a single scientist, let alone an American woman, undermine public confidence in its product. With the government as accomplice, the retaliation was swift. At the insistence of the Seafood Export Council, a quasi-government agency responsible for expanding demand for Norwegian seafood, the institute took the unusual step of releasing a statement criticizing its own scientist. "NIFES distances itself strongly from the contents of Claudette Bethune's media initiatives, where she speaks on issues she is not an expert on nor is responsible for," said the statement. "This scientist does not represent NIFES' scientific view on this issue. Consequently, Claudette Bethune's statements are her own private opinions. NIFES is unaware of why the issue is presented like this and why Norwegian food authorities are unjustly slandered in this way." Going further, an industry spokesman at the Seafood Export Council accused researchers who voice "negative" concerns about farmed salmon of "acting as fifth columnists." It was an emotionally laden accusation in a country where thousands of people had collaborated with Germany during its occupation of Norway in World War II.

Bethune fought back, explaining in a memo to her supervisors that she felt going to the press was her only recourse after her findings were suppressed at the institute. "I believe I acted in the interest of public health and safety," she wrote. Going public made Bethune radioactive in the government community, and her days were numbered. Even colleagues who agreed with her findings kept their distance and would not go public, for fear of losing their jobs.

In March 2006, Bethune met with the institute's senior leadership, accompanied by a union lawyer who came in from Oslo. Bethune was in tears for most of the meeting as her expertise was challenged without cause and she was criticized harshly for going public with negative information. She was told that she would have to resign from her contract early. As part of the resignation package, she was forbidden to speak out about any aspect of her work at the institute. With her work visa canceled and her contract now ended, Bethune would likely have to leave Norway.

Her fiancé and his family were supportive in the first days of the controversy, but they grew distant as criticism of Bethune continued. She and her fiancé soon broke up. "It was a life-altering, devastating consequence," she said, recalling the hurt sixteen years later. "I was summarily dismissed. I temporarily developed a nervous tic, a twitch, with the media coverage. I had loved living there. I worked hard and was loyal, and so thought I would spend my life there. But now I was considered a traitor to Mother Norway."

The controversy followed Bethune. She could not find employment in Norway, and when she tried to get a job with a company in the Netherlands, it was clear they did not want her. Disappointed and frustrated, she returned to the United States and spent nearly four years working essentially underground at a contract research organization, ghostwriting studies for other scientists to publish, to earn money as the dust settled. Eventually, she returned to clinical research on medicine at a small pharmaceutical firm in Southern California. She also rediscovered her voice and started writing and talking about her experience.

Bethune was not alone in challenging the quality of Norwegian farmed salmon. Jerome Ruzzin, a French scientist at the University of Bergen, told Nicolas Daniel and Louis de Barbeyrac, two French journalists making a documentary in 2013, that Norwegian farmed salmon had five times more toxins than wild salmon, echoing findings by other scientists. Ruzzin described one study in which mice fed a diet heavy in farmed salmon grew obese and their bodies were found to contain high levels of contaminants. He also said he had been turned down for a new job at a government institute in 2010 because of his findings. Unlike Bethune, however, Ruzzin did not lose his university job. A year after Bethune was forced out of her job, she worked with former colleagues in Norway to use her example to pass the country's first law providing university researchers basic protections for negative findings in research.

Concerns about contaminated salmon were also raised by Anne-Lise Bjorke-Monsen, a pediatrician and professor of medical biochemistry at the University of Bergen. She first grew worried about the potential dangers of salmon farms after her family bought land on the west coast of Norway. She saw pollution caused by a salmon farm just two hundred yards offshore, and it sparked her interest in environmental pollutants and their potential impact on children and pregnant women, her specialty. She became worried after parents of a boy on the autism spectrum came to her for a second opinion about tests conducted in the United States. Looking at the results, Bjorke-Monsen found that the boy had been tested for many of the same pollutants occurring in farmed salmon. After further study, Bjorke-Monsen suspected that contaminants in farmed salmon could be contributing to autism and other health problems in children.

Scientific research had repeatedly shown that toxins like the PCBs found in farmed salmon and other oily fish were associated with harm to fetuses and young children. Yet the Norwegian government was running a program to promote salmon consumption in the schools for children as young as kindergarten. "I do not recommend pregnant women, children or young people eat farmed salmon," Bjorke-Monsen told the Norwegian newspaper *Verdens Gang* in June 2013, after the study she had conducted with a colleague, Bjorn Bolann. "It is uncertain in both the amount of toxins salmon contains and how these drugs affect children, adolescents and pregnant women." Given the risks, the pediatrician recommended that pregnant women and women considering pregnancy get their omega-3 fatty acids from other fish, like mackerel and herring.

Senior government officials contradicted Bjorke-Monsen and advocated following the guidelines from the Norwegian Food Safety Authority, which was recommending that everyone eat salmon at least three times a week. Right before Christmas 2014, a major marketing period for salmon, the government's Scientific Committee for Food and the Environment issued a new report saying that farmed Norwegian salmon could be eaten safely even by pregnant women. "Furthermore, adults including pregnant women with fish consumption less than one serving per week may miss the beneficial effects on cardiovascular diseases and optimal neurodevelopment in the fetuses and infants [sic]," the agency declared. The advice contradicted the government's own warning that pregnant women and the young should limit consumption of oily fish like salmon to two meals a week to protect children from health risks. Other scientists recommended that children and pregnant women should be eating even less farmed salmon.

The extent of the joint campaign by the salmon-farming industry and the Norwegian government to block negative information was exposed in an extensive, well-documented series of articles published jointly in 2017 and 2018 by two Norwegian publications, *Morgenbladet* and *Harvest*. The series described the tensions created when the industry's commercial interests collided with independent research. The articles showed ties between salmon-farming companies and government agencies and recounted the stories of researchers like Bethune and Ruzzin, who felt harassed and saw their work misinterpreted or blocked. The reporters also uncovered internal documents showing that the Norwegian government had unsuccessfully lobbied the European Union to increase toxin limits in salmon feed for twenty years, right from the start of the European Food Safety Authority.

Norway has managed to reduce the use of antibiotics in farmed salmon. The 2020 annual report of the industry's Norwegian Seafood Council said only 1 percent of the country's total salmon harvest in 2019 received antibiotic treatments, part of a continuing decline in their use. Independent studies have confirmed that the use of antibiotics has declined sharply, but contamination problems remain. Thirty percent of the antibacterial agents still in use in Norway's salmon farms are classified by the World Health Organization as critically important for human medicine, raising the critical risk of increasing antibiotic resistance among people. Pesticide use remains substantial, and the sea lice transfer from farmed salmon to wild salmon poses an ongoing threat.

Today, the Norwegian government continues to recommend that everyone eat two to three meals of fatty fish a week. The Monterey Bay Aquarium's Seafood Watch disagrees, and Atlantic farmed salmon from Norway remains on its "Avoid" list, a stain on the reputation of the sacred salmon. Still, salmon remains the most popular fish in Norway, and consumption levels have remained steady for nearly two decades.

Faced with restrictions on expansion, rising license costs, and bad press at home, Norwegian companies shifted more operations to places like Canada, Chile, and Scotland. In all three countries, the Norwegians quickly emerged as the dominant player. And in all three, they use more antibiotics and pesticides than they do in Norway. For example, Cermaq received a permit from the provincial government in British Columbia in 2018 to discharge more than five hundred thousand gallons of a pesticide containing hydrogen peroxide into Clayoquot Sound to fight sea lice. Hydrogen peroxide is toxic for krill, a dietary staple for wild salmon and whales found in the sound, and it can harm juvenile salmon. The permit was granted despite a petition from

36,000 people opposing it, and the latest science from Norway confirms the threat to marine life. While salmon farms in Norway have reduced the use of antibiotics, the big companies have not made corresponding reductions in antibiotics or other chemicals outside their home waters. For example, the Global Salmon Initiative, which was set up by salmon-farming executives, reported that, from 2019 to 2020, Cermaq increased its use of antibiotics in Chile by 37 percent.

Responsible salmon farming offers one solution to meeting the world's increasing need for food. Yet the industry is dominated by hyperintensive open-net farms, which are damaging marine ecosystems and posing risks to consumer health. The fundamental question for governments and consumers at this point in the evolution of aquaculture is: Do the big open-net salmon-farming companies cause more harm than good?

CHAPTER 11

THE ANATOMY OF HARM

In the 1990s, anthropologists began paying more attention to the role of corporations in society. Spurred by leaps in technology and free trade, corporations were gaining outsize influence and power as the forces of globalization transformed the international economy. Among the challenges was how to govern multinationals, which had expanded beyond the control of any single government. Anthropology provided useful analytical tools for understanding the strategies of big business and suggesting ways to restrain its growing influence, especially in cases where the corporations caused harm. And corporations causing harm is a good summary of aquaculture over the last four decades.

In 2010, two anthropology professors, Peter Benson of Washington University and Stuart Kirsch of the University of Michigan, created a new lens through which to analyze corporate behavior in an article entitled "Capitalism and the Politics of Resignation," published in the journal *Current Anthropology*. The paper focuses on the harm caused by industry and the ways corporations shape public and government responses to perpetuate activities that fall under the broad rubric of "harm industry." The paper identified three primary stages in corporations' response to critics and examined how their response at each stage perpetuates corporate harm.

The first stage is denial, when corporate representatives argue that their actions cause no harm. During this stage, they often employ corporate-financed experts to create doubt and discredit critics.

If the criticism becomes impossible to deny, the corporate response escalates to stage two: acknowledgment and a pretense of accommodation. This occurs when the corporation takes token steps toward addressing the problem but does not make substantive changes.

The last resort comes at the third stage, strategic engagement. Backed into a corner by facts or public opinion (or both), the corporation must engage with critics and develop ways to neutralize regulators and quiet the public while continuing to operate profitably.

Benson and Kirsch connected these three stages to form a template for how corporations, even when facing criticism, can magnify harm by insisting on business as usual, with only token modifications or doing the bare minimum to get the public off their back. One result of this behavior is that the public is persuaded that corporations cause harm with impunity, creating what Benson and Kirsch called the "politics of resignation." As an alternative to resignation, the authors suggested that public dissatisfaction with harmful corporate practices could be transformed into a starting point for social change. Their article focused on two industries with well-known reputations for causing harm, tobacco and mining. In 2017, two professors and two graduate students at Memorial University in St. John's, Newfoundland, adapted the hypothesis to a less obvious business, salmon farming. In a paper published in *Marine Policy*, Professors Dean Bavington and Reade Davis, along with grad students Benjamin Rigby and Christopher Baird, examined the cycles of growth and crisis in salmon farming on the southern coast of Newfoundland. The authors described injections of taxpayer subsidies that nourished the industry while environmental problems that arose as farms expanded damaged fishing grounds for lobster, scallops, and other seafood, and the industry's response to the inevitable criticism. The pattern of aquaculture industry responses tracked the Benson-Kirsch template step by step. The paper added a new element: the role played by academic institutions that support the industry while wrapped in a cloak of dubious independence.

St. John's, the capital of Newfoundland and Labrador, Canada's easternmost province, sits on a harbor that has served the fishing trade for six centuries. Popular folklore holds that the city got its name from an Italian explorer, Giovanni Caboto, who arrived in 1497. By then, the Grand Banks fishery off the Atlantic coast of Newfoundland was already busy with fishermen from France, Spain, and Portugal in search of cod. The bounty lasted hundreds of years, attracting settlers and creating good livelihoods for generations of

Newfoundlanders. The rise of industrial fishing in the twentieth century, with its omnivorous trawler ships, led to overfishing of cod and other species, spelling the end of the Grand Banks fisheries. In 1992, Canada closed its commercial cod-fishing industry. Not long after, the salmon-farming industry sailed to the rescue—or so provincial and federal government officials imagined. Companies from Norway and Canada set up salmon farms on the southern coast of Newfoundland in the Gulf of St. Lawrence, directly on the migration route of wild Atlantic salmon.

Proponents of industrial aquaculture argue that the industry holds the key to preventing a global shortage of protein as the world's population grows. The World Bank and the UN Food and Agriculture Organization, both advocates of globalization, stress the opportunities that aquaculture offers for food security in lower-income countries. The industry in general, and salmon farming specifically, presents itself as a sustainable solution to feeding the world, despite the impact on the environment and the damage to wild fish and other marine life.

Sitting with us in the lobby of the Delta Hotel in St. John's, the place where Canada announced the moratorium on commercial cod fishing on July 2, 1992, Dean Bavington was intense and voluble in describing the economic impact of the loss of the cod industry on Newfoundland. The decision to shut cod down led to the largest single-day layoff in Canadian history, with forty thousand people losing their jobs, and it set the province on a precarious economic road. Bavington wrote a book, *Managed Annihilation*, that blamed the collapse of the cod fishery on government's failure to stop uncontrolled harvesting and its refusal to take the concerns of fishermen into account. Bavington believes that, despite the industry's claims to be feeding the world in an environmentally friendly and sustainable manner while providing jobs in remote coastal areas, similar failures have paved the way for the harm caused by salmon farming.

"Their idea of protecting the environment through sustainable production actually destroys fishing places and peoples, breeding grounds and habitats that have established unique ways of living with the ocean and its creatures. It is a death-producing industry, and it is causing serious harm," Bavington said.

The logic is undeniable. The corporations that control salmon farming fit neatly into the template set out by Benson and Kirsch and refined by

Bavington and his colleagues. What happened in Newfoundland over the past two decades follows the pattern of how these same corporations operate elsewhere.

Applying the Benson-Kirsch template to the salmon industry in the *Marine Policy* paper, Bavington and his colleagues highlighted the role played by the government and government-funded institutions like universities in financing and promoting the growth of salmon farming in Newfoundland despite evidence of the harm it was causing. Closer attention should be paid to the links among academics, government, and private industry, they wrote. Those links surfaced when the industry was joined by government and academics to fight claims that salmon farms harmed wild salmon, lobsters, and other marine life. The joint effort to discredit the industry's critics became clear in the fall of 2019, when the Newfoundland government and Mowi, the world's leading farmed salmon producer, tried to whitewash the deaths of roughly three million salmon at ten Mowi farms off the province's southern coast. The full story of what happened will be told in chapters 19 and 20.

Mowi is a master at projecting a positive image of itself and the industry. Every year, the company produces a glossy publication, called the *Salmon Farming Industry Handbook*, extolling the virtues of salmon farming. Photos of glistening salmon and pristine fjords adorn its pages. "The industry is a good fit with the global macro trends, as Atlantic salmon is a healthy, resource-efficient and climate-friendly product produced in the sea," read the 2020 edition. "In addition to its resource-efficient production, farmed fish is also a climate-friendly protein source. It is expected to become an important solution to providing the world with vitally important proteins while limiting the negative effect on the environment."

Tell that to Joachim Drew, whose fifteen years as a commercial scuba diver on salmon farms gave him a decidedly different picture of the industry. From the water's surface or the air, the ten or more cages that comprise a typical salmon farm appear benign as they float in a quiet cove or bay. Whether round or square, arrayed in rows or circles, the cages keep a low profile, just a few feet above the waterline. Occasionally, a fish leaps out of the water. Seagulls and birds of prey hover over the pens or perch on the netting covering the cages holding smaller salmon. The scene appears to fit Mowi's claim about limiting the environmental impact.

Below the waterline, however, Drew found a vile dystopian world. Cages extend thirty to fifty feet below the surface. They are jammed with salmon circling endlessly through water dark and murky with waste. Dead fish covered with hundreds of lice rot on the cage bottoms; live fish swim even though parasites have eaten away the tops of their heads, revealing skull. Some salmon are visibly deformed, with spines in an S shape. Fish have open wounds and fungus on their scales. Often, when Drew was sent down to clean the nets or remove dead fish from inside the cages, he could not see more than a few feet in front of him. Frequently, mussels clog the nets, cutting off new water and entombing the pens.

On the seabed below the cages, Drew encountered a thick carpet of feces, chemical residue, and uneaten feed that had dropped through the nets. Bacteria festering in this stew depleted the oxygen and increased toxicity, causing algal blooms, killing wild fish and other marine life, and turning ocean floors around the farms into biological deserts. The few signs of marine life were giant sea worms reaching out of the sediment.

"I dove in water so dirty that sometimes I couldn't see the guy next to me inside the cage," Drew said as he sat at a table in a pizza joint in western Newfoundland. "We had to let each other know what we were doing by touch. We were filling bags with dead salmon. Some days, there would only be ten or fifteen dead fish, and we could clean them out in twenty minutes. Other times, there could be a thousand dead fish on the bottom of the cage, and it would take all day."

Salmon farmers were attracted to the southern coast of Newfoundland by its long, narrow inlets, which provide shelter from sea ice in winter, a geography like Norway's fjords. The geographical isolation and availability of workers left behind when the commercial fisheries disappeared in 1992 added to the attraction. Drew built a thriving business diving at salmon farms along the coast. He shook his head as he recalled the things he saw. He blinked with regret as he remembered the things he did on behalf of his employers.

Drew grew up along the southern coast of Newfoundland, on the reservation of the Conne River Band of the Mi'kmaq First Nations people, the largest Indigenous tribe in eastern Canada. He attended a school for First Nations children that was run like a boot camp. Students who misbehaved were forced to kneel on pencils for long periods in a corner of the classroom, or were berated by teachers in front of the entire class. He remembered the burning humiliation when a teacher pulled him to the front of the class and told him, "You are going to grow up to be a bum."

Drew left school after the eighth grade, with only a rudimentary education but determined to prove the teacher wrong. He took a series of low-skill jobs in the timber industry and other places. Growing up on a wild river near the ocean, he had spent some of his happiest moments on the water. In his early twenties, he decided to become a professional scuba diver. The Conne River Band had money to train its people, and Drew moved to Prince Edward Island to attend a school for scuba diving. There was a hitch that could have stopped him cold. Before he could start, he was required to earn a high school graduate equivalency degree, or GED. Instead of diving school, he found himself in an adult education program on PEI, as the island is known. Unlike the schools on the reservation, he found inspiring teachers who encouraged him.

With his GED in hand, Drew enrolled in diving school on PEI, determined not to leave any aspect of himself or professional diving untested. He earned certifications for open-water scuba diving, night diving, and ice diving. He returned to Newfoundland for an advanced course in commercial diving. Armed with real skills and new confidence, he started his own diving company just as the salmon-farming business was starting to expand on the province's southern coast in the mid-1990s. He found plenty of work installing cages at new farms in the fjords and bays, diving fifty feet or deeper to attach anchor cables to concrete blocks on the seabed to stop the farms from drifting with the tide. Drew loved the job in those early days. He mended the tough plastic nets enclosing the fish when they were damaged by predators or storms. He cleaned mussels and kelp off the cages to allow the water to flow through. Almost every workday, he dove inside the cages to stuff dead and decaying salmon into nylon mesh bags normally used for scallop diving. The bags were hauled by rope to the surface and taken away by boat to be dumped in deeper water. Regulations required their disposal on land, but dumping them back in the water saved time and money.

The French name Bay d'Espoir translates as either "Bay of Hope" or "Bay of Despair," perhaps depending on your mood. The bay is a small body of water connected to the arm of the larger Hermitage Bay on the Gulf of St. Lawrence, off southern Newfoundland. The bay was made famous by one of Canada's iconic writers, Farley Mowat, who fell in love with its steep cliffs, idyllic coves, and fjords while working aboard a coastal steamer in 1957. The steamer *Baccalieu* carried supplies and mail weekly to dozens of centuries-old fishing villages, many of which were accessible only by boat. By necessity, people who lived there were largely self-sufficient, making their living generation after generation by fishing for cod and herring and by logging and seal hunting. In his autobiography *Bay of Spirits*, Mowat writes movingly about the bleak beauty of the landscape and the warmth of the people in isolated communities with names like "Come by Chance," "Heart's Desire," and "Chimney Tickle." Few of the villages remain. Most of them are ghost towns, emptied between 1954 and 1975 in a controversial resettlement program initiated after Newfoundland and Labrador changed their status in 1949 from Britain's oldest colony to Canada's newest province.

Joachim Drew encountered his own despair in the Bay d'Espoir. Two dives there are etched in his memory and on his conscience. The first occurred early in 2014. The winter was the coldest in a decade, and salmon farmers feared the impact was killing lots of fish. Like humans, fish are less active in the cold, as their metabolism slows and they eat less. The risk comes from what is called a "super chill" event, when the water reaches a critical temperature, usually below thirty-two degrees Fahrenheit. Anytime the air temperature dips near freezing, there is the risk of a super chill. Marine waters where salmon farms are located stay above freezing most winters, but sustained cold air temperatures can drop water close to the surface to the freezing point. Winter tides tend to be high and can flush the cages with super-chilled water, which can cause fish blood to freeze. Wild salmon are free to escape the cold water, but farmed salmon survive winter by remaining in warmer water near the bottom of the cages, which are about thirty feet deep. If they surface, the colder water can freeze their gills and their blood. When the air temperature is near freezing, workers know to stay away from the farms and stop feeding the fish to keep them from surfacing. Theory and practice are two different things, though, and super chills sometimes kill thousands of farmed salmon. For instance, when fishing boats or pleasure craft pass by the cages, the fish instinctively think, "Food," and head for the surface and likely death. Other times, fish starve to death or suffocate as they congregate at the bottom of the cages in search of warmer water.

In the winter of 2014, a thin layer of ice covered the coves and small bays within Bay d'Espoir and the adjoining coves. One bitter day, Drew and a colleague were sent to a farm in Marguerite Cove to check the cages to see how many fish were dying. Drew's first dive was inside one of the cages, where he discovered thousands of dead salmon clogging the bottom. Many more were circling slowly in what appeared to be death spirals. There were too many carcasses to haul them out in bags, particularly in the bone-chilling cold. Drew returned to the surface and telephoned the site manager to report what he had found. The manager told him to dive beneath the cages and dump the dead fish. And, the manager added, don't worry about the fish struggling to stay alive. Drew broke a hole in the thin ice, tied a rope to himself so he would not get lost under the ice, and headed to the first of ten cages.

"I had to dive under the cages and slice the net open, so the dead fish came out and slid to the bottom of the bay," he said, looking away as he remembered. He knew that the thousands of carcasses would pollute the bay and that disposing of them in this way violated the regulations at the farms. "I didn't want to do it, but they made me," he said. "If I didn't do it, somebody else would." Fish still alive could swim through the same holes to freedom.

When fish die in the wild, they provide rivers and streams with vital nutrients, a natural replenishment at a manageable scale. A mass of decomposing fish, however, represents a threat to other marine life by producing bacteria that consume oxygen. Young fish, lobsters, and crabs are particularly susceptible to the risks of oxygen deprivation, so they either die or are driven away. In addition to threatening marine life, the disposal of dead fish in the ocean without a permit violates the Canadian Fisheries Act. Records show the federal government has not issued a single permit for disposal of dead salmon, yet there is no evidence of a single prosecution.

There are alternatives to dumping in the water. Fish can be hauled to landfills, incinerated, or used by farmers as fertilizer. These alternatives are expensive and time-consuming, and they risk drawing attention to losses. Most salmon farms are in remote locations, so it is easier and cheaper simply to dump dead fish into the water, where they mix with the chemicals, excess feed, and other waste that builds up under and around the farms.

What happens underwater tends to stay underwater.

Drew's business expanded along with the industry. He hired and trained a dozen divers and bought a boat to ferry them to and from the farms dotting the bays and coves along the coast. Eventually, he had twenty employees and a profitable business. Most of the work involved cleaning cages and repairing nets, but he and his crew also dealt with the predators that broke through the nets to eat the salmon. One technique for dissuading predators is installing large hooks outside the cages in the hope of snagging the tuna and sharks before they get inside. Another method is to surround an entire farm with nets made of high-density polyethylene, particularly in winter, when seals and sea lions are more common in Canadian waters.

To get to the thousands of salmon trapped in a cage, determined predators sometimes chew through the netting. In one video he took in 2013, Drew floats in a gaping hole a predator made in a net, arms spread so wide he cannot touch the sides. He described entering cages to kill tuna that had chewed their way in; one time, he killed three tunas in a single cage, each fish weighing over a thousand pounds. Tuna that size would be worth big money on the market, but Drew and his divers were under orders to let the dead fish sink to the bottom to rot, because they had no tuna license. They could not even take the meat home, a painful choice for a member of a First Nations tribe, where every part of a fish is eaten or used in another way.

Tuna were not the only predators. One day, as he stood on the metal walkway surrounding a cage and preparing a dive to clear away mussels and other debris, Drew saw that the salmon had company, a lot of company. The water was too murky to count them from above, but an unusually large number of sharks were cruising in circles in the cage. Drew dove outside the cage, found the entry hole in the net, and then surfaced. Even in the dark water, he recognized from their slender bodies and bright coloration that the invaders were blue sharks, which are common in the waters of eastern Canada and New England. Generally, blues are considered more curious than dangerous. Drew had encountered them before and chased them out of the nets. When he went down to clear the cage of predators, he brought along two colleagues because there were so many sharks.

But getting them out of the cage proved tougher than the divers imagined. Sharks are the only fish that cannot swim backward, so pulling them out by their tails induced wild thrashings from angry sharks. The next tactic did not work any better. The sharks were not afraid of the divers, and they fought back when the divers tried to squeeze them into large nylon bags. In the end, there appeared to be only one way to clear the cage.

Drew and the other two divers returned to the surface. Grabbing pieces of metal, they fashioned six-foot long spears, sharp at one end. Returning to the cage, they killed nineteen blue sharks, some longer than ten feet. They dumped the carcasses outside the cage and watched as they floated to the bottom.

Killing sharks, seals, dolphins, tuna, and other predators is common at salmon farms, according to Drew and other workers. The U.S. Marine Mammal Protection Act prohibits the intentional killing of marine mammals in commercial fishing operations, including fish farms. For several years, animal rights groups and others have called for the United States to ban the importation of farmed salmon from Canada and Scotland because farmers can obtain a license to kill marine mammals like whales, dolphins, seals, and sea lions. The voices were heard, and as of January 1, 2022, countries with fisheries that interact with mammals must demonstrate they have taken steps to comply with U.S. law or be banned from sales in the United States. Canada and Scotland passed regulations to comply with the U.S. standard. In Scotland, the Ferret, an investigative website, said government documents showed that salmon farmers in the country killed seventy-five seals in 2020, the highest number since 2014.

Drew's second memorable dive in the Bay d'Espoir nearly cost him his life and did cost him his business. One day, while working at a Cooke Aquaculture farm, he was called upon to inspect some anchor lines. The job required him to dive much deeper than normal, about eighty-five feet. Shallow dives required a single tank of compressed air. Because this was a deep dive, Drew wore two tanks so he could stay down long enough to finish the job and avoid a trip back to the surface for a second tank. After his many years of diving, he felt as comfortable underwater as he did on land, and he was not worried about an extended period in the deep.

Air in scuba tanks is a pressurized mixture of oxygen and nitrogen. A diver's lungs use the oxygen, but the nitrogen dissolves into their blood and accumulates during the dive. When a diver swims back toward the surface after a deep dive, the water pressure decreases and allows the nitrogen to dissipate as the diver rises. If the transition occurs too quickly, however, the nitrogen does not have time to clear from the diver's blood. Instead, it forms dangerous bubbles in the blood and in tissue.

To give the blood time to rid itself of excess nitrogen, even inexperienced divers know to swim back up slowly, even from a dive as shallow as fifteen or twenty feet. As a rule of thumb, divers should rise to the surface no faster than thirty feet per minute, a foot every two seconds. A slow ascent is really a rolling decompression stop, which allows your body to flush out and exhale the dissolved nitrogen before bubbles form in the bloodstream. Ideally, a diver should pause for several minutes fifteen feet below the surface to purge any vestiges of nitrogen. The longer a diver is underwater, the more important it is to get rid of the nitrogen buildup.

Divers who go up too fast and do not give the nitrogen time to clear from their blood suffer from decompression sickness, commonly known as "the bends." Harvard Medical School compares the effect to what happens when you open a carbonated drink: the decrease in pressure inside the soda can causes gas to come out of the liquid in the form of bubbles. When this occurs too fast inside the human body as water pressure decreases, blood flow is blocked, and blood vessels and the heart can be severely damaged.

As Drew worked at the bottom on his dive, he became engrossed in the task. He worked fast, increasing the speed at which he used up his compressed air. He was too busy to check the gauge on his air tanks, and he never heard an alert from the surface, where an assistant was supposed to be monitoring his dive time. Suddenly, as he tightened an anchor line at eighty-five feet, the air stopped flowing. The tank was empty, a rookie mistake, the kind of thing every beginning diver is warned to avoid, the kind of thing that kills people or leaves them paralyzed. And he had no one to blame but himself.

In a normal ascent, Drew needed nearly three minutes to reach the surface safely, even if he skipped the pause at fifteen feet. But the empty tanks meant he did not have enough air in his lungs to go up slowly or safely. Unbuckling the weights around his waist and shrugging off the tanks, he shot to the surface in an emergency ascent. When he broke the surface, he was going so fast that he popped out of the water to his waist. He grabbed his heart, which felt like it was about to explode. He had the bends, and his life was in real danger.

Diver deaths at salmon farms are rare, but they do occur. There is no central registry for recording such deaths, and most are isolated incidents. But in 2019, the National Union of Divers of Chile reported that fifteen divers had died that year at the country's salmon farms. These deaths, though not necessarily the fault of salmon farming, are another indication of the peripheral dangers associated with the industry.

Treating a severe case of the bends requires hours inside a decompression chamber to replicate a proper assent by reducing the size of the bubbles and adding oxygen to the injured tissues. The only decompression chamber in Newfoundland was not operating the day of Drew's accident. He was flown to Halifax, Nova Scotia, an hour away, and spent nine hours in a chamber. Physically, he recovered. Mentally, he was finished with diving.

A few weeks later, Drew tried to return to the water for a shallow dive. He discovered that he could not descend more than seven or eight feet before panicking. No matter how many times he tried in the months that followed, no matter how much he loved diving and depended on the business he had built, he could not overcome the mental barrier. He sold the business, but not before he had proven how wrong his teacher on the reservation had been about him and not before he had seen the harm caused by salmon farms below the surface.

CHAPTER 12

"SORRY, GUYS"

Melvin Jackman sees the damage caused by salmon farms from a different perspective than Joachim Drew or the professors at Memorial University. He and his wife, Laverne, spend eight months of the year in a three-room cabin in Hardy's Cove, a remote spot on the shore of Hermitage Bay, in southern Newfoundland. They generate their own electricity from solar panels and a small windmill, draw water from surface pools, and have a freezer full of moose meat. A handful of other hardy souls live within a couple hundred yards, providing camaraderie and an occasional feud. What they all share is the serenity and beauty of Hermitage Bay. The bay is hemmed by steep cliffs, waterfalls cascade down from mountain streams, otters play in the coves, and moose stand regally on the plateaus above the cliffs. The landscape is dotted by small communities known as outports, some as isolated as in the days when Farley Mowat first fell in love with the region and its welcoming culture. But paradise has been spoiled for Mel Jackman: three salmon farms are spaced along the bay not far from Hardy's Cove. Jackman cannot wait to show visitors the damage they have wrought.

When Jackman's eighteen-foot aluminum boat left the cove, the sky widened, and the sun turned Hermitage Bay to gold. Dozens of bald eagles and osprey rose into the cloudless sky, a bevy of sea otters on the banks slipped into the water, gulls wheeled and dipped. Slowing and circling into Round Cove, Jackman shouted to be heard above the waves banging the boat. "Look at that, just look at that," he yelled, his anger surfacing, as if seeing the cove for the first time. "That makes me sick."

The small crescent-shaped stretch of beach tucked beneath cliffs and towering spruce trees looked like a junkyard. Styrofoam blocks the size of refrigerators littered the cove. Thick nylon rope, long pieces of black PVC pipe, and chunks of broken plastic tubing spread an ugly blanket across the sand. A circular cage about thirty feet in diameter made from black PVC tilted on its side at one end of the beach. Stepping ashore meant sinking ankle-deep into the debris. Jackman gestured at the mess in disgust. "This is all from the salmon farms," he said, still shouting even though the boat's engine was off. "It's everywhere. They refuse to clean it up. They say that you can't prove it came from their farms."

"They" are Cooke Aquaculture, which operates the three large salmon farms in Hermitage Bay, all within a few miles of Round Cove. Back in the boat, Jackman steered toward the closest Cooke farm and cruised slowly around the perimeter buoys encircling twelve cages. "They know me," he said. "If I get inside the buoys, they can take my boat from me for trespassing."

The Styrofoam buoys are identical in size and shape to the pieces littering the cove a few hundred yards away. The black PVC pipes enclosing the salmon pens are identical to the ones littering the beach. Up and down the bay, similar piles of rope, Styrofoam, and plastic piping defile the inlets and coves. So much debris from the salmon farms is present that clever residents have recycled some of it to build wharves and small swimming rafts. They jury-rig tracks of pipe for pulling their boats out of the water. "A lot of people are concerned about the trash and other impacts, but they won't say anything that might upset others," Jackman said, heading toward another Cooke farm, across the bay. "It's a small town, and a lot of folks need the jobs that come with the salmon farms." He navigated around the second farm, which was tucked into a small cove. A worker outside the shack attached to the farm flicked a cigarette into one of the salmon cages.

Farther up the bay, Jackman cruised into the harbor at Gaultois, a storied village on the tip of Newfoundland's Long Island, accessible only by boat or ferry and utterly dependent on the sea. Tall cliffs surround the harbor, and a shuttered fish plant dominates the little-used wharf. The natural harbor once made Gaultois a busy port. In the early 1700s, French fishermen lived off the thriving fishery in the area until they were displaced by English settlers. When Captain James Cook surveyed the Newfoundland coastline for the British Royal Navy in the late 1700s, he said Long Island's shore was the most beautiful he had seen. In those days, the town was home to wooden schooners that sailed to the Grand Banks and brought home cod, haddock, hake, pollock, and other fish. The work was hard, cold, and dangerous. Ships would stay at sea for weeks, and the crew would use baited lines made of tarred cotton two thousand feet long to catch fish. A whaling company was established in Gaultois in the early nineteenth century, and at the height of its operations in the late 1870s, it killed forty to fifty whales a year and brought the carcasses to the local plant for processing. In time, the whaling schooners were replaced by huge trawlers bringing cod to the processing plant. Mel Jackman remembers working on a trawler in the 1970s, when Gaultois was so busy that ships had to wait in line to offload their catch.

The plant meant Gaultois was better off economically than other small coastal communities of Newfoundland, so it was able to fend off the dreaded resettlement movement. The government established the controversial program to persuade people in the isolated outports to move to larger communities on the main island. At least 90 percent of the heads of household in a village had to sign a petition agreeing to the resettlement in order to get money to cover the costs of relocation: a thousand dollars for the head of household, two hundred dollars for each additional family member. Many outport residents took the money and literally floated their houses to new lives on the big island, known as "the Rock." Decades later, the program remains mired in a province-wide sense of dislocation, captured by folk songs known as sea shanties that are still sung at what the locals call "kitchen parties."

> He sits on the plank and the memories roll
> The spring sun is shining, there's a lop in the cove
> And the shoreline is dotted with lobster pot buoys
> But his boat's full of weeds and there's tears in his eyes
>
> Don't take a man from the life that he knows
> And tear up his roots and expect him to grow
> Cause if he's unwillingly forced to decide
> He'll move without leaving and never arrive . . .

Gaultois residents were the only people on Long Island who refused to go, and Gaultois was one of the few villages anywhere along the coast determined to stay put. The fish plant was still operating, and there was a small commercial center. As other villages disappeared, Gaultois attracted their residents, and its population swelled to about six hundred.

January 5, 1990, is remembered in Gaultois as "Black Thursday." That was the day the Canadian government imposed quotas to reduce the cod haul in a doomed attempt to save the fishery. As the catch went down, so did work at fish plants throughout Newfoundland. Workers protested, to no avail. On that Thursday, Fisheries Products International announced that it was taking thirteen trawlers out of service and closing three plants in the province. The list included Gaultois. The plant manager called the mayor and said workers could stay on the job for several weeks while operations wound down. Two years later, the government imposed a total ban on cod fishing that eventually led to the permanent closing of the plant. Today, Gaultois's population of about 130 is scattered among a few dozen white houses clinging to the hills surrounding the harbor. Victoria Academy, a school for kindergarten through grade twelve, overlooks the harbor and remains open, but with fewer than two dozen students.

For those who remain, Gaultois is a way of life, not just a place to live. Their ancestors adapted to hardship and isolation, forming bonds with one another and with the sea. Many of the few remaining jobs still depend on the sea, though not in the traditional ways. The lucky few with full-time jobs get onto boats each morning and head to the eighty or so salmon farms along the province's south coast. The shortest commute is about two minutes to the Cooke Aquaculture farm just outside the harbor. The farms do not provide many jobs, no more than thirty or so for Gaultois residents, by most estimates, but some say they make a difference. "Aquaculture is what has saved Gaultois and other small communities in the Coast of Bays," said Jane Pitfield, a former Toronto City Council member who runs the Gaultois Inn.

Gaultois symbolizes the fate of Newfoundland and Labrador. The 40,000 jobs the province lost when the cod fishery closed in 1992 have never been replaced—certainly not by salmon farms. The latest Canadian government figures list 355 jobs in the entire aquaculture industry in Newfoundland. The province faces a record budget deficit, a victim of fluctuations in resource-based industries like oil and gas, timber, and the dying fisheries. Attracting new business is tough. The province is nearly twice the size of Great Britain, and its road system is sparse, to be kind. The population of 520,000 residents is dwindling because people are dying at higher rates than babies are being born and because young people must leave to find work on the mainland. The question for Gaultois, and the province, is whether the few short-term jobs in salmon farming are worth the long-term risk to the environment that has sustained them for centuries. The folks in Gaultois knew their answer; they hunkered down and stayed.

Light drained from the sky as Jackman returned to Hardy's Cove. He piloted the boat to his small wharf, jumped out, and hauled it up two runners made of scavenged black PVC pipe. His anger was exhausted, worn down by what he has seen again and again in the bay and by his frustration with the refusal of the government or Cooke Aquaculture to make any effort to clean up the junk. He has written countless letters to government officials and Cooke executives, most without response and all without result.

Over a dinner of moose meat and potatoes at the kitchen table, Laverne Jackman described her thirty-six years at the fish-processing plant in Harbour Breton. The early years were the good ones. A steady supply of cod, herring, and sea trout kept the processing lines humming. The last years before she retired, when the cod were gone and other fish were in short supply, were devoted to processing farmed salmon. Often the fish were so covered with sea lice when they got to the plant that workers used industrial vacuums to remove the parasites. As the fish moved down the conveyor belt, many were deformed by crooked spines, double tails, strangely shaped heads, and open wounds. When she worked on the grading line, Jackman had to make split-second decisions about which fish were fit to process and which were so damaged they had to be discarded. It was best to err on the side of processing.

Shaking her head at the memory, Jackman said, "If it was only the head that was half eaten off, and the body felt firm, you could let it go on to be processed. If it was just the fins damaged, you could let it go. The fish that were decaying from head to tail were tossed into great big vats along with the trimmings of fins, to be ground into fish meal and fed back to the salmon at the farms. When the ISA started in the farms, they started bringing in diseased fish. My Lord, you have never seen anything like it. The fish were starting to decay from the inside, but it was still being processed. I was called in to work on a Sunday. I had to pick and sort through all this rotten fish. A lot of it went to trimming lines to be processed as fillets. You can't imagine it unless you see it."

Cooke's sloppy practices in dealing with abandoned and broken gear are not isolated to Hermitage Bay. In 2019, World Animal Protection ranked Cooke among the bottom tier of aquaculture companies in its global report on plastic, rope, and similar debris left in the ocean. The trash lining Hermitage Bay and the diseased fish arriving at the processing plant conflicted with the pledges on Cooke Aquaculture's website and in its advertising. "Protecting the ocean has always been essential to our business," the site says. "We understand that feeding future generations depends on what we do today, and we are dedicated to our role as environmental stewards." Given the promise to protect the environment, it seems fair to ask how Cooke's role as environmental steward fits not only with the mess around Hermitage Bay, but also with the practices exposed by an undercover worker at Cooke's hatchery in Bingham, Maine.

Hatcheries are a critical part of the industrial food chain. Hundreds of thousands of salmon eggs arrive in trays at the land-based plants. They are fertilized and placed in incubation trays, where a steady flow of freshwater moves over them as they develop. When the eggs hatch, the newborns, called alevin, nourish themselves on a yolk sac attached to their stomachs. When the yolk sac disappears after three to four months, the fish are known as fry, and they are moved to larger tubs of freshwater and fed tiny pellets of fish meal and grain. After ten to sixteen months, they are renamed smolts and eventually transferred to cages in salt water. A steady supply of smolts is essential to stock farms.

The industry boasts that its hatcheries are run by veterinarians and professional workers and that they are certified by the Global Aquaculture Alliance's "Best Aquaculture Practices" program, which says it enforces the highest standards for aquaculture facilities. An undercover video tells a different story about the Cooke hatchery in Bingham, one of three supplying salmon stock for the company's twenty-four farms throughout Maine.

The video was taken by an investigator for an animal rights organization who worked at the Cooke hatchery for three months. The five-minute clip first broadcast on YouTube in the fall of 2019 shows graphic instances of young salmon being abused in the hatchery. Fish are brutally cast aside if they show signs of fungal infections or deformities like two heads or twisted spines. Workers smash fish against posts, stomp on them, and throw live fish into buckets, where they slowly suffocate—if they aren't crushed first by other fish tossed in on top.

Workers, their faces blurred out, provide a running commentary of callous indifference. Holding a damaged salmon, one worker says, "Fungus ate his face away." In one exchange, a worker says, "He won't make it." His colleague responds, "No, he's gonna just suffer until he's fucking dead." In another scene, workers pluck squirming smolts out of a shallow tank to inject them with antibiotics. One worker warns about the danger of tearing a gaping hole in the squirming fish. "It's so rough," says another worker. "Over the years you kinda get desensitized."

The video was made by Animal Outlook, a nonprofit organization that makes no secret of its mission to persuade people to switch to plant-based diets. Erin Wing worked undercover in the hatchery for three months and took the video that exposed a side of the salmon industry that never makes it into the marketing brochures. Wing, who is in her twenties, decided a few years ago that she wanted to fight for animal rights and signed up for training in undercover work with Animal Outlook, then called Compassion Over Killing. She learned how to operate a hidden camera, how to blend in with the other workers, and how to expose the brutal conditions for animals in the industrial food chain of the United States.

After working undercover at two industrial feedlots for pigs, Wing applied for a job at Cooke's hatchery in Bingham, a small town on the Kennebec River in northern Maine. She was hired for an entry-level job. She received no training at the hatchery and was told she would learn on the job from her coworkers. For the next three months, Wing lived a painful dual existence. Days were spent alongside nine or ten blue-collar workers transferring young salmon from one tank to another within the hatchery. She watched in horror as the workers brutalized the fish. Reacting to the conditions and cruelty would have risked exposing her and ending the investigation, so she was stoic. At night, she went back to a small rented room and struggled to forget what she had seen. This dual existence continued through the heart of Maine's bleak winter, from late January until April 2019.

"It can be hard to live in isolation for long periods of time, coupled with all the cruelty you have to live with at the facility," Wing said. "You have a strong emotional connection to those animals, but you have to watch your demeanor. When I left the hatchery for the day, it was hard to be myself even when I was alone. When you're undercover, it's almost like surrendering your identity and reinventing yourself over and over again. It's very mentally and emotionally draining. You can't get too close to the workers because you don't want to risk blowing your cover."

Despite the cruelty she recorded each day, Wing did not regard her coworkers as monsters. Most of them had worked at the hatchery for years and carried out their jobs with a sense of remorse over the treatment of the fish. She said staffing was minimal, and workers had to move fast to keep up as they cleaned tanks, shifted fish from tank to tank, and disposed of the damaged ones. In one instance, she watched a worker as he cleared clumps of fungus from a filthy tank filled with young salmon. "Sorry, guys," he said, apologizing to the fish.

Wing left the job with hours of unedited video. Two months later, lawyers for Animal Outlook filed a complaint with the State of Maine citing what it called inhumane treatment of fish at the Cooke hatchery. They attached the full seventeen hours of video as evidence of the failure to properly anesthetize the fish before they were tossed aside or smashed against walls. Officials with the Maine Department of Agriculture told the lawyers they would investigate whether any anti-cruelty laws or regulations had been broken. But Animal Outlook did not wait for the state. In October 2019, a tightly edited version of Wing's video was released on YouTube. The result was a firestorm of criticism of Cooke Aquaculture on social media and in the press.

When viewed from the perspective of the Benson-Kirsch template for a harm industry, the video made it impossible for Cooke Aquaculture to execute stage one of the typical corporate response and deny the inhumane treatment. So, the company shifted immediately to stage two: acknowledgment and a pretense of accommodation. The day the video was released, Glenn Cooke issued a statement from the company's headquarters in New Brunswick calling the incidents "unacceptable" and promising to work with the

Maine Department of Agriculture to improve its hatcheries' practices. "I am disappointed and deeply saddened by what I saw today," he said. "Based on the information received from the department, and after reviewing the footage issued today by the activist veganism organization, it appears that unacceptable fish handling incidents occurred at the Bingham hatchery." Cooke could not resist taking a swipe at Animal Outlook, with his description of it as an "activist veganism organization." The "blame-the-messenger" theme was picked up by Joel Richardson, a Cooke Aquaculture spokesman, who took Glenn Cooke's veiled criticism a step further, characterizing the nonprofit as "a plant-based investment organization" involved with "fake seafood products."

A few months before the video was released, Martha Stewart, the lifestyle guru and television personality, had formed a partnership with Cooke Aquaculture to market a line of prepared fish meals, Martha Stewart for True North Seafood, whose name echoed the brand name of Cooke's consumer products. The salmon was described as "sustainably farmed in the clear waters of the Gulf of Maine." When approached later at a public gathering by a volunteer from Animal Outlook with a copy of the video on a computer screen, Stewart looked away. When pushed a bit, she snapped that the video was a "setup" and stalked off.

The state's response was not much different. Maine officials praised Cooke for acknowledging the problems and promising to correct them. The final investigative report, obtained through a Freedom of Information Act request, was done by the Agriculture Department's animal welfare section, which focused on cruelty to cats, dogs, horses, and land-based livestock. No one in the section knew how to deal with the mistreatment of salmon because the issue had never come up before. The inexperience showed in the results.

Liam Hughes, the director of the animal welfare section, turned for advice on how hatcheries should operate to the Global Aquaculture Alliance, the industry trade association whose three thousand members in sixty countries include Cooke Aquaculture. Companies that want to be certified by the trade association agree to follow its standards. Among the standards are specific practices for slaughtering damaged or unwanted salmon. One of them requires that "specific members of staff designated to carry out lethal control measures shall be trained in humane slaughter methods." Another said specific methods must be in place "for the slaughter of surplus, unwanted or compromised animals that minimize animal suffering. Records shall be available to show these methods are followed when animals are euthanized."

Although the Global Aquaculture Alliance had certified that Cooke adhered to its best practices, Hughes found that the hatchery did not meet the standards. But instead of holding the company accountable for its failure to follow the alliance's standards or to train its employees in humane techniques for slaughtering salmon, Hughes blamed the workers themselves. "Bad techniques for handling and euthanasia were taught by one worker to another," he wrote in the final report. He added an exculpatory line, writing that the workers did not "intentionally cause suffering to the fish." Perhaps Hughes missed the parts of the video in which the workers tossed live salmon into trash barrels to suffocate, or when they stomped on fish. No action was taken against the company. "Cooke Aquaculture did take responsibility for what happened and has taken appropriate action to improve training and operations," Hughes said in a public statement. The Global Aquaculture Alliance did not review or revoke Cooke's certification as a company that followed its best practices—and a few months later, as we will show, the trade group praised Cooke in response to another round of criticism on the other side of North America.

Animal Outlook was not walking away. In the summer of 2020, the nonprofit corporation filed a consumer protection lawsuit against Cooke Aquaculture and its True North brand in Superior Court for the District of Columbia. The suit, which grew out of the undercover investigation, accused the company of deceiving consumers in Washington, DC, by marketing its True North salmon as sustainably raised in a natural environment. The suit was filed by the Richman law firm, the same New York–based lawyers who sued Mowi for deceptive marketing. The complaint against Cooke listed what the suit claimed were false marketing phrases used by Cooke and other salmon farmers, like "sustainably raised," "naturally raised," "raised on a natural diet from sustainable sources," and "hormone, antibiotic, and pesticide free." The suit said the company's reliance on open-net pens jeopardized the environment, its use of antibiotics and chemicals in salmon feed to treat parasites and pathogens was unnatural, its crowded pens created stressful conditions that far exceeded the population density of wild salmon, and its brutal practices at the Bingham hatchery did not meet regulatory requirements.

After procedural delays and technical dodges, the company filed a motion to dismiss the suit. The motion did not dispute the issues raised in the complaint. Instead, Cooke said the suit should be dismissed because the company never intended to sell its True North brand in the District of Columbia. In April 2022, Judge Heidi M. Pasichow dismissed the lawsuit, ruling the court lacked jurisdiction because the suit identified only one sale of Cooke salmon in Washington, DC. But concerning Animal Outlook's claims about filthy open-net pens and fish left to suffocate in garbage cans, she said those conditions were "grotesque and reprehensible.".

When the aquaculture industry's actions and impact are examined, the ultimate question is a moral one: Do fish deserve to be treated humanely? Oxford University scientist Dr. Theresa Burt de Perera argued in a paper that fish learn faster than dogs and engage in various social activities. It is settled science that fish feel pain. Even a study commissioned by the Norwegian Food Safety Authority, which usually sides with the industry, found that farmed salmon reacted with clear signs of pain when bathed in hot water to remove parasites: they swam wildly, shaking and colliding with the side of the containment vessel, and the erratic behavior persisted until the fish lay motionless on their sides.

Despite such findings, the treatment of salmon at hatcheries and farms indicates that the industry treats the fish callously even as it claims to protect them. In an article in the journal *Animal Sentience,* New York University professor Jennifer Jacquet argued that fish represent the largest number of animals killed for food of any group. Jacquet proposed that they should not be treated "as commodities, caught, farmed, and eaten without much moral consideration." Guaranteeing fish welfare should be a moral responsibility, whether you are a vegan, pescatarian, or omnivore. Many people won't eat veal because of the barbaric way the calves are raised, and others refuse to consume eggs from chickens that spend their lives crammed in cages. A California referendum passed in 2018 prohibits the sale of pork, veal, and eggs from animals raised in confined spaces; eight other states effectively ban eggs from caged hens. But when it comes to fish, consumers and regulators have a blind spot that allows salmon farmers and other elements of aquaculture to mistreat these animals in ways we would not find acceptable for other species.

CHAPTER 13

THE OCEAN IS RUNNING OUT OF FISH

Look around at the damage caused by industrialized salmon farming, and aquaculture in general, and one place stands out. The 3,400-mile-long Atlantic coast of West Africa, once one of the world's richest and most abundant fishing grounds, has been overfished by fleets of trawlers from China, Russia, Korea, and EU countries. Some of these monsters of the ocean are nearly as long as a U.S. Navy destroyer and can hold 7,000 metric tons of fish. Their nets can swallow a 747 jumbo jet; they can scoop up 250 metric tons of fish a day, and they operate 365 days a year. The United Nations says half the fish stocks off West Africa are overfished and at risk of collapse. To add insult to injury, up to 40 percent of that fishing, according to the United Nations, is "illegal, unreported, and unregulated." Interpol, the international criminal police organization, says illegal fishing and associated criminal activities threaten the economic, social, and political stability of coastal communities, costing West African countries $2.3 billion a year.

As much as 70 percent of the catch off West Africa is small species, known as forage fish. These fish compensate for their small size and protect themselves from predators in the wild by swimming in large schools along coastlines, making them easy targets for trawlers that can scoop up whole schools. Most of the fish harvested by these giant ships wind up as fish meal and fish oil for export to the United States, Europe, and Asia to feed salmon, other farmed fish, terrestrial animals, and pets. Greenpeace counted more than fifty processing plants operating along the shores of Mauritania, Senegal, Guinea-Bissau, and the Gambia, most owned by Chinese companies. A single plant can pulverize 7,500 tons of fish a year—or 15 million pounds.

Small-scale fishermen who work close to shore once thrived on catching forage fish like mackerel, sardinella, and a fish called *bonga*. Today, they are forced to take their small boats farther into the ocean for longer periods. Mor Ndiaye lives in a fishing town in northern Senegal. He said life there was good until a few years ago, when the foreign trawlers and processing plants arrived. "The fish just vanished; what can we do?" he asked a BBC correspondent in 2018. "We used to catch enough fish in a day or two. Now we need to go out to sea for weeks to catch the same amount. It's terrifying; we can only rely on God." Many fishermen have taken another risky trip, trying to immigrate to Europe to find work. Women who once earned a living processing fish for local and inland markets have watched the fish and their work disappear, too.

Hundreds of millions of people who depend on fish for up to 75 percent of their protein are vulnerable to food and economic insecurity. The aquaculture industry often refers to the forage species as "trash fish," a derogatory description of a staple in the diets of many of West Africa's 380 million people. "You take the food from the plates of people in West Africa to feed the people of Europe and the United States and other countries," said Dr. Ibrahima Cissé, Africa's oceans campaign manager for Greenpeace. "If people have access to this fish, they eat it, they sell it. It is not a business. It is a way of life."

Food security is a challenge in many parts of the world. The term *food security* is generally defined as having access to a stable supply of enough food to live an active, healthy life. When industrial-scale trawlers sweep up millions of tons of native fish, they are not only taking nutritious food off peoples' tables but also robbing them of jobs. In Africa, the risk of food insecurity is particularly high because the continent is one of the few places where population growth is expected to increase in the coming decades. While populations in the United States, Europe, China, and India are stagnating or falling, families in sub-Saharan Africa are having four or five children, and Nigeria could surpass China in population by the end of the century. Protein from so-called "trash fish" will be more important than ever to make sure all these people have enough to eat.

The impact is not confined to West Africa. On the other side of the world, off the Pacific Ocean coast of Peru, the anchovy stock has been halved by similar overfishing, imperiling the ability of the species to replenish its population. The catch of these fish, which are about five inches long, weigh a few ounces, and are known as anchoveta, dropped substantially in recent years, and it is estimated that only 2 percent of what remains goes to feed people. Oceana, the nonprofit ocean advocacy group mentioned earlier in connection with mislabeled seafood, said much of Peru's fish meal production comes from businesses operating without proper licenses and from the systematic diversion of anchovies designated for human consumption to fish meal factories. In a country with sixteen hundred miles of coastline and one of the world's great fisheries, where seafood was once plentiful and affordable, anchovies now feed fish and animals in the United States and other places rather than feeding people in Peru and South America and supporting those local economies. A 2019 report by the Organisation for Economic Co-operation and Development found that governments spend an estimated $35 billion worldwide each year to support the fishing sector. According to the report, the worst type of subsidies provide support for cheaper fuel and gear for the giant vessels wreaking havoc on marine ecosystems and disrupting the food chain for marine life and people through overfishing and illegal fishing.

The problem of overfishing is not restricted to lower-income countries. Along the East Coast of the United States, overfishing from the Gulf of Mexico north to the Chesapeake Bay threatens a slender fish called a menhaden, a critical food source for commercially important fish and an integral player in minimizing algae blooms because it eats phytoplankton. A single company, Omega Protein, accounts for more than 70 percent of the menhaden harvested in the region. Planes spot schools of the fish and alert the trawlers, which then drop nets encircling the schools so hoses can suck the menhaden out of the water and into the bowels of waiting ships. Omega processing plants turn millions of them into fish meal and fish oil for salmon feed, fish oil pills, and fertilizer.

Cooke Aquaculture acquired Omega Protein for five hundred million dollars in 2017. Cooke CEO Glenn Cooke described the deal in a statement as part of his company's "strategy of responsible growth as a leader in seafood production. We are bringing together two innovative fishery teams with a passion for delivering superior products, service, and value to our customers in a safe and environmentally sustainable manner." The deal was completed about the same time that Omega was confronting the latest in a long series of criminal environmental cases.

In 2013, the Houston-based Omega had pleaded guilty to violating the U.S. Clean Water Act by illegally dumping bilgewater and fish wastewater into the Chesapeake Bay. Omega was fined $5.5 million and ordered to contribute $2 million to a foundation restoring Virginia's waterways. The company was placed on three years' probation and required to comply with federal environmental regulations. Four years later, in 2017, Omega pleaded guilty again to criminal charges and admitted violating the 2013 plea agreement by discharging pollutants into the Vermilion River, near its Louisiana plant, in 2014 and 2016. The company was fined $1.2 million.

The guilty pleas caught the attention of the Justice Department and federal financial regulators. Over the years, Omega had obtained loans through a U.S. Department of Commerce program to promote aquaculture, and other loans followed. The loans required the company to file regular financial reports with the government certifying that it was complying with environmental laws. After Omega's guilty plea in 2017, the Department of Justice filed a civil suit accusing the company of violating the False Claims Act by wrongfully claiming it was following environmental laws to avoid defaulting on its government loans. Omega paid a $1 million fine to settle the case in early 2019. The U.S. Securities and Exchange Commission followed up by declaring that financial reports submitted by Omega as part of the loan agreements were fraudulent. "To obtain these loans, Omega agreed to a number of covenants, including representations of compliance with applicable federal laws and regulations relating to environmental matters," the SEC said. "Omega, however, has been a repeat offender of the Clean Water Act." The agency fined Omega $400,000 and ordered it to stop breaking the law.

The aquaculture industry feeds billions of farmed fish every day, fueling the global demand for small fish like anchovies, sardinella, and herring to provide fish meal and oil. Nutritionists who design feed for fish have long relied on fish meal and fish oil because they contain an almost perfect balance of the forty or so essential nutrients that salmon and other fish need to be healthy and grow. In processing plants, forage fish are cooked, pressed, dried, and ground to make fish meal; oil is removed in the pressing stage, and excess water is discharged. The meal and oil are then mixed with other ingredients to form dry pellets for salmon feed. Studies show that approximately four to five tons of whole fish are required to produce each ton of fish meal. Based on that formula, the six million tons of fish meal produced annually for aquaculture requires twenty-four million to thirty million tons of fish, taking protein from people in lower-income countries to feed people in wealthier countries and disrupting the marine food chain by depriving larger fish, seabirds, and marine mammals of staples in their diet.

Some types of farmed fish, like tilapia and grass carp, are herbivores and rely on 100 percent vegetarian feed from crops and other agricultural by-products. The sustainability issue with Atlantic salmon is that they are carnivores and require animal protein. As demand for farmed salmon has grown, the price of wild-caught fish meal and oil has more than doubled in the past twenty years. Economics, rather than environmental concerns, is now pushing feed companies to explore alternative protein sources. Major feed companies have steadily reduced the percentage of wild-caught fish in feed in recent years, partly by expanding the use of plant-based ingredients. Two decades ago, as much as 90 percent of salmon feed comprised marine ingredients; today the percentage hovers between 25 and 30 percent, depending on the manufacturer, and efforts are underway to develop feed that is free of marine ingredients.

Yet, even as feed companies try to reduce the amount of wild-caught ingredients in feed, the rising demand for salmon continues the pressure on forage fisheries. The feed industry is aware of the criticism of its use of wild-caught marine ingredients, but its representatives see demand increasing in response to the need to feed the world's growing population. The United Nations' Food and Agriculture Organization predicts a need for twenty million tons of additional seafood before 2030. "This means that there's a need for an additional twenty-five to thirty million tons of additional feed ingredients in this decade," Petter Johannessen, director general of the International Fishmeal and Fish Oil Organisation, a private group that represents the marine feed industry, told a webinar in the spring of 2021. Johannessen and other industry participants in the session acknowledged the increasing public concern over wild-caught ingredients and advocated developing more sustainable marine ingredients.

Aquaculture's early efforts to develop alternatives to marine ingredients in feed focused on soybeans, corn, and other grains, but problems emerged in the health of salmon that, as we have seen, could translate into problems for the people who ate them. Farmed salmon get their omega-3 fatty acids from oily forage fish; the more oily, small fish in the diet, the higher the level of omega-3, a major health advantage for salmon. Oils from soy and similar plants do not provide omega-3 fatty acids, and levels of omega-3 in farmed salmon have declined as the percentage of plant protein and oils in feed has increased in the past decade, reducing the health benefits of salmon for humans.

Research on alternatives for sources of protein and omega-3 is being pursued in many places, from university labs and start-up companies to a repurposed sugar-processing plant in England and rice paddies in California. Much of the work has focused on insect larvae, oil from algae, and by-products from land animals like chicken meal, feather meal, poultry oil, and blood meal. Trimmings and bones from fish processing are also ground into meal and substituted for wild-caught fish.

Cargill, the American agribusiness giant, is a major supplier of feed to salmon farmers. The company has been experimenting with feed formulas that use soy and insect larvae as substitutes for wild-caught fish. Early results reduced the wild-caught content in salmon feed to 27.6 percent in 2018 compared with 31.7 percent in 2017. Cargill expanded its use of fish trimmings and animal by-products, which would otherwise be wasted. But the company said "poor consumer perception" limited the use of by-products. The shift to both plant-based proteins and animal by-products may lead to another problem. Some researchers have found evidence that linking seafood production to terrestrial agriculture poses health risks to consumers through indirect exposure to air, water, and soil contaminated by chemicals used in industrial farming.

At Norway-based Skretting, another big aquaculture feed producer, researchers developed salmon feed that contains no fish meal or fish oil. Called Skretting Infinity, the feed relies on algae oil to provide the omega-3 fatty acids that make salmon healthy for consumers. Skretting researchers focused on a suite of novel ingredients like algae oil, insects, yeast, and food-processing by-products to lower the environmental and social footprint compared to using wild fish to create feed. "If we are to increase food production sustainably and ensure that the rising world population has access to essential food, it is important that we seek to reduce the amount of human resources that are used in fish and shrimp diets," said Sophie Noonan, Skretting's global communications manager.

Rick Barrows has strong views about the necessity of producing sustainable salmon feed and sparing the world's forage fish. He spent fourteen years as a fish nutritionist for the U.S. Department of Agriculture, experimenting with replacements for wild-caught fish in salmon and trout feed. After retiring, he set up a small feed company in Bozeman, Montana, to continue his research on protein substitutes like larvae, algae, and bacteria. His science-based reasoning is straightforward: "Fish do not require fish meal. They require the nutrients that fish meal happens to contain. That is why fish meal has been used so much in aquaculture. If you take the fish meal out, you must supplement with other ingredients to get the necessary nutrients, so you need other protein sources."

For decades, Barrows said feed producers have been lazy and have relied on large amounts of fish meal to provide salmon with the required nutrients. Manufacturing feed that uses alternative protein sources is more demanding, requiring more ingredients and precise formulas. But the result can be a sustainable feed that reduces the demand for forage fish at the same time that it grows healthy salmon. Some substitutes do not sound appetizing. For instance, fish nutritionists are testing dried black soldier fly larvae as an alternative to fish meal. The people working with the soldier fly larvae do not call them "maggots," and they point out that salmon in the wild eat insects. Slightly more palatable from a marketing point of view, single-cell proteins like mold and yeast have also been tried, with mixed results. Algae, a diverse group of aquatic organisms at the bottom of the marine food chain, have shown promise as an alternative source of the omega-3 fatty acids found in fish oil. A study in the journal *Aquaculture* found that replacing some fish meal and fish oil with algae meal boosted weight gain and maintained fatty acid levels in striped bass, a carnivorous fish like salmon.

For the past few years, Barrows has been chief science officer at Future of Fish Feed, a collaboration among NGOs, academic researchers, governments, and the private sector. The goal is to encourage feed companies to develop replacements for wild-caught fish globally. Central to the organization's effort is the F3 Challenge, a series of three contests to produce alternatives that the industry will buy and use. The first contest challenged feed companies to develop and sell seafood-free feed for freshwater fish that are not carnivorous, like tilapia and carp, using innovative proteins. The winner of the two-hundred-thousand-dollar prize was Guangdong Evergreen Feed Industry Company, which sold 84,000 metric tons of a new feed that used only soybean meal, peanut meal, and rapeseed meal. F3 estimated that Guangdong's innovative feed saved 350 million forage fish.

The second contest required developing fish oil replacements that mimicked the fatty acid profile of forage fish. This two-hundred-thousand-dollar prize went to a Netherlands-based joint venture, Veramaris, which produced an algae-rich oil at pilot plants in Slovakia and Nebraska. The company said its algal oil contained twice as much omega-3 as fish oil and could help reverse the decline of those essential fatty acids in farmed salmon, a decrease directly linked to diets more reliant on plants. F3 estimated that the 850 metric tons of algal oil used spared the equivalent of 2 billion forage fish. Veramaris worked closely with Norwegian salmon-farming companies, and the biggest, Mowi, said it would test the algal oil in its feed. Anette Zimowski at the Norwegian Seafood Council said companies are looking for alternatives like algal oil and insects, but she said vegetable ingredients like soy meal currently make up 60 to 70 percent of aquaculture feed.

The third contest posed the greatest difficulty. The challenge was to develop substitute feeds for aquaculture's biggest consumers of forage fish: salmon, shrimp, and other carnivorous species. The goal was to accelerate the development and adoption of alternatives to fish meal and fish oil, with a one-hundred-thousand-dollar prize for the winner in each of the three categories of carnivorous fish. While the rules did not specify ingredients, the feeds were expected to diverge from the heavy reliance on marine ingredients in favor of the novel proteins being developed. Contest results are expected in the fall of 2022.

The F3 Challenge was designed to stimulate and reward innovations that could lead to large-scale reductions in the use of forage fish. But even prizes worth hundreds of thousands of dollars are a drop in the ocean for the twenty-billion-dollar salmon-farming industry. Economics will drive the reduction of fish meal and oil in aquaculture feed. If the price of fish meal continues to go up as fisheries continue to be depleted, and the price of alternative proteins goes down, the feed profile will change, and farmed fish might ultimately have a sustainable food that would allow forage fisheries and the people who depend on them to recover. Skretting's Noonan said novel ingredients offer a path toward sustainability, but they must be scalable and cost-effective, the default position for an industry focused on the bottom line.

John Risley got his start selling lobsters out of the back of a truck in Nova Scotia and went on to earn a fortune harvesting lobsters and shellfish from the deep ocean off the Atlantic coast of Canada. The company he founded in 1976, Clearwater, became the largest seafood company in Canada and pioneered exports of shellfish to Europe and Asia. In 2021, Risley sold the company to a coalition of Mi'kmaq First Nations. He was far from finished with the seafood industry, however. For many years, he had invested in start-up companies aimed at using technology to create sustainable products. One of them was Mara Renewables, which developed marine microbial algae oil for aquaculture. "Feeding fish with fish is not sustainable, and [it's] a barrier to the growth of the aquaculture industry," Risley said. "Salmon don't produce omega-three; they consume the fatty acids in their diets. So, we began looking for an algae organism that produces omega-three."

Risley's search for a robust form of omega-3 started in the tropical rain forests of South America, where biodiversity and the extreme environment have produced a quarter of the world's natural medicines. But the researchers eventually found the solution closer to home. The extreme tides in the Bay of Fundy foster a similarly challenging environment, which produces unique characteristics in the marine life that survives there. The team found a fast-growing micro-alga in the bay capable of producing high-quality omega-3. Risley described a simple fermentation process that grows the algae in tanks as large as seventy thousand gallons. When the algae become a gelatinous mass, an enzyme is introduced that breaks down their cell walls, allowing the valuable oil to drain out. Once the proof of concept was developed, Risley bought a former sugar refinery in Liverpool, England, which had the huge tanks required to produce omega-3 at a commercial scale.

Risley said the algae oil provides a sustainable substitute for salmon farmers and the entire aquaculture industry and that it could eliminate the depletion of forage fisheries worldwide. Comparing the salmon-farming industry to fossil fuels, he said both have refused to adapt to more sustainable production methods. Risley, like others, predicts that consumers will eventually force changes in salmon farming. "Consumers became aware that tobacco is bad for you, that seat belts are a good idea, and now people recognize that fossil fuels are not sustainable," he said. "Education will catch up with aquaculture. These guys just don't understand yet that this will catch up to them. Unless it changes, it should disappear."

In mid-2021, Risley issued a public challenge to the salmon-farming industry. In an essay published in a business publication, he called for a moratorium on ocean-based salmon farming for a range of reasons, from health risks and environmental damage to the impact on wild salmon. Per standard practice, the industry was quick to attack, falsely accusing him of misstating facts. Risley was philosophical about the harsh response, saying he wanted to stimulate a public discussion rooted in science. Uncertainty is inherent in science, but scientific uncertainty, according to Professors Anthony Carpi and Anne E. Egger, who study science education, is a quantitative measure of variables in data. In other words, science is objectively certain about its levels of uncertainty. The salmon industry, like fossil fuel apologists and climate change deniers, exploits this uncertainty by claiming falsely that it implies doubt the way it does in everyday life. "The consequence of being wrong in the case of salmon farming and its impact is that we are exterminating a species," said Risley.

Others are looking to the distant past for the salvation of forage fish. A fascinating pilot project is underway in California to raise small fish in flooded rice fields, providing the protein that salmon require and potentially solving a separate environmental problem: reducing emissions of methane, a greenhouse gas far more potent than carbon dioxide. The research is in its early stages, but fish nutritionists and environmentalists see promise.

Growing aquatic organisms in rice fields has a long history, particularly in Asia, where rice and fish are essential elements of food security. Ancient pottery from the Han dynasty, which ruled China from 206 BC to AD 220, depicted fish in rice fields, and a traditional saying in Vietnam likens rice and fish to mother and child. Today, roughly half the people in the world depend on rice as a staple food. Each year, the world produces more than 740 million tons of rice, second only to corn. The globe's two most populous nations, China and India, are also the leading producers and consumers of rice. Worldwide, 400 million acres are devoted to growing rice, an area four times the size of California.

Rice requires lots of water, so most of the crop is grown in flooded fields, creating the familiar rice paddies seen across Asia and the subcontinent. In the United States, rice is grown in Arkansas, California, Louisiana, Mississippi, Missouri, and Texas. During the fallow, or transition, period between rice crops, the fields often remain flooded, to help break down rice stocks and replenish the soil. In California, competition for access to water is fierce between farmers and urban areas. Rice is the most water-intensive crop produced in the state, accounting for roughly 6 percent of California's water use. Most of the 550,000 acres of rice planted each year are located along the Sacramento River and its tributary, the Feather River. Many farmers there have rights to river water dating back to the start of commercial rice farming in the area in the early 1900s. But there is constant pressure to use the water efficiently, even when the fields lie fallow between crops from late fall to spring.

Huey Johnson was an ardent environmentalist and founder of one of the nation's largest environmental organizations, the Trust for Public Land, started in 1972. The trust's goal was to expand public access to parks and trails in urban areas and national parks. A decade later, after serving as California's secretary of resources, Johnson adopted a more local strategy and established the Resource Renewal Institute, a small think tank in Mill Valley, north of San Francisco. The institute, known as RRI, was designed to be small and agile in pursuit of technology-drive innovations in land and water use.

One of Johnson's biggest ideas came in 2012, while he was hunting duck in Northern California. "I was hanging out in a Central Valley duck blind during hunting season—relaxed, content, peacefully waiting for a flock to fly by," he wrote in his autobiography, *Something of the Marvelous*. "As part of a joint program of rice farmers and the California Department of Fish and Wildlife, many farms along the Pacific Flyway flood their fields after harvest to promote the decomposition of rice straw and provide wetlands for migratory birds. As I sat waiting for the ducks, I began to wonder. What if all those fields of water could be put to another use, like shoring up the beleaguered California salmon population, made weak and scarce by dams and water exploration?"

Johnson's curiosity led to a project that involved putting juvenile salmon in fallow, flooded rice fields to see if they could grow on the zooplankton, microscopic animals that are abundant in the ocean and in freshwater. The experiment succeeded beyond Johnson's expectations, with the young salmon gaining five times their weight in six weeks. The next step was to determine whether fish could be grown commercially in the fallow rice fields. The project was named Fish in the Fields. Johnson envisioned multiple benefits, from providing a profitable and sustainable second crop for rice farmers to saving the world's forage fisheries. "We thought we could grow freshwater forage fish to replace the loss of forage fish in the ocean and allow the forage fish in the ocean to recover," said Deborah Moskowitz, a California native and public health expert who is president of the RRI.

The project evolved from replacing salmon to growing freshwater fish that could be sold to replace the huge numbers of forage fish being used in aquaculture feed. The fish of choice was the golden shiner, a freshwater species that is the most popular bait fish in the United States and is easily and cheaply available. The initial batch was set loose on thirty-five acres of flooded rice fields, where they thrived, grew fast, and reproduced rapidly. Johnson's vision of "fish in every rice field" appeared to be feasible. As prospects grew, the institute teamed up with the University of California, Davis and California Trout, a conservation group. A study found that fish grew ten times faster in the rice fields than in the wild. The future of the project looked promising—until an unexpected obstacle popped up.

Patagonia, one of the charitable foundations Johnson and Moskowitz hoped would finance the project, questioned the justification for promoting rice because the fields emit so much methane gas. When it comes to greenhouse gases and the climate crisis, carbon dioxide gets most of the attention, but methane is carbon dioxide on steroids. Over twenty years, a ton of methane gas will warm the atmosphere about eighty times more than the same amount of carbon dioxide. A study published in the journal *Environmental Research Letters* found that cutting methane emissions could slow the rate of Earth's warming by as much as 30 percent and reduce the most extreme impacts of the climate crisis. The largest producers of methane gas are livestock farming and the energy sector. But recent studies have blamed some of the sharp global increase in methane on microbes that produce the gas when they break down organic matter in wetlands like bogs and rice paddies.

Moskowitz understood the foundation's reservations, and she started searching for a solution to keep the project alive. The answer cropped up in an unusual place: a frozen lake in northern Finland. Methane gas is trapped under the ice in Arctic lakes. Drill a hole in the ice, and enough gas emerges that it can be lit. In 2016, Moskowitz found a scientific paper by Dr. Shawn Devlin, an aquatic ecologist at the University of Montana, who described using fish to reduce methane in lakes in Finland. Devlin and his colleagues had put a plastic curtain down the middle of a small frozen lake in Finland. On one side of the barrier, they introduced fingerling perch; the other side was left alone. The result on the perch side was a domino effect in the food web, called a trophic cascade.

This cascade can be broken into three steps. Methanotrophic bacteria occur naturally in water and are prodigious consumers of methane gas. Zooplankton feed on methanotrophic bacteria, eating enough to wipe out entire populations virtually and functionally. The result is that methane gas remains and is emitted into the atmosphere. The introduction of the perch changed this equation. The perch ate the zooplankton, which meant that the bacteria were free to consume all the methane they wanted. Devlin found that the side of the lake that contained the fish produced 90 percent less methane.

When Moskowitz read Devlin's paper, she realized she had found her solution. She sent an email to Devlin asking if he would be interested in applying the same concept to reduce methane in rice fields by introducing fish to eat the zooplankton. He agreed to help. When thousands of juvenile golden shiners were introduced to the rice fields that the RRI was using, they ate the zooplankton and left the good bacteria alone so it could eat the methane gas before it entered the atmosphere. The methane output of the fields with fish dropped by 65 percent. In an additional environmental bonus, the flooded rice fields provide food and sanctuary for tens of thousands of migrating waterfowl and seabirds in winter.

In July 2020, Johnson died peacefully at his home in Marin County, California, at the age of eighty-seven. But he lived long enough to see his idea start to come to life. Moskowitz and Devlin worked with a feed company and a land-based salmon farmer to determine whether the project could be expanded into a viable commercial source of marine ingredients for the aquaculture industry and if rice farmers would warm to the idea of a second crop in their fields. Trying to emphasize as much local content as possible, they started a hatchery for Sacramento blackfish, an oily fish native to California that thrives in warm, murky water and feeds on zooplankton.

Expanded to the world's four hundred million acres of rice fields, the innovative process could reduce global warming, provide protein for aquaculture feed, increase earnings for rice farmers, and grant a reprieve to the world's forage fish. "We're at a neat intersection between environmentalists, scientists, and rice farmers," said Moskowitz. "An important aspect of Fish in the Fields is it can be done anywhere that rice is grown. We have great hopes."

PART II

IN THE TRENCHES

CHAPTER 14

"SOMETHING IS SERIOUSLY WRONG"

"Skagit nine-one-one. What is your emergency?"

"I'm not quite sure if this is a nine-one-one emergency or not, but my husband and I are on our boat in Secret Harbor, and the middle fish pen is breaking apart, and we don't know who to call," Jill Davenport told the 911 operator for the police in Skagit County, about a hundred miles north of Seattle.

"What do you mean by the middle fish pen?" the operator asked.

"In Secret Harbor, on Cypress Island, there's three fish pens," Davenport explained calmly. "There's a bunch of equipment and stuff that, like a forklift and generators and stuff, that are potentially going into the water. And we don't see any humans around. It's huge, and the whole thing is buckling. There's a forklift that looks like it's about ready to go in the water."

"We are passing that information along," the operator replied.

Davenport and her husband, Jeff, were on their way with their young children to set crab pots off Cypress Island, in Puget Sound, at about three o'clock in the afternoon on Saturday, August 19, 2017. As they approached Cypress Island, they heard a loud clank from one of the three salmon farms in the small bay. They turned and saw a thick chain drag across the metal walkway linking the ten cages that formed one of the farms. As they watched, the underside of a cage rose out of the water, its nets covered with a thick layer of mussels and kelp. Davenport thought to herself, "When you see seaweed, something is seriously wrong."

The current was dragging the entire structure south, threatening to pull apart all ten cages and the metal structure holding them together. That was when Davenport got out her phone and called 911. Then she turned the phone toward the farm and took video footage of the buckling cages. She could not see beneath the water, where some of the ten anchor lines holding the farm to the seafloor were breaking loose, but the entire farm appeared to be on the verge of collapse. The landscape of salmon farming in Puget Sound was about to change dramatically.

About fifteen minutes after Davenport's 911 call, as their boat idled near the unfolding disaster, she spotted a worker and called out to him. He waved and shouted that he had called his boss and that help was one the way. A few minutes earlier, Daniel Farias, the lone weekend worker, had telephoned Sky Guthrie, the site manager, and urgently told Guthrie that walkways at Cypress Site 2 were buckling. He said he thought the entire structure could break loose and collide with one of the two other ten-cage farms in the cove.

"It's really bad," Farias said.

Guthrie understood the danger. Less than a month earlier, he had gotten a preview of the potential for disaster at the same farm. In response to the new call, he jumped into his car, drove two minutes to the nearby marina, grabbed a skiff, and took off for the collapsing farm. On the way, he telephoned Cooke's regional manager, Innes Weir, who relayed word of the impending disaster back to corporate headquarters in Blacks Harbour, New Brunswick, the home of Cooke Aquaculture, the owner of the Cypress Island farms.

Three individual farms were situated off Cypress Island, a largely undeveloped island about halfway between the mainland and offshore San Juan County. The farms there were identified as Sites 1, 2, and 3. Each farm consisted of floating steel rafts linking ten individual cages, arranged in two rows of five cages each. The floating collection of cages known as net pens was held in place by a mooring system comprised of chains and ropes attached to concrete anchors on the seabed. Cooke had bought the farms and five others in Puget Sound off the Washington State coast a year earlier from Icicle Seafoods. Already the dominant salmon farmer in Maine and New Brunswick and active in Chile and Scotland, the Canadian company was executing its plan for a major expansion in the Pacific Northwest. Cooke Aquaculture had grown aggressively to become the largest privately owned salmon-farming company in the world, but that drive to dominance was about to hit a road-block.

Guthrie got to the farm about twenty minutes after the call from Farias. Immediately, he knew his coworker had underestimated the situation. Walkways had twisted, some were submerged. Equipment had fallen into the water, and the large generator that provided electricity to the site was about to slide into the sound. A metal footbridge linking a floating office to the ten cages had broken loose. Nets were close to tearing open, about to send tens of thousands of Atlantic salmon into waters that were home to Pacific salmon. Weir arrived a short time after Guthrie and brought more workers. Guthrie got back on the phone and tried urgently to hire tugboats to stop the slowly drifting site from breaking apart completely and colliding with the two other farms, which were a few hundred yards away and filled with several hundred thousand fish.

Just as onlookers cannot take their eyes off a slow-moving train wreck, the Davenports watched from their boat as workers struggled to pull two portions of the heavily damaged middle cage out of the water. The *Lindsey Foss*, the first tugboat to arrive, got there at about five o'clock, two hours after Davenport's call. The four-hundred-ton tug is powered by twin diesel engines pumping out eight thousand horsepower. When she was built in 1993, the *Lindsey Foss* was the most powerful tug in the world. Its commissioning was a direct response to the *Exxon Valdez* disaster in 1989, when an oil tanker spilled eleven million gallons of crude oil into Alaska's Prince William Sound after tugs proved too weak to stop it from going aground. The slick covered 1,300 miles of coastline and killed hundreds of thousands of seals, whales, otters, and seabirds.

At Cypress Island, the huge tug maneuvered in order to swing in close to the pen, so workers could attach a line to the steel structure and allow the tug to try to pull the farm back into shape. As the *Lindsey Foss* neared the farm, its captain peered into the water from the ship's bridge. He saw nets below the surface heavily clogged with mussels, kelp, and seaweed. Instead of allowing water to pass through the cages, the fouling had turned the nets into massive sails that were being pushed by the current and tide. The bigger the blockage, the larger the sails and the greater the chance of the site's breaking loose entirely from its anchor cables. The risks of clogged nets were well known among salmon farmers and state officials in Puget Sound. Those risks were the reason

Cooke's lease with the state required the company to maintain its farms in clean and safe condition, with regular inspections and net cleanings. Later reports would show that the accumulation had occurred over many weeks.

A second tug soon joined the *Lindsey Foss* and began pulling from another direction to try to hold the farm together. The second tug lowered a boom to the deck of the farm and lifted away the forklift, which had been perilously close to going into the water.

While she and her husband watched the drama unfold, Davenport received calls from the county emergency services office, the state Department of Ecology, and the U.S. Coast Guard. Everyone wanted to know how bad things were. Bad, she replied. Davenport had the impression that the officials on the other end of the calls did not understand the size of the salmon farm or the potential environmental danger. She had emailed photos to the Coast Guard at about 4:30 p.m., but no government vessels had shown up by seven o'clock, when the Davenports headed home, assuming nothing could save the site from total collapse.

Guthrie and his crew worked alongside the two tugs through the night. Early Sunday morning, the structure was stable enough for workers to begin removing salmon from the damaged cages by hand. Divers were sent down to try to reattach the mooring chains that had broken loose from the anchors. But when the tide came in, more chains broke loose, the heavily fouled nets dragged along the bottom, and twisted walkways flipped as the site shifted position completely. Two cages tore open as the stress on the nets mounted . . . then four . . . then six. The site was no longer safe. The workers were ordered off. While the tugs struggled to avoid a total collapse, the effort turned into a salvage operation. Guthrie and his coworkers watched helplessly as tens of thousands of farmed salmon began escaping into Puget Sound.

As the farm was collapsing on Sunday, phones began to ring. Matthew Stratton, a special agent with the Criminal Enforcement division of the U.S. Environmental Protection Agency, was sitting at home not far from Cypress Island when he got three calls in quick succession. The first was from Seth Wilkinson, an assistant U.S. attorney in Seattle who specialized in environmental prosecutions. Then came the attorney general for Washington State.

Finally, a federal agent from the U.S. Fish and Wildlife Service. The message was the same: "Have you seen this?" "Are you on this?" "Let's get on this." He turned on the television and channel-surfed until he found a local news report on the disaster unfolding minutes from his home.

Stratton had spent thirty years as a federal criminal investigator working for the U.S. Fish and Wildlife Service and the FBI. Nine years earlier, looking for a quieter life away from Seattle, he had joined the Criminal Enforcement division of the EPA. On Monday, August 21, Stratton wanted a firsthand look at what had happened at Cypress Island, so he contacted Cooke Aquaculture's local office in nearby Anacortes. The person who answered took Stratton's number. When a lawyer for the company called back, Stratton said he wanted to go to the site. Not until the farm was stabilized, he was told. In the meantime, Stratton checked in with the Washington State Department of Natural Resources, which was leading the state's inquiry. He was told the episode looked like an environmental disaster.

Kurt Beardslee's phone also rang that Sunday afternoon. He had been about eight miles from Cypress Island, on Lummi Island, working with a crew from Patagonia, the outdoor clothing company, to film a ceremony conducted by the Lummi First Nation tribe, the original inhabitants of Washington State's northern coast and of southern British Columbia. Beardslee's Wild Fish Conservancy worked closely with Patagonia and its founder, Yvon Chouinard, on environmental projects. As soon as the ceremony ended, he aimed his boat south for Cypress Island.

Beardslee had been fighting salmon farms for many years, and he had seen plenty of damaged pens and debris. He understood the harm that could be done to the environment and to wild salmon from spilled chemicals, viral and parasitic outbreaks, and escaped farmed fish. He had become so concerned about the rising number of salmon farms along Puget Sound that the Conservancy had recently begun a public campaign called "Our Sound, Our Salmon." The campaign aimed to build public awareness about the threats posed by the farms and to encourage state lawmakers to end open-net salmon farming in Washington State. The petition drive quickly got more than ten thousand signatures. But none of what had motivated Beardslee to start the campaign equaled the destruction he encountered at Cypress Island Site 2. "I was expecting to see it broken, but it just imploded on itself," he said.

First thing Monday morning, Beardslee called Brian Knutsen, an environmental lawyer in Portland, Oregon, who had represented the Wild Fish Conservancy in several lawsuits against the federal and state governments, trying to get them to enforce environmental laws. Beardslee said he wanted to sue Cooke Aquaculture for violating the U.S. Clean Water Act by allowing nonnative salmon to escape and by polluting the water with debris from the collapse. Knutsen warned him that Cooke was a major company with deep pockets, so suing them would be expensive and time-consuming. Knutsen told Beardslee that the company would have every incentive, and the necessary resources, to drag out the proceedings and attack the Conservancy and its people.

The Wild Fish Conservancy had never had much of a budget. Knutsen had done most of his work for them on a pro bono basis, recouping costs only if he won the case. Even with lawyers working for free, the expense of taking on a major company with a combative reputation could reach seven figures for expert witnesses and scientific studies. From the start, Beardslee recognized that he was risking the future of the Conservancy, but he knew there was no alternative. This fight was the very type for which he'd founded the Conservancy. He authorized Knutsen to draft a letter formally notifying Cooke of the Conservancy's intent to sue, a requirement under the Clean Water Act. "I had no hesitation," Beardslee recalled. "We were staking everything we had on the suit. We knew there could be countersuits. You don't take this type of thing on lightly, but you also don't let these things go unchallenged because of the potential risks. That's how they get away with it. We were in it for the long haul."

Cooke had already been on Beardslee's radar. After the company bought out Icicle Seafoods, Beardslee read about its plans to expand in Puget Sound and up the coast into Alaska. He feared that Puget Sound would become "the new Chile," its coastline dominated by larger and larger salmon farms and greater and greater threats to native fish. Those fears had deepened a few months earlier, when Cooke applied to install fourteen circular cages at a new salmon farm in the Strait of Juan de Fuca, a narrow, ninety-six-mile-long passage between Washington State and Vancouver Island in British Columbia. The proposal would more than double the size of an existing farm, expanding the footprint on the water from four acres to nearly ten. Worse than the size of the proposed farm was the threat the location posed. The Strait of Juan de Fuca is a primary migration route for wild salmon returning from the Pacific

Ocean to spawn in autumn and the exit route for young salmon leaving the freshwater of Washington State and British Columbia in spring and early summer to reach the ocean. From Beardslee's perspective, it was the worst possible place for a massive salmon farm. The application was scheduled for its first public hearing in early September, just weeks away.

Events unfolded quickly in the days after the failure of Cypress Island Site 2, creating a tsunami of challenges for Cooke Aquaculture. Facing a public outcry and government investigations, Cooke denied responsibility for the incident and instead blamed natural causes. The company also downplayed the number of escaped fish and their potential impact on wild salmon.

A solar eclipse occurred on August 21, two days after the start of the collapse. Cooke claimed that it was the high tides and currents leading up to the eclipse that had torn apart the farm. "Tides and currents and tidal surges in the last weeks have been very strong," Nell Halse, Cooke's vice president of communications, said on August 21. "Our people are out there every day, and that is what they have been seeing. The tides were extremely high, the current 3.5 knots. People can believe it or not." When it came to the wild Pacific salmon population's imperilment by the escaped fish, Halse was dismissive. "It's primarily a business loss," she said. "The salmon will be food for the seals, and the fishermen can enjoy them."

The same day, the company filed its first official report on the escape of the salmon with the state, estimating that "upwards of 4,000 fish may have escaped." Cooke said the final number had not yet been determined. The official report also blamed the tides, claiming that "structural damage to pens [was] brought on by extraordinary strong tidal currents."

Cooke's initial attempt to point the finger at the eclipse fell apart for the simple reason that the tides were not unusually robust when the Cypress Island site collapsed. When she was on the scene in her boat, Jill Davenport saw no indication that the tides were responsible. "It has been suggested that the implosion was caused by unusual tides and currents," she wrote in an unpublished letter to her local newspaper in Anacortes. "Since we were right next to the pens and not experiencing anything abnormal, I don't believe either to be a legitimate cause." Tidal data and scientists debunked Cooke's attempt to blame high tides and currents. Parker MacCready, an oceanographer at the University of Washington, told the *Seattle Times*, "The data speak for themselves. There were large tidal ranges the day of the eclipse, but not out of the ordinary, and in fact, they were smaller than during some recent months." Weather records showed that the tides had been stronger at some point in every preceding month of the year.

In addition, the farm's location, in a protected bay only a few hundred yards from shore, diminished any tidal effects. The tide was strongest farther out in the channel. Adding to the dubiousness of the company's explanation, the site had broken apart *before* the strongest tides arrived with the eclipse on the twenty-first. Later, the state would declare that professionally designed and maintained salmon pens should have been able to withstand much stronger tides than those recorded on August 19 and 20.

Some state officials appeared unable to decide whether the escaped Atlantic salmon posed a threat to wild Pacific salmon. On August 23, the Department of Fish and Wildlife encouraged anglers to catch as many of the escaped Atlantic salmon as they could, to protect wild salmon, and they asked fishermen to report the number caught and their location. The alien fish were easy to spot because they are larger than their Pacific cousins and have distinctive black spots on their backs. In the same press release, however, the head of the department's fish program, Ron Warren, contradicted any suggestion that Atlantic salmon posed a threat to native fish. Warren said no evidence existed that the Atlantic salmon were a danger to the Pacific salmon and that there was no record of the two species interbreeding in Washington State's waters.

Despite Warren's attempt to smooth the waters, the danger posed by farmed salmon to wild salmon cannot be dismissed so easily. Salmon escape from pens in every country where they are farmed, sometimes in large numbers. Tens of millions of farmed salmon have escaped worldwide since the start of commercial farming in the early 1970s. Between 2010 and 2019, two million salmon were reported to have escaped from Norwegian farms; researchers argue that the actual number is likely much higher, because not every escape is reported, a gap that worries conservationists. Most countries designate a minimum number to trigger reporting requirements. For instance, farms on Canada's eastern coast in Newfoundland are not required to report escapes of fewer than one hundred fish. Yet, even small numbers add up, with the potential for big impacts.

Wild Pacific salmon and farmed Atlantic salmon are genetically different. Wild salmon have adapted over generations to changes in local river conditions like temperature, flow rates, and acidity levels in the water. Farmed fish, however, have been bred for fast growth in a closed environment, not for their ability to adapt. The negative effects of this divergence are well documented. Studies have showed that the interbreeding of farm salmon with wild salmon lowers the fitness of the hybrid offspring, weakens their ability to survive, and eventually reduces the overall wild population. Biologists studying salmon escapes fear the farmed version will eventually displace wild salmon, particularly in places like the Pacific Northwest, where wild salmon are in decline. Experts have found that farmed Atlantic salmon outcompete wild fish for food in some phases of their life cycle. In addition, there is ample evidence that the two species interbreed, and there are serious questions about the long-term sustainability of the resulting hybrids. In fact, scientists say a trickle of escapes may be more dangerous to wild populations than large-scale escapes. Interbreeding from a single large escape will weed itself out over a short time, because the escaped fish are less likely to survive and interbreed in any significant numbers. A steady stream of smaller escapes, however, provides a constant introduction of foreign genetic material, which means the local wild population never gets a chance to recover and is irrevocably nudged in a new direction as a species.

Another risk that farmed Atlantic salmon pose to wild Pacific salmon is the spread of parasites, viruses, and diseases not found in the native salmon or in the waters in which they swim. For example, a study published in *Virology Journal* after the Cypress Island collapse estimated that 95 percent of the escaped Atlantic salmon were infected with an exotic variant of piscine orthoreovirus, which had never been documented previously in Puget Sound waters. PRV causes heart and skeletal inflammation in salmon, which can lead to death. The virus apparently came from salmon eggs imported from Iceland. The study's authors included Alexandra Morton, Kurt Beardslee, and Fred and Molly Kibenge. A different study by a team of Canadian scientists, including from the federal Department of Fisheries and Oceans, determined that the virus arrived in the northwestern Pacific around thirty years ago, roughly the same time the first salmon farms showed up in British Columbia. The study said that evidence showed the virus had been transmitted from farmed salmon to wild Pacific salmon, where the disease had never been found before.

Farmed Atlantic salmon are also genetically different from wild Atlantic salmon, which means escapees from farms pose similar dangers by interbreeding with wild Atlantic salmon. That risk was clear in a study of a September 2013 escape of twenty thousand salmon from a Cooke Aquaculture farm in Hermitage Bay, Newfoundland. The timing of that earlier escape was particularly bad because it occurred at the height of spawning season for wild Atlantic salmon. The Canadian Department of Fisheries and Oceans found clear evidence that the escaped salmon interbred with wild salmon. Genetic material from the farmed fish was found later in one of every four salmon examined in the wild. "We looked at 19 rivers in the first year and hybrids were detected in 18 of those rivers," said Brendan Wringe, the lead researcher on the study. "We weren't surprised to find hybrids. We were surprised to find as many hybrids as we did and to find them as widely spread as we did." An analysis by the Atlantic Salmon Federation estimated that interbreeding from the episode had a direct impact on the wild population: the number of wild salmon in the Conne River in southern Newfoundland dropped from about eight to ten thousand to fewer than a thousand after the 2013 escape.

The Cypress Island collapse looked like a repeat, but at a far greater magnitude. Hundreds of Atlantic salmon were caught in Puget Sound and nearby rivers and streams in the days after the farm failed. Many anglers reported seeing large numbers swimming free in the water. "Fish continue to hug the beach in large schools," one angler told the state. "They seem to prefer staying in the sheltered bays." Ten fish were spotted near Lummi Island, 8 miles from the collapse. Seals and eagles were feasting on dead Atlantic salmon that had washed ashore all along the coast of the sound. Tribal fishers from Lummi and Samish First Nations caught 55,000 Atlantic salmon in an organized effort to stop the fish before they entered rivers and streams on tribal land. Weeks later, Atlantic salmon were found 130 miles south, near Tacoma, and 250 miles north, near Vancouver Island in British Columbia. In British Columbia's Sabine Channel, Atlantic salmon were caught with small native salmon in their bellies. Just like in Newfoundland, the mass escape from Cypress Island coincided with spawning season.

The numbers of alien Atlantic salmon caught in the days after the collapse contradicted Cooke's estimate of four thousand escapees. But the company stuck with the figure "several thousand," saying thousands of fish had been recovered with the damaged nets. Even as they refused to acknowledge that tens of thousands of fish had escaped, Cooke was forced to back away from its claim that the solar eclipse was to blame. The data on the tidal conditions could not be denied.

April Bencze is a professional photographer who lives on a sailboat off Vancouver Island in British Columbia. She specializes in documenting environmental degradation like shipwrecks, oil spills, and collapsed salmon farms. On August 23, four days after the start of the Cypress Island collapse, she was in Victoria when a documentary film producer called. He was working for Patagonia on a film about the impact of salmon farms in Puget Sound. The collapse of the Cooke farm was the drama every documentary needs. "We need underwater footage of this mess," said the producer. "How fast can you get here?"

Bencze's dive gear and underwater video camera were on her boat, which was eight hours away by car and ferry. She understood the urgency and drove through the night to get her equipment and passport, and then she caught a ferry for Puget Sound. She arrived on August 24. The Patagonia crew was waiting aboard a fifty-foot work boat called the *Galactic Ice*, which Patagonia had hired for its documentary. As soon as Bencze was aboard, they headed for the collapsed farm. When they arrived, they encountered, along with the twisted wreckage and ongoing salvage operations, a handful of sport fishermen responding to the state's call to catch escaped salmon and a U.S. Coast Guard cutter patrolling the waters around the farm.

Riley Starks, the captain of the *Galactic Ice*, maneuvered the vessel close to the collapsed farm. Suited up and gripping her underwater video camera, Bencze rolled backward into the water from a low platform on the side of the ship. She had dived the peripheries of salmon farms before, but she had never seen the level of destruction that greeted her sixty feet below the surface that day. As she drifted on the current along the length of the wreckage, she filmed heavily fouled nets with gaping splits, salmon cut in half and wedged in the twisted nets. A week after the collapse, a few fish were still gasping. What Bencze did not find was just as significant: the cages did not contain huge numbers of dead salmon; most of the fish had escaped through the massive rips in the nets or been hauled out by Cooke workers.

About half an hour into her filming, Bencze heard a metallic pinging from above, the universal signal for an emergency ascent. She could not tell if the tapping was coming from her own boat, from workers on the fish farm, or from the Coast Guard, but it could not be ignored, so she headed toward the surface, where she found a chaotic scene. Someone at the Cooke farm was using its loudspeaker to order her out of the water, claiming she was trespassing. She swam to the *Galactic Ice*, where crew gathered in her video camera and helped her aboard. It is not illegal to swim in the ocean, and the Cypress Site 2 had drifted beyond the boundaries of its lease, but prudence dictated that Bencze not return to the water. Anyway, she already had dramatic footage of what was happening beneath the surface.

Bencze was preparing to return home when she heard that Lummi fishermen were catching large numbers of Atlantic salmon in the Nooksack River, nearly thirty miles from the collapse. Intrigued, she headed out to meet the fishermen. About five thousand tribal members live on the Lummi reservation, which sits on a peninsula across from the island about one hundred miles north of Seattle. The tribe's director of natural resources, Merle Jefferson, says, "The Lummi are salmon people; salmon is culture, and culture is salmon." The decline of wild salmon endangers Lummi culture and livelihoods, and the tribe has been involved in many efforts to protect and restore the fish.

When the Cooke farm collapsed, Lummi leaders recognized the threat posed by the escaped Atlantic salmon. They declared an emergency and urged tribal fishermen to catch as many Atlantic salmon as possible to protect the native species from disease, interbreeding, and simply being eaten by the invaders. As Bencze watched and photographed, fishermen at the mouth of the Nooksack landed dozens of Atlantic salmon that appeared to have been deformed or damaged in the farm's collapse. When some of the salmon were sliced open, the Lummi found enlarged and discolored organs: signs of disease. These were clearly alien fish that threatened the native salmon.

Instead of 4,000 escaped fish of little concern to wild salmon, evidence pointed to *hundreds of thousands* of escaped fish and a far greater threat to the native population. The notification letter that the Wild Fish Conservancy had sent Cooke Aquaculture after the collapse accused Cooke of negligence in maintaining the farm and scoffed at the company's explanation for the collapse. The Conservancy estimated that as many as 305,000 salmon had escaped. "As had been widely reported," it said, "Cooke Aquaculture presided over the near-complete structural failure of a net pen facility located in Deepwater Bay off of Cypress Island over the weekend of August 19th and 20th, the failure of which has resulted in, and continues to result in, the discharge of Atlantic salmon, dead fish carcasses, and massive amounts of debris among other pollutants."

Instead of the solar eclipse, the Conservancy suggested that the cause was weakness in the structural integrity of the net pens. The Conservancy had discovered that emergency maintenance had been performed on the same pen after it nearly collapsed in July. It also challenged the claims by Cooke spokesperson Halse and by Warren, the state's fish program manager, that the escaped salmon did not jeopardize the imperiled wild salmon population. "The escapement of Atlantic salmon poses threats of competition to native juvenile and adult salmon and steelhead," said the Conservancy's fisheries scientist, Dr. Nick Gayeski. "The escaped fish still need to feed and thus are likely to compete with native juvenile Pacific salmon and steelhead, including preying on them. Like Pacific salmon, Atlantic salmon spawn in the fall. The escaped fish are capable of spawning and will begin entering Puget Sound rivers to attempt to spawn."

On August 27, Washington State governor Jay Inslee ordered a major investigation, establishing a multiagency command center like those created to respond to oil spills or wildfires. "Tribes and others who fish Washington waters deserve a comprehensive response to this incident, including answers to what happened and assurances that it won't happen again," Inslee said in a press statement. Once the state investigation started, Inslee said agents would look at all of Cooke's operations in Washington State. "The broad public outcry surrounding this net pen failure is understandable," he told a press conference. "So is the lack of confidence in how Cooke responded to the emergency, the recovery of fish and the management of future operations the company may pursue here in our waters."

Three Washington State departments (Ecology, Natural Resources, and Fish and Wildlife) assembled a panel of top experts in early September to determine the cause and evaluate the impact of the site's collapse. Investigators had been at work since the incident gathering evidence about the condition of the collapsed site and the real number of escaped fish. Three central questions confronted the investigators: Why did Cypress Island Site 2 collapse? How many salmon escaped? And what would it mean to the future of salmon farms in Washington State?

As state and federal investigators began their work, the picture that emerged was of a disaster with a far greater impact on the future of open-net salmon farms in Washington State and beyond.

CHAPTER 15

BATTLING ON MULTIPLE FRONTS

On September 2, EPA special agent Matthew Stratton took the Highway 20 bridge from his office on the mainland to Anacortes, a small city on Fidalgo Island and the closest access point to Cypress Island. There he joined Innes Weir, Cooke Aquaculture's regional manager, and Douglas Steding, one of the company's lawyers, for a short boat trip to the ruined farm. After a two-week wait, Stratton was finally getting to the scene of a potential crime. Weir was a big man, with a weightlifter's build, a heavy black beard, and a Scottish accent.

Before the boat pulled up alongside the remains of the salmon farm, Stratton thought he was prepared for the sight. People at the state agencies had told him the farm's nets had been clogged with marine material, and he had followed press accounts of the salvage work over the previous ten days. But the amount of fouling Stratton saw in the nets being hauled out of the water by divers made him doubt the nets had been cleaned for weeks or longer. The stinking, dripping nets were attached to a crane to be hauled onto a nearby vessel. As the nets rose out of the water, mussel shells and thick tangles of seaweed rained down on those below. Some nets were so heavy with debris that they had to be cut into pieces before the crane could lift them. The nets, a solid wall of marine life and debris, incredibly smelly from the fouling, were going to a landfill. When Stratton asked where the twisted remains of the floating steel structure that had enclosed the pens were going, Weir said they were being taken to a nearby salvage yard, where they would be reassembled like a puzzle into a rough approximation of the precollapse site, for further analysis.

It was the only question Stratton got to ask that day. A few days earlier, John Wolfe, a Seattle criminal defense attorney, had called Stratton to give him permission to visit the site. Cooke Aquaculture had hired the criminal lawyer when the company learned about the EPA investigation. Wolfe's only condition was that Stratton avoid questioning employees at the farm, because Wolfe would not be present. Stratton had gotten along well with Wolfe in the past, and he agreed. Stratton was in the early stages of gathering evidence, so his questions could wait. What was important was that he see the site before the debris was removed and that he take plenty of photos to record the scene.

Stratton had grown up on Puget Sound. He knew the water and the currents. Cooke Aquaculture's story about the solar eclipse and the tides made no sense to him. He found the claim darkly amusing. Cooke did not stop trying to blame the eclipse until a few days after the accident, when meteorologists and scientists began to scoff at the notion publicly. The scene at the farm, especially the clogged nets, raised questions in Stratton's mind about whether the company had been negligent in maintaining Cypress Island Site 2, a potentially important avenue of investigation.

EPA special agents such as Stratton investigate the most significant and egregious potential violations of environmental laws. A criminal investigation is a factual progression, from a hypothesis to a conclusion. The scene is visited; records are collected and analyzed; employees, former employees, and other witnesses are interviewed. In the case of a structural failure like the net pen collapse, the investigator needs engineers to explain how the system should have functioned in order to recognize how things went wrong. Other experts help investigators understand the impact on the environment. The investigative work is coordinated with a prosecutor and, in sensitive cases, others higher up the chain of command. When possible, the investigator conducts informal interviews with potential witnesses to prepare for formal versions when lawyers will be present. Most crimes require proving intent to break the law or negligence in not following the law. The investigator's goal is to present the strongest-possible evidence to the prosecutor, who decides in the end whether charges are appropriate. Each step can be unpredictable, and investigations that seem open-and-shut can take months, turning on a single witness or a technicality.

As his investigation started, Stratton's working hypothesis was that Cooke had violated the U.S. Clean Water Act, which regulates discharges of pollution into the waters of the United States. The EPA is the lead agency in setting standards for pollution and determining if discharges violate the law, but the EPA cooperates with state and local authorities. Stratton's theory was that fish released unintentionally, along with debris from the collapse, would likely be considered pollutants under the act. As is often true for legal issues, no one could make a final determination until the facts were gathered and analyzed.

If the Cooke collapse had been caused by extreme tidal currents, a criminal charge would have been unlikely, and Stratton's investigation might have ended quickly. Evidence of negligence, such as a failure to keep the nets clean or maintain the farm properly, made a potentially stronger case. In the initial stages of his investigation, Stratton focused on three broad and interrelated questions: First, were the invasive Atlantic salmon a threat to wild Pacific salmon and other marine life? Second, did the escaped salmon constitute pollution? Third, was there evidence of negligence by the company or its workers?

After his on-site visit, Stratton turned to experts on marine biology and environmental science to understand the impact of nonnative salmon on the population of Pacific salmon. By then, the estimated number of escaped fish had risen to the tens of thousands, making it the largest single escape in Pacific Northwest history. A biologist compared the site's collapse to an oil spill or massive sewage discharge because of its impact on the ecosystem and wild salmon. "The Pacific Northwest salmon are in a fragile and delicate ecosystem which has been severely damaged by development and climate change," the biologist told Stratton. "Anything which inhibits Pacific Northwest salmon from flourishing, including releasing non-native species into their habitat, affects everything." Foreshadowing an issue that would become important later, a second biologist warned that proving that the invasive fish threatened native salmon might be difficult. "The aquaculture industry has done an excellent job of lobbying lawmakers to prevent any serious research to be completed on inter-species breeding due to aquaculture escapes," he said. An engineer whose office was in the same building as Cooke's regional office in Anacortes and who was familiar with the site raised the issue of negligence. He told Stratton that Cypress Site 2 was a big bag of overcrowded fish and that Cooke knew its "time was up."

Early in their parallel investigations, Stratton and the Washington State investigators discovered that the August collapse was not the first serious episode at Cypress Island Site 2. On July 24, just four weeks before the August disaster, the site had nearly been destroyed by fouled nets and structural failures. The company had delayed reporting the earlier incident, and when it did file the state-mandated report two days later than it should have, it downplayed the seriousness of the episode. "The strong flood tides caused some movement of the Site 2 anchors and fish pen structures," Cooke wrote. But a starkly different picture emerged from interviews with Cooke employees and members of salvage teams that had struggled to save the farm over a four-day period in late July.

Cooke workers who had been on the scene told state investigators that the farm did more than move; it nearly collapsed. As the current pushed against badly fouled nets, they said, half the mooring lines securing the farm to its underwater anchors had broken, and the farm drifted several hundred feet. Workers said the nets had not been cleaned properly at the time of the first incident because two of the three cleaning machines had not been working in July, requiring a single cleaning machine to be shared with the two other Cooke farms at Cypress Island for up to six months. When the state investigators interviewed Innes Weir about cleaning the nets before the July incident, he acknowledged that some machines had been inoperable. But Weir said workers had pulled the nets up by hand and cleaned them to a satisfactory level.

State investigators heard a different story from other Cooke employees who described the condition of the nets. Biofouling (or the clogging of nets by mussels, seaweed, and other marine organisms on salmon farm nets) is ranked on a scale of one to ten, with ten being the worst and four out of ten considered normal. Cooke personnel told the investigators that the fouling of the nets at Cypress Island Site 2 was seven to eight out of ten, and a sign of potential trouble.

When Stratton interviewed him, Sky Guthrie said the biofouling at Cypress Island Site 2 prior to the July incident was between eight and ten on a scale of ten. He told Stratton that the site's nets had not been cleaned for two to three months before the July incident because the two inoperable machines had left the crews unable to remove the mussels, kelp, and other debris.

The dirty nets and other maintenance problems were also noticed by the crews of the tugboats and other salvage experts summoned to try to save the farm from collapse in late July. For instance, the tugboat *Millennium Star* was called to the site only hours after it started to drift on July 24. A crew member told Stratton that he saw rust holes in the metal structures holding the net pens together and that some of the walkways were buckling. The situation on the farm was so precarious that he refused to allow any other tug personnel to board the structure. The crew member told Stratton that the whole situation seemed to be in disarray, with Cooke workers running around "like chickens with their heads cut off."

On July 25, as workers struggled to keep the farm from collapsing, a second tugboat, the *Quilceda*, arrived. The captain told Stratton that he found the *Millennium Star* and several smaller boats trying to hold the site together. The captain, whose name, like that of other sources, was redacted in federal government records, said the site was "falling apart"—metal walkways holding it together were bent into a U shape, and the heavily fouled nets were being pushed by the current, dragging the site with them.

A third salvage expert from a marine construction company, who spent four days at the site in July, told the EPA investigator that Cypress Island Site 2 was in such bad condition that Cooke should have harvested the fish immediately to avoid its total collapse. Instead, he said, the company rolled the dice, hoping the farm would hold together long enough for the fish to grow to market size by October. Cooke "got greedy," he said, and should have pulled the fish out of the net pens in July, even though they had not yet reached market size.

And there had been a ready-made opportunity to take out the fish. On July 24, a ship called the FV *Harvester* was loading salmon from Cypress Island Site 3, just a few hundred yards from Site 2, to take them to a processing plant. A member of the ship's crew told Stratton that up to one hundred thousand fish could have been removed from the cages, reducing the drag on the fouled nets from the current. But he said Cooke personnel at Site 2 refused to harvest the fish.

The evidence from the witnesses indicated that the July incident was more serious than Cooke had disclosed to the state, giving rise to questions about whether the ultimate collapse of the farm in August could have been prevented. State investigators would say in their final report that corrosion had likely reduced the structural capacity of the site and that the stress on the nets had been caused by the failure to clean them according to Cooke's schedule.

For his part, Stratton wanted to find out more about the lifespan of mussels to understand just how long they had been growing on the farm's nets. So, he visited a research professor at the University of Washington who specialized in marine biology. Examining the photos Stratton had taken of the mussels at the farm on September 2 and listening to his description of the mussels raining down when the nets were pulled out of the water, the professor estimated that the mussels clogging the nets were full-grown adults. To reach that size, she explained, the mussels would have to have been attached to the nets far longer than the four weeks between the two incidents, meaning the nets were not properly cleaned after the July 24 incident.

The evidence lies in the life cycle of mussels. The larvae are about the size of a grain of sand and spend the first three to six weeks of their lives floating freely and feeding on algae. Eventually, the young mussels attach to a specific location—a pier, a boat bottom, or nets at a salmon farm. Once attached, the professor explained, mussels move very little through the remainder of their life span. She said the mussels in Stratton's photos would have required *six to eight months* to reach the size they were when they were recovered from the clogged nets at Cypress Site 2. Had the nets been cleaned properly in July, she explained to Stratton, there could not have been enough time for the mussels to reach the adult size found in August. Stratton was told the same thing by several other biologists he interviewed.

Facing public and political pressure, the investigation by the three state agencies moved at a faster pace than Stratton's one-man probe for his federal bosses. On January 30, 2018, the state agencies released a scathing 120-page report accusing Cooke of negligence that led to the catastrophic net pen collapse in August. The state found that between 243,000 and 263,000 Atlantic salmon escaped into Puget Sound, more than twice the number the company had finally reported, and sixty to seventy times more than the company's first reported number. Anglers had reported catching 57,000 escapees, which left about 200,000 Atlantic salmon at large. Data showed that tidal currents had contributed to the collapse, but the report said the tides were neither unprecedented nor altered by the solar eclipse. Instead, the investigators concluded that the anchors and mooring lines broke because they were heavily corroded and could not handle the strain created by the badly fouled nets. The conclusion was blunt: "The probable cause of both the July incident and the August failure was the failure of Cooke to adequately clean the nets containing the fish. Properly designed, sited, and maintained, salmon pens should be able to withstand combinations of tidal currents, wind, and wave forces that reasonably could be expected to occur at a site."

The state investigators estimated that up to 110 tons of mussels, kelp, and other sea life had accumulated on the nets before the August collapse. Excessive fouling caused the near failure of the mooring system at the farm in July, said the report, but Cooke "did not provide accurate and complete information to the state about the July incident." While the company officially maintained that there had been "some movement" of the pen in July, its internal emails told a different story. The day after the incident, Weir sent an email to Cooke headquarters saying, "We nearly lost the farm." By August, the additional buildup on the nets turned them into underwater sails that were dragged by the current and tide. The movement broke the anchor lines, and the structure twisted and collapsed.

At a press conference in Olympia, the state capital, top officials said Cooke had misled state agencies about the seriousness and cause of the July mishap and misrepresented the cause and the scope of the collapse in August. "The collapse was not the result of natural causes," said Hilary Franz, the state commissioner of public lands. "Cooke's disregard caused this disaster and recklessly put our state's aquatic ecosystem at risk." Maia Bellon, director of the Department of Ecology, also said Cooke was negligent. "What's even worse is that Cooke knew they had a problem, and they didn't appropriately respond to deal with the problem. They knew that there was an issue, and Cooke Aquaculture could have and should have prevented this incident."

The Department of Ecology fined Cooke $332,000 for the escape, concluding that the company had violated its National Pollutant Discharge Elimination System permit, which regulates discharges and requires monitoring and reporting of pollution. The Clean Water Act gave the state the authority to enforce the regulations, and its investigation determined that Cooke had violated the permits by failing to thoroughly inspect the farm's anchors, inadequately cleaning the nets, and negligently releasing farmed salmon.

Significantly for Stratton's investigation, the department declared that the escaped fish constituted a pollutant. A state finding was not binding on the EPA, but it provided momentum for Stratton.

A few days later, the state canceled Cooke's lease for all three of its Cypress Island farms and began to review its other operations in Washington State's waters, as Governor Inslee had ordered. The review led to the cancelation of the lease for a Cooke farm at Port Angeles and ended its plans for the new fourteen-cage farm in the Strait of Juan de Fuca that had alarmed Kurt Beardslee and others because of its proposed size and sensitive location.

The company denied wrongdoing and attacked the state's findings. "Cooke Aquaculture was shut out of this investigation by the state agencies," Joel Richardson, a public relations executive at Cooke, said in a press statement. "As a result, investigators with limited experience in aquaculture or net pen operations have produced an inaccurate and misleading document that appears intended to fuel the push by aquaculture opponents to put Cooke out of business in Washington state." Cooke appealed the fine and fought the cancelation of its leases, later losing in both instances.

Pushing back against the estimate that up to 263,000 salmon had escaped, Cooke adopted a strategy to deny and discredit its critics, entering stage one of the Benson-Kirsch template. The company said its employees counted fish remaining in the nets in August under state supervision, concluding that about 145,000 were missing. Richardson said the state used flawed estimates in claiming that twice as many fish had escaped as Cooke calculated. The company also disputed the amount of fouling on the nets and its impact on the collapse. "We acknowledge that the site fell behind in net hygiene prior to the mooring failures in July," said Richardson. "However, Cooke provided the investigators extensive documentation of the washing performed at Site 2 after the July incident. Although the report is correct that mussels were present in the bottom of the nets, the investigative panel lacked the expertise to make that judgment about the relationship between fouling and drag and did not rely upon alternative expertise when forming the conclusions reflected in the report."

Richardson's points were drawn from a twelve-page letter sent to the state agencies by Cooke's civil attorneys the day before the governmental report was released. The letter challenged many of the state's findings. The accusation that Cooke had misreported the number of fish recovered from its net pens drew an especially sharp attack from Cooke's attorney, Douglas Steding, who called the conclusion "nonsensical" and "a defamatory analysis that Cooke cannot tolerate." Steding said failure to correct what he called factual inaccuracies would prejudice Cooke's case in the state legislature, which had begun debating bills to ban salmon farms from Washington State's waters after the August collapse.

Cooke Aquaculture was fighting for its future in Washington. Public opposition to salmon farms had increased sharply, led by chiefs of the Lummi First Nation and other Native American tribes along Puget Sound. The grassroots movement extended beyond the Native Americans and environmental groups, drawing support from businesspeople, commercial and recreational fishers, scientists, and the public at large. The collapse of the Cooke farm galvanized large swaths of the public that had paid little attention to the growing impact of salmon farming in Puget Sound. A steering committee of fifteen groups, including the Wild Fish Conservancy, the Sierra Club, and the Audubon Society, began meeting weekly to mobilize support for legislation to ban salmon farms from Puget Sound and the surrounding waters. Representatives of the coalition collected signatures at county fairs and farmers' markets, ultimately drawing support from more than one hundred local businesses and tens of thousands of individuals. State legislators were swamped by calls from people demanding a ban. One state legislator said that he and his colleagues had not heard from as many of their constituents on a single issue since 2012, when Washington State voted to legalize same-sex marriage.

Several bills were introduced to ban Cooke and other salmon farmers from the state's waters. The most serious measure came from state senator Kevin Ranker, whose district included Cypress Island. His legislation specified that existing open-net farms could operate until their leases ran out, but no leases would be extended, and no new permits would be granted. The bill would require state agencies to keep a closer watch on the existing operations until they were phased out, which would happen no later than 2025. There was precedent: California, Oregon, and Alaska had prohibited open-net farms. Washington was the only state on the West Coast where the farms were permitted. In an unusual exhibition of solidarity, the leaders of twenty-one Native

American tribes combined forces to send a joint letter to every state lawmaker requesting that salmon farms be shut down to protect Pacific salmon.

Cooke responded by hiring a team of lobbyists and more lawyers and mobilizing spokespeople to defend its record and its operations. Forms filed with the state government showed that the company spent nearly three hundred thousand dollars on lobbyists in 2018 and 2019 to fight the legislation, far more than the cost of cleaning the cages at Cypress Site 2. Cooke's argument relied heavily on the 181 jobs it had created in the state and its seventy-million-dollar investment in its farms. As often happens when a company confronts restrictions, Cooke promised to upgrade and expand its operations and create more jobs. At one legislative hearing on Senator Ranker's bill, Cooke employees wearing rubber boots and work clothes were paid by the company to pack the room to demonstrate support for salmon farming.

Ranker was no newcomer to the risks of salmon farms. After he was elected to the State Senate in 2008 as a Democrat, he filed the first bill to ban salmon farms. He argued that the state and federal governments were spending millions of dollars to protect the environment at the same time that fish farms were polluting waterways and threatening native Pacific salmon. Ranker was ahead of the times; the measure never got out of committee.

Nearly a decade later, Ranker had been sitting in his home a few minutes from Cypress Island on Sunday, August 20, when a friend telephoned with the news that a nearby salmon farm was collapsing. Ranker hopped into his boat and arrived as Cypress Site 2 was coming apart. In all the years he had spent on the water, and even with the recent increase in the number of salmon farms in Puget Sound, Ranker had never seen anything like the collapsing site. In the weeks that followed, Cooke's claims about high tides and minimal salmon escapes fell apart, and so did the company's credibility in Ranker's eyes. "They lied," he said. "It was very clear to me that we had to have legislation to ban them." He dusted off his decade-old bill and started thinking about how far he could go under these changed circumstances.

A couple of weeks after the collapse, as word began to circulate that Ranker was preparing a new bill, he got a call from Cooke Aquaculture. The company's CEO was going to be in Seattle and wanted to meet with the senator. Ranker agreed, and a few days later he met Glenn Cooke in the lobby of the Olympic Hotel in downtown Seattle. The self-made millionaire was friendly and low-keyed, just the way his family-owned company portrayed itself in advertising and to the media. Cooke set out his position, saying the incident was caused by nature and that the company was not responsible. He reminded Ranker that the industry provided jobs for people in his district up and down the coast. Cooke said the company was planning a major expansion. Ranker appreciated hearing Cooke's views in person, but the legislator remained skeptical. He pointed out to Cooke that the more than two hundred thousand jobs in fishing and outdoor recreation in Washington State depended on maintaining healthy waters in and around Puget Sound. Ranker said he had not decided whether his bill would propose a complete ban on salmon farms, but he said a total prohibition was on the table. Ranker said Cooke responded that the collapse was "a fluke" and that the company had no responsibility for what had happened.

Ranker introduced his retooled bill in November. He proposed phasing out all salmon farms in the state's waters. The collapse had changed the political atmosphere, and this time the legislation moved quickly through committee hearings and was making its way to a vote with bipartisan support by mid-January 2018. The release of the report by three state agencies on January 30 provided the final push. On February 8, days after the investigative report was made public, Ranker's bill to phase out the farms was approved by the State Senate by a vote of 35 to 12. A week later, the House passed a slightly different bill, limiting the prohibition to "invasive species." The change would keep Atlantic salmon out, but it left the door open for filling existing farms with native fish like steelhead trout. The House version also required a review of the ban if new science found that farmed salmon did not harm wild salmon. The changes meant the bill was returned to the Senate for a new vote, which meant more time and more political capital would be required for passage. The end of the legislative session was approaching, and opponents were using the deadline to try to kill the bill by running out the clock.

Washington's legislature is a part-time operation. When the legislative session ended on March 2, any lingering bills would be kicked over to the next session in November. If Ranker's bill did not pass before the session's hard stop, the issue could not be raised again for months. The postponement would give Cooke time to expand its defense and increase its lobbying campaign. Perhaps the public outcry would go quiet, too. Ranker's best chance required moving quickly.

The days between the House vote and the mandatory reconsideration by the Senate were intense for Cooke Aquaculture, and its arguments betrayed its desperation. Glenn Cooke returned to Washington State to try to persuade senators not to phase out salmon farms. In conversations with lawmakers and in press interviews, he called the proposed ban an overreaction that would cost jobs and give the state a black eye in the business world. At one point, Cooke compared the proposed ban to "something you would hear in the Soviet Union." In a biology-defying, "alternative fact" moment, he denied that the mussels and other marine life had accumulated on the farm's nets for months. Instead, Cooke claimed the mussels and debris could have grown after the August failure in the few days before the nets were hauled out of the water. "We believe the cages were in good shape, the moorings were in good shape," he told a radio interviewer.

Richardson, Cooke's public relations official, threatened to escalate the proposed ban into an international issue. Unfurling the Canadian flag, he said that if the ban were approved, the company would recoup its investment through arbitration under the North American Free Trade Agreement. "There's a trade agreement that provides for relief in exactly this type of situation where a foreign company is treated worse than, and is disadvantaged against, its domestic counterparts," said Richardson.

The scary prospects of lost jobs and big-time litigation might have worked in less affluent places like New Brunswick or Maine, both locations where Cooke dominated salmon farming. But Washington State was home to major corporations like Boeing and Microsoft, and Puget Sound was a beloved recreation icon and tourist hub. Low-paying jobs in the salmon-farming industry were not as significant there as they were elsewhere.

On the afternoon of March 2, the last day of the session, the House-passed version of Ranker's bill came up for its vote in the Senate. Opponents tried to bury it in an avalanche of amendments as the seconds ticked toward five o'clock and mandatory adjournment. Each amendment required a roll call vote of the forty-nine-member Senate, each of which ran precious minutes off the clock. Each amendment required Ranker and his staff to counter the substance as quickly and thoroughly as possible to keep supporters in line. Some issues were technical, and the senator and staff members maintained an open phone line to get advice from Kurt Beardslee and his team at the Wild Fish Conservancy. It was a frantic scramble as the deadline approached.

A few minutes before five o'clock, it was clear that all the amendments could not be voted on before the session ended. Ranker and a fellow Democrat, Sen. Kevin Van De Wege, employed a last-ditch parliamentary maneuver to extend the time. Under Washington's legislative rules, the majority party could designate its last bill for a session, which required that debate continue until there was a final outcome, no matter how long it took. With time nearly out, the Democrats and their 3-vote majority identified the salmon farm bill as their last legislation for the session. The debate would continue until its fate was resolved.

As Cooke and Richardson watched from the Senate gallery, Ranker and Van De Wege defeated all twenty-one amendments offered by their opponents. As the vote on the bill neared, one of the Republicans rushed into the Senate chamber waving a piece of paper and shouting that the bill violated a Senate rule that required the name of the legislation to reflect its objectives. Sen. Sharon Nelson, the leader of the State Senate, offered a scathing dismissal. "Point not well received," she replied before calling for the final vote on Ranker's bill.

Finally, at six thirty in the evening, the bill passed 31–16 with bipartisan support. Atlantic salmon farms would be banned from Washington State's waters by 2025. No existing leases for salmon farms could be extended, and the state would step up its oversight of the industry for the remaining seven years. On March 22, Governor Jay Inslee signed the measure into law. He vetoed the House-added provision requiring a review if the science changed. "This bill will phase out non-native marine pens in Puget Sound," Inslee said. "These present a risk to our wild salmon runs that we cannot tolerate."

After denying what had happened, Cooke Aquaculture switched to what Benson and Kirsch would likely call "strategic accommodation." Richardson issued a statement saying, "While our company and our rural sea farming employees are deeply disappointed by the governor's decision to ignore science and sign the bill, we will certainly respect the wishes of the legislature." He added that the company would evaluate its operations and explore all options. Translation: Cooke was not done fighting.

Washington State's ban renewed the battle north of the border. Canadian biologist and wild salmon campaigner Alexandra Morton, the leaders of several First Nations tribes, and other opponents of salmon farms pushed for a similar moratorium in British Columbia. Fish do not stop at international borders, and some of the escaped Atlantic salmon had been discovered in waters off the British Columbia coast, raising new fears of interbreeding and the spread of disease there. Morton said Washington State's ban would have a positive impact on wild salmon throughout the Pacific Northwest. "My main concern with salmon farms is that they amplify pathogens," she said. "So, sea lice, viruses, bacteria simply pour out of these facilities at levels that the wild salmon are just not built to survive." In other words, to Morton's mind, the fewer salmon farms, the better.

A poll conducted for a Canadian conservation group three weeks after Inslee signed the ban found intense opposition to salmon farming in British Columbia. Nearly three out of every four respondents, 74.6 percent, said they supported an immediate ban on salmon farms; 48 percent of them said they "strongly supported" a ban. More than fifty candidates for federal office in British Columbia signed a pledge to shut down salmon farming in the provincial waters by 2025. The question was whether public opposition would translate into the kind of changes made in Washington State.

But the Canadian government was in no rush to follow Washington State's example. "We understand Canadians' concerns around aquaculture and are committed to science and evidence-based decision making," said Dominic LeBlanc, the federal fisheries minister who represented New Brunswick, Cooke Aquaculture's home province, in Parliament. He said a government panel would be formed to consider whether there was scientific evidence indicating that changes to aquaculture regulation were necessary. For Morton and others, the suggestion of a commission evoked memories of the strong recommendations made years earlier by the Cohen Commission, most of which had been ignored by the government.

The industry pushed back, too. Jeremy Dunn, executive director of the BC Salmon Farmers Association, said fears of a Washington-style disaster in British Columbia were overblown. "We do things differently here in B.C.," he said. "Our farmers have done the responsible thing and invested millions of dollars in technology and practices that have radically reduced escapes to the point [where] over the last decade, fewer than 100 fish have escaped from B.C. salmon farms each year." He added that fish farms contributed $1.5 billion to the province's economy and employed 6,600 people.

The public opposition to salmon farms was not lost on Canada's prime minister, Justin Trudeau. He had been elected in October 2015, replacing Stephen Harper, who had a terrible record on the environment. Trudeau had entered office as a young champion of liberal causes like protecting the environment. After nearly four years as prime minister and a series of personal missteps, he was fighting for political survival in October 2019. Polls showed his Liberal Party headed for defeat or, at best, a minority government with fewer than half the seats in Parliament. Scrambling for support, Trudeau sought to tap into the opposition to salmon farming in British Columbia. A pledge to move salmon farms from the water to closed-containment systems on land by 2025 was added to the party platform: "In British Columbia, we will work with the province to develop a responsible plan to transition from open net pen salmon farming in coastal waters to closed containment systems by 2025."

Opponents of salmon farming were thrilled. The industry was not, fearing the proposal would close dozens of farms in British Columbia and start a domino effect of bans in the Atlantic provinces of New Brunswick, Nova Scotia, and Newfoundland. The Canadian Aquaculture Industry Alliance called the idea reckless and warned that it would cost jobs across the country. The industry need not have worried. After the votes were counted and Trudeau's Liberals won the right to form a minority government, this promise, like a lot of campaign promises, was watered down. In December 2019, Trudeau instructed his new fisheries minister, Bernadette Jordan, to work with the BC government and First Nations communities "to create a responsible plan to transition from open net-pen salmon farming in coastal British Columbia waters by 2025." The prospect of a mandatory shift to closed-containment systems was gone, and having neither a timeline nor definitive goals meant action could be delayed indefinitely. "Going into the election, we were all pretty clear what the promise was," said Karen Wristen, executive director of Living Oceans Society, an ocean conservation organization based on a small island north of Vancouver. "There's no question that the language became somehow murky and ambiguous when the mandate letter was issued."

Opponents of salmon farms soon suffered another setback, but this one was temporary. In 2012, the Cohen Commission had recommended that the federal Department of Fisheries and Oceans examine whether disease from salmon farms might harm wild salmon around the Discovery Islands. If the government determined there was a risk, the commission said the farms should be shut down. After years of delay, DFO scientists rejected the recommendation in September 2020, saying nine scientific studies found that the farms posed minimal risks to the native sockeye salmon and could remain.

Opponents met with Jordan and pressed her to reverse her own scientists. In December 2020, the fisheries minister took the unusual step of overruling the DFO scientists and ordered that the salmon farms in the Discovery Islands be phased out by June 2022, when the licenses expired. The time frame allowed eighteen months for the three million salmon currently in the farms to reach market size, but the companies were prohibited from any restocking.

Tribal leaders and other opponents of the farms saw Minister Jordan's decision as a step toward returning wild salmon populations to health, but the aquaculture industry criticized the reversal. It claimed that removing the farms would do little to help the recovery of wild stocks while jeopardizing the jobs of workers in Vancouver Island's coastal communities and others across Canada. The Canadian subsidiaries of Mowi and Cermaq demanded a judicial review and reversal of the phaseout. The judge granted the farmers a limited reprieve, ruling that the ban on restocking the nineteen farms would impose financial harm on the companies and require destroying more than a million salmon already in hatcheries waiting to move to the pens. The ruling did not address the larger issue of the June 2022 ban, so it remained in effect.

Another disappointment was looming for Matthew Stratton back in Washington State.

CHAPTER 16

CASE CLOSED

Five months into his criminal investigation for the EPA, Matthew Stratton was still trying to determine how many Atlantic salmon had escaped and whether Cooke had purposely undercounted the escapees. A few thousand, as the company claimed, might not mean much to a jury. But a couple hundred thousand invasive fish mingling with native salmon would make an impact. Even when its initial claim of around 4,000 escapees was proven wrong, the company maintained that it had recovered 145,000 fish from the damaged farm, leaving about an equal number free in the wild. By the reckoning of the state investigators, the company's recovery estimate was way off. The state report, based on video footage of the recovery effort and testimony from site workers and outside experts, found that Cooke had salvaged only about 70,000 fish, which meant that between 243,000 and 263,000 Atlantic salmon had entered the waters and tributaries of Puget Sound.

Witnesses involved in the counting and photographs and video from the scene could turn those abstract numbers into a powerful image for a jury and cast doubt on Cooke's credibility. In the age of TV crime shows, a little drama could make a big difference. Innes Weir was at the top of Stratton's witness list for a formal interview. The Cooke regional manager had been in charge during the July and August incidents, and he led the counting when fish were pulled out of the collapsing cages in August. The first challenge was to find him.

Stratton was able to interview several Cooke employees informally, but he encountered resistance when he approached the company in February about talking to Weir. Cooke was slow to respond, and Stratton considered subpoenaing the Cooke manager. By mid-February, Stratton was worried his witness had skipped town, so he asked the Department of Homeland Security to put a "lookout" on Weir, which would show if he had left the country. A couple of weeks later, the department notified Stratton that Weir had indeed left the United States on February 25, destination unknown.

Stratton forwarded the information to Seth Wilkinson at the U.S. Attorney's Office. Why Weir had left was unclear, but the mystery of his whereabouts was solved in mid-March, when SalmonBusiness, an industry news service, posted an item on its website reporting that Weir had been hired as general manager of a salmon-farming company in Scotland. "Innes hit the ground running in late February," said the report. Stratton discussed traveling to Scotland to interview Weir, but the idea was dropped as too cumbersome. In the event of a trial, bringing Weir back to testify would also present legal difficulties with an uncertain outcome.

With Weir beyond his reach, Stratton focused on the next name on his list: Sky Guthrie, the young manager of Cypress Island Site 2.

Guthrie and his wife, Keegan, had been looking for peace and quiet when they arrived in Anacortes in 2006. Founded in 1879 on the north shore of Fidalgo Island, in Puget Sound, Anacortes was dominated in its early years by fishermen who sailed on schooners to the Bering Sea and returned with salted cod and huge salmon. For a time, the town boasted that it was the "Salmon Canning Capital of the World." When the commercial fishing industries dwindled, Anacortes reinvented itself as a mecca for recreational boaters and a gateway to the popular San Juan Islands.

Guthrie had three years of college and was working odd jobs when he met a scuba diver for the salmon farms in Puget Sound. The work sounded interesting, and Guthrie applied for a job with American Gold Seafoods, which operated the Cypress Island farms at the time. Hired as a fish technician at a salary of around $27,000 a year, he monitored the steel structures enclosing the cages and made sure the fish were fed properly. Meanwhile, he took classes on the side for his scuba certification. After he got certified and started inspecting farms from beneath the surface, Guthrie discovered he did not like working in cold water with limited visibility. He returned topside and moved slowly up the ladder to site manager. Guthrie was a strong supporter of salmon farming and of the aquaculture industry in general. He believed it was an environmentally safe means of providing protein for a fast-growing world. He stayed on when American Gold was sold to Icicle Seafoods and when Cooke bought the farms in 2016.

His mild manner, knowledge of the business, and willingness to do the hard work himself made Guthrie a good site manager. When the farm started to collapse in July, he spent days working to save it. In August, his efforts had been just as arduous, though the outcome was different. The collapse left Guthrie disheartened, and he quit the business in December. He took a temporary job at Sebo's hardware store in Anacortes and applied for work with the city's Parks and Recreation Department. He wanted to work outside, just not at a salmon farm.

Stratton found Guthrie at the hardware store, flashed his badge, and told him they needed to talk. Guthrie was nervous. He had already told his story to the state investigators and thought he had put Cypress Island behind him. The idea that a federal criminal investigator had tracked him down made his stomach churn, but he agreed to meet Stratton the next day at the Store in Anacortes, a popular restaurant and bakery.

After they sat down, Stratton explained that he was recording the session, identified himself for the record, and asked Guthrie a few basic questions. He sensed Guthrie's anxiety, and he went slowly and carefully, trying to sound like Guthrie's best friend. After showing photos of the attempts to save the farm in July and August, Stratton focused on Cooke's net cleaning.

Repeating what he had told the state investigators, Guthrie said three net-cleaning machines were shared among the three farms at Cypress Island. Two had been inoperable for more than a month before the July incident. He described the time-consuming efforts of pulling up the nets by hand and trying to brush off the mussels and other debris. Guthrie said that he and the other workers could not reach the mass of mussels on the bottoms of the cages, and he acknowledged that cleaning by hand was not an effective way to clear the nets of fouling material. When Stratton asked how dirty the nets were in July, Guthrie repeated what he had told the state inquiry: eight on a scale of ten. Guthrie said that Cooke had hoped to limp along until the salmon reached harvest weight in late fall before replacing the nets.

It was a lengthy interview, about two hours. Guthrie recounted in detail the efforts to save the farm in August.

As he reached the end of his questions, Stratton asked what every smart investigator knows should be the last question: "Is there anything I don't know about?" he said.

"Yes," said Guthrie. "They undercounted the escaped fish on purpose."

Stratton paused at the unexpected answer. State investigators had concluded that Cooke had vastly underreported the number of escaped fish initially and had overestimated the number of fish it had supposedly recovered from the wrecked farm. Until that moment, however, no one had suggested that the company had deliberately miscounted the number of fish salvaged from the cages to downplay the number of escapees.

Guthrie offered the type of detailed firsthand account that would make a jury pay attention and help them visualize the scene. He said some cages had torn open, and those fish were gone almost immediately. Other cages still contained salmon after the collapse.

Guthrie walked Stratton through the counting process, explaining how a hose sucked fish, dead and alive, out of the damaged cages and dumped them onto a conveyor belt. Workers used thumb clickers to count the fish as the belt carried them to a harvester vessel alongside the farm. Guthrie joined the counting at one point because the company wanted to dispose of the dead fish and transfer the live ones to a different site as fast as possible, so it was an all-hands situation. He described how workers called out the numbers of fish to the supervisor, who wrote them in a log.

"In your opinion, was the fish accounting part of it accurate or as accurate as could be?" Stratton asked.

"Um—ah, no," Guthrie said.

"Okay, what do you think was the problem?"

"Um—ah, there was one point, ah, that I recall, um, recording the number of fish, um, and I believe that that number was reported and elevated on the report form."

"Who was filling out the report forms?"

"Ah, I believe that was Innes Weir."

When Stratton asked by how much the recovery count was exaggerated as Weir recorded the numbers provided by the workers, Guthrie was not certain, but he said it was substantial. A few days later, Stratton tracked down another

Cooke employee who had been involved in the counting. The employee said he suspected Weir had purposely inflated the numbers of recovered fish reported to state officials.

Stratton was never able to interview Weir. In a series of emails with us in the summer of 2021, however, Weir said the counting process was observed by state officials and he denied exaggerating the number of recovered salmon. Weir said he simply collated the numbers provided by Guthrie and other workers who were counting the fish. He also said the decomposed fish added to the difficulty of getting an accurate count. "Regardless of what was or what was not counted, the recapture numbers and subsequent zero environmental impact from the escape as confirmed by the WA Department of Fish and Wildlife would perhaps suggest that the recovery process was as good as it could have been," Weir wrote.

On the larger issue of the farm's collapse, Weir said he suspected that the mooring lines and the safety chains attaching them to anchors had been sabotaged. He said the items had been repaired following the near collapse of the farm in July and should not have failed. "I have always found this odd," said Weir, who became a regional manager with Scottish Sea Farms, a joint venture of two big Norwegian companies in Scotland. Weir acknowledged that his suspicion was "pure speculation." When we asked Stratton about Weir's suspicion of sabotage, his response was blunt: "There is no way that someone sabotaged them. It is complete bunk."

As Stratton organized his case notes after his interview of Guthrie, he felt he had answered the threshold questions of whether the collapse had polluted Puget Sound and whether the escaped fish posed a threat. When it came to pollution, Stratton felt comfortable that the escaped fish and the debris that had fallen into the water constituted pollution under the law. Defining pollution in federal law seemed straightforward: Pollution is the introduction of harmful materials into the environment. The material can be natural like volcanic ash or created by human activity, as with trash or industrial effluent. The Clean Water Act defined pollution this way: "The term 'pollution' means the man-made or man-induced alteration of the chemical, physical, biological, and radiological integrity of water." The potential damage from Atlantic salmon in Pacific waters seemed to fit the requirement. On the latter point, around 250,000 nonnative fish had gotten loose, far more than Cooke had reported to the state, and experts were convinced the escapees threatened native salmon. Evidence of interbreeding between escaped farmed Atlantic salmon and wild Pacific salmon had surfaced already. Stratton felt that his interviews with the tugboat captain and others had corroborated the state's conclusion that negligence had contributed to the collapse. He also felt that the U.S. Attorney's Office was fully onboard.

Stratton was ready to bring Seth Wilkinson up to date and discuss next steps.

The twenty-three-story federal building in downtown Seattle occupies a city block and houses the U.S. District Court, the Office of the U.S. Attorney for the Western District of Washington, and other federal agencies. In mid-May 2018, Stratton rode the elevator to the fifth floor to meet with Wilkinson. The prosecutor, who specialized in environmental cases, had stayed current on Stratton's investigation into what remained a hot political issue in the state. He had doubts about whether criminal charges were warranted, but he kept an open mind as Stratton laid out the evidence. Wilkinson said he would take over some of the final questioning and set up formal interviews with Cooke employees.

A few days later, Wilkinson and Stratton interviewed a marine biologist who had been hired as a consultant by Cooke after the August collapse. The biologist, whose name was redacted from the records, said he was deeply concerned that the escaped salmon would establish themselves in Puget Sound and its rivers and streams on a long-term basis. He had already seen troubling signs. Escapees had dispersed north as far as Vancouver Island, and he believed it was only a matter of time before the fish learned to survive outside cages. One signal of early adaptation was the discovery of small fish bones in the stomachs of Atlantic salmon caught in the days after the collapse, evidence that the farmed fish had transitioned from eating dried pellets to eating small fish. These intruders would compete with native salmon for food and habitat and could transfer diseases to the wild fish, the biologist said. The assessment fit what others had told Stratton and appeared to establish that the escaped salmon presented a danger. Just as important, the biologist's opinions indicated that Cooke knew what its farmed salmon could do to the wild population, creating an incentive for the company to downplay the threat by underestimating the number of escapees.

Stratton waited for the formal witness interviews to be scheduled. Weeks passed, and nothing happened, leaving him in the dark. In late summer, Karla Perrin, a criminal attorney from the EPA General Counsel's Office, called Stratton back to the federal building. She told him the investigation was being closed without charges. Perrin said the U.S. Attorney's Office had decided not to proceed. Stratton was surprised. Up until Perrin's call, he thought he had put together a strong case and that Wilkinson was on board. Perrin told the investigator to write a memo officially closing the case.

Stratton's memo, dated October 15, 2018, read:

> This investigation was initiated after EPA CID became aware of a large Atlantic Salmon release in Puget Sound, within Skagit County Washington. These Atlantic Salmon were being raised in aquaculture net pens, owned by Cooke Aquaculture. Cooke Aquaculture is a Canadian-based aquaculture company, which is one of the largest in the world. The subsequent investigation revealed that the large amount of Atlantic Salmon were released into the waters of Puget Sound due to a lack of maintenance of both the net pen structure and the aquaculture nets attached to the structure. A series of large tides broke one of the Cooke net pens and released approximately 200,000 Atlantic Salmon. This release was in direct conflict with their NPDES permit and a violation of the Clean Water Act. Due to some recent litigation involving the EPA Civil division, it was decided by both RCEC Karla Perrin and members of the United States Attorney's Office in Seattle . . .

The lines that followed were blacked out in the version released to us by the EPA under the Freedom of Information Act. Public affairs officials in Seattle at the EPA regional office and the U.S. Attorney's Office refused to explain to us why the investigation had been dropped or to identify the "recent litigation" mentioned in Stratton's memo. After weeks of inquiries, Michael R. Fisher, a senior lawyer in the EPA Criminal Enforcement division in Washington, DC, responded by email. He said the "recent litigation" was a civil case from 2015 still pending in federal court.

By coincidence, the pending 2015 case identified by Fisher had been brought by Kurt Beardslee's Wild Fish Conservancy against the EPA and the

National Marine Fisheries Service. The lawsuit sought to overturn a 2008 decision by the two federal agencies that had found that salmon farms were not a threat to wild salmon. Under that standard, the escaped salmon from Cypress Island would not be considered a pollutant. No pollution, no underlying crime, no prosecution. The rationale for the government's 2008 decision was contained in two papers attached to Fisher's email. The papers had been submitted to the court by government attorneys in the 2015 litigation; one was written by the National Oceanic and Atmospheric Administration, and the other by the Washington Department of Fish and Wildlife. Both concluded that escaped salmon posed little risk to wild salmon and said that no evidence had been found of interbreeding.

The papers and their conclusions were hopelessly out of date and out of touch with the latest science. They had been published in 2001, a time when research on the impact of salmon farms was in its infancy. Seventeen years had passed, millions of farmed salmon had escaped from cages in multiple countries, and dozens of scientific studies had found evidence of interbreeding and other dangers to wild salmon posed by escaped farmed salmon. Despite new scientific evidence, the EPA and the Fisheries Service were refusing to update their position on a matter of critical importance to the survival of wild salmon. In fact, two months before Stratton was ordered to close his investigation, U.S. District judge Barbara Rothstein, who was hearing the Conservancy's case against the government, had ordered the EPA and Fisheries Service to start a new assessment of whether salmon farms constituted a threat to wild fish. The EPA vowed to fight the judge's ruling.

Was the decision to shut down the Cooke criminal investigation linked to Judge Rothstein's ruling and the EPA refusal? A senior government official involved in the decision to end the investigation, speaking on condition of anonymity, denied any connection. The official said the U.S. Attorney's Office had made its decision before Rothstein issued her ruling and that it had simply taken time to close the criminal investigation. Perhaps the decision to black out the name of the case was standard procedure. Was the decision to fold up the criminal case based on an order or on "advice" from EPA headquarters in Washington, DC? At one point, Stratton said he was told that the word to shut down the investigation had come from "back East." Perhaps the decision to drop the Cooke investigation, the judge's ruling against the EPA, and the involvement of EPA headquarters were a coincidence. Or perhaps, as

Kate Atkinson's fictional detective Jackson Brodie says, a coincidence is just an explanation waiting to happen.

Coincidence or not, it was clear that the EPA was dragging its feet in reassessing the threat from salmon farms. Rothstein was the second judge to order the agency to revisit its 2008 decision. In 2010, in response to another suit by the Wild Fish Conservancy, U.S. District judge John C. Coughenour had ordered the EPA to reconsider the effects of farmed Atlantic salmon on Puget Sound's native salmon and orca whales. Coughenour said the EPA should use the "best available" science in making its decision. For nearly a decade, the EPA had refused to comply with Coughenour's order, and the case had stalled in the face of the agency's inaction.

There were grounds under the federal Clean Water Act for declaring the escaped salmon to be pollutants, though legal scholars differ on the issue. States have the authority to enforce the federal act, and the Washington investigation referred specifically to the escaped salmon as pollutants. A leading authority on the federal law agreed that the fish constituted pollution. Robert W. Adler, a distinguished professor and former dean of the College of Law at the University of Utah, has taught and written extensively over four decades about the Clean Water Act and the underlying case law. After reviewing documents from the criminal investigation of Cooke Aquaculture and other material, Adler offered his views, specifying that they did not constitute a legal opinion: "Based on all of this, my preliminary conclusion is that the fish unintentionally released from the Cooke industrial fish farm, along with associated materials, would likely be considered 'pollutants' under the C[lean] W[ater]A[ct]," he said. "As is true for most legal issues, however, I would not say this with 100 percent certainty."

On its face, the decision to close the investigation contradicted settled science about the impact of escaped farmed salmon on the environment and on wild salmon. But science was not the deciding factor; policy was. The official involved in closing the case said bringing criminal charges when the official EPA position remained that salmon farms did not pose an environmental threat would have been unfair to the potential defendants. "When you prosecute a criminal case and make decisions about charging someone with a crime, we are dealing with issues of black and white," the official said. "No one should ever be surprised that what they did was a crime. No one should think the government is pushing the envelope. The last word from the EPA was that farm-raised salmon would not pose a threat to native salmon. We needed to be sensitive to that. It can seem opportunistic when all of the sudden you turn around and charge someone with a crime."

Cooke had won a battle, but the war was still being waged in federal court, where the rules of engagement were different, and Cooke would soon find itself on the ropes.

CHAPTER 17

RISKY BUSINESS

In the spring of 2019, Kurt Beardslee was on a roller coaster. More than a year earlier, Washington State investigators had confirmed the negligence he and his lawyers had suspected when they filed their federal lawsuit against Cooke Aquaculture Pacific, the company's subsidiary in Washington State, in November 2017. The phase-out signed by Governor Inslee was a significant victory. When it came to substance, Beardslee found plenty of positives. But the lawsuit was dragging on, just as his lawyer, Brian Knutsen, had predicted.

Eighteen months of legal back-and-forth had failed to bring the defendants to the negotiating table. Beardslee and his team had produced what they viewed as conclusive evidence of negligence at Cypress Island for the entire period Cooke had owned the farm. Yet Cooke was not budging. Company employees were uncooperative in Knutsen's depositions, the company was challenging the Conservancy's expert witnesses, and the trial was to start in September. Moreover, Cooke's attorneys were threatening to sue Beardslee personally for speaking out about the dangers of salmon farms.

Beardslee has the heart of an idealist and the head of a realist. He understood the risks from the start. The lawyers were working pro bono, but expenses for expert witnesses and related matters were rising. Beardslee confided to his wife, Candace, that they might need to take out a mortgage on their cabin to keep the suit, and the Wild Fish Conservancy, alive. A loss would have financial repercussions for Knutsen and his partner in the law firm, too; they would not be reimbursed if they lost. Beardslee believed he had a moral obligation to Knutsen and his law partner, and he calculated that he would have to devote himself full-time to raising money to repay them for the time they were investing in the suit. His bigger fear, however, was that losing would mean he had failed to hold a major salmon farmer responsible for polluting the environment and threatening the future of Pacific salmon, the killer whales that fed on wild salmon, and other marine life.

The Cooke team's legal strategy was to convince the judge to throw out the lawsuit on purely technical grounds. The Clean Water Act empowers the federal government to protect the nation's waters from pollution and to restore damaged waters and wetlands. Enforcement is the responsibility of the Environmental Protection Agency and can result in criminal penalties. The law also allows a private citizen or organization to file a civil suit under the Clean Water Act. But those suits must identify ongoing violations at the time of the filing. Past violations are not considered in public-interest suits because the goal is to address ongoing pollution that can be stopped through an injunction or similar action. This restriction is present only in the citizen suit provision of the law; polluters can't escape liability entirely, because the federal and state governments can still sue for past violations. In citizen suits, when ongoing violations are found, financial penalties can be compounded daily while the violations continue. Financial awards are used to repair the environmental damage and, in some cases, reimburse costs and fees for the lawyers who filed the case. Failure to identify ongoing violations could nullify a private citizen's suit, but in a 1989 case, the U.S. Supreme Court granted lower courts wide leeway to make their own determination of what constituted "ongoing."

The Wild Fish Conservancy contended that the more than two hundred thousand escaped Atlantic salmon still swimming in the Pacific waters and the debris still on the seabed beneath the farm constituted ongoing violations. Cooke's lawyers argued that the suit should be dismissed because the escaped fish were not ongoing pollution under the law and because the company had spent $3.5 million to remove remnants of Cypress Island Site 2 from the seabed. Cooke said no future violations were possible because it did not intend to rebuild the Cypress Island farm. "Site 2 is forever dead," the company said.

A core element of the Conservancy's complaint was that Cypress Island and other Cooke farms in Puget Sound had not been inspected properly by the company for at least five years, going back to before Cooke bought them. The pollution discharge permits for the farms required divers to inspect the chains and ropes that attach the net pens to anchors at least once a year. The requirement included dives of one hundred feet or more at sites with deep anchors like those at Cypress Island. The inspections were deemed essential to ensuring that a farm remained attached securely to the seabed.

The failure of the moorings and anchor lines at Site 2 in July and August raised doubts about whether they had been inspected as required. State investigators found no evidence that Cooke or the previous owner, Icicle, had conducted the required dives to one hundred feet. The state's conclusion was helpful, but Knutsen had to be certain about whether the dives had occurred. As part of the discovery process, he asked for the logs of every dive over the past five years at each of Cooke's eight farms in Puget Sound and for testimony from a witness who could authenticate the records.

Cooke identified its regional general manager, James Parsons, as the witness who could testify that the required dives had taken place. Two days before Parsons's deposition, Cooke's legal team delivered thirty thousand pages of documents to Knutsen. Its lawyers had told the judge that the logs proving the dives took place were among the documents. With the deposition approaching, Knutsen and his colleagues spent hours scouring the records. No evidence was found of a single dive to one hundred feet at any of the eight Cooke farms in the last five years. Spotty records were found for shallower inspection dives, but Cooke appeared to have violated the state requirement in a way that could be interpreted as negligence connected to the site's collapse—and negligence would sharply increase its financial liability.

When Parsons appeared for his sworn deposition, Knutsen asked for proof that the deep dives had occurred. Parsons tried to evade the question, saying divers who had gone down to forty feet were able to determine whether mooring lines were secure at one hundred feet.

"My question is with respect to whether or not divers dove below 100 feet as part of the mooring system inspections since 2012," Knutsen repeated.

"In order to understand that, I think we would have to go through the dive logs. I'm not aware of any," said Parsons.

"You're not aware of any?" asked Knutsen.

"I have not looked at every dive log," said Parsons.

Parsons was Cooke's designated expert on the dive logs, yet he acknowledged that he had not examined them thoroughly. Knutsen's team had found no record of a single one-hundred-foot dive. Parson's testimony followed a pattern of what Knutsen and his colleagues viewed as nonresponsive answers from Cooke witnesses in depositions that ran for hours and sometimes days. The company appeared to think it could avoid providing information without sanction from the judge. The exchange with Parsons proved to be a turning point.

Judge John Coughenour was overseeing the Conservancy's suit against Cooke in federal court in Seattle. He was a senior judge who had been on the bench since 1981. In that time, he had presided over many high-profile cases, including the trial of Ahmed Ressam, known as the "Millennium Bomber," who was convicted of attempting to blow up Los Angeles International Airport on January 1, 2000. More relevantly, Coughenour had ordered the EPA to review its determination that farmed salmon did not represent a threat to wild salmon in the Conservancy's 2010 suit against the EPA. He had a reputation as a no-nonsense jurist, which he demonstrated in response to a motion by Knutsen about the Parsons deposition.

Coughenour ruled that Parsons had not prepared adequately and had been evasive in his testimony. He ordered him to submit to another deposition to answer the Conservancy's questions about the dive records. The judge called the delivery of the thirty thousand pages two days before the deposition was scheduled "an eleventh-hour disclosure." More significantly, he postponed the start of the trial from September 23 to December 2, a clear message to Cooke's lawyers that the lawsuit was not going to be thrown out and that they should start settlement talks.

The second Parsons deposition was a variation on the first. Parsons said he had been unable to locate any dive logs recording inspections at one hundred feet or deeper and claimed that the absence of an inspection record did not mean no inspection had occurred. But without supporting evidence, the company's claim that the mandatory inspections had been carried out could not be proven, not just for Site 2 but for every Cooke farm in the state. The company's lawyers were forced to retract the claim and to acknowledge that there were no relevant dive logs. In a new motion, Knutsen asked that Parsons's testimony, which opened up the slim possibility of unlogged deep dives, be stricken from the record. Coughenour refused to go that far. Instead, he said he would weigh the testimony and the absence of supporting records at trial.

The logs weren't the only record-keeping issue giving Cooke trouble. The national discharge permits for operating salmon farms require that every escape, no matter how small, be reported each year, and that significant escapes must be reported immediately. The state's data showed that Cooke and its predecessor, Icicle, had made no reports of fish escapes most years, yet discrepancies between the number of fish put in the pens and the number harvested or dead indicated that there had been escapes.

Coughenour's ruling on the Parsons deposition and his delay of the trial indicated that the judge was running out of patience. The two sides agreed to see if they could work out a settlement.

In May 2019, lawyers for both sides gathered in a conference room at Cooke's lawyers' office in Seattle for the first settlement talks. Beardslee sat in the room with his lawyers. Glenn Cooke had flown in from New Brunswick and was sequestered in the conference room next door. Cooke was not introduced to the Conservancy team and presumably listened to the talks over the office communications system. Knutsen told the group that the judge's most recent ruling was a clear indication that discovery was turning up numerous violations by Cooke Aquaculture at its farms. Douglas Steding, Cooke's lead lawyer, countered that the company had no interest in a settlement and that he was confident they would prevail at trial. The talks adjourned in less than an hour, with no common ground in sight.

Brian Knutsen shared Kurt Beardslee's passion for the outdoors. After law school at Lewis and Clark University in Portland, Oregon, he was working at a big firm in Seattle when he met Beardslee in 2007. Over the years, they developed a friendship and a successful partnership. In 2010, they won a big lawsuit against the federal government for failure to enforce the Endangered Species Act. When Knutsen left to start his own firm in 2011, Beardslee went along as a client. Since then, they have won other cases against state and federal agencies. Knutsen and his partner in the new firm, Paul Kampmeier, have done a fair amount of pro bono work for the Wild Fish Conservancy and other environmental organizations over the years. They try to balance those risky cases with ones where the fees are certain to keep the firm afloat. The

Wild Fish Conservancy case against Cooke would not make or break the firm financially, but Knutsen had no intention of losing a case as high-profile and important to the environment as the one against Cooke Aquaculture.

After the initial settlement talks failed, Knutsen needed leverage to get Cooke back to the table, something to convince them that the risk of going to trial was too great. He needed Sky Guthrie. Knutsen was familiar with Guthrie's testimony from reading the state's report on the collapse, but he was unaware of what Guthrie had told Stratton. He also did not know where to find the former Cooke employee. Knutsen reached out to someone who would know his potential witness's whereabouts: Matthew Stratton. Recently retired from the EPA, Stratton agreed to track down Guthrie again and to serve him with a subpoena requiring his testimony in the civil case against Cooke.

Stratton's return to the hardware store turned Guthrie's day into a "good news, bad news" one. The former site manager had learned that morning that he had gotten a job with the city's Parks and Recreation Department, something he had been working on for months. His good mood evaporated, however, when Stratton appeared. What now? Guthrie was unaware of the civil suit until Stratton handed him a subpoena for a pretrial deposition. When he read the date on the subpoena, his mood sank further: the deposition was on the same day he was supposed to start his new job.

Before they sat down for the deposition in the presence of Cooke's lawyers, Knutsen wanted a sense of what Guthrie would say. A few days after having Stratton serve Guthrie with a subpoena, Knutsen had an informal chat with his new witness. (Knutsen had already changed the date for the formal deposition so it would not interfere with Guthrie's new job, a strategic peace offering.) After listening to Guthrie repeat what he had told the state and Stratton, Knutsen knew he had a credible and strong witness with an important story. Reserving Guthrie's name for the moment, he let the defense lawyers know that he had found an anonymous whistleblower and provided a summary of what he would say in his deposition and at trial.

Instead of returning to the negotiating table, Cooke Aquaculture became more aggressive, threatening again to sue Beardslee for speaking out. This was not necessarily an idle threat. Cooke had recently sued the state Department of Natural Resources and its commissioner, Hilary Franz, for terminating the lease for Cypress Island Site 2. That case was pending in state court despite Cooke's having told Judge Coughenour that the farm there was "forever dead."

Facing trial with a hostile insider, Cooke hired a new criminal defense attorney, Christopher Wion. Unlike Steding, who handled civil matters, Wion was an experienced litigator whose hiring signaled that Cooke remained determined to go to trial—or at least wanted the Conservancy to think so. Wion and his colleagues were evaluating the potential impact of the whistleblower when Judge Coughenour issued an order that cleared up any doubts about what would come next.

In civil cases, either side may file a motion for summary judgment. The motion asks the judge to weigh evidence submitted up to that point and decide whether it is sufficient to render a verdict for one side or whether specific issues can be resolved before the trial begins. Most often, a summary judgment motion allows a judge to streamline the proceedings by ruling on some issues in advance, allowing the trial to focus on disputed facts. Lawyers parse the judge's decision for clues about which way the court may be leaning, something that is particularly important when the outcome will be decided by the judge, not a jury.

On November 25, a week before the rescheduled trial was to start, Coughenour issued a twenty-six-page ruling in response to motions filed by both sides. The ruling cleared up some matters in preparation for the trial on December 2—and the overall message was much stronger than any of the judge's previous orders. The Wild Fish Conservancy lost on a couple of small issues, but on a half dozen key disputes critical to the outcome of the trial, the judge came down strongly on the Conservancy's side.

Coughenour agreed with the Conservancy that Cooke had failed to provide evidence that it had carried out the mandatory inspections of net pen moorings and anchors at its salmon farms in Puget Sound. The judge highlighted the disparity between Cooke's initial claims that it maintained records of all dives against its eventual admission that logs were missing. The written ruling provided a detailed breakdown of the inspection dives at the three farms at Cypress Island, listing a handful of dives dating to 2012 and noting that the divers failed to inspect most mooring lines. When it came to the mandatory deep dives, the judge ruled that Cooke had failed for several years to provide evidence of inspections of mooring components one hundred feet or deeper at any of its five farms with anchors at that depth.

The ruling was equally tough on Cooke when it came to reporting escaped fish. From 2012 to 2018, Coughenour said, Cooke (and its predecessor Icicle) violated the discharge permits for all the farms by failing to accurately monitor or report the number of escapes. The judge also rejected Cooke's motion to dismiss the testimony of Dr. Tobias Dewhurst, a marine engineer hired by the Conservancy, who said Cooke's remaining salmon farms were at risk of failure because the designs were inadequate for the tides and currents common to their locations. Coughenour had already ruled that Cooke had failed to develop necessary plans for inspecting cages, storing chemicals, and tracking fish in its pens. Cooke's regulatory failures, coupled with Dewhurst's testimony, meant that the company faced heavy financial penalties for the Site 2 collapse and at its other farms if violations were deemed to have occurred there.

Finally, Cooke had hoped to avoid trial by arguing that the lawsuit should be dismissed because there were no continuing violations at Site 2, as required by the Clean Water Act. The company said the site was closed and would not be rebuilt. The judge rejected this argument, too, finding that Cooke "continues its operations in Puget Sound. Thus, civil penalties still serve to deter future Clean Water Act violations." Implicit but unstated was the understanding that the escaped salmon constituted a pollutant under the federal law, subjecting Cooke to potential penalties for each escaped fish.

Cooke had lost on every substantive issue. There would be no jury to persuade otherwise. The rulings had been made by the person who would decide the company's fate at trial. Staring at a near-certain loss and the potential for large civil penalties, the company's lawyers responded quickly. Within hours, Christopher Wion called Knutsen.

"We got the message," said Wion. "We are ready to talk."

Wion wanted to meet the next day in the Seattle office of his cocounsel, Douglas Steding. Knutsen was in the firm's Portland, Oregon, office, but he was eager to sign a deal before Cooke's side reconsidered. He telephoned his partner in Seattle, Paul Kampmeier, who agreed to go to the meeting. Knutsen and Beardslee would participate via conference call. Looking back at the judge's ruling, Knutsen felt that Coughenour had almost dared Cooke to go to court.

That night, Beardslee struggled to figure out how much could be extracted from Cooke Aquaculture. In its final brief to the judge, the Conservancy said that Cooke was a major corporation and that a penalty of at least $12.5 million was required to send a message of deterrence. Now Beardslee worried that demanding too much would force Cooke to declare its Pacific subsidiary bankrupt, which could lead to a long legal battle in bankruptcy court. Still, the settlement had to be painful enough for Cooke to feel it and large enough to cover the costs of Knutsen and his colleagues. And it had to send a strong public message. Beardslee did not want a repeat of what had happened in 2013 in New Brunswick, when criminal charges against Glenn Cooke and two other company executives were dropped and the company was fined just $500,000, against a $19 million exposure, after using an illegal neurotoxin at fifteen of its farms in the Bay of Fundy. Beardslee wanted more than a slap on the wrist for Cooke.

In papers filed before the judge's order, Cooke had argued that a modest penalty should be assessed if the judge found wrongdoing. The company argued that no deterrent was necessary because Cypress Site 2 was closed and that any violations at its other farms were not serious. The company said it had spent millions cleaning up the wrecked farm, had lost $5 million worth of salmon when the cages collapsed, and had paid $332,000 as a fine to the state. Cooke's lawyers suggested $50,000 was a good benchmark for penalties.

The two sides met on November 26 for the settlement talks. Cooke opened with its argument for a modest penalty, a nonstarter for Beardslee and Knutsen, who were determined to get a settlement of seven figures. The negotiations went back and forth, on the money and on the steps Cooke would be required to take to improve operations at its remaining salmon farms before the leases expired under the state's new law. In the end, Cooke agreed to pay $2.75 million in exchange for dismissal of the suit. Beardslee settled for the smaller amount to avoid the chance that Cooke would declare its Pacific operations bankrupt. And the penalty was still enough to cause Cooke the kind of financial pain and public embarrassment that it had largely avoided in 2013 in New Brunswick.

The Rose Foundation, a public charity in Oakland, California, that specializes in administering settlement awards, would receive $1.15 million to finance projects to protect wild salmon and killer whales in Puget Sound. The remaining $1.6 million would cover costs incurred by Knutsen's firm and the

Conservancy. Cooke also agreed to upgrade its remaining facilities before restocking its remaining farms, correct the deficiencies identified during the lawsuit, and provide the Wild Fish Conservancy with copies of its reports to state agencies for the next three years.

The agreement required Judge Coughenour's approval, a formality that would not occur for a couple months. Beardslee did not wait before locking down the agreement. The next day, he issued a press release announcing the settlement and the penalty. "This is truly a victory for the future of our sound," he wrote. "Open water net pen aquaculture is a risky business, and thanks to this settlement we are one step closer to getting this dirty industry out of Puget Sound once and for all."

Despite agreeing to pay a substantial penalty, the company refused to accept responsibility for the collapse, instead trying to shift blame to state regulators. In a public statement, company spokesman Joel Richardson said Cooke had been planning improvements to the Cypress Island pens at the time of the collapse. He said permit applications for upgrades were sitting with regulators at the time of what he called "the unfortunate incident." State authorities said the company filed the applications in February 2017, a recognition by the company that its farm was in poor shape.

Confronting the loss of its salmon farms in Washington State, the company filed an application to triple the size of its existing operations in Nova Scotia, on Canada's Atlantic coast. In the aftermath of the settlement, Cooke had decided to open its next battle closer to home.

CHAPTER 18

"WE'RE REALLY PROUD OF WHO HATES US"

While the Wild Fish Conservancy was fighting Cooke Aquaculture in federal court, another skirmish in the salmon wars broke out. Patagonia, the outdoor clothing and gear company, released an eighty-minute documentary that presented a passionate indictment of fish hatcheries and open-net salmon farms. The film, called *Artifishal*, debuted at the Tribeca Film Festival in New York City in April 2019 and then shifted to YouTube, where it began chalking up tens of thousands of views and fiery comments. In response, the salmon-farming industry and its captive publications opened an attack aimed at discrediting Patagonia.

If you were looking for a hero and a villain in a clear contest, nothing could have fit the bill better than the tussle between Patagonia and the salmon-farming industry. Founded in 1973 by Yvon Chouinard, an avid outdoorsman, rock climber, and fly fisherman, Patagonia had grown into a billion-dollar global player with a reputation for high-end clothes and a long history of political activism on behalf of the environment. Chouinard and his family-controlled company have donated more than $110 million to environmental causes around the world and have pioneered business practices closer to the ideal of true sustainability.

Patagonia made its promise to balance profits and purpose legally binding in 2012, when it became the first California company certified as a B Corporation. B Corp firms agree to consider the interests of their workers, the community, and the environment in addition to those of shareholders. Certification requires a rigorous assessment of a company's environmental, social, and managerial performance by B Lab, a private nonprofit. Qualifying companies that want this certification are required to codify that their ultimate purpose is to operate for the benefit of all stakeholders, not just shareholders. They also commit to an assessment of their performance by the B Lab every two years and pay administrative fees tied to their annual revenue. In short, for companies that want to demonstrate, and deliver on, their status as good citizens, there is no certification more telling than being a B Corp.

In 2012, Patagonia branched out into specialty foods through a subsidiary, Patagonia Provisions. The objective was to provide environmentally responsible, regeneratively grown alternatives to modern industrial agriculture and its reliance on monocrops, herbicides, pesticides, and wasteful water use. Birgit Cameron, the head of Patagonia Provisions, described the mission this way: "Provisions is an example of showcasing a better path forward. The way the food industry has done things isn't necessarily how it should be done. If it's not right for the planet, there is no point in doing it. As conservationist David Brower liked to say, there is no business to be done on a dead planet."

Among the items sold by Provisions were wild-caught Pacific salmon from carefully vetted producers in Alaska and Washington State, which made the company a small competitor to the farmed-salmon industry, but a large symbol of a better way to eat salmon. Patagonia Provisions was an innovator in establishing standards for sustainable food. Like its clothing, Patagonia's food was high-end and high-priced. A "wild sockeye salmon box" was thirty-six dollars; the "responsible seafood sampler box" was ninety. What angered the salmon farmers, and particularly Cooke Aquaculture, were not Patagonia's products, which occupy a different price range, but its documentaries and the widespread attention they attracted.

Patagonia channels some of its activism into films about environmental threats. A 2014 documentary, *DamNation*, argued that the more than eight hundred thousand dams in the United States do more harm than good. In 2018, Patagonia financed *Blue Heart*, a film about efforts to protect the last system of wild rivers in Europe. The latest example of its cinematic activism, *Artifishal*, was being filmed when the Cooke farm collapsed in Puget Sound in August 2017. The documentary's primary focus was detailing the threats from hatcheries to wild salmon in the rivers of California, Idaho, Oregon, and Washington. Salmon farms in Chile, Norway, and Washington State were also singled out for the damage caused by escaped fish and the release of pesticides, organic waste, and chemicals. Kurt Beardslee, who had partnered with Patagonia on several projects, appeared in *Artifishal* talking about the collapse of the Cooke farm in Puget Sound.

One of the film's most dramatic moments is April Bencze's dive into the waters surrounding the collapsed farm and the response from the Cooke workers. Her video footage shows the devastation beneath the surface as she drifts with the current past empty split nets and the remains of dead fish. On the surface, Cypress Island's loudspeaker can be heard calling for her to get out of the water, claiming she is trespassing. Sitting on the deck of the *Galactic Ice* after her dive, Bencze is philosophical: "It seems like it's a big secret what's going on under there. The last thing these companies want is people to go under and see what's actually going on."

In a press release announcing the film, Chouinard said hatcheries and open-net farms were causing irreversible damage to wild salmon. "Humans have always thought of themselves as superior to nature and it's got us into a lot of trouble," he said. "We think we can control nature. We can't. If we value wild salmon, we need to do something now. A life without wild nature and a life without these great, iconic species is an impoverished life."

CleanFish, a wholesaler in San Francisco that promotes itself as a source for sustainable seafood, was among the first critics of the film. The company created a hashtag, #benefishal, that was picked up on social media by aquaculture companies and the Global Aquaculture Alliance, the lobbying association that represents salmon farmers and other aquaculture business interests. "Despite dramatic advances in the sustainability of aquaculture, new certifications, and standards, and recognition with improved ratings for farmed fish by groups like Seafood Watch, public perception lags behind the science," the allied interests said in a global statement. After attending a screening of the documentary at the Patagonia outlet store in Freeport, Maine, Steven Hedlund, the communications manager for the Global Aquaculture Alliance, wrote that the film was one-sided and heavy-handed, pointing out that no representatives of commercial fisheries appeared in it. He said the film ignored the benefits of aquaculture and left the audience with one conclusion: "that open net-pen aquaculture is destroying wild fish populations."

Artifishal was viewed more than three million times on YouTube in the months after its release. Denmark responded by ordering a halt to all future open-pen fish farms. The mayor of a ski resort town in Sweden banned

Norwegian farmed salmon from school lunches. In a Facebook post, Chouinard boasted about the impact: "We came out with a film that's against offshore, penned fish farms and hatcheries, *Artifishal*. It has had a huge effect,
particularly in Europe. Because of that film, a lot of schoolchildren in Sweden
are no longer fed farmed salmon. I just heard yesterday that Denmark is going
to stop licensing any more offshore fish farms. Chef Francis Mallmann, the
barbecue king in Argentina, has taken salmon out of nineteen of his restaurants worldwide. You see little victories like that, and it all adds up."

Those "little victories" increased the anger toward Patagonia across a
broad spectrum of the aquaculture industry. A second film Patagonia released
in the fall of 2020 was more targeted. *Take Back Puget Sound*, a direct indictment of salmon farming in the ocean, focuses on the collapse of Cooke Aquaculture's Cypress Island farm. The opening shots were taken by a drone flying
over the twisted wreckage of the salmon farm. As the drone pans the site, a
recording plays Jill Davenport's call to 911 about the unfolding emergency.
Beardslee is one of four experts who guide viewers through the many risks
from salmon farms in a film that is more like a seminar than a documentary.

Cooke Aquaculture is the villain of the video, which drew sharp criticism from the industry and from Cooke itself. The Global Aquaculture
Alliance praised Cooke as "a global leader in responsible aquaculture" and com-
mended the company for adhering to the alliance's best practices. The praise
was lavish in light of Cooke's having pleaded guilty to using a banned pesticide
that killed thousands of lobsters, its negligence in allowing the release of around
250,000 Atlantic salmon into the waters of Puget Sound, and its employees' bar-
barous mistreatment of juvenile salmon at its hatchery in Maine, which had
been exposed just a few months earlier. Both the illegal use of the pesticide and
the incidents at the hatchery violated the alliance's published standards for Best
Aquaculture Practices, which prohibit the use of banned chemicals and specify
humane methods for slaughtering unwanted or compromised fish. Yet Cooke
Aquaculture remained in good standing with the organization.

The Northwest Aquaculture Alliance, the industry association in the
Pacific Northwest and a primary lobbyist against the state legislation banning
salmon farms, focused on Patagonia's collaboration with the Wild Fish Conservancy and the company's specialty line of wild Alaskan salmon and other
certified-sustainable food products. Jeanne McKnight, executive director of
the Northwest Aquaculture Alliance, said, "Patagonia has taken up with an

anti-aquaculture NGO, the Wild Fish Conservancy, to launch one of the most scientifically unfounded and defamatory attacks on aquaculture by a competitor in the wild fish sector." McKnight raised two negative issues that have dogged Patagonia, the microplastics that are shed when its synthetic clothing is washed and its labor relations in lower-income countries where many of its products are made. The impact of microplastics on the environment was not a new criticism of Patagonia and similar clothing manufacturers.

Calling out Patagonia on the microplastics issue was fair, but it also highlighted the contrast between how Patagonia responds to its problems and the way environmental challenges are addressed by the salmon-farming industry. Patagonia readily acknowledges the environmental risks from microplastics and says it is investigating ways to minimize fiber shedding and financing studies about the ecological and health impacts of microfibers. Industrial salmon farmers, by contrast, are focused on denying the environmental damage caused by their farms, downplaying the health risks of their fish, and discrediting critics across the board.

Cooke Aquaculture attacked from another angle. Its chief spokesman, Joel Richardson, criticized Patagonia for manufacturing most of its clothing in foreign countries while boasting that Cooke had more than four thousand employees in twenty-two U.S. states. "Patagonia is in no position to challenge our family company and perhaps should spend its energy looking deeper within rather than attacking thousands of American fishing and aquaculture workers who work every day to supply U.S. grocery stores with healthy, affordable American seafood," said Richardson.

The industry responses to Patagonia generally tracked the first and second stages of the template laid out by anthropology professors Peter Benson and Stuart Kirsch: Discredit or ignore the science, attack the opponents, and gloss over your own shortcomings. Truth is sacrificed first when this happens. Patagonia is an unconventional company, not a perfect company. It has made long-term commitments to the environment and to improving its own operations. In the end, facts matter, and *Artifishal* and *Take Back Puget Sound* were based on settled science about the threats posed by salmon farms to wild salmon and the environment in general and the need to educate the public about those dangers. Or, as Dylan Tomine, the official fly-fishing ambassador and writer for Patagonia, put it, "If you judge a person or company by their enemies, we're really proud of who hates us."

CHAPTER 19

MILLIONS OF DEAD SALMON

In her elegiac, prize-winning novel *The Shipping News*, E. Annie Proulx described Newfoundland as an island of coast and cove, where travel by boat or snowmobile is much easier than by car or truck, a place of harsh storms, timeless beauty, isolated villages, countless lives lost to a dangerous sea, and chronic unemployment that forced an ongoing exodus. When she published her novel in 1993, one year after the closing of the commercial cod fishery decimated the island's economy and way of life, Proulx captured the essence of the place locals call "the Rock" in a single paragraph: "Everybody that went away suffered a broken heart. 'I'm coming back some day,' they all wrote. But never did. The old life was too small to fit anymore."

When John Crosbie, Canada's federal fisheries minister, arrived in Newfoundland from Ottawa on July 1, 1992, he may have hoped for a warm greeting in celebration of Canada Day. Instead, he was met at the Independence Day party held in a small fishing village by a furious crowd of 350 fishermen, fish-processing-plant workers, and their families. They had learned in advance that Crosbie planned to declare a moratorium on commercial cod fishing the next day, a response to cod stocks that had plunged to historic low levels off the Grand Banks of Newfoundland. The fishers blamed government mismanagement, but factors such as climate change and overfishing by Canadian and foreign trawlers had played major roles, too. Fisheries scientists hoped a two-year moratorium would spark a recovery for the cod.

The uproar got worse. On July 2, when Crosbie announced the shutdown at a press conference in a ballroom at the Delta Hotel in St. John's, the provincial capital, security officers inside the ballroom were forced to barricade the doors as about a dozen burly fishermen tried to break them down.

A year later, the government extended the moratorium indefinitely because the cod were not rebounding. The ban remains in place today and sparks as much bitterness as it did decades ago. Crosbie, who was born in Newfoundland, later said shutting down the cod industry was the toughest thing he had to do in his thirty years as a politician. An estimated forty thousand jobs disappeared overnight, and the impact on rural Newfoundland was profound. An industry that had supported Newfoundland for more than four hundred years ended abruptly, and there was nothing to replace it.

The Newfoundland and Labrador provincial government faced the daunting task of creating new jobs at the same time that other resource-based industries like paper mills and forestry were also declining. Offshore oil and gas discoveries held some promise, but they would not come online for years, and even then, the energy sector was expected to provide five thousand jobs at best. Just as their counterparts in New Brunswick had done a decade earlier, provincial officials embraced aquaculture as the economic savior. The fit seemed perfect: the fish farms would float in the many sheltered bays and inlets off the south coast, the same remote places where commercial fishers were losing jobs and where fish-processing plants were standing idle. Hatcheries on land would provide a steady supply of young cod and salmon smolts, which would be moved to open-net farms where they would grow to maturity. Instead of having to migrate to St. John's or the mainland for employment, fishers and plant workers could find work close to home. At least, that was the plan.

In fact, government support for fish farming had begun in the 1980s, when small-scale cod and Atlantic salmon farms began appearing along Newfoundland's south coast. The government hoped large-scale production would create jobs and secure votes. Millions of taxpayer dollars were spent building new wharves to serve the fish farms and upgrading roads to connect isolated bays with processing plants. An eight-million-dollar government-financed research center was established to develop new methods to keep farmed fish healthy and improve harvesting and processing. The government money spurred growth, leading to new and bigger farms. But success was limited. The number of jobs was far smaller than promised. Cod did not take to living in pens. In 2005, a Canadian business publication declared the government's effort to promote cod farming a failure. Few disagreed. "Today, no for-profit cod farms operate in Newfoundland," wrote *Canadian Business*. The government got the message, and the big cod farms disappeared. In a province where fishers in the 1980s routinely caught more than 200,000 tons of cod a year, cod farming's peak production of 227 tons in 2002 was a drop in the bucket.

Salmon farming did better from the government's perspective. Atlantic salmon had proven more adaptable to living in cages. By 2009, about eighty salmon farms were arrayed along Newfoundland's southern coast within a six-hour drive of St. John's, and they produced 13,625 tons of fish and provided only a few hundred jobs. Both totals were a fraction of the old cod fishery, but at least it was heading in the right direction. The provincial government doubled down, promoting and financing the industry, often with little regard for the well-known risks to existing lobster, scallop, and herring fisheries or to the pristine coasts and coves. As the number of farms increased, so did the problems.

At one time, Newfoundland prided itself on being home to some of the best salmon rivers in the world, but by 2009, the wild population had been declining for years. There was plenty of blame to go around, ranging from overfishing and climate change to timber operations that destroyed the salmon's habitat. The arrival of salmon farms only increased the threats to wild salmon from interbreeding and the spread of sea lice and pathogens. One of the most contagious viruses, infectious salmon anemia, was capable of not only devastating salmon farms, but also damaging wild salmon.

In July 2012, at a salmon farm operated by Gray Aqua Group in a small bay called Butter Cove, veterinarians detected the province's first known outbreak of infectious salmon anemia. While ISA is harmless to humans, it kills up to 90 percent of the salmon it infects, causing severe anemia, hemorrhaging in internal organs, and general lethargy. The federal government ordered the slaughter of 450,000 fish to contain the infection. Six months later, Cooke Aquaculture was ordered to destroy 350,000 salmon at one of its farms on Newfoundland's southern coast after another ISA outbreak. Both infected sites were located along a corridor used by wild salmon to get to and from the Conne River, increasing the risk that the disease would spread to wild salmon. The virus also threatened cod, herring, and mackerel, all of which were still found in Newfoundland's coastal waters.

The aquaculture industry likes to blame ISA infections on wild salmon. In response to the infections at Butter Cove, a spokesperson for the local aquaculture association said, "In the ocean, there's a lot of naturally occurring viruses and bacteria and other things that can impact our farming situations. And unfortunately, it appears that this may be the case at this site right now, maybe impacted by something it caught from the wild." Perhaps intentionally, the statement missed the point and ignored the differences between ISA in the wild and ISA in salmon farms containing a million fish. Studies have shown that the virus rarely infects wild salmon and that salmon farms are the superspreaders of the disease, which damages farmed salmon and endangers other species.

Think of the outbreak in the terms that became common during the COVID-19 pandemic: Walking outdoors and maintaining physical distance kept you relatively safe because the SARS-CoV-2 virus was not spread easily. Indoors, risks were far greater, especially when the room was crowded. Similarly, outbreaks of ISA are extremely rare among wild salmon, as infected fish either are killed by predators or simply die. Because the ISA infection of a wild fish takes place in the open water, there is no chance of mass mortalities. Not so for salmon packed into fish farms. As with SARS-CoV-2, the salmon virus flourishes in crowded conditions, often resulting in large-scale outbreaks and mass deaths.

Incidents of ISA, sea lice, and other diseases were increasing in direct proportion to the number and size of salmon farms along Newfoundland's coast. At the same time, the number of wild salmon was in sharp decline. Within a few years of the first ISA outbreaks, Canadian government scientists said wild salmon populations in seven of the fourteen rivers in Newfoundland had reached the "critical zone," raising the threat of extinction. The Conne River, which had salmon runs of ten thousand fish or more as late as the 1980s, counted two hundred returning salmon in 2020. ISA and other diseases were bad for both farmed and wild fish, but they posed no risk for Gray Aqua or Cooke Aquaculture.

Under Canadian law, the owner of an animal the government orders to be destroyed can apply for compensation. The law was originally passed for terrestrial farms, but salmon farmers can take advantage of it, too. A few months before the Butter Cove losses, the government paid Cooke $13 million after destroying infected salmon at its farm in Shelburne, Nova Scotia.

In Newfoundland, Cooke received $8.3 million for its 350,000 salmon, and Gray was paid $5.9 million for its 450,000 fish. Four more outbreaks followed on the heels of the initial infestations, two more at Gray farms and two more at Cooke farms. In total, the federal government paid the two companies $43 million in compensation based on the market value of the 2.8 million slaughtered salmon in 2012 alone.

The payments caused a nationwide outcry. Communities and conservation organizations objected to spending taxpayer money to subsidize what they regarded as poor fish-farming practices. In the spring of 2014, a coalition of groups led by the Ecology Action Centre in Halifax, Nova Scotia, calculated that the federal government had paid almost $139 million over two decades to salmon farmers in Canada's four Atlantic provinces to compensate them for ISA-related losses. In response to the criticism, the federal government tightened up its compensation plan and reduced the number and amounts of payouts, but the law remains on the books, and companies continue to take advantage of it to underwrite their risks.

Even millions in compensation were not enough to keep Gray Aqua afloat. The company declared bankruptcy in 2013, and its seven farms and a fish-processing plant in Newfoundland were sold in 2016 to Mowi. The new Norwegian owner applied for seventeen more salmon farm licenses, a request the provincial government welcomed as justification for its own commitment to salmon farming. Two years later, Mowi bought another Canadian company, Northern Harvest Sea Farms, adding forty-five more salmon farms to its roster in Newfoundland and New Brunswick. The world's biggest salmon farmer was placing a big bet across the ocean from its home in Norway, where the government had restricted growth. And its new venture would immerse the world's largest salmon farmer in a controversy commensurate with its size.

Keith Sullivan is a sturdy, intense, ginger-haired union leader. The son of a fisherman, Sullivan grew up in Calvert, a small cod-fishing village on Newfoundland's south coast, went to university in Nova Scotia, and returned home in 2002 with a degree in biology. His timing was not great: the fishing industry was crashing, and job prospects were bleak. So, Sullivan turned to what appeared to be the future of fishing and enrolled in postgraduate courses in aquaculture at Memorial University in St. John's. As part of the program, he spent a year working on a salmon farm in Ireland. Unlike many Newfoundlanders, he was unable to shake off the lure of the Rock and came home again.

Sullivan had seen enough of salmon farming in Ireland, however, to know it was not for him. Instead, he went to work for the Fish Food and Allied Workers Union, which represents inshore fishers, like lobstermen who work the waters close to shore, workers at salmon farms and fish-processing plants, and a mix of people in related trades. Sullivan worked his way up and was elected president of the fifteen-thousand-member union in 2014, at just thirty-four years old.

The job was never easy because the fishing industry was still shrinking, and so was union membership. But as he sat at his desk in the union's nondescript headquarters a few blocks from St. John's Harbour in mid-September 2019, Sullivan faced a problem that was making his job even harder. Since early August, lobster fishers and workers at salmon farms had been calling to report salmon dying in growing numbers at farms in Fortune Bay, a large bay about six hours away, on the province's southern coast. Workers on the farms blamed sea lice infestations for sickening salmon at farms owned by Northern Harvest Sea Farms, the Mowi subsidiary. Lobster fishers complained that dead and dying fish were floating outside cages and that their corpses were fouling the seabed.

The reports put Sullivan in a tough spot. Tensions already existed with the multinational corporations running the salmon farms. Pay was low for workers at the farms and in the processing plants, and the number of jobs promised in return for multimillion-dollar government subsidies never seemed to materialize. Still, plenty of union members bristled when Sullivan criticized the aquaculture industry. They worried the companies would pack up and move, taking the desperately needed jobs with them. By September, however, the reports from the field had become so persistent and serious that Sullivan felt he had no choice but to pick up the telephone and call Northern Harvest to try to get to the bottom of the mystery in Fortune Bay. He was about to touch off the sort of corporate response that defines a harm industry.

Sullivan spoke with Jamie Gaskill, the managing director of Mowi's Northern Harvest operations in St. John's, explaining that his members were reporting major fish die-offs at the company's farms in Fortune Bay and nearby

Harbour Breton Bay. He told Gaskill that his main concern was making sure the company was aggressive in dealing with the problem. Gaskill assured him that the situation was under control and that the provincial government had been notified. But Sullivan was not convinced, and he had little faith in the government to protect fishing grounds. Over the years, Sullivan believed that the fisheries ministry and other provincial and federal government agencies had proven themselves more interested in promoting salmon farms than in enforcing regulations. He was not sure what his next step should be. In the meantime, the calls from the coast kept coming.

Northern Harvest and its parent company, Mowi, had informed the provincial government on September 3 of the fish die-offs in Fortune Bay and Harbour Breton Bay. The company blamed the deaths on an extended period of high temperatures that warmed water in the cages to a catastrophic level. Salmon are cold-water fish, and they suffer stress when temperatures rise into the midsixties Fahrenheit. The fish had responded by congregating in the cooler water to be found at the bottom of the cages. The congregating fish meant there was not enough oxygen to go around, and fish died in large numbers—although the company told the fisheries ministry it was uncertain of the exact numbers of dead fish. Some fish had floated out of the cages, making an exact count impossible. Most, however, were lying dead at the bottom of the cages, where there were so many decomposing fish that divers could not make an accurate count. According to government workplace safety reports, the water was so murky that two divers lost track of their depth and ascended too fast, winding up hospitalized in a decompression chamber.

Despite the mounting concerns at the farms, neither the company nor the government alerted the public. But Newfoundland is too small to keep a big secret. People living along the south coast had been aware of the unfolding disaster since early August, well before Mowi said the warm water had arrived. Throughout the month and into September, dead fish had been washing up onshore. Workers from the farms were talking among themselves and with their families. Word spread that something bad was happening in the bays, but no one wanted to go public. Since the call with Gaskill, Sullivan had been wrestling with whether to break the silence and alert the public at large.

On Friday, September 20, a union member called Sullivan to tell him that the situation was getting worse. Sullivan telephoned Gaskill and left a message on his phone: "We have a problem. Please call me back as soon as possible." He heard nothing over the weekend, and there was no message when he arrived at work on Monday. That afternoon, he issued a statement to members on the union website, saying the union had received reports of significant numbers of dead farmed salmon on the south coast of the island, which raised concerns about a major die-off and its environmental impact. Sullivan said the union had asked Mowi for a more aggressive cleanup operation.

On Tuesday morning, calls from the media poured into the union office. Sullivan's remarks to reporters were stronger than his statement of the day before. He said millions of pounds of salmon may have died, posing a threat to fertile lobster grounds and to other fish in the bay. He suggested the deaths raised questions about whether the farms should be allowed to continue operating in fragile coastal areas where they threatened other marine life. "Maybe the answer is on-shore salmon farming," he told CBC News. "We can't afford to have things like this happen that are going to threaten the environment for fish harvesters." Sullivan said he did not understand why the union had to be the one to notify the public, rather than the government or the company.

What followed was a joint exercise in defensive maneuvers and concealment by the company and the government. It was clear that Sullivan had caught the government flat-footed, and the public was angry about having been kept in the dark. Gerry Byrne, the fisheries minister for the province, tried to take the high ground by climbing on top of the company, claiming Mowi had refused his advice to make the die-off public. "The truth is the company, by not proactively coming out and talking about this in a sensible, measured way, providing facts, they've caused some of this confusion," he said.

Byrne, a seasoned politician and member of Prime Minister Justin Trudeau's Liberal Party, took no responsibility for the government's failure to alert the public in the nearly three weeks since Mowi had notified him about the die-off. Instead, he pledged that new regulations would be drafted to increase oversight of the industry. The statement bypassed the real questions: Why had the government failed to alert the public at the beginning of September? What sort of oversight had the government been conducting for two decades? Was the big investment of taxpayer dollars in salmon farming a smart bet? Behind the scenes, Byrne was urging Gaskill and other company officials to get out in front of the wave of bad publicity and take the heat off him.

That same day, Mowi issued its first public statement, a press release blaming the die-off on high water temperatures over a period of several days in late August and early September. The company did not mention sea lice as a potential contributing factor, nor did it confirm the reports from union members that the deaths had started in early August. Instead, it blamed environmental factors outside its control. The statement provided no estimate of how many fish had died, but Mowi said it was using all available dive teams and equipment to remove the dead fish. Jason Card, the subsidiary's spokesman, said the dead fish would be transported to a rendering plant and used for other purposes, like pet food or fertilizer. Card said Mowi was considering redesigning its salmon cages to extend deeper into the water, to allow the fish to stay cool. "We have to act as though this temperature spike is not an isolated incident," he said. "We have to accept it as a new normal so that we are ready to deal with it."

Even though it was misleading in context, Card's mention of a "new normal" contained an element of truth. Since the 1950s, the amount of oxygen in the world's oceans has declined because of global warming. The climate crisis is warming the world's oceans, and warm water contains less oxygen than cold water. The reduction in oxygen is sharpest near the surface, where the water is warmest. The warm water and the oxygen depletion increase stress on fish, which means they need even more oxygen to survive—a vicious circle. Scientists have blamed die-offs of salmon and other fish in many places on water temperatures approaching seventy degrees Fahrenheit, a challenge the salmon-farming industry has yet to confront effectively.

Mowi blamed the mass mortalities on a prolonged period of ten days or more when water temperatures were abnormally high, a position supported later by the province's chief aquaculture veterinarian. Some biologists and other experts continued to point to the dead fish and the large numbers of sea lice first reported in early August and throughout the month, ahead of the temperature increase the company cited. They theorized that the sea lice had killed some fish before the temperatures spiked and had weakened others, making them more susceptible to the warmer water and ratcheting up the deaths when such temperatures arrived.

The day after defending itself in the press, the company and the local aquaculture association went after Sullivan, the person who exposed the die-off to the public. Card praised the company's disclosures, saying it had been in regular contact with the government, local leaders, and the Fish Food and

Allied Workers Union. He claimed he had been blindsided by Sullivan's assertions that the company had not been transparent. Mark Lane, the executive director of the Newfoundland and Labrador Aquaculture Industry Association, went a step further in attacking Sullivan: "He lied. He says the company wasn't transparent. How much more transparent can you be?"

The claims by Card and Lane were a distraction from the disaster still unfolding on the coast. Despite the assertions of transparency, the company had delayed making the episode public until Sullivan forced their hand, and it still refused to estimate the number of dead fish or how long the cleanup would take. The responses fit neatly into the denial stage of the Benson-Kirsch template on how corporations react in a crisis.

Industry representatives accused Sullivan of timing his disclosure to coincide with the start of the annual international conference on aquaculture in St. John's. Sullivan said it was a coincidence, but the news cast a pall over the gathering. Rather than showcasing the province's innovation, technology, and receptivity to aquaculture for hundreds of delegates from around the world, the conference became a venue for discussing the fish deaths and the beating Mowi was taking in the press. Byrne, the fisheries minister, used his opening address at the conference to provide some details of the plan for tighter regulations on aquaculture, not a message the industry wanted to hear. A few days later, Byrne tried to walk back his tough talk. Addressing the companies facing being shut out of British Columbia and Washington State because of environmental concerns, Byrne urged them to look east. "Newfoundland and Labrador are places where much of that salmon production should consider locating," he told the press.

Byrne's plea ran into hard facts: millions of farmed salmon were dying in Newfoundland from ISA and from the Mowi die-off, and the toll was rising.

CHAPTER 20

KEEP YOUR MOUTH SHUT

Gary Snook did not need the media to tell him a disaster was occurring in Fortune Bay. Born and raised in Harbour Breton, a postage stamp–size village that is the unofficial capital of the Fortune Bay region, he had spent his life on the water, like almost everyone he knew. Snook left high school at sixteen to go to sea, following earlier generations on big ships fishing for cod off the Grand Banks. One winter, he lost part of the left side of his face to frostbite, but he still recalled the period with fondness. These days, his brother and other relatives work in various jobs at nearby salmon farms or for the big processing plant in town.

When the cod fishery closed in 1992, Snook became an inshore fisherman. He stayed close to the coast, fishing for scallops and herring. Eventually, he bought a lobster license and started setting baited traps for lobsters. During the intense, three-month lobster season, Snook and his wife, Georgina, took their forty-foot boat, the *Sara Ann*, into the waters of Fortune Bay and the surrounding area to collect lobsters from their 185 traps, the legal limit. The boat had a propane stove, a generator to refrigerate the lobster, and a small sleeping alcove. For years, Gary promised Georgina that he would install a shower. From mid-April until mid-June, they lived on the boat, going ashore weekly only to unload their catch and take the opportunity to shower. It was good money, about a thousand dollars a day, and a good life. They owned a home, two nice pickup trucks, and three other boats. The number of lobster licenses sold is capped by the province to manage the lobster population, which makes the licenses valuable. Snook planned to sell his lobster license and the boats to finance his and Georgina's retirement in a few years. Recently, however, he had begun to worry that his investment was losing value. Wild fish and lobsters were becoming scarce around the bay. In the privacy of their own homes, he and his neighbors blamed the salmon farms for polluting the water with feces and chemicals that drove away marine life. Snook said lobsters caught near salmon farms smelled so bad that people refused to eat them. Scallops and herring, his other money crops, were disappearing, too.

"Our life and our retirement are invested in fishing," Snook told us as he and Georgina sat at their kitchen table. "It's worth five hundred thousand dollars. I have four boats and the lobster license. What are they going to be worth if the salmon farms kill the fishing? If the lobster fishery goes down, everything I've invested is gone. Young people who come after won't have anything. Our three sons don't want to be fishermen."

Snook heard about fish dying in Fortune Bay in early August, the same time as Keith Sullivan. Workers from the farms gossiped among family and friends about finding as many as three hundred sea lice on a single fish in overstocked cages. A diver told Snook that so many fish were dying that orange masses of flesh were falling through the nets and piling up beneath the cages. Everyone was talking about it, but no one wanted to do anything. When Snook suggested going to the government or the press, relatives and friends warned him to remain silent. They did not want to antagonize the farms, for fear of losing their jobs. "People came to Gary and told him to keep his mouth shut," said Georgina. "These were friends and family."

Toward the end of September, after the die-off became public knowledge, Snook got a telephone call from Bill Bryden. A former editor and writer at a science magazine, in recent years Bryden had devoted himself to trying to force the reform of the salmon-farming industry in Newfoundland. Armed with a keen sense of outrage and informed by a wide network of disgruntled workers and worried fishers, he was constantly petitioning the federal and provincial governments to protect the environment and haranguing journalists to pay attention to the environmental damage occurring along the south coast. But there is a lot of nowhere in Newfoundland, and Bryden found it hard to attract the attention of the press six hours away in St. John's, much less media from outside the province. His luck was no better with the government, provincial or federal. But he was indefatigable.

Bryden had started getting reports of the die-off in Fortune Bay from his contacts via Facebook and telephone calls at about the same time that Snook and Sullivan were learning about the issue. One caller told Bryden that his wife worked at a farm where they were experiencing massive mortality rates. The fish were dying, the caller said, and the cause was a mystery. Bryden relayed this information to reporters in St. John's, but they were not interested. He offered to hire a boat to take them to the farms, but they were not interested. It seemed the south coast was too far to go for a few dead fish.

After the die-off made provincial headlines in mid-September, Bryden wanted a firsthand look and started calling people on the coast, looking for a boat to take him to the farms. He was turned down half a dozen times until he reached Snook. When Snook told friends that he was going to take Bryden to see the damage, he was again warned not to get involved. With jobs at stake, people tend to overlook the long-term impact of environmental problems, an attitude that is not unique to those living in the isolated villages of coastal Newfoundland. Better to keep those jobs and hope the future takes care of itself. Everybody has to eat, after all. But as we've seen, today's needs can destroy tomorrow's resources.

On October 1, Snook and Bryden met before dawn in Harbour Breton. The days were getting shorter, the sun was not up, the harbor was still dark, and the water was flat and opaque. Bryden was eager and apprehensive as the *Sara Ann* chugged toward Fortune Bay. Nearing the first salmon farm, Bryden saw dead fish floating outside the cages and watched as a salvage vessel pumped dead salmon out of a cage straight into the ocean. Snook had to keep his distance from the farm; violating the boundary marked by the large buoys could lead to an arrest for trespassing and confiscation of his boat. Edging closer, Snook took a sonar reading, which showed a staggering *seventy feet* of dead salmon on the seabed. Bryden dropped an underwater drone over the side and saw fish carcasses floating in water milky with decomposing fat and waste.

Bryden knew the images would propel the story onto the national news. He telephoned CBC News and other news outlets and described the gruesome scene. With Mowi's problems already making headlines in St. John's, the story was getting too big for the press to ignore. CBC News dispatched a reporter and video crew to hook up with Bryden and Snook in Harbour Breton the next day. The group was joined by Don Ivany, the Atlantic Salmon Federation's representative in the province and a longtime ally of Bryden.

Ivany, a biologist, had spent nearly thirty years working for the ASF, fighting to preserve wild salmon in the rivers of Newfoundland and Labrador. He had grown up on a bay outside Corner Brook, in the western part of the province, and married a woman "from away," which to close-knit Newfoundlanders meant the other side of the bay. Like most of their friends, they had a cabin in the woods and fished for salmon, always releasing whatever they were lucky and skilled enough to land. To Ivany, salmon were not dinner, and they were certainly not a commodity. They were living animals worthy of respect and humane treatment. He dreaded what he was about to encounter as Snook's boat pulled out of the harbor with the TV crew.

On the way to the farms, the boat passed beaches covered with six inches of fat from decomposing salmon. When the *Sara Ann* arrived at the first farm, Ivany was moved to tears. Now two salvage vessels were pumping dead salmon out of the cages and into the water. "The first thing that hit me was the scale," he said later, sitting in his small, windowless office in Corner Brook. "This wasn't in just one cove, but every area. It was the sight of it, the impact of it, knowing the government was trying to cover it up. It was pretty gruesome stuff. They were pumping fish out of cages and sending them overboard. They said to the media they were cleaning the environment, but what they were doing was cleaning out the cages. I was overwhelmed, choked up. It was enough to make you heave over the side of the boat."

The CBC crew taped the scene as gallons of thick, pink liquid and chunks of what appeared to be decomposed fish flowed freely out of hoses on the sides of the ships. Three men on a small barge used handheld nets to retrieve pieces of salmon floating on the surface. The men could not keep up, and the current spread the remnants hundreds of yards beyond the farm. Snook moved closer to the shore, which was covered with a thick layer of the fish fat as far as they could see. According to biologists, the fat acted like an oil spill. Farmed salmon is a fatty fish, and its fat has the consistency of butter. When combined with seawater, it turns into a thick, sticky substance that suffocates marine life and coats seabirds. The danger was higher here because the pollution was concentrated in narrow bays and protected coves, where it would take time to be swept away by the tide and current.

Back in St. John's, the company took a strikingly upbeat view of the gruesome scene. Card, the spokesman for the Mowi subsidiary, said the liquid
dumped into the ocean was not blood or fish viscera, but merely pink coloring
from pigment added to salmon feed. He said the fat covering the shoreline
was a natural part of the decomposition process and would dissolve eventually. The explanation did nothing to soften the impact of the CBC broadcast
that evening.

The graphic CBC footage forced the provincial government to respond
again. Employing the usual strategy, Gerry Byrne attacked the messenger.
He called the CBC images propaganda and compared the video to the images
of baby seals being clubbed that had been used in an international campaign
against seal hunting decades earlier. The anti-seal campaign remains an
emotional issue for many Newfoundlanders, who were angered by what they
regarded as the distortion of a long tradition of seal hunting. "I've seen some
very, very emotive issues when it comes to the seal hunt, which do not reflect
the realities," Byrne told a CBC interviewer. "So, I would caution, before anyone draws a conclusion. Just think through how certain industries have been
victimized by the production of images which may be far in excess of what is
the truth of what's happening here."

Environmental groups and opposition politicians objected to the tone
and substance of Byrne's comments. He suddenly found himself referred to
in the press as "the beleaguered minister"—never a good sign. James Dinn, a
legislator from the opposition New Democratic Party, demanded an investigation into the die-off by either Environment Canada, the federal agency, or
an arm's-length environmental consulting firm. "We want an independent
investigation into what happened here, that's taken out of the hands of Minister Byrne and the government," said Dinn. "The minister is sounding more
and more like a cheerleader for the industry than a person who should be
exercising oversight."

Byrne was looking for a life preserver, and it came a few days later, when
Mowi informed him that the information it had provided the government
on September 3 was incomplete. Instead of six farms, the die-off involved
ten farms, affecting millions of salmon. Byrne immediately suspended the

licenses of the ten Mowi farms until the company satisfied the province that it was operating in a safe manner. In a new statement, Byrne defended his decision not to inform the public after the first report of the die-off, saying he had no authority to release such news. He said new regulations would require salmon farms to disclose similar incidents to the public.

The day Byrne suspended its licenses, Mowi revealed to the public that the tally of dead fish had reached 2.6 million, one of the worst mortality events in salmon-farming history. Gaskill, the managing director for the Mowi subsidiary that owned the Newfoundland farms, acknowledged that the company should have been more transparent. "I want to state for the record that we should have advised earlier of these additional mortalities as they occurred over time," he said. "I take responsibility for this personally. . . . We were too focused on the cleanup efforts, and we have learned from this experience."

In private, Gaskill's attitude was sharply different. In a letter to Byrne after his public apology, Gaskill argued that the government exceeded its authority in suspending the licenses and demanded that they be reinstated immediately. He said most of the deaths were reported as soon as they were confirmed by divers, keeping the company in compliance with the conditions of its leases. At four of the ten sites, he said, the fish died over a longer period, so it took time to grasp the full extent of the die-off.

Mowi's public face remained conciliatory. In early November, Alf-Helge Aarskog, the chief executive officer of Mowi, traveled to St. John's and met with Byrne and the province's premier, Dwight Ball. He apologized for the company's handling of the die-off and pledged that Mowi and its subsidiary would take steps to improve transparency, build cages that let salmon swim deeper, monitor their farms better, and develop new emergency plans for dealing with any similar incidents in the future. The next day, Aarskog returned to Bergen and resigned as CEO. The company said the move was unrelated and that Aarskog had informed Mowi's board of directors six months earlier of his plans to leave the company.

Bowing to the pressure, Byrne announced that there would be what he called an independent inquiry into the causes of the die-off. Instead of the federal government, Byrne said the investigation would be carried out by the Fisheries and Marine Institute at Memorial University. The institute was not independent from the government or the aquaculture industry, though.

Most of its funding came from the provincial and federal governments, and the institute was a key partner in the province's plan to promote aquaculture. The institute was also closely aligned with the farming industry. The head of its aquaculture program, Cyr Couturier, was an ardent champion of the industry who was serving his second term as president of the Newfoundland and Labrador Aquaculture Industry Association, the lobbying group for salmon farmers. Institute scientists received research grants from the industry. Further, while the institute was affiliated with Memorial University, its researchers and other staff did not have tenure, which meant they had no protection if they objected to the conclusions of the review. The Fisheries and Marine Institute was not exactly arm's-length, as Dinn had demanded.

When it came to assessing damage to the environment, the province took an even more suspect route. Byrne allowed Mowi to select the entity to conduct the evaluation and to define its parameters, and the company would pay for the assessment. Mowi hired a First Nations organization called Mi'kmaq Alsumk Mowimsikik Koqoey Association, which translates to "Mi'kmaq Aquatic Resource and Oceans Management," and is known as MAMKA. The organization had been set up in 2005 as part of a federal government effort to increase the role of Indigenous people in managing their own aquatic resources. Aligning itself with a First Nations organization afforded Mowi a level of insulation from public criticism. From the start of MAMKA's inquiry, there were doubts about its capacity to evaluate the impact of the die-off. It had a staff of five, two of whom were administrative assistants.

The two-part assignment was to measure the impact of the salmon die-off on the environment and to monitor the recovery of the surrounding waters and shoreline. MAMKA did not begin work until the end of October, long after tides had swept away some of the mess. The organization blamed the delay on bad weather and a lack of boats and workers. Even when the work started, MAMKA relied heavily on water samples collected near a handful of the farms and on photographs taken from drones rather than on-site examinations. Still, the group said it was confident in its findings. An interim report in January 2020 said the impact on the coastline was not widespread and that damage was minimal. Dean McDonald, who worked with MAMKA on the inquiry and was the brother of its executive director, downplayed the idea of environmental damage. "There was a bit of grease on the shoreline, no doubt," he told CBC News. "Certain places it did gather up, which kind of looked bad. But after visiting the sites several times, we seen [*sic*] it dissipate significantly."

The Fisheries and Marine Institute report was released in March 2020. Sensitive to his close association with the aquaculture industry, the institute did not identify Couturier as part of the review. Instead, the work was led by the director of the institute's Centre for Aquaculture and Seafood Development, and its findings were reviewed by two professors from outside Newfoundland. The report was based on reviews of water temperatures at the time of the die-off, the findings of provincial officials, data from the company on lice counts, and satellite images of the bays. The provincial veterinarian, Daryl Whelan, had rejected suggestions that sea lice played a role in weakening the fish, blaming the die-off entirely on unusually warm water. The panel acknowledged that the institute did not conduct its own scientific research; the report was more an interpretation of existing data than an independent inquiry.

The findings were couched in strained language, indicating that the panel had not reached a firm conclusion on the die-off's cause. "We speculate that the following series of events created a spiral of worsening conditions inside the net pens," the executive summary read. The primary cause listed was an increase in water temperature in the bays, which had stayed as high as sixty-four degrees Fahrenheit for several days in late August. The report said the high temperatures depleted the oxygen in the water and drove salmon to the bottom of the cages in search of cooler water, where tens of thousands of them suffocated. The accumulating weight of the dead fish lying on the bottom of the net pen tightened the net, causing more deaths. The assessment matched statements by the company and the provincial veterinarian.

Rather than accepting the explanation of Mowi and the veterinarian that warm water alone had caused the die-off, the Fisheries and Marine Institute's review identified other factors that it said contributed to the scale of the deaths. First, chemical treatments for sea lice at the farms prior to the warm temperatures had stressed and weakened the salmon. Second, algae blooms in the bays had depleted the oxygen in the water before the warm temperatures arrived. The report said salmon disease played no role, except at one farm, where ISA was detected before the die-off. Criticism of Mowi was relegated to the absence of a robust contingency plan and of sufficient equipment to deal with an emergency on the scale of the mass die-off. The institute agreed with the company that the final toll of dead salmon was 2.6 million; six of the affected farms lost 100 percent of their fish, and the other four lost between 33 and 50 percent. The number of dead salmon in the institute's report, though, did not match the number cited in documents we obtained from the province through Access to Information Act requests. Those records put the number 15 percent higher—at around 3 million.

In its final report in April 2020, MAMKA minimized the impact of the die-off. The report said that only about 2 percent of the shoreline was affected, and it claimed that the decomposing fat had dissolved quickly. It said drones had spotted no evidence of harm to seabirds and that underwater cameras had found no accumulation of organic matter on the seabed. Much of the report's executive summary was devoted to criticizing conservation groups and the media. "The subjective media onslaught was both graphic in its presentation and alarming in its stridency," the report read. As Byrne had done, the report singled out CBC News, the highly respected national broadcaster, for what MAMKA characterized as aggressive and unbalanced coverage. The media criticism was unusual for an assessment of environmental damage. The tone was closer to the language of the provincial government and Mowi than to a scientific paper.

Backed by reports from the two handpicked groups, the government reinstated the licenses at the ten farms. Byrne issued a brief statement saying Mowi had established new protocols and practices to reduce the chance of a similar event. He praised the openness and transparency of the companies in regaining the public trust.

Even before the Fisheries and Marine Institute and MAMKA issued their findings, questions had been raised about their independence. The institute was widely respected in academic and industry circles, but its ties to the local industry and its dependence on government funding created doubts about its autonomy. MAMKA's independence was compromised from the start because Mowi, the subject of the investigation, was paying the investigator's bills.

Among those who challenged the inquiries was Bill Montevecchi. A familiar figure in academic and political circles in Newfoundland, Montevecchi is a longtime professor of biology and ocean sciences at Memorial University. In 2020, he created a stir when he resigned in protest from a government advisory committee set up to protect wilderness areas. "The environment in this province doesn't have a priority," he told the press in explaining why he was quitting after twenty-five years on the committee. Montevecchi felt the same way about the government's response to the die-off, and he knew from experience that it could have been far better.

After the monumental Deepwater Horizon oil spill in the Gulf of Mexico in 2010, Montevecchi spent weeks in Louisiana rescuing seabirds. The magnitude of that disaster was far greater than the salmon die-off in Fortune Bay, but what struck Montevecchi was the contrast in official responses. In the immediate aftermath of the Deepwater Horizon disaster, U.S. president Barack Obama appointed an independent commission with no ties to the oil industry to investigate the cause. Obama blamed the blowout on what he called a "scandalously close relationship between the regulator and the industry." In Newfoundland, Montevecchi pointed out, Byrne and the provincial government assigned the inquiry to a government-funded institute and allowed the industry to select the entity to conduct the environmental review and pay for the work. Once the predictable results were published, he said, the government returned to business as usual, missing an opportunity to hold the industry accountable.

"Could the Northern Harvest die-off have been prevented? I don't think so," Montevecchi said. "This is an industry that comes with collateral damage. Waste products, toxins, escaped fish, ISA, this will continue. The collateral damage is always rationalized in terms of jobs, feeding a hungry planet, when in fact it is corrupting ecosystems. It is clear they lie and that is part of the industry modus operandi. Fabricating, stretching, exaggerating, and outright lying. They love the good news—we are creating jobs, we fund tuition for students. It is a ransom, that is what it is."

Another biology professor at Memorial University, Ian Jones, had been one of the first responders when the *Exxon Valdez* dumped more than ten million gallons of oil into Prince William Sound, off the coast of Alaska, in 1989. He rescued injured wildlife and counted the dead birds and other mammals. He drew a similar comparison between the Newfoundland episode and what he had seen in Alaska, while acknowledging the dramatic difference in scale. "Is this pollution?" Jones asked rhetorically about the dead salmon.

"It is a substance containing a concentration of rotting fish. It is gooey, so it sticks to things like beaches and wildlife. And it contains hydrogen sulfide, so there is a horrific stench. It will break down over time, but the initial effects are serious. Birds get coated and fly away, so we don't know how many die. Other marine life is affected."

Fish kept dying. In the twelve months after the Mowi die-off, at least fourteen farms in Newfoundland sustained major outbreaks of infectious salmon anemia that resulted in the slaughter of an estimated 3.5 million more salmon. Most ISA infections were at Cooke farms, but several were at Mowi sites. The overall mortality rate for salmon in farms off the coast of Newfoundland was a staggering 54 percent in 2019, according to provincial government figures. In other words, more salmon died than were harvested. In 2020, the government said the death rate improved slightly, to 40 percent, which is still at least twice the global mortality rate of 15 to 20 percent. In September 2021, Mowi reported the deaths of 450,000 salmon at a single farm off the Newfoundland coast, roughly half the total at the site. The company blamed the die-off on weather conditions, including low oxygen in the cages, and repeated that it was developing ways to deal with what it called "environmental pressures."

The mass deaths at its Newfoundland farms cost Mowi nearly $45 million between the end of 2019 and the end of 2020. Its chief executive, Ivan Vindheim, blamed the high death rate on water temperatures and sea lice, and he said the company would take new measures to combat the challenges of salmon farming in the province. After the losses, Mowi and Cooke reduced the number of salmon farms operating along the coast, and some industry analysts thought the heavy losses might cause Mowi to leave Newfoundland.

But the provincial government had no qualms about doubling down on its financial commitment to salmon farming. In July 2020, Byrne announced $725,000 in government funding to support expanding salmon farming, and he praised the industry for providing jobs in Newfoundland and helping feed the world. The province also approved final licenses granting a subsidiary of Norway's Grieg Seafood exclusive rights to develop a huge salmon-farming facility at Placentia Bay, an eighty-mile-long body of water on the province's southern shore that is most famous as the place where U.S. president Franklin D. Roosevelt and UK prime minister Winston Churchill met secretly in August 1941 to begin hammering out the Atlantic Charter, the shared Anglo-American strategy for World War II. The bay was virgin territory for salmon farming, and Grieg planned eleven open-net farms and had already started building a fish-processing plant. In 2019, Byrne moved to immigration minister, and his successor as fisheries minister, Derrick Bragg, said the province was opening an additional one-hundred-mile stretch of coastline to salmon farms for the first time. Bragg was defensive about criticism of the industry, telling a CBC interviewer that there was no research linking salmon farms to the decline in wild salmon.

The tepid response to the Mowi die-off from Newfoundland's government and the public contrasted sharply with the reaction in Washington State to the escape of around 250,000 salmon in Puget Sound. The brief suspension of Mowi's licenses in Newfoundland was a slap on the wrist intended more to save face for a government official than to punish the company, while Washington State banned salmon farms and effectively kicked them out of its waters. Why were the responses so different?

First, the economics of Newfoundland and Washington State are starkly different. Salmon farms are a minor part of Washington's economy. Major corporations like Boeing and Microsoft employ thousands of people, and the state's gross domestic product is more than six hundred billion dollars a year, more than twenty times higher than Newfoundland's. Few economic alternatives exist in Newfoundland. Revenues from the oil and gas industry have declined, commercial fishing has diminished, and the provincial government regularly confronts a multibillion-dollar deficit. Faced with tough economic conditions, politicians are loath to take actions that could cost jobs.

Second, environmental activists and conservationists are part of the cultural fabric of Washington. Puget Sound is a mecca for people who love the outdoors and who recognize the value of protecting it. Lots of wealthy people maintain homes on its shores and islands, and few have any love for the salmon farms that mar their view and spoil the fishing grounds. The collapse of Cooke's farm ignited latent kindling and sparked a broad opposition movement that pushed the state legislature to act. In Newfoundland, environmental groups have been regarded with suspicion since the days of the anti-seal campaign in the 1980s. More significantly, the province's south coast is remote, and those who dare speak out are often unheard. The few lonely voices raised in protest did not spur anything close to widespread outcry.

Third, the governor and legislators in Washington were responsive and progressive. Environmental champions like Kurt Beardslee and state senator Kevin Ranker emerged to lead the charge, and an aggressive press covered every twist and turn in the battle. In Newfoundland, the government had invested too much of its credibility and taxpayer money to step back.

In Nova Scotia, where Cooke and Cermaq were making big plans, a public outcry like what happened in Washington State was about to play out. The question was how Nova Scotia's provincial government would respond.

CHAPTER 21

LOBSTER IN THE CROSSHAIRS

Under a brilliant blue sky, Peter Stewart cast off the mooring ropes and gently guided his boat out of Moose Harbour and into Liverpool Bay, on Nova Scotia's South Shore. The Atlantic Ocean beckoned from just beyond, but Stewart's target was closer as he cleared the breakwater and gunned the engine. Soon enough, he was steering through a slight chop and toward a black smudge on the water's glistening surface, a salmon feedlot that held tens of thousands of fish next to Coffin Island.

Cooke Aquaculture operates the farm near Coffin Island, one of its twelve open-net farms along Nova Scotia's coast. In early 2019, as it was losing its salmon farms in Washington, the company proposed expanding the farm at Coffin Island to twenty cages from fourteen and adding two new farms in the bay, each with twenty cages. In its application to the provincial government, the company said the new farms would cover more than two hundred acres of Liverpool Bay and at least triple the number of penned fish. Stewart was unhappy about the prospect of industrial-scale salmon farming in his home waters.

Stewart is a tall, muscular man in his midfifties, with a face weathered by two decades at sea. His boat, the *Shelley and Lindsay*, is weathered, too. Her scarred rear deck, filled with lobster traps during the six-month season, is empty this day. The helm is utilitarian but surprisingly high-tech. By law, boats must carry paper nautical charts like those that guided ships for hundreds of years, in case the technology fails. Standing at the wheel, Stewart pointed to four computer monitors, each showing a different navigational chart. These monitors depicted full-color configurations of the shoreline and the seafloor, providing depths in fathoms and locations of dangers to navigation. Despite the modern equipment, Stewart tapped a battered compass screwed down next to the wheel and said, "That's still the best technology onboard."

As the boat moved through the water, a pair of grey seals swam past. The previous summer, a fin whale, the second-largest mammal in the world after the blue whale, spent three days feeding on herring in the shallow bay. The whine of the engine changed pitch as the boat slowed, and Stewart pointed to the spot on the screen where one of the new farms would be located. "In spring, that's my bread and butter," he said. "That's where I set my traps, and the salmon cages will be right there, in a prime lobster habitat. That will be our downfall. This farm and others will push all of us into a smaller and smaller area. It won't take long to create problems in what's now a tight-knit community. The whole future of this place will be in danger." Cooke's expansion would reduce the lobster grounds available to boats from Moose Harbour and other locations around Liverpool Bay, squeezing them into smaller territory and creating friction among the nearly seven hundred lobster fishers licensed to fish in that specific district.

We have our own history with these waters. In the early 1990s, Catherine's parents retired to a small house in Eagle Head, on a bay next door to Liverpool Bay. Her father, Paul, had watched with fascination as the first salmon farm was installed next to Coffin Island a few years later. A lifelong fly fisher, he thought raising salmon in a closed pen might help take the pressure off the wild salmon. He enjoyed the occasional trip out to the island with a neighbor who had jury-rigged an old wooden boat into a glass-bottom boat, perfect for taking in the sights on the ocean floor. Within a couple of years, though, the shoreline around the island was littered with trash, and Paul said the seabed beneath the farm was dead. Paul, like so many others who had hoped for better, believed salmon farms were doing more harm than good.

Nova Scotia was shaped by the sea, and by lobsters. Myth says lobsters were not trapped or eaten by the first inhabitants of North America, a notion debunked by historians. For hundreds of years, the First Nations Mi'kmaq tribe speared and ate lobster throughout their ancestral lands in what are now the Atlantic provinces of Canada: Nova Scotia, New Brunswick, Newfoundland-Labrador, and Prince Edward Island. The Mi'kmaq lived by the seasons, migrating from winter camps in the interior to the coasts in spring and summer. They harvested the abundant cod and lobster, relying on hooks made of bone for cod and three-pronged spears to catch lobsters in shallow water.

The abundance of sea life drew Europeans to Nova Scotia in the sixteenth century. The waters were rich with halibut, lobster, salmon, and other fish, but cod was king. Dried or salted, it kept for months for transport to Europe. Fishing led to shipbuilding, trading, and in the case of the French and the British, a fierce battle for the future of the empire. Europeans had harvested lobsters along the Mediterranean coast since Roman times. In the New World, they found the crustaceans so plentiful that they were considered a poor person's food, suitable for prisoners, apprentices, and slaves. In the fishing and boatbuilding town of Lunenburg, on Nova Scotia's South Shore, a judge ruled in the late 1700s that it was cruel to feed prisoners lobster more than three times a week.

In the mid-1800s, attitudes started to change. Lobster flesh came to be regarded as a delicacy, a shift that led to the first commercial lobster fishing industry in Nova Scotia. The invention of the airtight tin can at about the same time opened new markets, allowing cooked seafood to be canned and then shipped long distances. Small lobster canneries popped up across the province, where no place is far from the water. In those early days, fishermen would row to the ocean in small ochre-colored boats known as dories, to set traps baited with herring, mackerel, and other small fish. Two men normally operated a dory and fished about two hundred traps, hauling them up by hand. Fast-forward a century, and modern lobster fishers run up to four hundred traps, moving among them on diesel-powered boats with crews of four to six. As the cod and other traditional fishing stocks were depleted, the lobster industry became a lifeline for fishers, and lobsters became Canada's most valuable seafood export, worth about two billion dollars a year. Like its farmed salmon, most Canadian lobsters go to the United States, but China and Japan are important markets, too.

In recent years, business boomed as markets expanded, prices rose, and the lobster harvest increased steadily. Biologists are uncertain what led to the increased haul. Two reasons cited often are warming water temperatures, which encourage growth in some marine life, and the decline of cod, which prey on juvenile lobsters. Licenses for lobster fishing have risen in value, too. Banks will loan up to four hundred thousand dollars for a license, and some licenses have sold for close to a million dollars in the most productive fishing zones. For some, their lobster license is more valuable than their house. Stewart and his fellow lobster fishers along Nova Scotia's shores worry that if the number of salmon farms increases, the good times could be at an end.

Moose Harbour is typical of the small-scale operations that dominate the lobster industry in the province. Tucked behind border rocks to protect it when Atlantic storms send thirty-foot waves crashing onshore, the harbor shelters twelve lobster boats. Together, the boats contribute three to four million dollars a year to the local community. "That money stays right here, with local businesses," said Peter Stewart. "It's local jobs, not just in the lobster industry, but it ripples through the economy. And don't forget, lobster is a sustainable industry."

Stewart had never set foot on the water until he moved from Alberta, in western Canada, to the small town of Liverpool. His father, a banker, had been transferred there a decade earlier; when he retired, he bought the *Shelley and Lindsay* and her lobster license to start a second career. In April 1991, Stewart's father suffered a heart attack, and Stewart and his wife, Janine, rushed east. Janine had been born in Alberta and never planned to leave the west. Soon after they arrived, Stewart asked her to give Liverpool five years.

Lobster season on Nova Scotia's South Shore runs from the end of November to the end of May. The spring months provide the bulk of the catch, like Christmas in the retail industry. When he arrived, Stewart realized that his father would suffer a major financial loss if his boat sat idle for the final weeks of the season, so he joined the crew of the *Shelley and Lindsay* and learned on the job; eventually, he took his place as captain.

In the early days, the family survived largely on Janine's salary as a bookkeeper, while Peter's earnings went back into the business. His income increased gradually as he learned that lobster fishing is more art than science. Lobsters can live up to fifty years, and because they never stop growing, they can reach twenty pounds or more. They shift their feeding grounds in concert with the weather and the condition of the seabed. When it is calm, they are found closer to shore, roaming the rocky bottom, foraging on eelgrass. When a storm comes in, they shift to deeper water, where the bottom is smoother, helping them weather the rough seas. Regardless of weather, lobsters tend to shun areas where there is heavy pollution, like the dead zones around salmon feedlots. So, finding the best spots for setting traps requires knowledge and a fair bit of intuition.

When the lone salmon farm first arrived in Liverpool Bay in 1992, the lobster fishers did not worry much. There were six small cages, and the impact on the lobster grounds appeared minimal. Over time, however, even the small farm drove away lobsters and other marine life. In 2011, Cooke Aquaculture's Kelly Cove subsidiary bought the farm and expanded it to fourteen larger cages, containing about seven hundred thousand salmon. A big salmon farmer gobbling up a small one and increasing production had become the industry standard. The fishers grumbled and moved their traps to other parts of the shallow bay, but lobster fishing remained a bright spot for Liverpool's economy.

The shipbuilding industry had disappeared years earlier, after the moratoriums on commercial fishing for cod and salmon. The forestry business was in decline, and in 2012 the Bowater Mersey Paper mill, the community's biggest employer, shut down, and three hundred people lost their jobs. The site was auctioned off in pieces, leaving the local economy in pieces, too. One of the mill's warehouses is now a cannabis farm. But the number of jobs has never recovered.

For years, young people had been fleeing Liverpool in search of better jobs, leaving a population significantly older than the rest of Nova Scotia. More than half the residents have no education beyond high school, having relied on jobs at the paper mill and in the shipbuilding and forestry industries. The lobster business was strong, but it was hard to find young people to crew the boats. Community leaders had to figure out how to survive, or risk becoming a ghost town.

Blessed with a beautiful coastline, Liverpool decided to reinvent itself as a retirement center. It advertised across Canada and in the eastern United States, slowly attracting new residents. Land and houses were cheap compared with Ontario, Quebec, and New England. The town had history and charm, along with a medium-size hospital. New houses were built around Liverpool Bay, creating jobs for carpenters and business for shopkeepers. Real estate prices began to rise, providing hope for the land-rich locals. Peter and Janine Stewart had bought five acres of wooded land overlooking Peter's favorite lobster-fishing spot. They built a house, which peeks above the towering spruce trees to provide a water view and is a nest egg for their retirement.

The lobster business remained healthy through the 2010s, but in early 2019, the proposed expansion by Cooke created a major threat. When Cooke's Kelly Cove Salmon subsidiary filed its application with the Nova Scotia government to more than triple its operations in Liverpool Bay, the locations it chose in the bay were virtually on top of the best productive lobster sites. The same currents that drew lobster made prime spots for salmon feedlots, and that was where Cooke wanted to put its new farms. Cooke Aquaculture, with its headquarters on the western shore of the Bay of Fundy, might be neighbors with Nova Scotia, but there was nothing neighborly about the locations of the proposed farms; the bay was to be a zero-sum struggle.

As Stewart's boat headed slowly back to Moose Harbour after a tour of the proposed locations for the new farms and Coffin Island, he mused about his future. There would still be lobsters, but the proposed farms would occupy prime habitats, driving the lobsters and the lobster boats into smaller spaces as the pollution spread. He expected to go farther to get fewer lobsters. Then there were the five acres on the waterfront that he and Janine had bought. What would that land be worth when what you saw from shore was not a coastal idyll, but two salmon feedlots, with their loud generators, bright lights, and ugly pens?

Stewart had joined the growing and increasingly vocal public opposition to Cooke's plans, linking up with local business leaders, environmental activists, and worried citizens to try to save the bay. The province's decision was delayed for months by COVID-19 restrictions on public gatherings, and as of this publication, there was still no final word.

To this day, the Canadian government maintains that salmon farms create new jobs and do not harm the environment. The government's own data say otherwise on jobs. In 2018, according to government statistics, there were about 13,000 jobs in the fishing industry in Nova Scotia, 4,800 jobs in fish processing, and 240 other jobs in all types of aquaculture. The number of jobs in salmon farming was not broken out, but studies put it at fewer than 150 full-time jobs and 50 part-time ones. The lobster industry, by contrast, directly employed more than 3,000 people, and the relatively few jobs from salmon farming risk a net loss in employment by endangering many more jobs in lobster fishing and tourism.

When Cooke filed its application to broaden its operations in Liverpool Bay, the company said its expansion there would create twenty new jobs and provide indirect benefits for the province's economy. Glenn Cooke told the Halifax Chamber of Commerce that the company would build a fish-processing plant that would provide hundreds of jobs. The promise had a familiar ring to it. In 2010, Cooke promised to build a processing plant in Shelburne that would create three hundred jobs. At the time, Cooke had pending applications for four new salmon farms there. Two years later, applications approved, the company received $25 million in government loans and grants as part of its expansion plans. But the processing plant was never built.

As for the federal government's contention that salmon farms do not harm the environment, many scientists, including the government's own biologists, disagree. A study by the Canadian government in 2015 found that two pesticides commonly used to fight sea lice could harm lobsters and other marine species hundreds of yards from a farm. Studies conducted a few miles south of Liverpool, in another picturesque spot, Port Mouton Bay, echoed those concerns.

In 1995, the first year a salmon farm was established in that bay, locals reported that lobsters and crabs migrated toward the farm, presumably to scoop up the nutrients in the excess feed falling through the cages. By the second year and every year after, the lobster haul declined sharply. In June 2018, Inka Milewski, the marine biologist who worked for the government in the 1980s and later moved to Dalhousie University in Nova Scotia as a researcher, and several other biologists published an analysis of the impact of the salmon farm on Port Mouton Bay. The results were the culmination of research that began in 2007, when the biologists recruited fifteen of the forty lobster boats moored in Port Mouton to report their catches during the lobster season. The study lasted for eleven years and confirmed the anecdotal evidence from the lobster fishers: when the farm was active, lobster catches in the bay dropped an average of 42 percent, and the number of egg-bearing lobsters in the area decreased by an average of 56 percent. The study found that antibiotics and pesticides from the farm had collected on the seafloor, turning it toxic and driving away lobsters and other marine life. One easily observed impact was the death of eelgrass, a flowering underwater plant that is an essential part of a lobster's preferred habitat and a barometer of water quality.

Good practices require salmon farms to lie fallow for several weeks after the fish are harvested for market. This period is supposed to break the cycle of sea lice and disease and allow the seabed to recover. Studies have found that these brief respites are not a permanent fix and that the cycle starts all over again when the farm comes back online.

At a public meeting in Port Mouton in July 2018, Milewski explained that odor plumes and fecal waste from the salmon farm had driven away the lobsters. Odors are cues used by lobsters to locate food, identify mates and predators, and choose where to live and breed. "It's not just by chance that we're seeing these differences," she said. "The low oxygen conditions and dissolved sulfides and ammonium that can be produced in large quantities as a result of the waste released from fish farms are known to have behavioral and toxic effects on lobsters."

Ricky Broome, who had fished for lobster out of Port Mouton for more than four decades, told a reporter for the local *Lighthouse* newspaper that the study confirmed what he saw on the water. "We knew something wasn't right," he said. "Our bay used to be one of the best bays there was for lobster fishing, but we definitely saw a decline after the farm went in. It's been doing damage for sure."

Sometimes the argument over the impact of salmon farms gets personal, even among scientists who are supposed to follow the facts. One area of contention is who is paying for the research.

In June 2019, Milewski and Ruth Smith, a local researcher in Port Mouton, published an update on the earlier study, focusing on poor regulation of salmon farms by the federal government. Milewski found herself criticized publicly by the industry and its defenders. Jon Grant, an oceanography professor at Dalhousie University in Halifax, claimed Milewski's work was influenced by her collaboration with a Port Mouton citizens group opposed to salmon farms. "When you have an agenda that drives your research, and goal, it does not speak well to objectivity," he told the Halifax *Chronicle Herald*, a serious insult in the world of academia, especially when aimed at a colleague at the same university.

Grant supported his argument by pointing to his own eight-year study of lobsters beneath a salmon farm in the New Brunswick part of the Bay of Fundy. He had concluded that the farm had no impact on the abundance or size of the lobsters there. Milewski fired back in the press, saying comparing the two studies was like comparing apples and cabbages. The location Grant studied was subject to strong currents that flushed the gravelly seabed and diluted material from the farm above, she said. Port Mouton, for its part, has a narrow entrance to the Atlantic, weaker currents, and a silty bottom, where contaminants are concentrated. The findings of Milewski's peer-reviewed papers have not been contested. A later study of three salmon farms in the Bay of Fundy by unrelated scientists found that lobsters had disappeared from the area in substantial numbers around two of the farms, appearing to contradict Grant's findings.

Then there was the issue of who paid for the dueling studies. Grant claimed Milewski's association with opponents of salmon farms tainted her conclusions. True, she had briefed the community group, and local lobster fishers had cooperated with the initial study, but the financing came from the OceanCanada Partnership, an independent coalition of nineteen research partners, community organizations, and the Canadian DFO. Grant, however, was a direct recipient of aquaculture industry money. Not only was his study in the Bay of Fundy financed by the industry lobbying association and two private businesses in the industry, but one of his coauthors worked for one of the businesses. At Dalhousie University, Grant occupied the Cooke Industrial Research Chair in Sustainable Aquaculture and trained students for jobs in aquaculture. Cooke had helped finance Grant's chair, his research, and the training program.

Grant is a reliable advocate for salmon farming and aquaculture in general. In an interview with us, he acknowledged that the industry and Cooke Aquaculture have made what he termed "missteps," including Cooke's use of cypermethrin in the Bay of Fundy more than a decade earlier. But he said salmon farming gets too much blame for damaging the environment and harming wild salmon and lobsters, and he has published papers laying out steps that he says would further reduce the impact of salmon farms. Grant told us he sees no conflict in having industry money finance his studies and work. He said the source of the money played no role in his conclusions, and he praised the collaboration between industries and academics. "I have people say to me directly that companies have no place in an academic environment," he said. "I say, 'Are you kidding?' I just don't see it as a bad thing. There are all sorts of synergies that are beneficial to society."

Aquaculture is not the only industry that finances scientific analyses of its own business and uses paid scientists to try to discredit its critics. Pharmaceutical companies do it. Oil companies do it. Big Tobacco did it for decades. And it's not just the companies who initiate this dubious relationship. Universities play the game, too, soliciting money from industries to finance research and even entire departments. Professors receive grants from companies with direct interests in the results of their studies. These practices have become routine in many universities.

Studies have documented how industry-sponsored research tends to be biased in favor of the sponsor's products. An extensive review published in the *American Journal of Public Health* concluded that corporate interests drive research agendas away from questions that are highly relevant to public health. This finding was particularly significant because industry funding for medical research has increased globally while money from government and nonprofits has decreased. Corporate financing does not taint every study, but its influence can make it difficult to differentiate objective conclusions from biased ones and to pursue avenues of scientific inquiry without regard for any bottom line but the planet's.

Cooke was not the only big salmon farmer looking for a new location in Nova Scotia. Rising public opposition to salmon farms in British Columbia, coupled with the Liberal Party's pledge to phase out open-net farms there by 2025, left Mitsubishi Corporation's Cermaq subsidiary searching for more welcoming ground. The company had already pulled two British Columbia farms out of production and was reconsidering the future of six others when it began to look east. Unlike Cooke, the Japanese-owned company lacked a foothold in Nova Scotia, but it planned a big splash. In the spring of 2019, Cermaq received approval from the provincial government to explore locations for fifteen to twenty new farms along the province's coast. To sweeten its appeal, the company promised to invest five hundred million dollars in new wharves and in two fish-processing facilities in the province.

Cermaq's choice of potential sites left locals scratching their heads over the illogic. Several proposed locations were in two of eastern Canada's most beloved and picturesque spots, Mahone Bay and St. Margarets Bay. While Liverpool was a working-class community where Cooke already had a farm, St. Margarets Bay and Mahone Bay were home to influential business leaders from nearby Halifax and wealthy summer people from far away. Cermaq's plans for up to twenty farms raised eyebrows even among supporters of salmon farming like Grant. "Twenty fish farms are too many, even for me," Grant said. "To think you should put them in St. Margarets Bay, that's crazy."

Residents from distinctly different parts of Nova Scotia were confronting the same question: If salmon farming was being phased out in British Columbia and banned in Washington State, why should it be permitted to expand to Nova Scotia? The answer would come in the next few months, with Cermaq facing the initial interrogation from angry residents.

CHAPTER 22

"SHIT HAPPENS"

In Nova Scotia, a grassroots movement rose up to oppose Cooke's and Cermaq's expansions. Lobster fishers, housewives, teachers, shopkeepers, innkeepers, artists, and retirees attended public meetings to express their concern, sometimes in angry voices. They worried about their livelihoods, the health of their children, the views from their homes. Signs proclaiming "Save Our Bay! Say No to Open-Pen Fish Farms" dotted front yards and storefronts across the province.

In its counterattack, the industry resorted to its standard playbook. Susan Farquharson, the executive director of the pro-industry Atlantic Canada Fish Farmers Association, captured its corporate spirit in an opinion piece in the Halifax *Chronicle Herald*. In the article, she warned the public and politicians to ignore "the usual dump of misinformation by several small but vocal anti-fish farming activist groups." She accused opponents of promoting misinformation and engaging in fearmongering. "Stand up to these anti-salmon farming sentiments that are based on the politics of fear rather than the realities of science," she wrote.

Corporations and politicians like to make *activist* a dirty word. In his book *Blessed Unrest*, environmentalist Paul Hawken has a different definition, describing activists as "Earth's immune system." Cora Swinamer, who lives in St. Margarets Bay, did not like Farquharson's tone and responded with a guest column in the same newspaper a few days later. She described her job history in bank management and landscape design, "so others can establish whether I am a 'radical fear-mongering activist' or a level-headed citizen." She wrote that her father, a scientist who specialized in salmon with the federal DFO, had taught her to rely on facts and science. For a time, she had worked as an aquaculture researcher. Swinamer said she opposed salmon farms based on research about their impact on wild fish and lobsters and on their widespread use of pesticides and other chemicals. She said she had recently retired, and added, "I didn't think I was also an activist. I don't want to be—I'd much rather return to tending my garden, reading good books and planning my next sailing vacation."

Grassroots movements need someone to plant and tend the seeds. Syd Dumaresq runs an architecture firm in Halifax started by his great-grandfather in 1860. A first-time visitor to his office gets a tour of the "museum," as Dumaresq refers to the photographs of four generations of architects and their buildings lining the walls of the entry. *Halifax Magazine* described the Dumaresq clan as "the family that built this city." Dumaresq's passion for architecture is matched only by his determination to protect the waters of his native Nova Scotia. When he learned that Cermaq wanted to put salmon farms in Mahone Bay near Chester, the affluent sailing community where he lives, Dumaresq immediately telephoned a friend who had been a senior official in the provincial government.

"Don't worry," said the friend. "It's never gonna happen."

"It's gonna happen if we don't get off our butts," Dumaresq replied.

A few days later, he met with Geoff Le Boutillier, a filmmaker and environmental activist who lives on land along St. Margarets Bay occupied by his family since 1780. The two met at a coffee shop along the highway that connects St. Margarets Bay and Mahone Bay. Le Boutillier agreed that the fate of the Twin Bays could not be left to chance or to the government. Their strategy was two-pronged: First, they wanted to assemble a team of local activists and people with knowledge of aquaculture and marine environments to gather facts. Second, they wanted to use those facts to mobilize public opposition to Cermaq, particularly at the public meetings the company was required to hold across the province. The plotters organized under a catchy name, "the Twin Bays Coalition."

Mahone Bay and St. Margarets Bay are two of the wealthiest communities along Nova Scotia's five thousand miles of coast. To the south, Liverpool scrapes by economically, and Lunenburg maintains a working harbor and attracts tourists as a UNESCO World Heritage Site. But many who live in Mahone Bay and St. Margarets Bay are professionals who work in nearby Halifax. The area also has its share of wealthy retirees. Chester, a picturesque town on Mahone Bay, is a sailing mecca with a history of international regattas dating back more than a century. St. Margarets Bay is tucked between two peninsulas, and its shores are lined with large houses and small fishing communities. The best-known village is Peggy's Cove, whose iconic lighthouse is the most visited and photographed location in Canada. Nearby is a memorial to the 229 people who died on September 2, 1998, when Swissair Flight 111 crashed into the Atlantic at the entrance to the bay. Relatives of the victims who arrived in the days after the crash were so taken by the region's sympathy and hospitality that many bought homes there and stayed.

The communities provided the Twin Bays Coalition with recruits who had skills to accompany their commitment and contacts to get their views heard. Swinamer signed up, and so did lots of her neighbors. They were joined by fishers who had lived on the shores of the two bays for generations. The coalition built a professional website, established outreach to media, enlisted young people, and arranged financing to fight Cermaq. A mortgage banker who grew up in the area offered his expertise to raise money, but he got a call from his supervisor at the big bank where he worked. He was told he would have to withdraw from the coalition and stop working against Cermaq, a potential client. The banker weighed the risks and continued to help, though he did so anonymously.

Along with organizing the opposition, Dumaresq and Le Boutillier wanted to persuade the provincial government to take a skeptical approach to Cermaq's proposal. But they quickly wrote off changing the mind of Nova Scotia's fisheries and aquaculture minister, Keith Colwell. On a recent taxpayer-financed trip to visit salmon farms in Norway, Colwell had told the press that aquaculture would transform the economy of Nova Scotia the way oil had transformed Alberta. It was a claim quickly challenged by Wendy Watson Smith, president of a conservation group known as the Association for the Preservation of the Eastern Shore. "This shows you how far behind the times he is," Watson Smith wrote in a letter to a local publication. "The Alberta economy is in a slump due to its continued reliance on an outdated, dirty, environmentally destructive industry. That is the only way that open

pen fish farming can be compared to the Alberta Oil Industry." In giving Cermaq permission to explore up to twenty farm sites, Colwell had also praised the company as a model of respect for communities and the environment; he would clearly not be the savior of the Twin Bays. As a workaround for getting the government's ear, Dumaresq and Le Boutillier arranged for fourteen business leaders to make their case to Stephen McNeil, the premier of the province.

There was good reason to be skeptical of the Nova Scotia government. Public anger after outbreaks of ISA at Cooke's salmon farms in Shelburne and Liverpool Bay and government reimbursements to them had led to a moratorium on new fish farms in 2013. The province created an independent panel to make recommendations for new regulations before the moratorium could be lifted. The review was led by two environmental law professors from Dalhousie University, Meinhard Doelle and Bill Lahey. They conducted public hearings in twenty-one coastal communities over eighteen months, listening to a range of complaints about the damage caused by salmon farms and the government's bias toward the industry and its support for the economic benefits and jobs the industry brought to the province.

The industry's biggest fear was that the panel would recommend a permanent ban like the one in Washington State. The chance that the provincial government would accept such a harsh action was zero, but even raising the possibility could inflame public opposition to the farms. The panel's report did not go that far and, instead, proposed regulatory changes to restore public trust and the industry's credibility. A key recommendation was to take authority for protecting the ocean away from Nova Scotia's Department of Fisheries and Aquaculture and transfer it to the provincial Department of Environment, the same proposal to separate promotion and protection that the Cohen Commission had recommended to the federal government years earlier. The report also recommended establishing a science-based system of zones to determine which parts of the coast were suitable for salmon farms, akin to the green, yellow, and red zones used in Norway to tether production to levels of sea lice. When evaluating applications for licenses and when setting terms on new licenses, the Nova Scotia system would prioritize the standards dictated by biology and marine science. Finally, Doelle and Lahey proposed a permanent regulatory advisory committee representing First Nations people, coastal communities, the aquaculture industry, and environmental groups to monitor future regulation of salmon farming.

The provincial government was not willing to give up any power. The panel's recommendation of a zone system was rejected, as was the proposal to separate protection from promotion. When it came to giving the public a voice, the government said companies would be required to conduct public hearings in locations where they proposed new farms. But in a bizarre twist that amounted to encouraging censorship, the companies would be allowed to decide which public comments were passed on to the government for consideration in the licensing process. Final decisions on licenses would rest with a new body, the Aquaculture Review Board, comprised of three members appointed by the fisheries minister, Keith Colwell at the time.

The response of Nova Scotia's government to the panel's recommendations made rather plain its primary allegiance. The industry was happy. The moratorium was lifted. Environmental groups were unhappy. Their main criticism focused on the refusal to adopt the traffic light system. As the Halifax-based Ecology Action Centre argued, allowing the government to decide on a case-by-case basis amounted to creating only green zones.

Cermaq called its mandatory public hearings "Hello Nova Scotia," and the first road show was in early 2020, in Digby, a community on the province's southwestern coast, famous for its scallops and high-quality lobsters. Cooke Aquaculture already operated two salmon farms near Digby, in St. Mary's Bay, on the Nova Scotia shore of the Bay of Fundy. Lobster fishers had long complained that debris from the farms fouled their gear, and residents objected to the odor and sight of the farms. A few years earlier, an empty pen was found floating free in the bay. Cooke blamed vandals, but critics chalked it up to poor maintenance.

Halfway through the inaugural meeting, local resident Shirley Langpohl raised previous problems with Cooke farms when she addressed the Cermaq representatives: "You have just met people who have a vested, long-term interest here. We live here. It's our community. We want you to understand we didn't invite you here. We love our fishing industry and our community, and St. Mary's Bay is an environmental nightmare with you. One broken cage and we have a horror. We want you to go." Another local worried about the risks that "dead zones" around the farms posed to lobster and scallops, the big moneymakers in the bay and surrounding waters. Linda Sams, Cermaq's director of sustainable development, said the industry does not call them dead zones. They are "areas of impact," she said. "If you're farming properly and managing your impact," she said, "you should be able to predict how big it is, and usually the farthest we see it is about one hundred meters from cage out, and it is reversible." Sams tried to be reassuring, saying only about half of Cermaq's proposed farms would operate at any given time, lessening the environmental impact.

Two weeks after the initial session, a noisy crowd filled the municipal council chambers in Digby. Most had come to support a councilor's motion to oppose Cermaq's plans. The official debate was marked by interruptions and occasional shouts. When a council member said the region needed the jobs that Cermaq promised, the comment was met with loud groans. In the end, the council voted 3–2 to oppose Cermaq's plans. The vote was purely symbolic, but it reflected the sentiment growing across the province.

As Cermaq prepared for a round of public meetings on the other side of Nova Scotia, the Twin Bays Coalition organized an information session to rally the opposition before the company began its mandatory public hearings. More than three hundred people showed up at the Twin Bays meeting on March 1, 2020, a Sunday evening, to hear three environmental leaders from British Columbia recount their struggles with Cermaq and other big salmon farmers. The speakers described sharp declines in wild salmon populations after fish farms arrived, saying the farms spread disease and used pesticides and other chemicals that damaged marine life. Rather than an economic boom, only between fifty and one hundred people were employed at Cermaq's fourteen sites in British Columbia's Clayoquot Sound. Public opposition had persuaded the British Columbia government to consider phasing out salmon farms as neighboring Washington State had done. "That's why they are headed your way," Bob Chamberlin, the chief of Kwakwaka'wakw, one of the First Nations in British Columbia, told the audience.

The drumbeat of public criticism continued the next night, when about three hundred people gathered in nearby Chester, the affluent community on Mahone Bay and home to Syd Dumaresq and other leaders of the Twin Bays

Coalition, for the first official "Hello Nova Scotia" session on the province's Eastern Shore. Some of the initial questions to David Kiemele, the managing director for Cermaq's Canadian operations, focused on the potential ban on open-net salmon farming in British Columbia as a reason for the company's plan to move to Nova Scotia. Kiemele downplayed prospects for the ban, blaming the concept on the silly politics of an election season. He had a tougher time when a member of the audience rose to his feet and questioned the high mortality rates for farmed salmon. "You want to raise fish here so they can all die?" the person asked. "With climate change, what do you think you're going to do in this province? You're going to raise fish? No, you're going to kill fish."

Kiemele replied, "Mortality happens on salmon farms. We have a dedicated team of professionals, but shit happens. It's farming. It's not easy."

Criticizing politicians was one thing. A flip response about the deaths of salmon in a community where many earned their living from the ocean was another. Julie Chiasson, who comes from a fishing family in Mahone Bay, took Kiemele to task. "I came here tonight with an open mind to hear how you would respond to what you did in those areas and to hear, quite frankly, that 'shit happens' is not really fair to the people in this room who make their livelihood from fishing," she told him. "We are a working shoreline. We have fishermen that make their livelihood off our coast, and we really need to know how you are going to assure us that when this 'shit happens' that you have a process in place, that you have done your due diligence to make sure that you can handle that so we can protect our fishing rights."

Kiemele apologized, saying his language was inappropriate and assuring the audience that Cermaq was working to reduce risks to its fish and to the environment.

The tone was much the same the following night, when "Hello Nova Scotia" moved to the firehouse in the fishing community of Blandford, which sits on a peninsula jutting into the Atlantic Ocean between St. Margarets Bay and Mahone Bay. The parking lot was jammed with pickup trucks and SUVs. Inside, nearly three hundred people sat solemnly on folding chairs and stood shoulder to shoulder along the walls. A table of snacks and coffee, normally a magnet at community gatherings, remained untouched. At the front of the hall, Kiemele and a half dozen other Cermaq employees milled about as they waited to start the meeting. Cermaq wanted the meeting to focus on the benefits of salmon farming in order to open the door for the company's expansion to the province's Eastern Shore, but the session soon went sideways.

Kiemele kicked off the proceedings with an upbeat description of Cermaq's plans to create new jobs and work with people to find the right path forward. He said Cermaq wanted to add a new chapter to the iconic seafood story of Nova Scotia, touting what he called the company's successful operations in British Columbia. Missing were maps and charts that could have showed where the company proposed to locate its farms. Kiemele explained that teams were still evaluating tides, currents, and water depths to identify the best locations.

Emotions were running high among an audience dominated by lobster fishers and other local residents. Some of them had attended the earlier information meeting, and the warnings from Chamberlin and his colleagues had left a strong impression. When the floor was opened for questions, a man said he was surprised to hear Kiemele list Cermaq's experience in British Columbia as a good example. He pointed out that scientists had linked declines in wild salmon populations there to diseases spread from farms run by Cermaq and other big companies. Kiemele replied that the impact on wild fish was an area where science came down on both sides of the issue. The industry, Kiemele said, was a scapegoat for broader issues endangering wild salmon, and he bemoaned the public's lack of trust in Cermaq.

A woman raised her hand and got the microphone. "Is it true that Cermaq received an emergency permit to use a new insecticide on their farms in Clayoquot Sound, one that's not approved for use in Canada?" she asked, returning to a topic that had been discussed at the session two nights before. "And that this chemical is so toxic that you cannot eat fish for three hundred and fifty days after the fish has been treated?"

The question left no room for Kiemele to hedge. The environmentalist contingent from British Columbia had shared government records showing that Cermaq had received official permission to apply the chemical, called lufenuron, at three of its farms. Kiemele acknowledged that Cermaq had used lufenuron with government approval, but he said that this did not mean the fish were unsafe for human consumption.

The records told a different story. Almost two years before, in April 2018, Cermaq had applied for and received approval to mix lufenuron with feed for its salmon, to treat sea lice infestations at three sites. The company said the powerful chemical was necessary because parasites had developed resistance to its usual pesticide. Contrary to Kiemele's strong claim that the fish were definitely safe for humans, the emergency approval from Health Canada said the government had not evaluated the safety of the pesticide and specified that no fish treated with lufenuron should be consumed by humans for at least 350 days. Like cypermethrin, the banned chemical used by Cooke in the Bay of Fundy two decades earlier, lufenuron is particularly lethal to crustaceans like lice but also to lobsters, shrimp, and crabs. Because of its risks, lufenuron is not approved for use in Norway, Cermaq's home country.

Speaker after speaker denounced the company and its plans. One man did not want the noise of farm generators ruining the quiet of his oceanfront home. Another reprised a familiar refrain in demanding to know why salmon farms were good for St. Margarets Bay and Mahone Bay if they were being shunned in British Columbia and banned in Washington State.

Vincent Boutilier, a lobster boat captain who had spent forty years fishing the waters of St. Margarets Bay, stood and said forcefully, "We don't want you here. Go home." Before the applause died down, another man grabbed the microphone and asked, "Does anyone in this hall want Cermaq here? Raise your hand if you do." Not a single hand went up, though the sound of many hands clapping resounded through the hall. The Cermaq contingency sat in stony silence.

Boutilier got the microphone back and offered Cermaq a deal: open its farms on land, instead of in the ocean. If they did that, Boutilier promised to rally lobster fishers to support the company. Kiemele dismissed the idea, saying it was economically impractical, the same position held by all the big companies operating salmon farms on oceans around the world.

As the meeting neared the two-hour mark, a lobster fisherman sitting near the back of the room rose, got the microphone, and addressed Kiemele. "You should know that bad things happen here to people who are unwelcome," he said. "Their boats burn. Their wharves float away."

The remark was met with uneasy silence. There was history behind the thinly veiled threat. In 1983, a hundred lobster fishers angry over enforcement practices chased, burned, and sank two patrol boats belonging to the federal Department of Fisheries and Oceans in Shelburne. In 2017, two lobster boats belonging to First Nations fishers were set ablaze as part of tensions with non–First Nations fishers about lobster-fishing rights.

There was no realistic way the meeting could continue after that comment. People grumbled and shook their heads as they filed out of the firehouse. The table of cookies and coffee was still untouched.

As one woman reached the exit, a local hired by Cermaq rushed over to her, apologized for the tone of the meeting, and said she hoped these differences would not affect their friendship. The woman looked at her and said, "We're not friends anymore."

The next day, Cermaq posted its assessment of the Blandford meeting and two previous sessions on its Facebook page. "We have been meeting with residents of Mahone and St. Margarets Bays this week and would like to thank everyone who has attended. We have heard a mix of support and vocal opposition, and we will continue to reach out and engage in the coming weeks." But the post went on to announce that an upcoming meeting had been canceled. Cermaq appeared to have heard enough. Its next step was expected to be a hearing on its final applications before the Aquaculture Review Board.

A month after the fiasco in Blandford, Cermaq waved a white flag. The company said in a press release that it could not find enough suitable locations for its salmon farms in Nova Scotia and that it was withdrawing all licensing applications. It would not be coming to Nova Scotia. In a nod to public opposition, Sams, the sustainable development director, acknowledged that the company had been unable to convince some groups and parts of the province that its presence would help the existing commercial fishing business. The company said it would close its local office and allow its lease options to expire. Aquaculture experts scoffed at Cermaq's claim that there were not enough suitable locations. The company had gotten the message that it was not wanted. "Hello Nova Scotia" had turned into "Goodbye Nova Scotia."

Syd Dumaresq was euphoric. "It's a total victory for Mahone Bay and St. Margarets Bay," he said later in his Halifax office. "They picked the wrong place. No salmon-farming company will ever come to Mahone Bay or St. Margarets Bay now."

But Cooke Aquaculture was not going away. The day Cermaq announced that it was withdrawing, Cooke said it had no intention of pulling out. The fight was moving south along the shoreline, to Liverpool Bay. Dumaresq thought stopping Cooke would be harder, because the company already operated salmon farms in Nova Scotia, but the Twin Bays Coalition and other opponents were ready to join their compatriots down the coast. In Liverpool

Bay, opposition to Cooke's expansion had galvanized a population that normally would have cheered any project that promised jobs. A broad collection of residents, local businesspeople, and fishers had created an opposition group, the Protect Liverpool Bay Association. The county Chamber of Commerce voted unanimously to oppose the expansion, and the municipal council voted 5–3 against Cooke's plans. Both votes were symbolic, but they reflected growing public opposition.

Still, Cooke remained committed to testing exactly how friendly local waters might be.

PART III

THE NEXT WAR

CHAPTER 23

SAVING WILD SALMON

Graham Chafe reached down to pull the Atlantic salmon out of the net gently. The fish had navigated many miles to arrive at the point where the Magaguadavic River flows into the Bay of Fundy in southwestern New Brunswick. From that estuary, the fish traveled up the gorge to a concrete fish ladder. Swimming and leaping nearly seventy feet up a series of low steps, the salmon reached the end of its journey: a metal trap submerged in the water. The trap was part of a rudimentary fish-monitoring station tucked beneath the dam on the Magaguadavic at the town of St. George. As Chafe examined the fish, the question was whether this was the end of its journey or a temporary stopover.

Chafe, a tall, balding biologist with the Atlantic Salmon Federation, had arrived at the monitoring station that morning to find the thirty-inch-long salmon moving listlessly in the trap. He triggered the electric hoist that brought the cage up ten feet to the metal grate that formed the floor of the station and caught the fish in a net at the end of a long pole. Cradling it in his bare hands, Chafe next had to determine whether the salmon was a fugitive from one of the one hundred or so salmon farms in the Bay of Fundy or a much rarer visitor, a wild salmon.

The Magaguadavic once teemed with wild salmon, but the numbers had been dropping steadily for decades. The story has been repeated in rivers and streams across Atlantic Canada and the northeastern United States. The number of returning wild Atlantic salmon had been in decline since the 1950s as a result of pesticide spraying and loss of habitat to the timber industry. The arrival of salmon farms in the Bay of Fundy was another blow to the population.

By 1983, a paltry nine hundred wild salmon entered the Magaguadavic to spawn, and the number has declined almost every year since, as the number of farmed salmon has increased. Today, for all practical purposes, wild salmon have disappeared on the Magaguadavic. None arrived in 2017; one in 2018; two in 2019; one in 2020. Instead of finding wild salmon in the traps, Chafe now finds escapees from farms in the bay, which contain about five million salmon. No one knows whether the arrivals from the farms are following some inbred homing instinct to return to their river of origin, despite being raised from eggs in hatcheries, or if they're simply arriving by chance.

Chafe examined the overnight guest for clues about its origins. The fins were damaged, and a dozen sea lice were attached to its skin, despite the climb through freshwater, which should have knocked them off. All signs pointed to an escapee. Taking a pair of tweezers, Chafe plucked a scale off the fish, put it on a glass slide, and carried it to an old-fashioned microfiche machine on a table attached to the wall. (Chafe laughed about the microfiche machine, explaining that university students who visit the station have never seen one before.) Pushing the slide under the machine's magnifying lens, he confirmed his hunch: the scale displayed the concentric growth circles unique to a farmed fish. Uniform concentric rings signify a fish that has been fed constantly and grown consistently at a farm. Rings on wild salmon vary in shape and distance, reflecting variations in the diet of a fish that forages for food, the way tree rings tell us about the life of the tree. "The key is the scales, which are like fingerprints," said Chafe.

Chafe would have taken a prized wild salmon to the other side of the dam and released it into the river to resume its migration. Based on the evidence presented by its scales, though, the farmed fish faced a death sentence. Chafe dropped the salmon into an ice chest half full of water. His assistant, Ellen Mansfield, put a few drops of clove oil into the water to sedate the salmon. Once it was quiet, Chafe lifted it out and gave it a single smack on the head with a wooden club. Mansfield was new to the job, and she winced. Chafe explained that it was important to kill the fish humanely, with a single, sharp blow. The dead fish was measured and weighed. A tissue sample was taken and placed in a small plastic bag to go with the scale and sea lice that had been scraped off the fish. The bag would be sent to a laboratory where tests would determine whether the fish carried any diseases. The results would be fed into a national survey being conducted by Dr. Kristi Miller-Saunders at the

DFO lab in British Columbia. Early results from her survey found that escapees from the farms in the Bay of Fundy carried a strain of piscine orthoreovirus associated with pathological conditions like heart and skeletal inflammation. The virus was the same strain of PRV discovered in salmon that escaped from the Cooke farm in Puget Sound in 2017. Miller-Saunders had also identified the variant in British Columbia waters, and her study was trying to determine the extent of risk from PRV to wild salmon.

The virus was one more danger to add to the list of possible threats to wild salmon. Studies by the Atlantic Salmon Federation and the Department of Fisheries and Oceans found that interbreeding between farmed salmon and wild fish in the rivers feeding the Bay of Fundy contributed to the wild population collapse. Studies have found that hybrid offspring are less able to survive in the wild and that the interbreeding constitutes genetic pollution that reduces the evolutionary fitness of the already declining wild population. In 2014, the DFO declared salmon farms a "marine threat of high concern" to wild salmon, which are classified as endangered in the bay. Similar findings have been documented in every other country where salmon farms are located near wild salmon migration routes. Conservationists contend that timely notice of escapes is essential to reducing the risk to wild salmon, particularly in spawning season, when the migrating fish are passing salmon farms. The Atlantic Salmon Federation has said that no new salmon farms should be allowed in proximity to wild salmon rivers anywhere in North America. Industry representatives contend that aquaculture is unfairly blamed for the demise of wild salmon.

The full scope of escaped salmon in the Bay of Fundy is unknown. Cooke Aquaculture dominates salmon farming there, but Mowi and other companies operate farms in the bay, too. New Brunswick law requires companies to report escapes only when more than one hundred fish have been lost. The reports are treated as confidential by the government, and the information can be released only with the consent of the companies, raising the obvious question: What good are the numbers if they are not shared with the public so that the extent of the problem can be understood?

When doing an autopsy on wild salmon populations, there is plenty of blame to go around. In his elegant book *King of Fish*, David R. Montgomery offered a web of responsibility: "Not surprisingly, there is no shortage of finger-pointing: Land developers blame the fishing industry. Fishermen blame the timber industry. Loggers blame land developers. Everybody except dry-land farmers blames the dams." Since Montgomery, a professor at the University of Washington, published his book, in 2003, two significant new threats have been added to the list: the climate crisis and the proliferation of open-net farms. Unfortunately, the risks are linked, and the effects are cumulative.

Climate change has created a cascade of threats to salmon and their habitats. More than 90 percent of global warming over the past fifty years has occurred in the oceans. Increased ocean temperatures raise the temperature of freshwater rivers and streams where salmon spawn and spend their early life. Oxygen levels decline in warmer water, weakening the salmon and making them more susceptible to predators and to parasites and diseases spread by open-net farms. Sea lice and many viruses thrive in warmer water, resulting in a double whammy for wild salmon. Warming oceans also send predators like killer whales, seals, and sea lions north in search of cooler climes, increasing risks to salmon and other cold-water fish. Global warming reduces snowpacks, causing glaciers to retreat and starving rivers and streams of water. Lower water levels make it harder for salmon to travel and survive in warmer temperatures. From New England and Atlantic Canada to Norway and the United Kingdom, researchers have documented the connection between the climate crisis, aquaculture, and the disappearance of wild salmon.

To understand decades of human impact on wild salmon, and find a glimmer of hope, drive three hours north from the St. George Dam on New Brunswick Highway 8 and turn left onto Howard Road. A few miles down the narrow blacktop, turn left again at the small hand-lettered sign that reads, "Curtis Camp." Follow the dirt lane a couple hundred yards to a cluster of cabins. Step out of your car, and you'll encounter the broad, mystical beauty of the Miramichi River, a legendary waterway known in eastern Canada as the mother of all salmon rivers.

Baseball Hall of Famer Ted Williams had a fishing lodge on the banks of the Miramichi. So did Pennsylvania's Hershey family, of chocolate fame, and many other wealthy anglers from the United States and Canada. They were drawn by the beauty of the river and the size of the Atlantic salmon, which reached thirty pounds or more. The halcyon days of the Miramichi are long gone, and the Hershey camp is in disrepair, but the magnetic pull of the river and its small population of salmon remains.

No one understands the river's cycles better than the man who lives at the end of lane. Jason Curtis is the seventh generation of his family to make his home and his living as a fishing guide on the Miramichi. His house sits on a rise, with a screened porch overlooking the water and a dock extending out fifteen feet. His father, guide turned novelist Wayne Curtis, lives in a cabin on one side of Jason's home. An uncle and a brother have cabins on the other side of Jason's. For 150 years, this has been Curtis family land, a thousand feet of riverfront and the river itself. Under an old legal concept known as "riparian rights," along with the land, the family owns the rights to the surface water out to the center of the river. Others can drift by in their boats, and a few cast a fly, but they cannot stop to fish or swim.

Jason Curtis remembers fly-fishing for salmon on the Miramichi from the time he was old enough to hold a rod. The sport that has bedeviled anglers for centuries is second nature to the Curtis clan. "The river was a playground," Curtis recalled. "It never used to be a big deal to catch a fish. We'd get one or two and consider it a bad outing." His father, Wayne, remembers salmon fishing as a way of life, long before he became a writer. "In my time," he said, "we caught them with fishing rods after school. We would anchor a canoe in the middle of the river and cast both ways and hook a salmon on the fly. Each of us would walk up the hill with a salmon. My grandfather would salt them. The river was like a garden."

By the mid-1970s, the number of fish had dropped so low that Wayne Curtis told his three sons they would have to start releasing the salmon they caught in order to maintain the population. The seemingly infinite supply of wild salmon had been declining steadily for years. Wayne, who was born in 1943, was old enough to remember the beginning of the end. "I remember the spraying of DDT," he said. "They always sprayed early in the morning, when there was no wind. We could smell it through our windows. They used old World War II planes. You could see the spray. There was an old airstrip near the river, and they hired a crew of pilots to spray."

No one set out to destroy the salmon in the Miramichi or a hundred other rivers and streams from eastern Canada to New England. They were victims of ignorance and greed, collateral damage in a giant effort to protect valuable timberland from pests. Dichlorodiphenyltrichloroethane, commonly known as DDT, was used widely from the 1940s to the 1960s to combat budworms, caterpillars, and other insects threatening the softwood forests. DDT was the first synthetic pesticide invented after World War II, hailed as a breakthrough in the fight against bugs that brought Swiss chemist Paul Hermann Müller the 1948 Nobel Prize for Physiology or Medicine.

The environmental damage caused by DDT was obvious immediately. The extensive, indiscriminate spaying of millions of acres did kill the insects that threatened the timberland. But it also poisoned fish and birds by the millions and contaminated the environment with a chemical that would remain for decades. Governments knew about the risk to fish and wildlife, but they chose to save trees instead. A paper published in February 1959 by the Canadian Department of Fisheries and Oceans described the trade-off this way: "When spraying presents the only means of protecting a forest from serious loss it becomes necessary to use it." The airstrip Wayne Curtis remembered was dubbed "Budworm City," and its planes made hundreds of flights.

Rachel Carson exposed the dangers of DDT in 1962 in her book *Silent Spring*. One of Carson's prime examples was the near elimination of salmon on the Miramichi River. In the book, she describes the journey of the Atlantic salmon to their spawning grounds along the Miramichi, which she calls "one of the finest salmon streams in North America." Carson recounts how the spraying killed young salmon and trout immediately and sealed the fate of succeeding generations by wiping out the insects on which the fish depended for food. She describes similar effects on salmon runs in Maine where fish blinded by DDT were so disoriented that they could be grabbed from the water by hand. By the time *Silent Spring* was published, salmon runs throughout eastern Canada and New England were in sharp decline. The United States and Canada banned DDT in 1972, but the damage had been done. And some countries still use the pesticide.

When Jason Curtis graduated from high school in 1988, he went to work as a guide and a fish camp manager on the Miramichi. That is why he knows the river by heart. From the stern of his motorized wooden canoe, Curtis pointed out where wild salmon still lurk, the deep pools where they search for cool water, the boulders where they rest just below the surface of the rapidly moving water. He slowed the canoe beside a collection of boulders forming a pool in the middle of the river between his property and land on the opposite side owned by his friend, Brad Burns, an American writer and salmon activist. Curtis and Burns had hired a hydrologist to help construct the pool to provide a resting spot for the salmon and a fishing spot for them. The expert told them exactly where to place the boulders and what size they should be to form the optimal attraction for wary salmon. The boulders, which just reach the surface of the river, were large enough to slow the current to give the salmon a resting spot in their trip upstream. Curtis had gone to a quarry to pick out each boulder and then placed them according to the design. "Rocks that work work all the time," he said.

Farther along the river, the canoe passed a collection of wooden buildings in disrepair, the once-thriving fish camp built by the Hersheys. Other Americans own the place now, but they rarely visit because there are so few salmon, a fact of life that has led to a sharp drop in visiting anglers over the past two decades. Some anglers have stopped fly-fishing for salmon completely because of concerns that the fish can be damaged in the process of being released. Passing a lone fisherman, Curtis cut the canoe's motor and called out, "How's it going?" The man shrugged. "He hopes," Curtis said quietly. "You come out and fish, and you hope for a miracle."

Water levels were so low in many stretches of the river that Curtis got out and dragged the canoe over shallow spots. He has installed Kevlar on the bottom to avoid damage from the rocky riverbed. A few hundred yards beyond the lone fisherman, Curtis anchored at the Black Brook pool, one of the most famous fishing spots on the Miramichi. Cold water from the spring-fed Black Brook flows into the river, creating a natural cooling-off spot for salmon seeking respite from warm water in the shallows. Dozens of salmon were visible, idling near the bottom of the pool. Occasionally, one broke the surface and jumped into the air. Three young men in waders eagerly cast their flies into the pool, but the fish showed no interest. The serenity is seldom disturbed by anyone catching anything.

Theories abound as to why salmon jump, ranging from practicing to get over obstacles in the river to genetics. Robin Barefield, a fishing and hunting guide in Alaska who has a master's degree in fish and wildlife biology, speculates that the fish would not make it to their spawning grounds if they couldn't jump. But she concedes, "The correct answer to the question 'Why do salmon jump?' is 'No one knows.'"

Conservationists have tried to battle the impact of global warming on the Miramichi by constructing pools like the one in front of Curtis's house that provide relief from the rising temperatures. Conservation efforts along the river have had some success, drawing a few hundred wild salmon back each fall to spawn. But it is a fraction of the historic salmon runs, and Wayne Curtis worries that Jason will be the last Curtis to earn a living on the Miramichi. Jason is more optimistic. "We certainly have enough fish in our river to sustain and build a population of wild salmon," Curtis said as he pulled the canoe alongside his dock. "The stock is in there. We just have to control other factors."

CHAPTER 24

PRESERVATION ON THE PENOBSCOT

One of the largest and most innovative efforts to save wild salmon unfolded over sixteen years on the Penobscot River in Maine. The river, named for the Penobscot Nation, whose members have lived by its waters for thousands of years, runs for more than one hundred miles from the mountains of northern Maine to the Gulf of Maine on the Atlantic Ocean. Two hundred years ago, there were no dams or industry on the river, and one hundred thousand or more Atlantic salmon swam upstream every year to spawn in the river and its tributaries. Millions of shad, river herring, and other sea-run fish that lived both in freshwater and in the ocean came to the river.

Beginning in the 1830s, paper mills and other factories were constructed along the river as the Industrial Revolution took root in the United States. The mills and textile factories needed power, and Maine's rivers offered ample water to generate it. Dams on the Penobscot prevented salmon from reaching their spawning grounds. In the early days, fish died of exhaustion because they could not get past the dams. The numbers were so large that newspapers were filled with stories about the smell of the decaying corpses. Water quality deteriorated as factories and towns dumped waste into the Penobscot and the streams that fed the river, and clear-cut logging damaged the overall habitat. Eventually the fish stopped coming.

Maine prospered in the industrial age; its fish did not. By the early twenty-first century, the number of returning fish had dwindled to almost nothing. The federal government took the obvious step of placing Atlantic salmon on the Endangered Species List, bringing salmon fishing to a halt on Maine's rivers and streams. The last major salmon-fishing grounds in the northeast-ern United States were closed.

Alarmed by the decline and fearing the end of wild salmon and other sea-run fish in New England, a consortium of six conservation groups formed the Penobscot River Restoration Trust in 1999. The consortium comprised American Rivers, the Atlantic Salmon Federation, the Audubon Society, Trout Unlimited, the Natural Resources Council of Maine, and the Nature Conservancy's chapter in Maine, which was started in 1956 by Rachel Carson. The consortium joined the Penobscot Nation and state and federal agencies to unplug the river in the hope that the fish would retrace the routes imprinted in their DNA. The trust's goal was to purchase and remove those dams whose elimination was deemed most essential for opening the river and its tributaries. A free-flowing river could bring salmon and other fish back to their historic habitat and create economic and recreational opportunities for local communities. For the Penobscot Nation, the project offered a chance to restore cultural traditions tied to the spiritual and physical well-being of its members. After identifying three dams for removal, the group faced three tough tasks: convincing Pennsylvania Power and Light to sell the dams, raising the money to buy them, and persuading political leaders and residents that it was a good idea.

Early negotiations were tedious, revolving around how much the dams were worth, how the payments would be structured, and what additional benefits the hydroelectric company would get in return for selling the dams. The company put a high price tag on the dams and also demanded that the state allow it to generate more electricity from other dams to compensate for the loss. When it came to residents along the river, consortium members held public meetings and went door-to-door to explain the benefits and to try to overcome fears of what might be lost. It was an exercise in graceful grassroots development.

"When peoples' fears came up around the project, we needed to determine whether they were founded and if so, how best to address them," Laura Rose Day, the director of the restoration project, said in *From the Mountains to the Sea*, a collection of nonfiction stories about the years-long effort. In trying to persuade people to accept the removal of the dams, Rose Day and other leaders framed the project as a greater good.

One of the residents who was concerned was Barbara Leonard, whose home overlooked the Veazie Dam, which was slated for removal as part of the project. Shortly after the project was announced, Rose Day found herself sitting at Leonard's kitchen table looking through a big window at the dam, which was twenty feet high and stretched one thousand feet across the Penobscot. Leonard served Rose Day lemonade and cookies and then nodded toward the dam. "Do you know what my grandkids call that?" she said. "'Grandma's Waterfall.'"

Rose Day said there was no reason for Leonard to support the project, because she liked things the way they were. But Rose Day explained to her that the dam's removal would help open a thousand miles of rivers and streams to salmon, herring, and other fish and bring new recreational opportunities to Veazie, a small town southwest of Bangor. A few years later, Rose Day received a donation to the project on behalf of Leonard's grandson. A note said the donation was a Christmas gift from his grandmother. "When you listen to people, you can move out of an 'us against them' mindset," Rose Day said. "I believe most people who disagreed with us respected us. I never said no to anyone who wanted to talk about the project. I treated people the way I'd treat my neighbors."

Talks with the hydro company and local businesses and political leaders dragged on. The then governor, Angus King, opposed the project because of worries about the loss of power from the dams, which are regarded as a clean, renewable energy source. Months into sometimes-contentious talks, negotiations had stalled. The logjam was broken by an incident that assumed the status of legend in the annals of the restoration.

John Banks, the natural resources director for the Penobscot Nation, and Laura Rose Day were the two lead negotiators for the consortium. "We were at an impasse with all these government lawyers, NGO attorneys, and businesspeople," Banks told *Maine* magazine. Banks tried to focus the debate on the river, not the people at the negotiating table. He asked for some time, unwrapped an eagle feather, and walked behind each person. Recalling the existence of the eagle and the salmon in the river for millennia, he said, "We are their voice." The episode was a turning point, one that changed the perspective of the participants and contributed to the need for cooperation to reach a settlement that would protect the river.

The agreement required the trust to pay the hydroelectric company $25 million in compensation for the removal of the Veazie Dam and Great Works

Dam and for the right to build a bypass channel that mimicked a salmon stream to allow the fish to swim around the Howland Dam, farther upstream. The consortium raised money from the public and from the National Oceanic and Atmospheric Administration, allowing construction crews to begin dismantling the dams in 2012. The channel at the Howland Dam was designed as a natural-seeming passive stream to allow salmon and other species of fish to travel upstream and downstream without encountering the dam. The channel was finished in 2015. By the time the final phase was completed, the price tag had reached $62 million. Thousands of miles of spawning habitat were reconnected to the Penobscot River for the first time in nearly two centuries.

The project won international acclaim and became a model for river restoration. Along with opening the Penobscot to fish, the work restored critical ecological functions that have allowed native plants, birds, and animals to flourish. Barbara Leonard told the Nature Conservancy that her grandchildren love to see the eagles, ospreys, and fish that have returned to what used to be "Grandma's Waterfall."

The return of wild Atlantic salmon has been slow but promising. In 2014, only 240 Atlantic salmon were counted on the Penobscot. By 2019, the consortium counted 1,076 salmon on the river; in 2020, the number had risen to 1,603. Despite being far lower than the historic runs, these returns still represent the largest Atlantic salmon run in the United States and a glimmer of hope. To monitor the progress, radio tags were attached to some salmon so they could be tracked through their ocean migration and return to the Penobscot. The tags tracked salmon exploring deeper into the newly opened rivers, scouting for new spawning locations in response to damage to their traditional habitats. River herring, a term that covers the alewife and blueback herring, have also returned in far greater numbers, with nearly 3 million counted in the most recent spring migration. The small, oily fish are a boon to the ecosystem because they are eaten by birds and because they protect salmon by providing alternate prey for predators. Another promising sign is the return of the sea lamprey, a primitive, eel-like fish considered by some to be an invasive parasite but which has a beneficial effect on the salmon population. Joshua Royte, an ecologist and senior scientist with the Nature Conservancy in Maine, said the lamprey are modifying streams with their nest building in ways that make the streams more hospitable to salmon spawning.

For the last few years, Royte has been monitoring the returning fish and the creation of new habitats across the one thousand miles of rivers and streams now open to them. He praised the restoration but called the results a qualified success to this point. Even with the new, improved route, the young salmon returning to the ocean still face a gauntlet of predators and, as they pass salmon farms, large groups of sea lice before they can start the long journey to feeding grounds off the western coast of Greenland. Despite the concerns, Royte and his colleagues remain hopeful that more salmon will return in response to the salmon scouts that have headed upriver in search of new spawning grounds.

What happens in the Atlantic waters off western Greenland plays a role in determining the ultimate success of the Penobscot's restoration in Maine, two thousand miles away. For thousands of years, Atlantic salmon have followed deep ancestral instincts and left the rivers and streams of North America and Europe for parts unknown. After two to four years, the fish return to their rivers of origin, where they spawn and create a new generation. There was magic and mystery to the migration that added to the romance of the salmon. In the 1950s, the mystery was solved when huge schools of Atlantic salmon were discovered off the western coast of Greenland, feeding on capelin, squid, and shrimp. The discovery proved to be a monumental disaster for the salmon.

Greenland is the world's largest island, about half the size of all Europe, and home to fewer than sixty thousand people. In 1960, the Danish administration in Greenland opened an intensive commercial fishery for Atlantic salmon. A thousand metric tons of salmon were caught in 1966, compared with only two tons in 1957. The harvest led directly to a sharp decline in the number of salmon returning to rivers in the United States, Canada, Britain, and Europe. In December 1968, the British House of Lords engaged in a lively debate on the need for an international solution to restrict the salmon harvest off Greenland. Part of the focus was on the use of drift nets by commercial fishing boats from Greenland, Norway, and Denmark to scoop up thousands of salmon as small as two pounds in a single sweep of the ocean and on the corresponding reduction in returning salmon. "Meanwhile, my Lords, the tide flows strongly towards a final extinction of Atlantic salmon in a few years," warned Harold Balfour, the Lord of Inchrye. "When that happens, those in charge of our affairs at that time will say, 'How did this ever occur? Why was it not stopped before?' But it will be too late then."

No agreement was reached, and the harvest peaked in 1971 at more than 2,700 metric tons, the equivalent of about 810,000 fish. Salmon returns continued to drop sharply in the United Kingdom, Norway, and other European countries. But the decline was most acute in New England and in Canada's Bay of Fundy, where wild populations had already been pushed to the brink by decades of dam building and pollution. By 1990, the number of salmon returning to Canada and the United States had dropped from nearly two million in the 1970s to fewer than five hundred thousand. Conservation groups desperate to save the wild salmon developed an innovative strategy: they would pay fishers to keep salmon in the water in a type of ransom scheme.

An international group called the North Atlantic Salmon Conservation Organization had been created in 1984 to manage and protect the declining stock of Atlantic salmon. Its members eventually included Canada, Denmark and other European Union nations, Norway, Russia, and the United States. It took a decade to negotiate an agreement with Greenland and the Danish government, which owns the island, to reduce its salmon catch in exchange for payments to train Greenland fishers for jobs that did not involve catching Atlantic salmon. The payment was five hundred thousand dollars a year in the beginning, all raised from private donors by the Atlantic Salmon Federation and the North Atlantic Salmon Fund, a nonprofit founded in Iceland and active in the United States. Indigenous people in western Greenland were permitted to continue subsistence-level fishing.

In response, Greenland reduced its salmon take, which led to a slow increase in salmon returning to the rivers and streams in New England and eastern Canada. But continuing to limit harvests to levels that would allow restoration of the fish proved difficult. As Greenland's haul increased, the number of returning fish began to drop again. In 2010, the harvest was forty tons, twice the target negotiated under the 1994 agreement. The deal was canceled. Greenland argued that the limit was unfair because Atlantic salmon were being harvested by commercial operators and recreational fishers in greater numbers in other countries, notably Canada, Norway, and Scotland. Without an agreement, fewer than 30 percent of Greenland's commercial fishers reported their catch in 2017, and the situation was regarded as dire enough that the groups returned to the negotiating table.

In 2018, after a year of talks, the Atlantic Salmon Federation and the North Atlantic Salmon Fund reached a new twelve-year agreement with the Association of Fishers and Hunters in Greenland. In exchange for reducing commercial salmon fishing to twenty metric tons, the two nonprofit organizations pledged to finance scientific research, initiatives to conserve marine resources, and extensive alternative economic development in Greenland. In addition, Greenlanders with fishing licenses could apply for small grants to diversify employment opportunities. Most of the money has been used to buy gear to fish for more sustainable species like halibut. Commercial fishers who failed to report their salmon catch to local authorities risked losing their license. The cost of the agreement was around four million dollars over twelve years.

In 2019, despite the new agreement, Greenland reported a commercial harvest of more than forty metric tons of salmon, twice the agreed target. Authorities blamed the excessive catch on failures to coordinate among fishers. Instead of walking away, the Atlantic Salmon Federation and the North Atlantic Salmon Fund hired a Greenland resident to work from the inside to help fishers fill out applications for the retraining fund and to report catches accurately. The move worked so well that they eventually hired ten more people to help monitor the process. Since then, the reported catches have been closer to the limit.

The agreement has had a positive impact on Atlantic salmon returns to North America, including the Penobscot River in Maine and the Miramichi River in New Brunswick. The returns remain far short of the historic numbers but still count as a success. "Significantly reducing the harvest of wild Atlantic salmon on their ocean feeding grounds is meaningful and decisive," said Bill Taylor, president of the Atlantic Salmon Federation.

Ensuring the survival of wild Atlantic salmon will require similar decisive actions in other realms. Chief among them may be embracing the disruptive new technology that is moving salmon farms onto land, where such businesses can no longer infect wild salmon with disease or allow escaped fish to interbreed.

CHAPTER 25

JUDGMENT IN NEW YORK

Tracey Clarke surveyed the dimly lit dining room. The table, dressed with a starched linen tablecloth, was laid with fine china and silver cutlery. The crystal wineglasses were polished to a high gloss. The portrait of a stern bulldog kept watch from above the fireplace. It was the perfect setting to stage a revolution.

Clarke had been a senior relationship manager for IBM and PricewaterhouseCoopers before starting the Perfect Cast, a specialty business that helped corporate executives build relationships through fly-fishing trips. She understood personal dynamics and applied them when she chose the dinner guests, a collection of investment bankers, private equity investors, and their spouses. All were sportsmen with both a keen interest in the environment and hefty bank accounts. The setting reflected their status. The dinner was held at a private, men-only club in an unmarked brownstone just off Park Avenue in New York City. The club attracts wealthy men from across the country who hunt and fish and enjoy a discreet, exclusive setting, a place so private that we cannot use its name. Dogs are welcome, and women are allowed as guests.

The menu was the reason for the gathering that snowy night in February 2016. The guests would sample five brands of fresh farmed Atlantic salmon in a blind tasting. Three of the mystery salmon had been raised in innovative land-based facilities; the other two were from ocean-based farms. Beside each plate was a scorecard on which the diners would rate each anonymous brand. The goal was to see if land-raised salmon tasted as good as fish raised in cages in the ocean. The diners did not know the origins of any of the fish.

Forty years earlier, the crème de la crème of the French wine establishment sat at a long table in Paris for a blind tasting that compared some of the finest wines in France with bottles from California. The tasting was conceived as a publicity stunt for a wine shop in Paris, but the results shattered the myth that only France could produce great wine when California vintages performed surprisingly well. The event, known as the Judgment of Paris, revolutionized the wine world. Tracey Clarke, an avid angler and a board member of the Atlantic Salmon Federation, was concerned about the impact of salmon farms on the diminishing population of wild salmon. She hoped the dinner would disrupt the world of open-net salmon farms and emerge as a turning point in promoting salmon raised in land-based facilities.

The United States imports about 350,000 tons of salmon worth three billion dollars each year, far more than any other fish and second only to shrimp in all seafood. Nearly 90 percent of the imported salmon comes from farms located on the coasts of Norway, Chile, Scotland, and Canada. Farmed Atlantic salmon is America's favorite fish despite the impact the farms have on the environment and the health risks of eating salmon treated with chemicals. These factors spurred a search for new technologies that would decrease salmon farming's environmental impact and reduce the need for chemicals and antibiotics.

At the time of Clarke's dinner, the most promising alternative to the traditional ocean-based approach was land-based, closed-containment technology known as recirculating aquaculture systems, or RAS. Land-based RAS involves growing salmon in tanks in closed buildings to maintain a secure and nearly sterile environment. The tanks are usually round and hold about as much water as an Olympic-size swimming pool, about 650,000 gallons. The freshwater and salt water used at different stages of the salmon's life cycle are sterilized through ultraviolet light and biofilters to prevent the transfer of diseases and contamination that might harm the fish. The water flows in a constant circular pattern, imitating ocean currents. As much as 99 percent of the water is recirculated, and aeration and filters remove carbon dioxide and waste generated by the fish, while adding oxygen. Sensors monitor water temperature and oxygen and pH levels in the tanks, and alarms alert workers to potential problems. As salmon do in the wild, most RAS fish spend their first months in freshwater tanks before shifting to saltwater tanks, where they grow to a market size of ten to twelve pounds.

RAS fish never touch the ocean, and neither does their waste, which solves a range of environmental and health problems. In RAS tanks, salmon are not exposed to seaborne diseases or parasites, making antibiotics and pesticides unnecessary. The fish have no avenue for escape, eliminating threats to wild salmon. Waste is treated and turned into fertilizer, hauled to landfills, or burned for biofuel. Open-net farms are located in fragile, often remote coastal waters, but RAS plants can be anyplace with enough water to fill the tanks and enough energy to keep them running. Building plants close to major markets reduces transportation costs and the carbon footprint of eating salmon.

In most ways, RAS systems are more efficient and productive than ocean-based farms. The controlled conditions allow salmon to grow faster in tanks, usually requiring two years to reach market size compared with up to three years in ocean-based farms. The absence of viruses like ISA or PRV, or of parasites like sea lice, and the well-tuned environment inside the tanks, mean healthier fish and lower mortality rates. In RAS plants, water temperature and levels of oxygen and carbon dioxide are monitored by sensors and adjusted continuously. Fish are not fed at night, so their need for oxygen goes down, and less is pumped into the tank. The level of control allows a greater density of fish in the tanks compared with ocean cages, where farmers must leave more space to combat rising water temperatures and the resulting decreases in available oxygen. Higher density in the RAS tanks, however, carries some risk. A glitch in the computers that run the systems can create a domino effect of problems that can wipe out an entire tank of fish.

Land-based farmers don't have to worry about winter, when cooler temperatures in open-net cages slow the metabolism of fish, so they eat less and grow slower. In addition, ocean farms need to be left fallow for weeks after harvest to break the cycle of sea lice and diseases and allow the seabed to recover from the waste and feces. *Recover* is a relative term, one that translates into allowing currents and tides to sweep the filth into the wider ocean. The overall benefit is that land-based salmon grow more consistently and can be harvested more regularly.

RAS is a disruptive technology with the potential to upend the way the industry operates and what consumers eat. Such technologies often begin in chaos and then, over time, sweep away the previous practices. When Johannes Gutenberg, a German goldsmith, invented the printing press in 1436, he forever transformed the way knowledge was disseminated and unlocked the modern age. More recently, the internet revolutionized how we communicate with one another. Each of these technologies took years to develop, each created winners and losers, and each changed the world permanently. Once invented, neither could be stopped.

The pace of change seems faster today, but futurists like Paul Saffo of Stanford University say it takes about twenty years to go from raw technology to transforming lives and industries. The key for a new technology is a mix of obsession, intuition, and timing. People make too much of the early bird getting the worm. Better to remember that the second mouse gets the cheese. However, transformation can accelerate when a new technology confronts an industry under stress.

By most measures, RAS offers a cleaner and healthier alternative to ocean pens, and it is being developed when the traditional industry is under increasing pressure from environmentalist groups, the public, and some governments. The transition to the land will not occur overnight, and setbacks are inevitable with any new technology. Jobs will be lost or transformed. Think of the scribes replaced by Gutenberg's printing press. Ultimately, if the new technology prevails, open-net salmon farms could go the way of hand-written Bibles.

The technology is so nascent that the start-ups are more concepts than companies. RAS adoption has followed a common path for new technologies: construction and operating costs are high compared with those at ocean farms, technical bugs have caused setbacks, and investors are wary. But the basic idea of raising salmon on land has been around for decades. Brood stock for salmon farms is grown from eggs to smolts in freshwater tanks at land-based hatcheries. The juvenile salmon usually spend twelve to eighteen months in freshwater at the hatchery while they mature enough to survive in salt water. The young salmon, called smolts, are then moved to pens on the ocean, where they spend two to three years reaching market size.

RAS pushes the hatchery concept to another level. Young salmon in RAS facilities start out in freshwater tanks and are transferred to saltwater tanks to grow to market size. The major hurdle is scale, producing enough fish to offset the higher costs of construction and operations on land and to make a profit. Proponents say costs are coming down and that the environmental and health benefits already outweigh the additional start-up costs. At this stage, the higher-cost RAS technology must compete with freeloading ocean-based farms, which benefit from minimal initial investments and cheap leases of public waters. Ocean farms also keep costs down by dumping their waste in the water, with the costs borne by the public and other marine users. In contrast, closed-containment systems on land recycle water, treat and reuse waste, and apply far fewer chemicals.

Despite the advantages, RAS plants are not an environmental panacea. They have a large footprint on land and use a lot of water and energy. Critics worry about the carbon footprint of constructing and operating the plants and the drain on local water supplies. In Maine, concerns about proposed plants have focused on the impact of effluent on the sensitive environmental balance in the Gulf of Maine, home to some of the world's richest lobster grounds. RAS farmers describe discharges as minimal and say the water is cleaner than when it was brought into the system. Nonetheless, critics worry that even small differences, such as the temperature of the released water, will disrupt the gulf's delicate ecosystem.

One of the three land-based salmon brands on Tracey Clarke's menu came from a complex of concrete buildings and metal structures in rolling hills about forty miles northeast of Halifax, Nova Scotia, and five hundred yards from the eastern shore of the Bay of Fundy. To find the plant, visitors must watch carefully for a sign that reads "Sustainable Fish Farming Ltd." as they drive down a narrow gravel road. The story of how salmon raised on fifty acres in the middle of nowhere made it to that exclusive club in New York City is emblematic of the trials and triumphs of a maturing disruptive technology.

Kirk Havercroft, the chief executive for Sustainable Fish Farming, loves to show off the buildings and the technology. To maintain biosecurity, big rubber boots are mandatory in the concrete buildings where the fish tanks are located. Freshwater is pumped from the ground, and salt water is drawn from the Bay of Fundy; both types are sterilized before being pumped into the fish house. The air inside smells like the ocean, but the background noise is not the waves on the shore. Instead, visitors hear pumps sending sanitized, oxygenated water into the tanks. The best vantage point is up a metal ladder to a walkway. From above, one can see about four thousand salmon swimming counterclockwise against the manufactured current in one of the tanks. Occasionally a renegade goes in the opposite direction. Havercroft pointed to a fish with a bump on its head and explained that it had jumped too high during feeding and banged itself on the rotating metal arm that distributes the pellets from several feet above the water. Back down the ladder, through two sets of metal doors, is the control center, a temperature-controlled room replete with banks of computers, circuit-breaker switches, and lights and gauges signaling conditions in the giant tanks. Beyond the control room is a cavernous hall with twenty-foot ceilings and rows of blue tanks linked by a series of pipes that connect with the salmon pens two floors up. Photos are prohibited in this part of the plant because the recirculating system is proprietary.

Havercroft moved to Nova Scotia from the United Kingdom in 2009, drawn by what he saw as a combination of environmental consciousness, preference for local seafood, and an abundance of inexpensive land. He was the money guy, and his business partner, Jeremy Lee, was the science guy. Lee, also British, spent more than twenty years designing public aquariums. The goal was to demonstrate that Lee's recirculating technology could be adapted to raising fish on land. The basics were like other RAS, with a key difference from an environmental perspective. Most closed-containment systems treat and discharge around 5 percent of their water. Lee's technology recycles almost 100 percent of the water through a combination of advanced filtration methods, including an ozone treatment to disinfect the water. The only discharge is a small amount of organic waste, which is collected and trucked to a nearby biofuel plant, where it is burned to generate energy. It's almost magically sustainable.

Together with a handful of conservation-minded investors, Havercroft and Lee started growing sea bass in 2010 in Nova Scotia. The fish sold well to restaurants and wholesalers, but the company had trouble getting a steady supply of juvenile sea bass. They switched to sea bream, widely considered by chefs to be the tastiest of all fish. But they could not give it away. Their customers were unanimous: sea bream was ugly and did not look anything like local favorites—salmon, halibut, and cod. In 2012, Havercroft polled retailers and influential chefs in Toronto who had been good customers about what they would like Sustainable Fish Farming to grow. Nearly 90 percent wanted Atlantic salmon. At the time, Cooke Aquaculture and other open-net salmon farmers were getting a lot of bad publicity in the Canadian press because of sea lice infestations and disease outbreaks, and some restaurants and wholesalers wanted a new, cleaner product. So, in 2013, Sustainable Fish Farming built its own salmon hatchery to ensure a steady supply of fish. The effort got off to a great start, and the first crop was scheduled to go to market in 2014, under the label "Sustainable Blue." Hopes were high that the third fish would be a charm.

Disruptive technology can bring surprises. Successful innovators learn to adapt. Companies that start out developing one product often wind up producing something else. One Saturday morning in March 2014, Havercroft was driving to the plant when his cell phone rang. A distraught employee had gone into the main fish house and found it completely dark. The electricity had failed, the computer controlling temperature and oxygen had shut down, and the backup batteries and generators had never kicked in. The entire first batch of twelve thousand salmon had been wiped out, just a few weeks before harvest. The cause was a mystery that had to be solved to avoid a repeat, but technicians could not find a reason for the failure of the electricity and the backup system. Suspecting sabotage, Havercroft brought in an outside company to investigate what had gone wrong. The outside team spent several days doing diagnostic tests and concluded that the only way the entire system could have failed was if someone had pressed keys on the keyboards of multiple computers. In other words, the failure could not have happened without human intervention.

Was it sabotage? Sustainable Fish Farming had been promoting the pending harvest of its first batch of salmon in the press. Havercroft thought the prospect of this new technology might have frightened competitors in the open-pen end of the business. Determined to find the cause, he called the Royal Canadian Mounted Police. The RCMP conducted a brief investigation but found no evidence of a crime. The cause was never determined, the system was rebooted, the tanks were restocked, and business returned to normal. In September 2015, the first successful harvest was shipped to restaurants and wholesalers in Toronto and Halifax. It sold out, a trend that has continued ever since as production has ramped up without further failure.

"We represent an ethical model compared to an unethical model," said Havercroft. Still, he acknowledged that "Sustainable Blue" is a misnomer at this point in the company's evolution. Issues remain before land-based salmon farmers can lay honest claim to being truly sustainable. Nonetheless, some of the problems are shared with ocean-based farming, chiefly finding an alternative to fish meal and fish oil in the feed, so the sticking points that remain aren't unique negatives to a land-based system.

David Roberts, director of special projects at Sustainable Fish Farming, has been working with feed producers and researchers to develop protein substitutes for fish meal. One promising replacement is black soldier fly larvae. Recent studies have found that salmon fed larvae raised on kelp and organic wastes grew at roughly the same rate as those fed feed containing marine ingredients. A blind taste test found that consumers could not identify which fish had been raised on insect meal. While such replacement methods are important, there are doubts that enough insect meal can be produced to put a dent in the demand for fish meal and fish oil.

The color of the salmon flesh is another problem land-based farmers share with their ocean-based brethren. In the wild, salmon get their characteristic pink-to-red hue from their diet of carotenoid-rich shrimp and krill. The flesh of fish raised in ocean cages or land-based tanks is an unappetizing gray because of their feed. Studies have shown that consumers expect, and will pay more for, salmon that appears pink or red. So, salmon farmers add red pigment to the feed to turn their fish red. "Don't call it 'dye,'" Roberts insisted. "It is yeast-based. But we know that consumers won't buy fish that isn't red."

Consumers will not buy fish that does not taste good, either. In rare instances, salmon raised in tanks taste slightly earthy or musty. What is known euphemistically as an "off flavor" comes from two compounds, geosmin and 2-methylisoborneol, produced by bacteria in the tanks. The compounds are harmless to humans but can accumulate in the tissue of the fish and change its ultimate taste. The most common way to eliminate these compounds, and the resulting unwanted flavor, is by forcing the salmon to purge. Just before harvest, the fish are moved to a separate, sanitized tank devoid of the bacteria. Over several days, as the fish fast, they throw off the unwanted compounds and get back "on flavor."

Havercroft and Roberts thought they had avoided the need for purging through a proprietary method, but sporadic customer complaints sent them back to the drawing board. The result was the construction of a facility in 2021 in which fish were cleansed of the unwanted flavor through a new technology. Understandably, the company is reluctant to provide more specifics.

Salmon from Sustainable Fish Farming Ltd. and a second Nova Scotia land-based farm, Cape d'Or, are in the display case at Dory Mates' Seafood Shop in Lunenburg, a small town on Nova Scotia's southeastern shore. The expression "dory mates" dates to the nineteenth century, when schooners sailed out of Lunenburg Harbour to the Grand Banks in search of cod, halibut, and other fish. Small, flat-bottomed wooden boats called dories were lowered into the Atlantic Ocean, each with a crew of two men who used hand lines to catch up to a ton of fish. The "dory mates" depended on each other in the dangerous and unpredictable waters. Testaments to the risks stand near Lunenburg's main wharf: eight three-sided black granite columns inscribed with the names of hundreds of mariners who died at sea from 1890 to the present. The schooners and dories are gone, but Lunenburg remains a fishing and shipbuilding village, home to big scallop trawlers and a fleet of boats that ply the surrounding waters for lobster, halibut, cod, haddock, and mackerel—and to a lot of people who know their fish.

Locals shopping for fresh seafood stop at Dory Mates', where owner Kelly Conrad is happy to explain to customers exactly when the lobster scrabbling around the tank came out of the sea, who among their neighbors caught the haddock, and whether she made fish cakes that morning. Conrad is just as precise when it comes to the provenance of the bright pink salmon fillets in her shop. She sells ocean-farmed Atlantic salmon from Cooke Aquaculture and salmon from Sustainable Blue and Cape d'Or. The RAS brands are about 50 percent more expensive than Cooke's True North salmon, but they are the first to sell out.

Conrad has a personal stake in the future of farmed salmon. Her husband, Jason, is a lobster fisher who catches herring in the off-season. Both have seen the damage caused by salmon farms and do not want it to spread. When it comes to eating salmon, Conrad keeps her preferences to herself for the sake of neighborly relations. Still, she confesses that she occasionally gets that earthy smell from some of the RAS-raised salmon. "It's sort of like walking in the forest when the leaves are wet," she said.

Sustainable Blue and Cape d'Or were on the menu at Clarke's dinner in New York City. The third RAS-raised salmon that night represented a departure from the others. It came from the Freshwater Institute in Shepherdstown, West Virginia, a pilot project focused on sustainable domestic seafood run by the Conservation Fund. Raising salmon in a landlocked state might seem odd, but RAS plants have been popping up in places like Dubai, in an alpine village in Switzerland, on former tomato fields near Miami, and on a farm in Wisconsin. This portability is one of the most exciting aspects of the technology, because the land-based farms can be located close to markets.

The Freshwater Institute salmon was different in two ways.

First, the fish were raised only in freshwater. Wild and, typically, farmed salmon start their lives in freshwater and shift to salt water to mature. At the institute, the salmon start and finish in freshwater, which adds to the flexibility of RAS farms by allowing them to be built far from the ocean. The concept is not completely alien. A type of wild Atlantic salmon called "landlocked" has adapted to living only in lakes and rivers. No one, however, had tried to grow salmon to market size only in freshwater.

The second difference was their diet: the institute developed feed that used fish meal and oil from trimming and scraps from a whitefish-processing plant in Oregon and from some animal by-products instead of wild-caught ingredients. Substituting by-products for wild-caught fish translated into a sustainable feed. But how would the fish taste? Clarke's dinner in New York City was one of its first major tests.

The two open-net salmon on the menu were Cooke Aquaculture's True North brand, which is widely available, and Black Pearl Scottish salmon. Black Pearl is raised in low-density open-net cages near the Shetland Islands, about one hundred miles off the northern coast of Scotland, and is certified as organic under UK standards.

Like her, Tracey's husband, C. D. Clarke, a painter and a member of the private club, was also on the board of the Atlantic Salmon Federation, as were several of the guests that evening. Without knowing which salmon they were eating, the diners were asked to rank the five fish in four categories: taste, texture, fat, and color. Clarke was not sure how the evening would turn out, though she had her fingers crossed that the land-based versions would prevail as the diners marked their scorecards.

To prepare the salmon, Clarke had recruited Kerry Heffernan, a prominent chef who had worked at several top-rated restaurants and was currently chef at Grand Banks, a seasonal oyster bar on a former cod-fishing schooner moored at Pier 25 in New York City. Heffernan believed that chefs had an important role in educating customers, and part of that role was promoting sustainable salmon. "They trust our palates and judgments and ethics," he said. "If consumers want to buy based only on price, RAS salmon cannot compete right now. Consumers have to be willing to make that jump for the sake of their moral compass."

The first course was *crudo*, or "raw." To highlight the flavor and texture of the salmon, the fresh fish was dressed only with a light olive oil. The second course was roasted salmon, a more common preparation. The conversation was lively as the judges tried to figure out what they were eating and compared notes about what they liked. Like Clarke, Heffernan did not know how the scoring would turn out. Most Americans are accustomed to fatty ocean-farmed salmon, which makes them more forgiving to cook. RAS-raised salmon, like wild salmon, are leaner because they are constantly swimming against strong currents in a tank. As a result, the fish requires more attention in the oven or on the grill to prevent it from drying out.

After the meal was over and the guests had departed, Clarke tallied the scores. When it came to taste for cooked salmon, the organic Black Pearl tied with one of the RAS salmon for the top spot. In every other category, the land-based versions took two of the top three spots. In an email to participants after the dinner, Clarke declined to identify the winners, except to say the land-based salmon fared very well, sweeping most of the top spots. Clarke told us later that she did not want to reveal the winners because the event had taken place six years ago, when the RAS industry was in its infancy.

Still, the dinner confirmed that when it came to taste, texture, fat, and color, salmon raised on land were equal to or better than their ocean-raised counterparts.

"Land-based, sustainably raised Atlantic salmon compares very favorably in all respects to open-net (unsustainably raised) salmon," she wrote after the dinner. "The sustainably raised salmon that was fed the sustainable diet (zero wild fish) compared very favorably in all respects to both the open-net salmon and the land-based, sustainably raised salmon. This is especially encouraging since using a sustainable diet means that no fish are removed from the ocean to feed farm-raised fish and therefore there is zero impact on wild Atlantic salmon or any other wild ocean fish."

The dinner was more evolution than revolution, but the judgment was an important milestone: all three land-based systems had demonstrated to discerning diners that RAS salmon was at least as tasty as Black Pearl's premium organic fish and superior to the traditional fare from ocean-based farmers like Cooke Aquaculture. Foremost among the remaining questions was whether land-based salmon farming could carve out a substantial share of the market in the competitive world of salmon farming. "Scale is going to make the difference," said Sustainable Blue's Havercroft.

Overcoming the twin hurdles of scale and price is tough right now, in part because the acknowledged leader of the organic food movement, Whole Foods Market, is not selling salmon raised on land at its roughly five hundred stores in the United States, Canada, and Britain.

On the plus side, Whole Foods requires suppliers to follow a set of strict guidelines that forbid the use of antibiotics and toxic chemicals, restrict the density of salmon in the pens, and prohibit the use of by-products from land animals like chickens in the feed. The standards are enforced by third-party auditors with the authority to stop using suppliers. Carrie Brownstein, the principal adviser on seafood standards at Whole Foods, said the guidelines debunk the myth that all salmon farming is bad. She said the farmed salmon sold by Whole Foods comes from a handful of open-net farms in Norway and Iceland that meet Whole Foods Markets' evolving and constantly improving standards. "We knew customers were looking to us to find a way to get it right," said Brownstein, who traces her relationship with seafood to a great-grandfather who sold fish from a cart in Philadelphia. Moreover, the experience of Whole Foods shows that customers are willing to pay premium prices for products that they believe are healthier and that adhere to higher environmental standards.

Whole Foods, a subsidiary of Amazon, is doing a better job than most retailers when it comes to farmed salmon, but trade-offs remain. First, flying fresh salmon from Iceland and Norway to distribution centers and trucking the product to stores nationwide increases its carbon footprint, contributing to the greenhouse emissions that are damaging the planet. Second, the company's prohibition on the use of animal by-products in salmon feed intensifies the salmon-farming industry's reliance on fish meal and fish oil from wild-caught fish. As we have seen, this practice contributes to the depletion of subsistence fisheries off the coasts of West Africa and South America and, because of the fuel used by vessels to catch wild fish, once again raises the carbon footprint of the salmon. Prohibiting poultry by-products on a widespread basis would lead to wasting viscera, bones, and other material containing valuable nutrients, thereby decreasing overall sustainability. Biologists and the National Oceanic and Atmospheric Administration, which has researched salmon feed extensively, concluded that a diet of poultry by-products and algae oil could be just as healthy for salmon as marine ingredients.

Finally, despite the chemical-free, environmentally friendly nature of salmon raised on land, Brownstein said the higher cost, the use of by-products in feed, and the relative scarcity of a steady supply are why the company doesn't sell the product. Defending the ban on animal by-products, Brownstein said, "There are some consumers that eat fish but don't eat poultry or other meat and don't want blood meal in their seafood. They prefer just fish." Brownstein indicated that the situation could change. For instance, she said, Whole Foods was open to feed that substituted insects and algae oil for wild fish ingredients. "I don't think anyone would complain about algae," she said.

The search is well underway for alternative sources of protein for farmed salmon, often led by land-based farmers. In the meantime, an ambitious attempt to respond to the challenges of price and scale has taken root in a most unusual location.

CHAPTER 26

GROWING SALMON IN FLORIDA

Johan Andreassen grew up on a cattle farm on the remote northwestern coast of Norway. The region's only city, Alesund, founded in the ninth century, had a history as a major fishing port and a central market for the cattle and sheep raised in the valleys of the Sunnmore Alps. By the time Andreassen was a schoolboy in the 1980s, the oil and gas industry was thriving in the North Sea. A decade later, the region's coastal waters were home to Norway's burgeoning salmon-farming industry. Andreassen's grandfather had been a fisherman, and it was from him that Johan learned to love and respect the sea. Young Johan spent hours maneuvering small boats in and out of the towering fjords etched by glaciers along the coast. He watched the salmon farms popping up in the fragile coastal waters and heard about the growing problem of sea lice infestations. Most farms were applying pesticides to fight the infestations, but some were experimenting with wrasse, a "cleaner fish" that eats the lice off salmon without damaging the fish or the environment.

Andreassen was fifteen years old when he and a cousin, Bjorn Vegard-Lovik, began fishing for wrasse to sell to the salmon farms. This niche business grew, and three years later, in 1995, the pair formed a company to supply cleaner fish to farms along Norway's western coast. A few years later, they sold the business and started their own salmon farm using only wrasse to fight sea lice. The company, Villa Organic, was Norway's first organic salmon farm, and its biggest customer became Whole Foods Market.

Despite his environmental concerns, Andreassen learned quickly that even an organic farm discharged waste and threatened wild salmon in Norway's rivers. He wanted to find a better way, so in 2010, he and Lovik sold Villa Organic and started Atlantic Sapphire with a Danish aquaculture expert, Thue Holm. They built a pilot plant on the west coast of Denmark, employing a recirculating aquaculture system to raise salmon on land from hatchery to market. They called it the Bluehouse, a nod to the controlled conditions in greenhouses. Bluehouse salmon would be raised without chemicals or antibiotics and without threatening wild salmon.

Within a few years, Atlantic Sapphire was selling two thousand tons of RAS-raised salmon a year at premium prices to customers in Europe and the United States. The volume was small, but the plant showed it could be done. Andreassen envisioned a next-generation plant that would change the global market, and he started searching for a place to build the world's biggest land-based salmon farm in the country with the world's biggest appetite for farmed salmon, the United States.

Open-net farms need to be on the ocean, so they are often remote from major markets. Andreassen wanted to build his new farm near population centers in order to provide fresh products fast and to reduce transportation costs. The trick was finding a place close to a big metropolitan area, with access to good highways, with a pool of skilled technicians to manage the plant's complex computerized systems, and with easy access to large amounts of salt water and freshwater—about one hundred times the amount used at the pilot operation in Denmark.

Like many disruptive technologies, RAS is more complex and initially expensive than the process it seeks to push aside. RAS operators must buy land, build large plants filled with expensive filtration and computer systems, treat water coming in and out, and pay large energy bills to maintain the microenvironment. Open-net farmers have few of these capital expenses or operating costs, a factor that Bill Taylor discovered makes them reluctant to consider changing their ways, despite some of the upsides that RAS offers.

Taylor, the president of the Atlantic Salmon Federation, has dedicated his career to protecting and restoring wild salmon. He and his daughters fish for salmon to catch and release in the same New Brunswick rivers where his grandfather fished, though there are far fewer fish these days. He had just started at the ASF in the late 1980s when the organization realized its mistake in supporting open-net farming as a way to take the pressure off fishing for wild salmon a decade earlier. Since then, Taylor and the federation have championed a shift to closed-containment systems on land. Convincing the titans of salmon farming to make the transition has proven difficult, however, as Taylor found out when he talked with Glenn Cooke in 2016 about a joint pilot project to raise salmon on land.

The Atlantic Salmon Federation's headquarters are in St. Andrews, New Brunswick, not far from Cooke Aquaculture's headquarters. Taylor knew Cooke had a lot of influence in the industry, and he wanted to enlist his neighbor in starting a RAS project with the federation to show that it could be profitable. He thought that getting support from the industry might make the concept more acceptable.

"Let's run a small program to test the financials," Taylor said to Cooke. "Let's do it with the open-net industry and make all the information transparent. Let's make it work."

Cooke shook his head. "I make fifty-two percent profit on open-net," he said, according to Taylor. "Why do something where we would be lucky to break even?"

Cooke's attitude was a common one among executives facing a disruptive technology. The bigger companies grow, the more resistant they are to change. But this stubbornness makes them vulnerable to the very technologies they spurn. The most dramatic example is Kodak. The American company invented digital photography in 1975 but remained wedded to its film business, a strategic failure that led to years of decline before the company's eventual obsolescence.

Johan Andreassen almost did not build his plant in the United States. Beginning in 2015, he searched for a location that met all his criteria. He traveled to Maine, which resembled Norway, but he worried that obtaining government permits would be too big a challenge because of the power of the lobster industry. He visited coastal Virginia, but feared that a backlash from the oyster farmers who dominate aquaculture there would block his plant. After two and a half years of searching across twelve states, he was on the verge of investigating other countries when he discovered the solution. "I was just googling, and I stumbled across this film on YouTube," he said. "It was a history of the Florida aquifer system, and the location sounded perfect." Hot, humid South Florida seemed a most unlikely place to raise cold-water fish, even on land. But the video described a vast underground network of aquifers containing pristine freshwater and ancient salt water. It sounded perfect for the next-generation Bluehouse.

Around thirty million years ago, sea levels began to drop, and what is now Florida emerged from the ocean. The shrinking ocean left behind a thousand-foot-thick layer of limestone rock. Over the millennia, water eroded the limestone to form cracks, passages, and huge underground spaces that filled with rain. Known as the Floridan aquifer, this natural reservoir contains billions of gallons of freshwater beneath 82,000 square miles of Florida and four other southern states. The freshwater from the aquifer is constantly recharged by precipitation and provides Floridians with most of the seven billion gallons of freshwater used every day to water their lawns, irrigate their crops, and operate their factories and power plants.

Trapped beneath the freshwater layer is an ancient saltwater sea. The pressure of the freshwater above and the layers of impermeable clay, mud, and limestone between hold the salt water in place, creating an unspoiled subterranean saltwater sea. RAS plants spend a lot of money to filter out pathogens and other contaminants from salt water, but the salt water beneath Florida had never been polluted by industry, touched by pathogens, or tainted by microplastics. It was ideal for raising salmon.

Below the salt water is a third layer, called the "boulder zone," an irregular series of caverns more than half a mile below sea level, beneath an overlay of limestone and dolomite that confines water. Miami, Fort Lauderdale, and other municipalities in South Florida inject treated municipal wastewater into the boulder zone, where it is cleaned naturally over time and returned to the ocean.

It seems that nature had designed the perfect spot for a recirculating aquaculture system. Drawing the freshwater from the top layer would allow Atlantic Sapphire to re-create the river stage in which young salmon start their lives. The ancient salt water would provide abundant clean water for the grow-out stage that occurs in salt water. The boulder zone would provide infinite storage for the discharge of treated wastewater.

Miami became the obvious choice for the plant. The city consistently ranks at the top of lists of the best places to start a business. The economy was thriving from tourism, finance, and international trade. The labor force was skilled. Land was cheap, particularly the flat, open agricultural fields within the greater Miami-Dade County metropolitan region. Plus, Interstate 95 connected South Florida with the entire Eastern Seaboard. Andreassen met with regional officials to outline his plan. He explained that the plant would draw from the freshwater aquifer, but most of the water would come from the saltwater layer. Sludge generated from the process would be sent to landfills in the initial phases, but he planned to desalinate the waste for fertilizer eventually. Despite the plant's size, he said it would not have a negative impact on water supplies. To the Norwegian's surprise, he encountered only encouragement. Officials said the salt water had no commercial value, and he was welcome to use it without a cap on the amount.

Andreassen zeroed in on Homestead as the site of the new Bluehouse. The company bought eighty acres of former tomato fields about forty miles south of Miami and fifteen miles from the Atlantic Ocean. Construction was planned in three phases over a decade, starting in early 2018 with a hatchery and a 390,000-square-foot building to house the first thirty-six fish tanks. The building looked like just another warehouse from the exterior, but inside were miles of piping, dozens of huge filters, and computers keeping fish alive. The final plan envisioned more than one hundred two-story cylindrical fish tanks in multiple buildings, fed by sixty-five independent wells drawing water from the two aquifers at a rate of two thousand gallons a minute. About 95 percent of the water would be recycled, with injection wells sending the remaining 5 percent down to the boulder zone after treatment. A plant to provide oxygen and a facility to manufacture biodegradable packaging were also on the drawing board. The buildings would be hardened to withstand Florida's powerful hurricanes.

Andreassen planned to produce 220,000 metric tons of salmon a year by 2031, the equivalent of about a billion salmon meals. American consumers currently eat about 600,000 metric tons of farmed salmon annually, and that figure is expected to rise to 1 million tons by 2030. Given those projections, Atlantic Sapphire could control more than 20 percent of the world's biggest salmon market. The project was wildly ambitious and wildly expensive. Final costs were estimated at about two billion dollars, far more than any existing RAS plant. Operating costs would be higher, too, because of "the

Miami factor," a reference to the extra electricity required to cool the water from nearly eighty degrees Fahrenheit to between fifty-seven and fifty-nine degrees, a suitable temperature for the fish.

With big ambitions come big risks. To succeed requires facing those risks squarely and learning from them. The parent company of the Florida operation is listed on the Oslo Stock Exchange and raised several hundred million dollars from investors to finance the Homestead Bluehouse. As phase one neared completion in the spring of 2020, a new stock offering to investors warned about the risks involved in a technology that had not reached commercial scale anywhere. It acknowledged the engineering and biological challenges and said the pilot plant in Denmark had lost 90 percent of its fish due to hydrogen sulfate poisoning when biofilters clogged in 2017. Later, the plant lost more fish when too much nitrogen was pumped into the tanks. The company said it responded to the incidents by improving designs and maintenance, but it cautioned that similar episodes were possible.

Hope remained high that operations in Florida would be smoother. In the summer of 2020, four million salmon in various stages of growth were swimming in the thirty-six two-story tanks inside the huge fish house. Until late July, the dream was looking good. This time, COVID-19 would get the blame.

The pandemic had delayed construction. Workers could not get to the job site, critical components did not arrive in time, and an installation team from Chile was barred from the country. The work should have been finished months earlier, but nothing could stop the fish from growing. Stress causes high mortality rates in farmed salmon, and technicians worried about the impact of the incessant noise and vibrations from the construction. The dilemma was whether to harvest the fish before they reached market size and lose money or hope the salmon survived the construction. Andreassen took the risk and left the salmon in the tanks.

In late July, four weeks from harvest, technicians saw salmon struggling in one of the tanks. The stressed fish could have been transferred to an emergency harvest building, where they could have been salvaged, but the building was not finished. With no place to move them away from the construction, two hundred thousand salmon had to be destroyed. Fish in other tanks were not affected, but Atlantic Sapphire lost half its fish. The slaughter cost the company five million dollars and sent its stock down 6.8 percent. In the spring of 2021, the operation lost another half a million salmon when a failure in the biofilters allowed gases to build up in the system. The fish were in the early stages of growth and weighed about 2.2 pounds each, representing 5 percent of the planned annual harvest. Again, the stock price fell.

COVID-19 struck the plant indirectly again at the end of August 2021. As the fourth wave surged across Florida, crowded hospitals ran short of the liquid oxygen used to treat the patients. In response, authorities asked businesses and residents to reduce water use. Because liquid oxygen is also used to treat water, Atlantic Sapphire cut its consumption of oxygen by lowering the temperature of the water in its tanks, stopping feeding fish, and harvesting one hundred thousand salmon early. The company's stock took a big hit, but within days, an alternative supply of liquid oxygen was secured, and regular operations resumed. Still, the episode demonstrated the challenges confronting the world of RAS salmon farms.

Four large die-offs of salmon at its two plants and other problems raised questions about whether Atlantic Sapphire could make the leap to commercial-scale production. Christian Nordby, a financial analyst in Oslo who tracks the seafood industry for the Paris-based Kepler Cheuvreux investment house, said the company's fate would play a significant role in determining the future of land-based salmon farming. "Atlantic Sapphire needs to prove it can do this," said Nordby. "If Atlantic Sapphire gets a lot of problems, we are not going to see the industry go in the direction of these land-based systems because banks will not support it. It is not free money. They need to excel."

Andreassen was philosophical about the setbacks. "If you don't fail, you are not innovating," he said. "We have done all the mistakes you can imagine. Every time, you learn something. We are good at adapting the new learning into new procedures. Ten years of trying and failing is one of the biggest assets we have in this company. It is part of the business of creating a new industry and doing something that has never been done. The fish in our tanks are completely dependent on us. If we fail, if a pump stops or the power goes off, the fish are at risk immediately. We have only minutes to react. So, we are learning from every mistake and creating redundant systems that know how to manage this every minute of the day. I like to compare it to other industries where things cannot fail, like the nuclear power plant in Homestead."

The transition to land-based salmon farming presents opportunities and challenges. By controlling water temperature, oxygen content, and other factors, RAS tanks can have about twice the density as open-net cages. This means growing more fish, but it also magnifies the damage when things go wrong. The pollution of open-net salmon farms and the deaths of millions of fish in those cases occur in more remote areas. RAS plants, however, are highly visible in their large warehouses, which garner attention from the media and those in the financial world interested in the new technology.

Moreover, when it comes to feed, RAS systems suffer from the same challenge that affects the open-net industry. Both types of aquaculture rely on feed that contains fish meal and oil from small forage fish. Efforts by the industry to replace wild-caught fish have brought the content down to 25 to 30 percent, but the salmon raised on this diet cannot be considered sustainable. Like many other RAS operators trying to change the industry, Andreassen understands the need to phase out marine ingredients from feed by substituting insect larvae and other land-based proteins. Though RAS-produced salmon are not yet sustainable, Seafood Watch, the consumer watchdog, ranks them as a "Best Choice" because they are grown without antibiotics or pesticides and without risking escapes that endanger wild salmon.

Water presents a different sustainability dilemma for Atlantic Sapphire and other RAS operators. The Floridan aquifer provides 90 percent of the state's drinking water, but the supply is being depleted as demand grows and the climate crisis raises sea levels. The main risk is overextraction, which might weaken the barrier between the freshwater aquifer and the saltwater aquifer beneath it, which would allow salt water to rise into the freshwater, according to numerous studies. So far, Atlantic Sapphire's system is working and even drawing praise. "To the extent that all businesses and development have an environmental impact, the operation is not without a footprint," said Dr. Rachel Silverstein, executive director of Miami Waterkeeper, an NGO focused on protecting water supplies and marine habitats in South Florida. "But in our review, we found that they are making every effort to reduce their impact and to employ sustainable practices."

From a personal perspective, Atlantic Sapphire's ambitions are paying off in a tasty product that is available widely. Salmon from the Bluehouse is being sold by several food chains in the United States. We found some at a Wegmans grocery outside Richmond, Virginia, in the summer of 2021, while visiting our youngest daughter, Rebecca, and her family. At the seafood counter, Atlantic Sapphire salmon was sitting next to fillets from Cermaq's open-net farms in British Columbia. They were priced roughly the same, and we bought some of each for a side-by-side, semiblind taste test with our daughter and son-in-law, Keith, that evening. None of us is a chef, but all four of us preferred the Atlantic Sapphire fish, which was firm, tasty, and easy to cook on the barbecue. The Cermaq salmon was mealy and fatty, a poor second.

Not every RAS operation has been greeted warmly. As in real estate, the biggest issue is location. A twenty-five-hour drive north on I-95 from Miami to central Maine, a proposal for another big RAS operation ran into a wave of public opposition. In 2018, Nordic Aquafarms, a Norwegian company, announced plans for a five-hundred-million-dollar salmon farm in Belfast, on the central coast of Maine. The plan was to produce 33,000 tons of salmon for the northeastern United States on about sixty acres of wooded land and fields along the Little River. The plant would draw freshwater from the local aquifer and sea water from nearby Belfast Bay. Treated wastewater would be discharged into Penobscot Bay at a rate of 7.7 million gallons per day.

Local politicians, the business community, and some conservation organizations supported the proposal, but individual citizens and influential conservation groups like the Sierra Club were opposed. Backers pointed to the promise of roughly one hundred jobs and an injection of tax revenue into the local budget. The proposed farm also fit with the state's efforts to promote Maine as a center for land-based aquaculture. Maine's two U.S. senators, Susan Collins and Angus King, came out in support of the plan. In a letter to Maine environmental officials, the Atlantic Salmon Federation praised Nordic Aquafarms for proposing the most advanced technology available and predicted that the plant would have no negative impact on the coastal and marine environment.

Opponents focused on what they saw as an unreasonable risk to the environment and the existing economy of Penobscot Bay and nearby communities. Several lawsuits were filed challenging the permits issued by the state and related matters. The Sierra Club of Maine's executive committee voted unanimously to oppose the project, saying its discharges would endanger coastal water quality and threaten lobster and other fisheries. The Sierra Club vote came after a feisty debate over balancing the role of salmon farms in feeding the rising world population with the risks to Maine's two-billion-dollar lobster and fishing industry and six-billion-dollar tourism business. Some members also worried about the carbon footprint of the construction and operation of the ten buildings that would comprise the farm.

"There were too many questions about how the Nordic Aquafarms system would work," said Becky Bartovics, a member of the executive committee. "You want to know that the system works before you dump millions of gallons of wastewater into the best lobster grounds in the state." Bartovics and other opponents pointed out that conservation groups and federal and state agencies had spent $62 million restoring the Penobscot River. Atlantic salmon and other fish were finally returning to the river, progress that they feared could be reversed by outflow from the salmon farm Nordic Aquafarms was planning.

The criticism surprised Erik Heim, the chief executive of Nordic Aquafarms. He said the company was working on land-based fish farms in six different locations, including in Northern California, and those projects were progressing smoothly. "The only place we have faced real opposition is in Maine," he said. "It is hard to explain. Politically, we have one hundred percent support. Academics and environmentalists are supportive. So why is a small group of people opposing it?"

It was a reasonable question, with many different answers. Half an hour north from Belfast, in Bucksport, Maine, Whole Oceans was building an RAS facility expected to produce up to fifty thousand tons of salmon a year, more than Nordic Aquafarms was planning. The proposal drew less criticism, in part because Whole Oceans planned to build on the site of a former paper mill in an area that was already industrialized. Nordic Aquafarms, though, was threatening wooded acreage, the views of seasonal residents and retirees, and the widely praised recovery of sea-run fish in the Penobscot River and its tributaries.

As Whole Oceans prepared to start construction, questions arose about whether the facility would have to meet basic building and energy codes. In response, and at the request of Governor Janet Mills, a bill was introduced in the Maine legislature to exempt all land-based aquaculture plants from state building and energy regulations. The measure would have granted land-based salmon farms and other aquaculture facilities the same exemption allowed for barns in which livestock are raised. Environmentalists objected, arguing that a complicated, computer-managed salmon farm was not the same as a simple barn, and in mid-2021 the bill was defeated.

The state's receptive attitude toward land-based salmon farms extended to granting ten-year tax exemptions and reduced electricity rates to aquaculture firms that created new jobs. Nordic Aquafarms and Whole Oceans were among several salmon farmers trying to open big plants in Maine. American Aquafarms, a company founded by a Norwegian, proposed operating two salmon farms covering sixty acres in Frenchman Bay, a fifteen-mile strip of water on the central coast of Maine. In a description that sounds like the world's largest diaper, the fish would be raised in floating net pens wrapped in synthetic sacks to collect the waste and excess feed. The waste would be filtered and discharged in deeper waters, according to the company. The proposal drew immediate objections from residents who said the farms would compete with existing lobster fishers and threaten the bay and nearby Acadia National Park. "This is simply a matter of the wrong place, the wrong technology, and the wrong people," James Paterson, a resident, said. The state rejected the proposed farm, saying the company had failed to identify a source for salmon eggs that would protect against diluting the gene pool of wild salmon if farmed fish escaped.

Concerns flared again in late summer of 2021 when Cooke Aquaculture reported that more than one hundred thousand fish died at two of its farms off the Maine coast near Bar Harbor, only a few miles from Frenchman Bay. Critics of salmon farming said suspicions were raised by the eleven-day gap between Cooke's discovery of the die-off on August 16 and its reporting of the incident to the Maine Department of Environmental Protection on August 27. In a statement, the company blamed the deaths on "uncommonly low oxygen levels in the cages," but offered no explanation for why the oxygen levels were low.

An internal email from the Department of Environmental Protection indicated that one of Cooke's site managers told authorities that the nets "had a lot of algae growth and were cleaned immediately after the die off," before the incident was reported to the state. Biofouling on nets often reduces oxygen levels in high-density salmon cages by restricting the water flow and inhibiting the removal of excess feed and waste. The results increase stress levels on fish, increasing the risk of death. The reporting delay left state authorities unable to conduct their own examination of the nets, according to another internal email, and a month after the die-off, the Department of Environmental Protection said it had found no infractions at the Cooke sites.

Investigators for the State of Washington had found that excessive bio-fouling of nets contributed to the collapse of Cooke's salmon farm in Puget Sound in August 2017.

"Maine is the wild west for industrial aquaculture," said Crystal Canney, executive director of Protect Maine's Fishing Heritage Foundation, an ocean conservation group. "Maine lacks a strategic plan for aquaculture. The rules and regulations have not been updated for years. State government has aligned closely with aquaculture lobbyists at the expense of lobstering, fishing and recreating on the water."

CHAPTER 27

REVOLUTION IN WISCONSIN

Reports started appearing on the internet about mysterious purple lights in the night sky along Interstate 94 near tiny Hixton, Wisconsin, population 611. As often happens with social media, wild speculation quickly followed. Some suspected alien ships, others pointed reassuringly to the Northern Lights, one person explained the lights were a haunting from the late rock star Prince, who was from neighboring Minnesota and whose best-known song was "Purple Rain."

The truth was stranger than fiction. The enigmatic glow in the sky emanated from thousands of LED grow lights inside a sleek glass-and-metal greenhouse twice the length of a football field. Beneath those lights were row after row of organic romaine lettuce, kale, bok choy, and other leafy greens. Underground pipes brought the plants filtered, nutrient-rich water from large tanks in a modern warehouse a hundred feet away, where about six hundred thousand Atlantic salmon and steelhead trout were swimming endlessly against a steady current in crystal-clear freshwater. Not quite E.T.'s spaceship, but an unexpected discovery in a place where dairy cows outnumber people.

The greenhouse and nearby building are the core of Superior Fresh LLC, a visionary project trying simultaneously to reshape the way the world farms Atlantic salmon and to reduce America's reliance on imported leafy greens. The operation is 100 percent organic and sustainable: no chemicals, no antibiotics, no pesticides, no fish meal or fish oil from wild fish, no genetically modified ingredients. The small amount of water discharged during the process is put to good use irrigating fields on the farm. Most remarkably, Superior Fresh salmon reach a market size of ten to twelve pounds twice as fast as salmon raised in ocean pens, and the vegetables grow faster and use 90 percent less water than their terrestrial counterparts.

Superior Fresh is a new twist on two old technologies. Hydroponics has been used for centuries to grow plants and crops without soil, with water-based nutrients. Aquaponics is employed widely to raise freshwater fish like tilapia, trout, and catfish and to reuse the nutrient-rich water from the fish to grow plants. What sets Superior Fresh apart from other commercial RAS operations is that it is raising a saltwater fish solely in freshwater.

Salmon are among a small number of anadromous fish that are born in freshwater and mature in sea water. Most RAS plants mimic nature by growing young salmon in freshwater and transferring them to saltwater tanks to grow to market size. In most RAS operations, the recycled saltwater cannot be used for plants because the salt kills vegetation. The excess water must be treated and returned to the ocean. Superior Fresh tapped into a research breakthrough that unlocked the potential for what could be a major shift in salmon farming.

The innovative technology behind Superior Fresh started at the Freshwater Institute in Shepherdstown, West Virginia, the institute created by the Conservation Fund to encourage land-based domestic aquaculture using freshwater. The lead aquaculture researcher at the institute was Steven Summerfelt, who first joined the institute as a doctoral student. As part of his work for his dissertation, he conducted extensive research on freshwater aquaculture at the Freshwater Institute. That work coincided with Summerfelt's growing concern over the damage caused by salmon farms to the environment and to wild salmon. In 2011, Summerfelt and the institute teamed up with the Atlantic Salmon Federation to test whether salmon could be raised in freshwater only, which could make it easier to build land-based farms away from the environmentally sensitive coastlines.

The institute had been using RAS technology for twenty-five years to grow freshwater fish like trout, arctic char, and yellow perch. With salmon, instead of shifting juveniles from freshwater tanks to saltwater tanks, the pilot program kept the fish in freshwater from start to finish. Summerfelt believed this approach would be possible, in theory, based on the existence of what is known as "landlocked" wild salmon. A small percentage of Atlantic salmon spend their entire lives in freshwater, moving from rivers and streams to lakes in an abbreviated migration pattern. No one had tried to raise Atlantic salmon on a commercial scale without using salt water, and it was uncertain what the impact would be on fish health and growth rates.

The team also wanted to develop a sustainable salmon feed by eliminating fish meal and fish oil from wild-caught fish. Big feed companies like Cargill in Minnesota and Skretting in Norway had been trying to reduce marine ingredients in salmon feed for years, but progress was slow. Summerfelt and Rick Barrows, then a scientist at the U.S. Department of Agriculture, started experimenting with a novel feed by replacing wild-caught ingredients with fish meal and oil from trimmings from a whitefish-processing plant in Oregon and with by-products from poultry. The results met the Monterey Bay Aquarium's Seafood Watch definition of sustainable salmon feed while still testing high in omega-3 fatty acids. Again, the question was how the salmon would respond.

Early results were promising. Atlantic salmon adapted to living fully in freshwater, and the sustainable diet worked. After just a year, the institute reported that its fish had grown twice as fast as salmon in ocean pens and that the mortality rate was 5 percent, well below the 15 to 20 percent average at open-net farms. The next step was finding out if consumers would buy it. The fish went to select grocery stores and restaurants. When the salmon from the Freshwater Institute competed successfully at Tracey Clarke's dinner in New York City in 2016, Summerfelt was elated. His optimism turned into a desire to see if the process worked on a commercial scale. Explaining why he left research for the business world, he said, "I didn't want to sit behind a desk doing research and watch things crash and burn."

Summerfelt found the perfect landing spot. A few years earlier, Brandon Gottsacker, a young graduate from the University of Wisconsin, had spent a year at the Freshwater Institute, where he had learned the basics of RAS technology and worked on several research projects. At the end of the year, Gottsacker returned home and joined an ambitious project to restore 750 acres of farmland and 50 acres of man-made lakes in a remote part of west-central Wisconsin. The land was owned by Todd and Karen Wanek. Todd was chief executive officer of Ashley Furniture, a firm founded by his father that had become the world's largest manufacturer of furniture. The Waneks wanted to return native plants and wildlife to the 800-acre farm outside tiny Hixton. They also wanted to explore whether raising fish and growing organic vegetables might play well with the restoration. Gottsacker's experience at the institute was going to be put to the test when he was tasked with building an integrated facility to raise salmon and organic vegetables.

The Freshwater Institute routinely shared its technology and research with start-ups, and Summerfelt had continued to work with Gottsacker as planning proceeded for the project in Wisconsin. In the fall of 2017, the combined fish-and-vegetable operation opened under the name "Superior Fresh." A few months later, Summerfelt signed on as chief science officer.

Superior Fresh sits on fifteen acres of the farm, and it is divided into two distinct parts, the fish house and the greenhouse. A closed-loop recycling system constantly circulates water between the buildings. The recirculating aquaculture system in the fish house is like those at other land-based salmon farms, except it uses only freshwater, drawn from two wells on the farm. The absence of salt water allows the water to be recycled to feed the organic vegetables next door in the greenhouse in a multistep process.

Here is how it works: First, groundwater is pumped into the fish tanks, creating a current for them to swim against. As the water leaves the fish tanks and before it gets to the greenhouse, it undergoes a two-step filtration system. A mechanical filtration device extracts the solid waste, generally fish feces and feed particles. A biofilter uses beneficial bacteria to break down and remove toxic chemicals like ammonia, resulting in nitrate-rich water that is then circulated to the greenhouse. The plants absorb the nutrients and clean the water in the process. The clean water is circulated back to the fish house to begin the cycle again. Any water spilled throughout the process is captured in containment trays, moved to storage ponds, and used on the farm to irrigate alfalfa fields and perennial grasses, which are cut for hay. The organic matter extracted during the mechanical filtration phase is transferred to wetlands, where it composts with the native plants. In other RAS systems, solid waste and water are contaminated by salt water and must be trucked off to landfills or disposed of in other ways. Superior's system recycles 99.9 percent of the water and doesn't even waste the waste, creating a symbiotic ecosystem of fish, crops, and land.

The salmon require two years to grow from eggs to market size, faster than ocean pens and most other RAS operations. The baby greens and head lettuce take just a few weeks from seed to harvest. As many as one million seeds are planted daily in a high-humidity germination room within the greenhouse. Once they sprout, the young plants are moved to the main greenhouse, where they float on food-grade polystyrene rafts going from one end of the building to the other. The plants mature within twenty-one days and are processed and packed on-site and shipped to local stores and markets. The process worked so well that new greenhouses were added in 2019 and 2021, bringing the greenhouse growing and processing space to nearly thirteen acres. Instead of the purple LED lights from the first phase, the new greenhouse uses white LED lights, adding a white glow to the night sky. The lights supplement sunlight on cloudy days, particularly in the fall, winter, and spring. The LED lights are calibrated to provide the precise intensity that supports optimal photosynthesis, the process by which green plants use light to synthesize food from carbon dioxide and water.

At the nearby fish house, biosecurity measures designed to protect the fish from outside pathogens require visitors to don blue plastic booties and wash their hands before entering the warehouse-like structure where salmon are grown from eggs imported from Iceland and Norway to market-size fish that are sold in stores in Wisconsin and neighboring states. The building is spotless, the temperature carefully controlled, the air crisp. As the fish grow, they are moved to ever-larger metal tanks. The biggest tanks are ten-feet deep and contain 22,000 gallons of water, smaller than most RAS tanks. Inside each large tank, forty thousand Atlantic salmon and steelhead trout swim against the ever-present current.

"This system solves so many problems," said Summerfelt. "We have zero water discharge and one percent fish mortality. Net pens lose twenty percent of their fish when they put them in the ocean. We are growing not only high-quality fish but also certified organic vegetables, all while restoring the land."

The relationship is remarkably efficient: for every five pounds of sustainable fish feed, Superior Fresh says it produces five pounds of salmon and twenty-five pounds of organic greens while replenishing the surrounding land with compost and water, far more efficient than the ratio for farmed salmon raised in the ocean. Superior Fresh produces about 160,000 pounds of Atlantic salmon and steelhead trout a year and 3 million pounds of leafy greens.

The current plant is the first step toward producing Atlantic salmon and

organic vegetables together in an efficient and sustainable manner. The system has provided consistent results, allowing the company to ship salmon to
customers every week since the first harvest in March 2018, when it became
the first land-based salmon to reach the U.S. market. The challenge now is
moving to the next level of production, which has the potential to transform
the markets for both salmon and leafy vegetables in the United States, where
consumers currently depend heavily on imports of both products. Plans call
for ramping up salmon production by a factor of ten, to seven hundred metric tons a year in Wisconsin and building new plants on the West and East
Coasts of the United States.

The race to build commercial-scale alternatives to open-net salmon farms
is like a gold rush, moving fast and attracting hordes of prospectors. In addition to Sustainable Blue and Cape d'Or in Nova Scotia, Atlantic Sapphire's
big project in Florida, and Superior Fresh in Wisconsin, more than seventy
RAS projects are in various stages of development in places ranging from
Mount Fuji in Japan and Fujian province in China to the desert outside Dubai
and the Alpine mountains of Switzerland. Most projects expect production
volumes of 5,000 to 35,000 metric tons a year, far smaller than the game-
changing ambitions of Atlantic Sapphire.

Adapting RAS technology to commercial salmon farming presents a
host of challenges. The technology is touchy, and missteps can wipe out whole
tanks of fish, as Atlantic Sapphire and Sustainable Blue have discovered. Capital can run out before the first harvest brings in cash. In the early days of the
technology, there were enough failures that the website SeaWestNews published
an article about the challenges under the clever headline "RAS in Peace."

Mainstream salmon farmers dismiss RAS technology as too expensive
and too small. On December 4, 2018, at an extraordinary meeting in Bergen,
Norway, Marine Harvest's executives announced that they intended to change
the company's name back to Mowi to honor its founder, Thor Mowinckel.
Among the shareholders in the audience was Johan Frederik Mowinckel, a
member of the founding family. When he stood to speak, most people probably expected him to thank the company for remembering his family. That
was not what happened.

Mowinckel had watched the industry and its footprint expand in ways that had left him uncomfortable. As a result, a descendant of one of the industry's creators had become an advocate for transformation. He and his family had no influence over the direction of the company, but they had been trying to persuade its executives to shift its production to environmentally friendly, land-based farms using RAS technology. But Marine Harvest and the other big Norwegian companies had little interest in making the transition, arguing that the capital investment in a land-based farm was too high and that the commercial viability remained in doubt.

This did not satisfy Mowinckel. Standing before the company's executives and other shareholders at the annual meeting, he spoke briefly and clearly. "We think it's completely wrong that the Mowi name is associated with the way you and others, in our opinion, pollute nature, wildlife's habitat, ecosystems, and threaten the future of future generations," Mowinckel said, adding that he and his family would vote against naming the company after them. Mowinckel's remarks and the "no" vote were a stunning rebuke that generated some negative press for the company. In practical terms, the complaint was nothing more than a bump in the road. The shareholders approved the name change, and Mowinckel's remarks were not even included in the meeting's minutes.

This being the modern era, Johan's son, Frederik W. Mowinckel, in his fifties, followed immediately with a tweet on his Twitter account: "No to MOWI. Members of the Mowinckel family have at the EGM today voted against Marine Harvest's plans to change its name to MOWI. We do not wish [to] be associated with what we consider an unsustainable way of farming salmon. Completely closed farms is the only way forward."

By 2021, Mowi had softened its view slightly, saying it was reconsidering the prospects of land-based systems. Two other major Norwegian companies have taken tentative steps as Norway's government develops ways to promote a shift to land-based systems. Grieg Seafood invested in a joint venture to grow salmon on land in western Norway, though company officials stressed that land-based farms would only supplement its traditional sites, not replace them. The second was Leroy Seafood Group, one of the world's largest integrated seafood companies, with a fleet of trawlers to catch cod and haddock in addition to its salmon farms in Norway and Scotland. In early 2021, Leroy said it was negotiating to develop a RAS facility in three phases in western

Norway. Again, there were caveats. "This learning will possibly, if desired, also be used for the realization of land-based projects also in other regions," Henning Beltestad, the chief executive officer, told *Fish Farmer* magazine.

Other alternative technologies are being explored. One is open-ocean farms, which keep the fish in cages but move them miles offshore, where strong currents disperse waste widely and where interactions with wild salmon are minimized. The tests are being conducted up to thirty miles from shore, which means these farms must deal with brutal ocean conditions, requiring construction standards like those for an oil platform. In 2018, the big Norwegian salmon-farming company SalMar built the world's first open-ocean salmon farm three miles off the coast of Norway, a three-hundred-million-dollar facility constructed to withstand fifty-foot waves. Called Ocean Farm 1, the pilot facility delivered ten thousand tons of Atlantic salmon to markets in its first two production cycles, working well enough for the company to plan to build a larger ocean farm. Salmon farms on the open ocean have certain advantages over open-net cages close to fragile shorelines, but the costs of construction and ongoing access are high. So, other alternatives are being pursued. One involves raising salmon in holes blasted out of rock at the shoreline. Known as "open-flow systems," these systems draw salt water from wells below the survival limits of sea lice to fill the rock pool. The water is treated before it is discharged into the ocean. In another alternative technology, a sewage treatment company north of Tokyo is raising Atlantic salmon on land using artificial seawater. The plant adds salt to freshwater from the municipal water system and cycles it through a two-stage, bacteria-based filtration system on its path to the fish tanks. In the mountains of Switzerland, Swiss Alpine Fish is creating salt water for its RAS operations in much the same way as the Japanese.

While the pioneers of land-based salmon farming are competitors, there is also a sense of collegiality as they work to overcome obstacles and change the way the world gets its farmed salmon. Every three months, top executives from the some of the big RAS facilities have a Zoom call to share ideas and information. Among the participants are Superior Fresh, Nordic Aquafarms, Sustainable Blue, Swiss Alpine Fish, Whole Oceans, and Kuterra, a farm on the northern tip of Vancouver Island started by the Namgis First Nation. "We talk about the issues and challenges while avoiding the exchange of proprietary information," said Havercroft of Sustainable Blue. "It's a friendly and collaborative group." Missing from the calls was Atlantic Sapphire, which chose not to participate. But the potential of the multiple die-offs at its two plants to affect financing for the fledgling industry is a frequent topic of conversation. In this "gold rush," the dramatic scale of Atlantic Sapphire makes it a bellwether for the industry. If it reaches and sustains commercial-level production, the company will prove that Atlantic salmon does not have to be raised in pens on the ocean in order to supply the world. Similarly, the success of Superior Fresh in raising Atlantic salmon on a sustainable diet in freshwater and producing organic vegetables offers a viable path forward.

In all its emerging forms, land-based salmon farming accounts for only a fraction of the global supply, and its fish cost more than open-net salmon. But the business has taken on an identity and appears poised to grow rapidly as its ocean-based competitors face public opposition and as governments impose greater restrictions on where and how they can raise their fish. For those searching for a more environmentally acceptable method of providing the world's protein, RAS technology offers more hope for a better way of farming salmon as the technology improves.

CHAPTER 28

NOW WHAT?

What you do makes a difference,
and you have to decide what kind of difference you want to make.

—JANE GOODALL

Over the last four decades, Atlantic salmon farming has changed the way the world consumes fish. A handful of modest pens in the fjords of Norway morphed into industrial feedlots along the coasts of three continents. Millions of meals of farmed salmon are eaten every day at restaurants and dinner tables. Salmon farming is the world's fastest-growing food-production system. In 1970, most salmon in stores and restaurants had been caught in rivers and oceans. Today, after overfishing and other assaults pushed wild salmon into the danger zone, roughly 70 percent of the world's salmon comes from crowded cages floating in fragile ocean ecosystems. This revolution in production tripled the worldwide supply to 2.6 million tons of farmed salmon annually, while lowering the price and creating a twenty-billion-dollar oligopoly dominated by a handful of multinational corporations.

The rise of farmed salmon changed lives in many lower-income nations. The increasing global appetite for cheap salmon created a parallel demand for forage fish like anchovies, sardines, menhaden, and mackerel. The aquaculture industry disparages these species, often referring to them as "trash fish." Tell that to people who depend on them for their livelihood and their food. Forage fish account for more than a third of the fish taken from the world's oceans each year, and 90 percent of the catch is processed into feed for aquaculture, livestock, and household pets. Industry efforts to reduce the wild fish content of salmon feed have had limited success, and the demand for forage fish is expected to grow as salmon production increases.

Millions of people buy farmed salmon every day without thinking about where it came from, the environmental impact of how it was raised, or whether claims about its sustainability and health benefits are accurate. This book was written to help consumers understand how salmon gets to their plate and the consequences of its journey. It was written to expose the hidden costs of salmon farming, the real price that never shows up at the seafood counter or on the restaurant menu—and which is not necessarily measured in dollars and cents. It is not intended to be an obituary for salmon farming but, rather, a way to encourage more responsible practices. Even if we were to wish to do so, closing a multibillion-dollar industry is not realistic. Perhaps it is not even necessary, provided the open-net salmon-farming companies adopt practices to protect the environment, stop damaging forage fisheries, and deliver a healthier product.

As with the tobacco and auto industries, the giants of the salmon-farming business will not abandon their profitable ways without pressure. Ravaged wild salmon populations have not forced traditional salmon farmers to stop spreading parasites and pathogens or to keep their operations away from salmon migration routes. Losses of tens of millions of fish every year have not caused them to reconsider conditions in cages. Warnings about health threats from chemicals, PCBs, and other contaminants have led to only modest changes. The public pays the price for the damage while the companies and their investors reap the profits.

There are signs that the public is beginning to pay attention. In mid-2021, the Environmental Defense Fund, an advocacy group in Washington, DC, conducted a poll of eight hundred Americans that identified the scope of consumer discontent with aquaculture. The results found that consumers are concerned about how farmed fish are raised, worried about the impact of fish farming on the environment, and doubtful about whether government is protecting consumers from health risks. The poll also offered aquaculture companies a glimmer of hope for the future, but only if they clean up their business.

The statistics were crystal clear:

- Sixty-nine percent of respondents said they were concerned about the origin of the seafood they eat;

- Seventy-three percent said they would eat more seafood if consumer protections were strengthened and if safety standards for how fish are farmed were improved;

- Seventy-one percent said they would eat more seafood if environmental standards for fish farms were raised and if the fish came from sustainable sources.

The choice for salmon farmers is clear: the industry can prosper by adopting higher health and environmental standards, or it can jeopardize its future by ignoring its customers.

The shift to more responsible, environmentally friendly, and healthier farming methods will take time, and the outcome depends on consumer awareness, increased government regulation, technological advances, and industry accountability. Alternatives to "business as usual" are increasing, from feed that ends the use of wild-caught fish to land-based systems that eliminate chemicals and escapes. By the end of 2022, more than one hundred RAS projects were underway around the world. Some analysts projected that land-based salmon production could equal that of open-net pen farms within the decade.

Not all innovations are drawing support from public health experts. In 2020, the U.S. Food and Drug Administration approved the sale of genetically modified salmon, prompting both praise and concern. Advocates argued that the GM fish grow twice as fast as normal farmed salmon. The GM version can also be raised in land-based farms, reducing the risk of pollution and interbreeding with wild salmon. Critics, on the other hand, worry that what they call "Frankenfish" are being marketed without sufficient testing on potential health risks for consumers and without adequate disclosures about the origin of the fish, a similar complaint about farmed salmon. Already, some stores have said they will not sell the GM version.

The moment has arrived to focus on the future, on feeding the planet in ways that will not kill the planet. The oceans are running out of fish. The United Nations' Food and Agriculture Organization said a third of the six hundred fish stocks it evaluates are either overfished or depleted, and most of the remainder are approaching their limit. History has demonstrated that with proper management, these stocks can recover, often quickly. Salmon farming has played a role in the depletion of wild salmon and forage fisheries. Sustainable salmon farming can play a role in their recovery. Adopting new technologies takes time, and the sclerotic industry will neither disappear nor change its practices overnight.

How do we make the transition? Fortunately, there is a road map to a more responsible and healthier way. The journey's first three steps are clear.

First is for consumers to understand the risks and rewards of eating farmed salmon. We should insist on greater transparency from grocery chains, restaurants, and salmon-farming companies. Taste preferences, price, and nutritional benefits influence consumer purchases. When it comes to farmed salmon, information about those factors can be deceptive or simply absent. For instance, the U.S. Department of Agriculture does not have standards for what constitutes "organic" salmon. So, almost all brands sold as "organic" in the United States are automatically mislabeled. Studies have found that farmed salmon is often marketed falsely as wild salmon, which is healthier and more expensive. Salmon farmers rarely disclose their use of pesticides, antibiotics, and other chemicals. Many certification programs identifying farmed salmon as healthy, sustainable, or naturally raised are operated by self-interested organizations financed by the industry.

You are what you eat; you are also what the fish you eat eats. When people look over a menu or approach the seafood counter at the local market, they should know what they are buying. Was the fish treated with antibiotics or other chemicals? Was it raised in an ocean feedlot or on land with minimal environmental impact? Labels should be required by law to make the same disclosures found on many other food products. Until that happens, consumers should demand honest information from seafood retailers and restaurants and rely on the handful of reputable seafood guides like the Monterey Bay Aquarium's Seafood Watch. Or they should stop buying farmed salmon.

The second step is transforming individual responsibility into coordinated action. Educated consumers can team up with environmental organizations, scientists, nutritionists, and government reformers to build a movement that requires salmon farmers to protect the environment and ensure the health of their fish and of consumers. Many groups and individuals, the people we call the resistance, have raised awareness about the risks from open-net salmon farming without sparking major reforms or a large-scale shift to land-based farms. Collective action can drive change. Harnessing policies to pocketbooks can influence the industry's behavior or lead to its extinction.

There are precedents. In the early 1950s, scientists found a statistical link between smoking and lung cancer. The tobacco industry's internal research confirmed the relationship. But Big Tobacco buried its evidence and mounted a sustained campaign to discredit critics. The deception did not end until public pressure and the exposure of internal documents forced governments to issue warnings for and increase taxes on cigarettes. Today, smokers know the impact of their choice.

Another example is the history of seat belts in automobiles. The first patent for a safety harness in a car was granted in 1885, but carmakers did not offer them until the mid-1950s, and they were a twenty-seven-dollar option (equivalent to three hundred in today's dollars). Then came Ralph Nader and his seminal book, *Unsafe at Any Speed*, which showed how automakers were risking lives for the sake of profit by neglecting safety advances. Five years later, in 1970, Congress created the National Highway Traffic Safety Administration, which overruled industry objections and required seat belts in all cars. The death rate from accidents dropped from 5.7 fatalities for every one hundred million miles traveled to 3.6 by 1975. Since then, seat belts have saved more than 375,000 lives in the United States and, with the addition of air bags and other improvements, the fatality rate has dropped to 1.11 deaths per one hundred million miles.

The point is not to equate salmon farming with deaths from smoking or car accidents. Rather, the lesson is that industries do not alter profitable behavior without coordinated public pressure and strong government action. The decision by Washington State to phase out salmon farms in its waters after the Cooke Aquaculture farm collapse in 2017 was propelled by a grassroots campaign demonstrating that collective action and a responsive government can lead to real change. Activists make a difference by speaking out. Consumers can refuse to collude.

The third step is for governments to stop putting a thumb on the scale when weighing economic interests against public well-being. Governments should take responsibility for protecting both the environment and public health. They should adopt strict curbs on the use of chemicals by salmon farmers. They should require the notification of all relevant authorities of every escape or suspected escape, and those reports should be made public. Food labels should be thorough and accurate and should reflect how the salmon was raised. Data about contaminants and additives should be transparent and available, particularly because of their impact on pregnant women, infants, and children. Local, state, and federal agencies need more resources to oversee food safety and public health. The fact that the U.S. Food and Drug Administration inspects only a tiny fraction of imported farmed salmon is just one indication of the urgent need to ramp up oversight. We recently saw that government action can lead to big changes. As of January 1, 2022, countries with fishing industries that interact with mammals must show that they are in compliance with U.S. laws protecting seals and other animals or be banned from selling their seafood in the United States. Canada and Scotland have passed laws to comply, and other seafood-producing countries are considering action.

There must be similar global efforts to protect the public health and the welfare of salmon. Action in major consuming countries is critical, but countries with the most responsibility for ending the untenable status quo are the ones where salmon is raised in the ocean. Governments in those countries should ensure that the responsibility to protect the environment and public health is separate from the mandate to promote salmon farming and other forms of aquaculture. Allowing a single agency to protect and promote sacrifices the public good. Regulations need to be strengthened and enforced; penalties should be significant enough to deter repeated violations. Scientists must be free to publish their findings and speak their minds. What happens in the producing countries affects everyone who eats farmed salmon.

The science is clear: salmon farming endangers wild salmon by spreading disease, pollution, and sea lice and allowing millions of alien fish to escape. Wild salmon are a barometer of the planet's health. They can survive only in clean, cool water, and their presence in a river has traditionally signaled to anglers that the water is safe to drink. Their decline shows that it's more than just recreational fishing that is being threatened, but life on earth as we know it. The creeping loss of this keystone species should be a clear warning to all of us. Wild salmon are on the verge of extinction in every country where intensive salmon farming exists near their migration routes. Protecting and restoring the wild stocks should be a legislative priority and an industry mandate. Regulations should keep farms away from migration routes and set reasonable distances between farms to reduce the spread of disease and parasites. Operators should be required to adopt comprehensive plans to stop fish escapes and to report every escape to regulators and the public, no matter how small. Existing fisheries for lobster, crabs, and other marine life should be protected from the impact of salmon farms, and people who make their living from the ocean should have a voice in where farms are located. For too long, these floating feedlots have polluted fragile coastal waters and endangered other marine life without consultation or consequence. In the past, whole species were destroyed, and no one noticed. Today, we know what we are doing, and we know how to stop it.

The choice for the public, government, and the industry is not between whether to feed the world or save the environment. We can do both. We can balance protecting the environment and providing jobs and food. Ultimately, governments need to rise to the challenge and support RAS and other land-based technologies through incentives that encourage the shift to land and through fees that discourage open-net farms, which have gotten a free ride for too long. The multinationals will object and will lecture officials and the public about generating jobs and feeding the world. They will lobby politicians, rail against activists, and smear credible scientists. In the end, the public good requires transforming harm industries when possible and abandoning them when necessary.

While reforming the old, we need to treat the new with optimism and humility. The power of technology to transform can blind innovators to unexpected results. When farming salmon in ocean pens was first introduced, conservationists imagined that the process would help take the pressure off wild salmon. Governments poured hundreds of millions of dollars of taxpayer money into nurturing the industry, and many countries still underwrite the business through low licensing fees, permissive waste disposal, and subsidies to the huge fishing vessels disrupting the food chain for humans and marine life. The unexpected result was a global industry that has demonstrably contributed to the decline of wild salmon. Predicting how a technology will affect the future or what surprises are waiting around the corner is tricky. Innovators, regulators, and the public should pay attention as RAS technology and other innovations change the way salmon is farmed.

When it comes to salmon farming, however, some conservationists and animal rights advocates argue that all the methods are cruel, whether the fish are in cages floating in the ocean or swimming in circles in tanks on land. Wolfram Heise, a conservationist in Chile, put it succinctly when he said, "There is no right way of doing the wrong thing." People for the Ethical Treatment of Animals calls land-based salmon farming inhumane, comparing the density in a RAS tank to twenty-seven fish crammed in a bathtub. In response to these ethical concerns, growing salmon and other seafood directly from cells and plants that mimic the taste and texture is rising in popularity alongside veggie burgers and fake bacon. A San Francisco start-up called Wildtype is working to transform the seafood industry by cultivating salmon from cells. The company has produced what it describes as "sushi-grade" salmon with the same amount of omega-3 fatty acids as wild salmon.

While vegans and animal rights activists have a right to object, abandoning salmon farming or aquaculture in general could create more problems than it solves for the global population. The challenge of saving the planet and feeding its people should be a strong incentive to bolster new technologies and strategies, from sustainable feed to biosecurity and disease control. Salmon farming remains a relatively new industry, and already there are signs of improvement in formulas for feed and in lowering contaminants. There is still time to reform its methods in ways that benefit the planet and the people.

We all make choices in deciding what to eat, and those choices have consequences for our health and the health of the planet. Bill Taylor made his choice. As president of the Atlantic Salmon Federation, Taylor heads an organization with twenty-five thousand members and volunteers in the United States and Canada dedicated to conserving and restoring wild Atlantic salmon. "We shouldn't be eating any salmon that is raised in open-net-pen feedlots," said Taylor. "The average person going into a grocery store sees Atlantic salmon everywhere. It's often the cheapest fish. The average person doesn't grasp the magnitude of the problem or the influence of their choices as consumers. Wild Atlantic salmon are in serious trouble, yet people see farmed salmon at fish counters and on menus all the time, and wonder, how can Atlantic salmon be in trouble? They don't square the difference between farmed and wild. The facts and the truth pull back the covers on the industry. The industry is filthy. A few people are making a lot of money, and the environmental costs are just huge."

Options exist, and change will come only when individual decisions are transformed into public demands, regulatory action, and a responsible salmon-farming industry.

We do have to choose.

SOURCE NOTES

This is not an academic book, and we have avoided using footnotes. Our primary sources were interviews, news and research articles, public meetings, and thousands of pages of court records and government documents. Most records and articles are available publicly, but some were obtained through Freedom of Information Act (FOIA) requests to the U.S. government and Access to Information Act requests to the Canadian government.

The work of these scientists, researchers, and journalists influenced our thinking and contributed to our conclusions. Listed in this section, by chapter, are the people we interviewed and the principal scholarly studies, news articles, and government records on which we relied. For readers who want more information, we have provided many of the website URLs.

Missing from the book are responses from Cooke Aquaculture and Mowi ASA. Both companies refused to answer written questions or allow executives to be interviewed. To provide the fullest portrait possible under the circumstances, we relied on news articles, court records, and public statements by the companies. Many of these documents are available on our website, www.salmonwarsbook.com.

INTRODUCTION

We first encountered salmon farming in the early 1990s. Catherine's parents owned a property in the small community of Eagle Head, near Liverpool Bay, on the South Shore of Nova Scotia. One year, a salmon farm was constructed a short boat ride away from the house, just off Coffin Island. Catherine's father, Paul, a fly fisherman, welcomed the farm in the hope that it would relieve pressure on the disappearing wild salmon. The small farm grew into a large one, ultimately owned by Kelly Cove Salmon, a subsidiary of Cooke Aquaculture. Neighbors described the dead zone created around the farm and complained about the debris, night lights, and loud generators. Paul's hopes disappeared like the fish he had spent his life chasing.

Salmon farms produce waste, but estimates of how much vary greatly and depend on many factors. A 1989 study of Norwegian salmon farms estimated the organic waste in the fjords generated by the production of 150,000 tons of fish equaled 60 percent of the waste generated by Norway's total population of 4.7 million people. Today, Norway produces more than 1 million tons of farmed salmon, and global production exceeds 2.6 million tons. In a February 9, 1990, *Science* magazine article, Marcia Barinaga compared waste from a two-acre salmon farm to effluent from a town of 10,000 people. The Pure Salmon Campaign, an international advocacy group, said a single salmon farm with 200,000 fish discharged fecal matter equivalent to a city of 65,000 people. The study is at https://nsapes.ca/sites/default/files/attachments/waste_0.pdf. Salmon industry experts and some academics argue that salmon farms have little or no impact on the surrounding environment.

The figure of two hundred yards for the reduction in biodiversity is from a study cited at https://seafood.ocean.org/wp-content/uploads/2016/10/Salmon-Atlantic -Scotland.pdf.

The underwater photo of the yardstick buried in waste was taken in Port Mouton Bay, Nova Scotia, by Kathy and Dave Brush, and can be found at https:// commonsensecanadian.ca/fish-farm-sewage-dfo-expansions-cost-money/.

Mortality rates, like waste estimates, vary. The estimated worldwide mortality rate of 15 to 20 percent is based on multiple academic and news sources. Only Norway and Scotland regularly report mortality rates. Norwegian figures are from the Norwegian Fish Health Report for 2020. Scottish government data was reported by Rob Edwards, "Farmed Salmon Deaths from Disease Reach Record High," The Ferret, July 13, 2020. The report is at https://theferret.scot/farmed-salmon-deaths-disease-reach-record-high/. The Ferret provides excellent coverage of Scotland's salmon farms. Newfoundland mortality rates came from provincial data obtained through an Access to Information request.

CHAPTER 1

John Fredriksen played a central role in transforming salmon farming into a global behemoth. He is also a fascinating character, as is evident in numerous articles about him and interviews with people who know him. Mowi declined our request to interview Fredriksen. The most thorough account of his career was by Bloomberg News reporters Edward Robinson and Michelle Wiese Bockmann, "Shipping Magnate John Fredriksen Sticks to His 'Gut Feeling': Invest," *Washington Post*, September 22, 2012.

Fredriksen's short-lived concern about the impact of salmon farms on wild salmon was reported by Rune Ostlyngen, "Move Salmon Farms Out of the Fjords," *Altaposten*, July 19, 2007. Ostlyngen confirmed Fredriksen's remarks in an interview. The letter from thirty-three organizations has been taken offline but is still available at https://donstaniford.typepad.com/files/fredriksen-backgrounder-for-der-fliegenfischer.pdf.

A description of the aircraft at the Alta airport in salmon season is from an article by Nina Berglund, "Alta Salmon River Lures the Wealthy," *Norwegian News in English*, July 17, 2014.

The dramatic growth of the farmed-salmon supply from 1995 to 2020 is on page 48 of the *Salmon Farming Industry Handbook 2021*, a useful annual compilation of data published by Mowi ASA: https://corpsite.azureedge.net/corpsite/wp-content/uploads/2021/05/Salmon-Industry-Handbook-2021.pdf.

Multiple sources have told the history of salmon farming in Norway, including Aslak Berge, "The Salmon Farming Pioneers: The Vik Brothers," SalmonBusiness, September 20, 2017; and numerous books and articles by Trygve Gjedrem, a Norwegian who studied at Iowa State University with Jay Laurence Lush, a pioneer in animal genetics. Lush's work is detailed at https://www.ans.iastate.edu/about/history/people/jay-l-lush. A timeline for Mowi's history appears on the company website: https://mowi.com/about/.

The 747 lice on a single salmon is from an excellent documentary by Lucy Adams, "Is There a Problem with Salmon Farming?," *Panorama*, BBC, May 20, 2019, https://www.bbc.com/news/uk-scotland-48266480.

The 2021 report on the economics of salmon farming, *Dead Loss: The High Cost of Poor Salmon Farming Practices*, is at https://www.justeconomics.co.uk/health-and-well-being/dead-loss.

CHAPTER 2

Glenn Cooke's appearance on *Undercover Boss Canada* aired January 3, 2014, and can be found at https://www.youtube.com/watch?v=EEpnkAGvyd8.

Numerous biographical articles have been published about Cooke. The most thorough were by Gordon Pitts, "Maritimer Dreamed of Casting a Global Net," *Globe and Mail*, October 6, 2008; Kevin Bissett, "Seafood Giant Cooke Aquaculture Joins Irvings, McCains as New Brunswick Business Royalty," *Canadian Press*, December 12, 2018; and Stephen Kimber, "Perseverance and a Social Conscience," *Atlantic Business*, March/April 2019. Cooke provided a personal account of his business career on May 20, 2011, when he received an honorary doctorate from the University of New Brunswick, which can be found at https://www2.unb.ca/chopinlab/imta/news/glenncooke_doctorate/index.html.

Inka Milewski was interviewed numerous times in 2020 and 2021. Her account of how Canada came to support salmon farming was confirmed in government reports and interviews with officials at the Atlantic Salmon Federation and other organizations.

Don Ivany was interviewed in 2020.

CHAPTER 3

Bryant Green was interviewed in August 2020. His recollections match details in court records in the criminal case against Cooke and his company.

The criminal investigation of cypermethrin use by Cooke Aquaculture's Kelly Cove Salmon subsidiary was described in several hundred pages of court records provided by a person involved in the case. The documents present a detailed chronology of the investigation and include a forty-nine-page affidavit by Robert Robichaud, affidavits by other enforcement officers, and results of tests that found cypermethrin at fifteen Cooke salmon farms. The court records were augmented by an Agreed Statement of Facts filed with the Provincial Court as part of Kelly Cove's guilty plea.

The plea, the near-empty scene in court, and Glenn Cooke's public statement are from "Aquaculture Company on the Hook for $500K for Pesticide Use," CBC News, April 26, 2013.

Robichaud's private view of the plea agreement came from a former colleague at Environment Canada; Robichaud declined an interview.

The huge number of viruses in the ocean is described by Ann C. Gregory et al., "Marine DNA Viral Macro- and Micro-diversity from Pole to Pole," *Cell* 177, no. 5 (May 16, 2019): 1109–23; and other studies.

The discovery of ISA at Cooke's salmon farm near Shelburne was described in interviews with local residents and news accounts, including Jack MacAndrew, "Canadian Food Inspection Agency Investigating ISA Presence in Cooke Salmon Farm," *South Coaster*, February 21, 2012; Timothy Gillespie, "More Salmon Kills Ordered at Shelburne Fish Farm," *South Coast Today*, March 27, 2012; and "Fish Farm Quarantined After Suspected ISA Outbreak," CBC News, June 20, 2012.

The $13 million payment to Cooke after it slaughtered a million salmon at its Shelburne farm is from "$13M for Cooke Aquaculture After Infected Salmon," CBC News, January 8, 2014.

The report on $100 million in compensation to salmon farmers in Canada's eastern provinces was produced by the Atlantic Salmon Federation. In 2014, the Ecology Action Centre in Halifax concluded that $139 million in taxpayer money had been paid in compensation to salmon farmers in New Brunswick, Nova Scotia, and Newfoundland; the information is at "Groups Call for End to Public Bailouts for Open-Pen Salmon Feedlots," Ecology Action Centre, March 19, 2014, found at https://ecologyaction.ca/press-release/groups-call-end-public-bailouts-open-pen-salmon-feedlots.

Glenn Cooke's quote "It's an incredible journey" is from *Undercover Boss Canada*.

CHAPTER 4

We conducted multiple interviews with Alexandra Morton. She also maintains an active presence on social media, including with her blog, *Resist Extinction*, https://

alexandramorton.typepad.com/. Morton described her husband's death in an interview and in news articles. Among the best articles about her are "Into the Wild," *Vancouver Magazine*, November 2, 2008; and Cornelia Dean, "Saving Wild Salmon, in Hopes of Saving the Orca," *New York Times*, November 3, 2008. Morton was featured in the 2013 documentary *Salmon Confidential*, written and directed by Twyla Roscovich. Morton has also published a memoir, *Not on My Watch* (Toronto: Random House Canada, 2021).

Kurt Beardslee described founding and running the Wild Fish Conservancy in interviews and email exchanges in 2020 and 2021. Additional information is at www .wildfishconservancy.org. Emma Halverson of the Conservancy shared additional insights.

Mary Ellen Walling's quote about Morton appeared in an article by Mark Hume, "One Woman's Struggle to Save B.C.'s Wild Salmon," *Globe and Mail*, April 20, 2012.

The Black Cube incident was recounted by Morton in an interview and in her memoir. The first article about it was by Cole Kelly, "'Black Cube' Mix-up Muddies Waters over 'Martin Sheen' Surveillance," *MyCampbellRiverNow*, July 27, 2018.

Morton's comment about publicizing the salmon issue is from Dean, "Saving Wild Salmon, in Hopes of Saving the Orca."

Don Staniford described his career in interviews and email exchanges. His blog, *Green Around the Gills*, is at https://donstaniford.typepad.com/my-blog/ and provides links to documents on salmon farming.

Staniford described his interaction with Jackie MacKenzie in an interview. The article about MacKenzie is by Antony Barnett, "'Illegal Poison' Used on Salmon," *Observer*, April 29, 2000.

Staniford's legal conflicts were described in interviews and media articles. His departure from Canada appeared in "B.C. Salmon-Farming Critic Vows to Keep Fighting from Norway," *Canadian Press*, March 5, 2012.

Staniford's legal battle with Cermaq appeared in "Anti-Salmon-Farming Activist Wins B.C. Court Victory," *Canadian Press*, September 28, 2012. The Court of Appeal order that Staniford pay $75,000 to Cermaq is discussed by the law firm McCarthy Tétrault LLP at https://www.martindale.com/legal-news/article_mccarthy-tetrault-llp _1923084.htm.

Staniford's response to the fine came from an interview.

CHAPTER 5

The 2004 article in *Science* was the starting point for this chapter. It was augmented by other scholarly articles and interviews. The article is at https://science .sciencemag.org/content/303/5655/226/tab-figures-data. The study by the Environmental Working Group is at https://www.ewg.org/research/pcbs-farmed-salmon.

John Webster's comment about "scaremongering" was reported by Michael Hopkin, "Farmed Salmon Harbour Pollutants," *Nature*, January 9, 2004.

Walter Willett's comment about the *Science* study is from Walter C. Willett, "Fish: Balancing Health Risks and Benefits," *American Journal of Preventive Medicine* 29, no. 4 (November 2005): 320–21. Ronald Hites responded in an interview in 2020.

"We did get a bit of heat" is from the Hites interview.

The description of the Scottish Quality Salmon campaign came from David Miller, a British sociologist, professor, and cofounder of the nonprofit Public Interest Investigations. His report is at https://www.academia.edu/2939514/Spinning_farmed_salmon. The attempt to discredit critics exposed by Miller fits a pattern of industry tactics that continues today.

The analysis of ExxonMobil's messaging strategy is from an article by Geoffrey Supran and Naomi Oreskes, "Rhetoric and Frame Analysis of ExxonMobil's Climate Change Communications," *One Earth* 4, no. 5 (May 13, 2021): 696–719.

CHAPTER 6

"It is confusing" is from an interview with Dr. Leonardo Trasande in 2020. We also relied on his book *Sicker, Fatter, Poorer* (Boston: Houghton Mifflin Harcourt, 2019).

The risks to children from food additives is described by Leonardo Trasande, Rachel M. Shaffer, and Sheela Sathyanarayana, "Food Additives and Child Health," *American Academy of Pediatrics* 142 (August 2018).

The findings of Sandra and Joseph Jacobson have been the subject of many scholarly works, including a report by John D. Schell Jr., Robert A. Budinsky, and Michael J. Wernke, "PCBs and Neurodevelopmental Effects in Michigan Children: An Evaluation of Exposure and Dose Characterization," *Regulatory Toxicology and Pharmacology* 33 (June 2001): 300–312. The original study was by J. L. Jacobson, S. W. Jacobson, and H. E. Humphrey, "Effects of Exposure to PCBs and Related Compounds on Growth and Activity in Children," *Neurotoxicology and Teratology* (July–August 1990): 319–26.

Seafood Watch's methods and recommendations were described in interviews with its staff and on its website, at https://www.seafoodwatch.org/recommendations/search?query=%3Aspecies%3BAtlantic%20salmon.

Oceana's survey on mislabeled salmon is at https://oceana.org/press-center/press-releases/new-oceana-study-reveals-scary-news-about-americas-favorite-fish.

Arizona State University's analysis of antibiotics in seafood is at https://sols.asu.edu/news-events/news/new-study-antibiotics-finds-something-fishy.

Warnings about antibiotic resistance in humans are described by the WHO at https://www.who.int/news-room/fact-sheets/detail/antibiotic-resistance.

In 2021, Seafood Watch rated 50 percent of Chile's farmed salmon as "Avoid,"

based on the use of chemicals. The recommendation is at https://www.seafoodwatch
.org/our-projects/farmed-salmon-in-chile.

Fred Kibenge's study of ISA in Chile appears at https://www.researchgate.net
/figure/Distribution-of-the-ISA-outbreaks-in-Chile-Chart-showing-the-distribution
-of-the_fig2_26322892.

"It turned this scientific field upside down" is from the Trasande interview.

The dangers from chlorpyrifos were described in a study published in August
2019 in the journal *Society of Environmental Toxicology and Chemistry*, at https://setac
.onlinelibrary.wiley.com/doi/10.1002/ieam.4199. The U.S. government's proposed ban
is from Dan Charles, "Government Scientists Say a Controversial Pesticide Is Killing
Endangered Salmon," *The Salt*, NPR, January 11, 2018.

Findings about reduced omega-3 fatty acids were reported by M. Sprague, J. R.
Dick, and D. R. Tocher, "Impact of Sustainable Feeds on Omega-3 Long-Chain Fatty
Acid Levels in Farmed Atlantic Salmon, 2006–2015," *Scientific Reports* 6 (February
22, 2016).

The U.S. Public Health Service and EPA paper on PCBs in humans is at https://
www.epa.gov/sites/default/files/2015-01/documents/pcb99.pdf.

The dueling opinions from the Mayo Clinic are at https://www.mayoclinic
.org/healthy-lifestyle/pregnancy-week-by-week/in-depth/pregnancy-and-fish/art
-20044185 and https://www.mayoclinic.org/healthy-lifestyle/nutrition-and-healthy
-eating/expert-answers/fish-and-pbcs/faq-20348595.

CHAPTER 7

The three lawsuits against Mowi and Mowi Ducktrap are Organic Consumers
Association v. Mowi ASA, Mowi USA LLC, Mowi Ducktrap LLC, Case No. 2020 CA
003368, Superior Court of the District of Columbia Civil Division; Neversink General
Store v. Mowi USA LLC and Mowi Ducktrap, Case No. 1:2020cv09293, United States
District Court, Southern District of New York; and Abigail Starr v. Mowi ASA, Mowi
USA LLC, and Mowi Ducktrap LLC, Case No. 2:20-cv-00488-LEW, United States Dis-
trict Court, District of Maine.

The suit by the Organic Consumers Association is at https://law.justia.com/cases
/federal/district-courts/district-of-columbia/dcdce/1:2016cv00925/179106/40/. The
suit by Neversink General Store is at https://www.classaction.org/media/neversink
-general-store-v-mowi-usa-llc-et-al.pdf. The suit by Abigail Starr is at https://www
.truthinadvertising.org/wp-content/uploads/2021/01/Starr-v-Mowi-complaint.pdf.

The quote beginning "Most consumers choosing," from Ronnie Cummins, is
from an Organic Consumers Association press release, August 4, 2020.

The antitrust investigations were described by several news outlets, including Kevin
Keane, "Salmon Farms Raided as Part of EU Competition Probe," BBC News, February

20, 2019; and Foo Yun Chee and Nerijus Adomaitis, "EU Raids Salmon Farmers in Suspected Cartel Inquiry," Reuters, February 19, 2019. The U.S. Justice Department investigation was described by many news outlets, including Mikael Holter, "U.S. Joins Antitrust Push Against Norway Salmon Farmers," Bloomberg News, November 15, 2019. As of publication, the antitrust inquiries were ongoing.

Similar accusations were made in a class-action civil suit filed in 2019 in federal court in Miami against five major salmon-farming firms, Mowi, Grieg, Cermaq, Sal-Mar, and LeRoy. In March 2021, the judge ruled that the plaintiffs had provided sufficient information to proceed and scheduled the trial for May 2023. The judge's order and background on the suit are at https://casetext.com/case/in-re-farm-raised-salmon -salmon-prods-antitrust-litig.

Scottish government records on the use of hydrogen peroxide by Mowi and other salmon farmers appear on Don Staniford's blog at https://donstaniford.typepad.com /my-blog/2020/12/sick-scottish-salmon-foi-reveals-toxic-chemical-use-via-wellboats -in-2019-.html. The investigation was described by Lucy Adams, "Salmon Farming Giant Mowi Probed over Chemical Use," *Panorama*, BBC, May 20, 2019; and Charlie Gall, "Scottish Salmon Farms Under Investigation for Potential Misuse of Chemicals," *Daily Record*, May 21, 2019.

Mowi was one of several salmon farmers blamed by the Scottish Environment Protection Agency in 2017 for contaminating at least forty-five lochs with toxic pesticides, according to Rob Edwards, "Fish Farm Pesticides Have Polluted 45 Lochs," *The Ferret*, February 28, 2017, at https://theferret.scot/45-lochs-polluted-fish-farm -pesticides/.

The death of 737,000 fish was reported by Rob Edwards, "Salmon Company Mowi Rapped over Fish Welfare after 700,000 Deaths," *National*, November 10, 2019.

Court approval of the $1.3 million settlement in the *Neversink v. Mowi* case is at https://www.casemine.com/judgement/us/60aecd964653d052f477d30e. The judge's order includes a description of the dispute between the law firms suing Mowi.

The "Salmofan" color chart is at https://www.dsm.com/anh/products-and -services/tools/salmofan.html.

Egil Sundheim's quote about farmed-salmon coloring is from an article on the Costco website, at https://www.costcoconnection.com/connection/201902 /MobilePagedArticle.action?articleId=1461267#articleId1461267.

CHAPTER 8

The GAO has called attention to the inadequacy of FDA inspections for more than a decade. The earliest report, "FDA Needs to Improve Oversight of Imported Seafood and Better Leverage Limited Resources," is at https://www.gao.gov/products

/gao-11-286. The latest report, "FDA Should Improve Monitoring of Its Warning Letter Process and Better Assess Its Effectiveness," published March 19, 2021, is at https://www.gao.gov/products/gao-21-231.

The figure of eighty-six inspections of 379,000 tons of salmon by the FDA is from a table in a 2017 report by the GAO at https://www.gao.gov/products/gao-17-443; and from an article by G. B. Smejkal and S. Kakumanu, "Safely Meeting Global Salmon Demand," *npj Science of Food* 2, no. 17 (2018), available at https://www.nature.com/articles/s41538-018-0025–5#citeas. Zach Corrigan's comments came from an interview in 2020.

The Food and Drug Administration did not respond to written questions after multiple inquiries.

CHAPTER 9

Norwegian parliamentarian Jon Lilletun's comments are from an article by Nancy Macdonald, "Something Fishy in B.C.," *Maclean's*, February 11, 2009, and other sources.

Transcripts of the Cohen Commission hearings and news articles provided the bulk of the material for this chapter. The official record is at https://publications.gc.ca/site/eng/432516/publication.html.

Margaret Munro of Postmedia News exposed the muzzling of Canadian scientist Kristi Miller-Saunders in "Feds Muzzle Scientist over Salmon Study," *Vancouver Sun*, July 27, 2011. Based on 792 pages of internal government records, Munro's article sparked a wave of reporting on efforts by the government to silence scientists. Among the best was one by Janet Davison, "Are Canada's Federal Scientists Being 'Muzzled'?" CBC News, March 27, 2012.

The journalist appalled by Con Kiley's conference call trying to discredit Fred Kibenge was Damien Gillis, "Food Safety Agency Should Protect Public, Not Cover Up Virus for Salmon Farming Industry," *Common Sense Canadian*, December 12, 2012.

The October 2011 press conference by Alexandra Morton and Rick Routledge was reported by Cornelia Dean and Rachel Nuwer, "Salmon-Killing Virus Seen for First Time in the Wild on the Pacific Coast," *New York Times*, October 17, 2011.

Don McRae's disparagement of the media was reported by Damien Gillis, "US Senators Demand Action on Salmon Virus While BC Counterparts Go into Denial Mode," *Common Sense Canadian*, October 20, 2011. The article also cited concerns expressed by Washington State U.S. Senator Maria Cantwell about the threat from ISA.

Justice Cohen's final remarks are at https://www.newswire.ca/news-releases/cohen-commissions-final-report-says-fraser-river-sockeye-salmon-face-an-uncertain-future-511079471.html. Cohen declined a request for an interview.

Stewart Hawthorn's response to the recommendations was in a press release from the BC Salmon Farmers Association on October 31, 2012. His remarks were also part of a broader summary of reactions to the final report by Crawford Kilian, "Wild Salmon Advocates Cheer Cohen Commission Report," *The Tyee*, October 31, 2012.

The decertification of Fred Kibenge's lab was covered most thoroughly by CTV Atlantic News at https://atlantic.ctvnews.ca/scientists-concerned-over-chill -in-reporting-of-salmon-virus-after-lab-delisted-1.1357850/comments-7.413591 /comments-7.413591/comments-7.413591.

CHAPTER 10

Multiple interviews and correspondence with Claudette Bethune in 2020 and 2021 were instrumental for this chapter. We also benefited from award-winning reporting by Simen Saetre of Norway's national newspaper *Morgenbladet*; by Kjetil Ostli of the online magazine *Harvest*; and from access to U.S. government documents on the safety of Norwegian salmon.

The impact of genetic erosion from interbreeding is well documented. The study that found interbreeding in more than 70 percent of Norway's rivers was by Sten Karlsson et al., "Widespread Genetic Introgression of Escaped Farmed Atlantic Salmon in Wild Salmon Populations," *ICES Journal of Marine Science* 73, no. 10 (November 2016): 2488–98, https://doi.org/10.1093/icesjms/fsw121. Researchers at the Norwegian Institute for Nature Research found widespread genetic erosion in 77 of 147 rivers where salmon were sampled.

The Norwegian Directorate of Fisheries figures for escaped salmon were reported by Bent-Are Jensen and Demi Korban, "Two Million Escaped Salmon in Norway Since 2010," *Intrafish*, September 9, 2020.

The harm to salmon from high water temperatures has been documented in academic studies, including Jonatan Nilsson et al., "Sudden Exposure to Warm Water Causes Instant Behavioural Responses Indicative of Nociception or Pain in Atlantic Salmon," *Veterinary and Animal Science* 8 (December 2019); and Anne-Lise Stranden, "Salmon in Pain when Warm Water Is Used as Delousing Treatment," *ScienceNorway*, February 5, 2020.

Anette Grottland Zimowski was interviewed via email in 2021.

Ola Braanaas's comment about the "sacred salmon" is from an article by Stephen Castle, "As Wild Salmon Decline, Norway Pressures Its Giant Fish Farms," *New York Times*, November 6, 2017.

Bethune provided records of conversations with her superiors and union representative.

The Russian ban was reported widely by the press, including, "Russia Widens Ban on Imports of 'Cooled' Salmon from Norway," *Fish Farmer*, December 20, 2005. U.S. government alerts were issued on December 29, 2005, and January 6, 2006, by the embassy in Stockholm. The 2006 message read, "Once again, the safety of Norwegian salmon is making headlines in the Norwegian and Swedish press. The Russian ban on Norwegian salmon imports and a Cornell University study on the risks of farmed salmon are amongst the most recent challenges to the Norwegian farmed salmon industry."

Bethune described finding risks of contamination in Norwegian seafood, Norway's successful effort to persuade the European Union to raise acceptable levels for cadmium, and the Russian ban on Norwegian salmon in *Environmental Chemistry*, May 31, 2006.

Jerome Ruzzin first told his story in the excellent 2013 French documentary *Fillet Oh Fish*, by Nicolas Daniel, available at https://www.youtube.com/watch?v =FiYHhzYAQmU.

An English translation of the article quoting Anne-Lise Bjorke-Monsen in *Verdens Gang* is at https://alexandramorton.typepad.com/news_from_norway/2014 /02/below-is-a-collection-of-articles-largely-from-norwegian-newspapers-on-the -toxicity-of-farmed-salmon-how-norway-hid-this.html. The full report is at https:// vkm.no/download/18.2994e95b15cc54507161ea1a/1498222018046/0a646edc5e.pdf.

We interviewed Bjorke-Monsen in 2021.

The drop in antibiotic use reported by the Norwegian Seafood Council is at https://en.seafood.no/news-and-media/news-archive/norwegian-salmon-farming-sees -continued-drop-in-antibiotics-use/.

Norwegian salmon consumption is from https://www.statista.com/statistics /643484/per-capita-consumption-of-fish-and-fish-products-in-norway/.

Cermaq's use of hydrogen peroxide was reported by Judith Lavoie, "B.C. Grants Cermaq Permit to Apply 2.3 Million Litres of Pesticide to Clayoquot Sound Salmon Farms," *Narwhal*, May 3, 2018. The continuing controversy was reported by Carla Wilson, "Concerns for Whales Are Raised over Plan to Use Hydrogen Peroxide against Sea Lice on B.C. Fish Farm," *Victoria Times Colonist*, May 18, 2021.

CHAPTER 11

Insights by Peter Benson and Stuart Kirsch were essential to this chapter and to chapters 12 and 13. Their paper, "Capitalism and the Politics of Resignation," *Current Anthropology* 51, no. 4 (August 2010): 459–86, is at https://www.journals.uchicago.edu /doi/abs/10.1086/653091.

The Benson-Kirsch concept was applied to salmon farming by a Memorial University team, Benjamin Rigby, Reade Davis, Dean Bavington, and Christopher Baird, in "Industrial Aquaculture and the Politics of Resignation," *Marine Policy* 80 (June 2017): 19–27.

Dean Bavington was interviewed in 2020.

Joachim Drew was interviewed in 2020. His underwater videos can be found on his YouTube channel: https://www.youtube.com/channel/UCPeq5Cyy2H5DurbT5TlVkcQ /videos. In March 2009, Drew was among several graduates of the adult literacy program honored by the PEI Literacy Alliance, http://en.copian.ca/library/learning/peilitall/stories09/se09.pdf.

Farley Mowat's remembrances of Bay d'Espoir are recorded in *Bay of Spirits: A Love Story* (Toronto: McClelland and Stewart, 2006).

The Harvard assessment of decompression sickness is at https://www.health.harvard.edu/a_to_z/decompression-sickness-a-to-z.

Deaths of Chilean divers at salmon farms were reported by Karla Faundez, "Chilean Divers Bid to End Salmon Farm Death Toll," FishfarmingExpert, January 7, 2020.

CHAPTER 12

We spent two days with Melvin and Laverne Jackman, touring Hermitage Bay and the surrounding area.

Gaultois history can be found at https://www.gaultoisinn.com/about.html; covered by Terry Roberts, "Hands Up for Resettlement in Gaultois as Island Community Braces for Winter," CBC News, November 26, 2017; and "Land & Sea: Gaultois in 1990 on the Day They Call Black Thursday," CBC News, December 2, 2017.

Jane Pitfield was interviewed in 2021.

The undercover video at the Cooke Aquaculture hatchery in Maine is at https://animaloutlook.org/investigations/aquaculture and https://www.youtube.com/watch?v=8tpd3Y1X7pQ. The website also lists news articles about the response to the video.

Erin Wing was interviewed multiple times.

The complaint from Animal Outlook, at the time called Compassion Over Killing, was obtained through an FOIA request to the State of Maine.

Glenn Cooke's statement appears at https://www.cookeseafood.com/2019/10/07/statement-from-glenn-cooke-regarding-fish-handling-at-a-cooke-aquaculture-hatchery-in-maine/; and in Paul Withers, "N.B. Seafood Giant Vows Change After Hidden Camera Shows 'Unacceptable' Treatment of Salmon," CBC News, October 7, 2019.

Martha Stewart's encounter with Animal Outlook was described by Erica Meier, "Martha Stewart: It's Not a 'Set Up'—The Cruelty Lurking in Your Seafood Line Is Real," Medium, December 13, 2019.

Liam Hughes was interviewed in 2020.

The final report to state authorities was obtained through an FOIA request.

The Animal Outlook suit against Cooke Aquaculture is at https://animaloutlook.org/wp-content/uploads/2020/06/true-north.pdf.

Dr. Theresa Burt de Perera's research on the intelligence of fish, "Fish Can Encode Order in Their Spatial Map," is at https://pubmed.ncbi.nlm.nih.gov/15475332/. Since then, she has said consistently that fish experience pain, an assertion supported by other researchers.

A robust analysis of the pain issue is in an article by Troy Vettese, Becca Franks, and Jennifer Jacquet, "The Great Fish Pain Debate," *Issues in Science and Technology* 36, no. 4 (Summer 2020), at https://issues.org/the-great-fish-pain-debate/; and Jacquet was interviewed in 2021.

CHAPTER 13

The size of big trawlers is from https://www.greenpeace.org.au/blog/monsters-oceans-7-criminal-super-trawlers-threaten-waters/ and https://usa.oceana.org/blog/friday-infographic-what-trawling.

The OECD report on subsidies by Roger Martini and James Innes, *Relative Effects of Fisheries Support Policies*, February 2019, is at https://issuu.com/oecd.publishing/docs/relative_effects_of_fisheries_suppo.

The plight of forage fish off the coast of West Africa has been covered extensively in scholarly articles, in reports by the United Nations and the World Bank, and by the media. Among the many useful sources were Greenpeace International, "Fishmeal Industry Stealing Regional Food and Livelihoods in West Africa," June 19, 2019; Hannah Summers, "Chinese Fishmeal Plants Leave Fishermen in the Gambia All at Sea," *Guardian*, March 20, 2019; Alfonso Daniels, "'Fish Are Vanishing'—Senegal's Devastated Coastline," BBC News, November 1, 2018; and Global Environmental Facility, UNDP, and UN University, "From Coast to Coast: Celebrating 20 Years of Transboundary Management of Our Shared Oceans," at https://www.undp.org/publications/coast-coast-celebrating-20-years-transboundary-management-our-shared-oceans.

Mor Ndiaye's quotation is from Daniels's report.

Dr. Ibrahima Cissé was interviewed in 2021.

The food security challenge was described by Damien Cave, Emma Bubola, and Choe Sang-Hun, "Long Slide Looms for World Population, with Sweeping Ramifications," *New York Times*, May 23, 2021.

Cooke's acquisition of Omega Protein was described in a press release on December 19, 2017. Omega Protein's violations of the Clean Water Act and the False Claims Act were found in court documents and press releases from the Department of Justice, including https://www.justice.gov/usao-edva/pr/fish-processing-company-omega-protein-inc-sentenced-environmental-crimes and https://www.justice.gov/opa/pr/omega-protein-companies-agree-pay-1-million-resolve-allegations-they-misrepresented. Chris Moore described Omega Protein's conduct in "It's Time to Take the Politics Out of Fisheries," *Washington Post*, January 17, 2020. The issue was covered by the *Sport Fishing* Staff, "Hold Canadian-Owned Menhaden Harvester Accountable," *Sport Fishing*, November 15, 2019.

Petter Johannessen was quoted by Nicki Holmyard, "IFFO's Johannessen: Use of

Marine Ingredients in Aquafeed 'Will Not Decline in the Foreseeable Future,'" SeafoodSource, September 23, 2020.

Efforts to develop alternative sources of omega-3 fatty acids are recounted in numerous scholarly reports, interviews, and media accounts, including Ben Goldfarb's, "Can Plant-Based Feeds Make Aquaculture Sustainable?" *High Country News*, January 6, 2016; a report by the National Oceanic and Atmospheric Administration, "The Future of Fish Feed May Lie in Insects, Mold, and Algae," NOAA, October 26, 2020; and John Davidson et al., "Effects of Feeding a Fishmeal-Free versus a Fishmeal-Based Diet on Post-smolt Atlantic Salmon *Salmo salar* Performance, Water Quality, and Waste Production in Recirculation Aquaculture Systems," *Aquacultural Engineering* 74 (September 2016): 38–51.

Evidence of potential harm from plant-based feed is in a report by Jillian Fry et al., "Environmental Health Impacts of Feeding Crops to Farmed Fish," *Environment International* 91 (May 2016): 201–14.

Cargill described its efforts to improve feed at https://www.cargill.com/doc /1432142322239/cargill-aqua-nutrition-sustainability-report.pdf.

Sophie Noonan was interviewed in 2021.

Rick Barrows was interviewed in 2021.

The Future of Fish Feed program and contest are described at https://carnivore .f3challenge.org/.

John Risley was interviewed in 2021. His article in *Atlantic Business* and the industry response are at https://atlanticbusinessmagazine.ca/article/john-risley-calls -for-moratorium-on-ocean-based-salmon-farming/. Mara Renewables is at https:// www.maracorp.ca/contact-us.

Huey Johnson founded the Resource Renewal Institute in 1985, https://www.rri .org. His memoir is *Something of the Marvelous* (Wheat Ridge, CO: Fulcrum Group, 2020).

"Fish in the Fields" was described by Deborah Moskowitz of RRI in interviews, on the organization's website; and by Heather Fraley, "Fish in the Fields," Flathead Lake Bio Station, University of Montana, November 19, 2018, at https://flbs.umt.edu/newflbs /outreach/news-blog/posts/fish-in-the-fields/.

Climate damage from methane gas emissions is well documented. A recent call to action came from Ilissa B. Ocko et al., "Acting Rapidly to Deploy Readily Available Methane Mitigation Measures by Sector Can Immediately Slow Global Warming," *Environmental Research Letters* 16, no. 5 (May 4, 2021). The *Economist* described the impact in "Put a Plug in It," March 31, 2021; and Brady Dennis and Steven Mufson wrote about the Ocko study in "Swift Action to Cut Methane Emissions Could Slow Earth's Warming by 30 Percent, Study Finds," *Washington Post*, April 28, 2021.

Shawn Devlin and coauthors described the Finland experiment in "Top Consumer Abundance Influences Lake Methane Efflux," *Nature Communications* 6, no. 8787 (2015), at https://www.nature.com/articles/ncomms9787. Devlin's relationship with RRI was described by Moises Velasquez-Manoff, "The Fishy Fix to a Methane-Spewing Crop," *Wired*, April 1, 2020; and by Moskowitz in interviews.

CHAPTER 14

The recording of Jill Davenport's 911 call was in an article by John Ryan on KUOW, the National Public Radio affiliate in Puget Sound, on November 6, 2017, at https://www.kuow.org/stories/911-call-on-atlantic-salmon-farm-the-whole-thing-is -buckling.

The collapse of Cypress Island Site 2 was reconstructed from many sources. News coverage of the incident and the later investigation by state agencies was extensive, particularly by Lynda V. Mapes of the *Seattle Times* and by CBC News. We interviewed Sky Guthrie, Innes Weir, former EPA criminal investigator Matthew Stratton, Kurt Beardslee, former Washington State senator Kevin Ranker, April Bencze, and additional people who asked to remain anonymous.

Through an FOIA request, we obtained internal records of the previously unreported criminal investigation by the U.S. Environmental Protection Agency and the U.S. Attorney's Office in Seattle. More details came from the final report by three Washington State agencies. The state report, *2017 Cypress Island Atlantic Salmon Net Pen Failure: An Investigation and Review*, January 30, 2018, is at https://www.dnr.wa.gov/sites/default/files/publications/aqr_cypress_investigation _report.pdf. The appendices, which contain analysis and notes of interviews, are at https://www.dnr.wa.gov/sites/default/files/publications/aqr_cypress_investigation _appendices.pdf.

The captain of the *Lindsey Foss* was interviewed by Stratton, and the transcript was among the FOIA documents.

Stratton was interviewed in 2020 and 2021.

Beardslee was interviewed in 2020 and 2021.

Halse's comment on the eclipse is from Lynda V. Mapes and Hal Bernton, "Please Go Fishing, Washington State Says After Farmed Salmon Escape Broken Net," *Seattle Times*, August 25, 2017, and other news reports.

Davenport's description of the tides and her unpublished letter are on p. 26 of the appendix to the Washington State investigative report; the EPA documents contain an account of Stratton's interview of Davenport.

Ron Warren's contention that escaped Atlantic salmon posed no threat to Pacific salmon and the invitation to anglers to catch the escaped fish are from a press release, "WDFW Encourages Anglers to Fish for Escaped Atlantic Salmon," published on August 22, 2017, by the Washington State Department of Fish and Wildlife.

The study of piscine orthoreovirus after the Cypress Island collapse is from Molly J. T. Kibenge et al., "Piscine Orthoreovirus Sequences in Escaped Farmed Atlantic Salmon in Washington and British Columbia," *Virology Journal* 16, no. 41 (April 2, 2019).

The finding by DFO scientists is from an article by Dirk Meissner, "Farmed Fish the Source of Virus Spread Among Wild Salmon, B.C. Study Suggests," *Canadian Press*, May 26, 2021. The study was by Gideon J. Mordecai et al., "Aquaculture Mediates Global Transmission of a Viral Pathogen to Wild Salmon," *Science Advances* 7, no. 22 (May 26, 2021).

The study of interbreeding in Newfoundland rivers is by Brendan F. Wringe et al., "Extensive Hybridization Following a Large Escape of Domesticated Atlantic Salmon in the Northwest Atlantic," *Communications Biology* 1, no. 108 (August 9, 2018).

Reports of catching escaped salmon are in Washington State's final investigative report into the collapse at Cypress Island.

April Bencze was interviewed in 2021.

The Wild Fish Conservancy notification letter to Cooke Aquaculture is at https://wildfishconservancy.org/60-days-to-cooke-aqua-press-release/view. The Conservancy website also provides links to key court records related to its successful suit against Cooke.

CHAPTER 15

The EPA criminal investigation was reconstructed from the FOIA records, including transcripts of interviews by Stratton and descriptions of his findings. The names of Stratton's sources were blacked out by the EPA, but some were discernible. Stratton, Guthrie, and Weir were interviewed.

The Washington State investigation was reconstructed from the final report and the appendices.

The *Millennium Star* crew member who saw the walkways buckling on July 24 was interviewed by Stratton on November 22, 2017.

The condition of Cypress Island Site 2 and the accusation that Cooke "got greedy" came from a salvage expert for Culbertson Marine Construction interviewed by Stratton on March 21, 2018.

Richardson's contention that Cooke was shut out of the state investigation was in a company press release, which also provided a link to the lawyer's letter disputing the state's findings. The press release is at https://www.cookeseafood.com/2018/01/30/cooke-aquaculture-pacific-dismisses-states-investigation/.

Former Washington State senator Kevin Ranker described his bills, his meeting with Glenn Cooke, and the timeline that led to the passage of the legislation in interviews in 2020 and 2021.

Packing one hearing with Cooke employees was described by Lynda V. Mapes,

"Puget Sound Fish Farmers Say Banning Atlantic Salmon Operations Would Be Unfair," *Seattle Times*, January 9, 2018.

Cooke's last-ditch lobbying efforts and Richardson's threat to invoke the North American Free Trade Agreement were covered by Lynda V. Mapes, "State Kills Atlantic Salmon Farming in Washington," *Seattle Times*, March 3, 2018.

Glenn Cooke's comment about the Soviet Union and his defense of the company and industry were from an interview by Glenn Farley on KING 5 Radio on February 8, 2018. It is at https://www.king5.com/video/tech/science/extended-video-cooke -aquaculture-ceo-glenn-b-cooke/281-8003565.

Passage of Ranker's legislation banning Atlantic salmon farms in Washington State was described by Ranker, Beardslee, and Halverson, and in media articles.

Dominic LeBlanc's comments were published in "Washington's Net-Pen Fish Farm Ban Has Canadian Consequences," *Canadian Press*, March 3, 2018.

Jeremy Dunn's comment is from "B.C. Salmon Farmers React to Washington State Ban," *Canadian Press*, March 3, 2018.

Trudeau's pledge to ban salmon farming was part of the Liberal Party's 2019 platform. The decision to weaken the pledge was covered extensively by the press and augmented with interviews with Karen Wristen and others.

CHAPTER 16

This chapter draws heavily on FOIA documents, on interviews with Stratton and Guthrie, and on an email exchange with Weir.

Stratton's search for Weir was from an official EPA report dated March 2, 2018, which also indicated that Stratton had informed the U.S. Attorney's Office.

Guthrie was interviewed in 2020, but direct quotes attributed to him are from the sixty-four-page transcript of Stratton's interview with Guthrie on March 29, 2018. The exchange about Weir's alleged role in undercounting the recovered salmon is taken verbatim from the transcript.

The second Cooke employee who described inflating the numbers of recovered salmon was interviewed by Stratton on May 9, 2018.

Weir raised the possibility of sabotage in an exchange of emails in 2021. Stratton rejected Weir's suspicion in a subsequent interview.

The interview with the Cooke consultant by Stratton and Assistant U.S. Attorney Seth Wilkinson occurred on May 18, 2018, and is described in the EPA documents.

Stratton's memo closing the investigation was among the FOIA documents.

Michael R. Fisher identified the litigation redacted from Stratton's closing memo in an email exchange in 2021.

The senior official involved in the investigation agreed to an interview on the condition that their identity be withheld.

Robert W. Adler was interviewed in 2020 and 2021. His interpretation was supported by legal scholars.

CHAPTER 17

Principal sources for this chapter were interviews with Kurt Beardslee, Brian Knutsen, and court records from the federal lawsuit by the Wild Fish Conservancy against Cooke, Case No. 2:17-cv-01708-JCC in United States District Court for the Western District of Washington. The complaint is at https://storage.courtlistener .com/recap/gov.uscourts.wawd.252225/gov.uscourts.wawd.252225.1.0_3.pdf. Related documents are available on various websites, including https://www.courtlistener .com/docket/6316730/wild-fish-conservancy-v-cooke-aquaculture-pacific-llc/; and through the Wild Fish Conservancy website, at https://wildfishconservancy.org/search ?SearchableText=cooke%2A&path=/wildfishconservancy/wildfishconservancy.

James Parsons was deposed on February 28, 2019, and on May 24, 2019.

The May 2019 settlement meeting was described by Beardslee and Knutsen.

Stratton's return to the hardware store was described by Stratton and Guthrie.

Judge John Coughenour's summary judgment ruling on November 25, 2019, is at https://wildfishconservancy.org/1125120.order.pls.and.defs.2nd.msumm.jud.pdf.

The quote from Wion was from the Knutsen interview.

Beardslee shared his considerations on the settlement amount and described the November 26 meeting in interviews.

The Conservancy press release is at https://wildfishconservancy.org/cooke -aquaculture-to-pay-2.75-million-ending-wfc-lawsuit-over-net-pen-collapse-1.

Judge Coughenour's final consent decree is at https://wildfishconservancy .org/126.consent.decreeentered.2020.02.11.pdf/at_download/file.

CHAPTER 18

Artifishal is at https://www.youtube.com/watch?v=XdNJ0JAwT7I. *Take Back Puget Sound* is at https://www.youtube.com/watch?v=b9H-1X03-V0.

Brigit Cameron was interviewed in 2021. The Patagonia Provisions website is at https://www.patagoniaprovisions.com/.

The criticism of Patagonia by CleanFish is from an article by Jeff Beer, "Patagonia's Fight to Save the Planet Continues with New Film on Wild Fish, Launching at Tribeca," *Fast Company*, April 25, 2019, at https://www.fastcompany.com/90340240/patagonias -fight-to-save-the-planet-continues-with-new-film-on-wild-fish-launching-at-tribeca, and in various salmon industry publications.

Steven Hedlund's criticism of *Artifishal* is from an open letter at https://www .aquaculturealliance.org/blog/open-letter-to-patagonia/.

The Global Aquaculture Alliance defense of Cooke Aquaculture is from its web-

site, "GAA Defends Cooke Aquaculture's Bid to Farm Steelhead Trout in Puget Sound,"
October 27, 2020, at https://www.aquaculturealliance.org/blog/cooke-aquaculture
-steelhead-trout/.

Jeanne McKnight's criticism of Patagonia is at https://www.nwaquaculturealliance
.org/nwaa-issues-challenge-to-patagonia-and-wfc-for-their-no-net-pens-campaign/.

Richardson's criticism of Patagonia is from an article by Owen Evans, "'Patagonia
Is in No Position to Challenge Our Family Company,' Says Cooke over Icicle Seafoods
Snub," SalmonBusiness, October 28, 2020.

Dylan Tomine was interviewed in 2021.

CHAPTER 19

John Crosbie's visit to St. John's and the decline of commercial cod fishing are
well chronicled in the archives of CBC News, at https://www.cbc.ca/archives/entry
/1992-newfoundlanders-protest-cod-moratorium; and by David Berry on August 6,
2020, in "Cod Moratorium of 1992," at https://www.thecanadianencyclopedia.ca/en
/article/cod-moratorium-of-1992; and https://www.cbc.ca/archives/entry/cod-fishing
-the-biggest-layoff-in-canadian-history.

The failed attempt to farm cod is from an article by Lindsay Royston, "Aquaculture: Cod Walloped," *Canadian Business*, November 21, 2005.

The first case of ISA in Newfoundland was disclosed by the Canadian Food
Inspection Agency and the provincial government on December 18, 2012, at https://
www.releases.gov.nl.ca/releases/2012/fishaq/1218n06.htm. Additional details, including compensation paid to Gray and Cooke, were from a background paper prepared by
the Atlantic Salmon Federation.

The call to end public bailouts of salmon farmers is from a press release by the
Ecology Action Centre, at https://ecologyaction.ca/press-release/groups-call-end
-public-bailouts-open-pen-salmon-feedlots.

Keith Sullivan was interviewed in 2020. The union statement about the die-off
is at https://ffaw.ca/the-latest/news/reports-significant-farmed-fish-mortality-south
-coast/.

Sullivan's suggestion to move salmon farms onshore is from "FFAW Says Die-off
Was 'Massive'—Company Blames Warm Water but Says Total Number Unknown,"
CBC News, September 24, 2019. The article also contains Byrne's comment that the
company should have told the truth. Byrne declined to answer our questions.

Jason Card's comments and additional comments from Byrne and Sullivan are in
the CBC News report, "Northern Harvest's Failure to Report Die-off in Salmon Pens
Hurts Public Trust: Byrne," CBC News, September 29, 2019, at https://www.asf.ca/news
-and-magazine/salmon-news/northern-harvest-die-off.

Mark Lane's accusation that Sullivan lied and that he timed the die-off disclosure to coincide with the international conference is from an article by Terry Roberts, "Aquaculture Conference Overshadowed by Fish Die-off, Bickering," CBC News, September 25, 2019.

CHAPTER 20

We interviewed Gary and Georgina Snook in 2020.

Snook's story was recounted by Brett Bundale, "2.6M Salmon Deaths Reignites Fish Farming Debate," Saltwire Publications, November 16, 2019.

Bill Bryden was interviewed in 2020 and 2021 and provided extensive documentation, including the results of his Access to Information requests to the Newfoundland provincial government.

Snook described seventy feet of dead salmon in the interview.

Don Ivany described his reaction to the dead salmon in the interview.

Along with Snook, Bryden, and Ivany, the boat trip to the cleanup site was described by Garrett Barry, "Pink Liquid Flows in Fortune Bay as Cleanup of Massive Salmon Die-off Continues," CBC News, October 2, 2019; and by Chris O'Neill-Yates, "No Dead Salmon Numbers Confirmed; Photos Not 'Very Pretty' but Not the Whole Picture: Gerry Byrne," CBC News, October 9, 2019. The October 9 article contained Byrne's comments comparing the CBC footage to tactics by the anti-seal campaigners.

James Dinn's call for an investigation is from a press release from the New Democratic Party, at https://www.nl.ndp.ca/post/province-must-launch-independent -investigation-into-massive-fish-die-off-ndp.

The private letter from Gaskill to Byrne was provided to us by someone involved in the investigation and is described by Peter Cowan, "Contrite in Public After Salmon Kill, Company Fights Behind the Scenes to Get Licenses Back," CBC News, November 21, 2019.

Dean McDonald's claim that there was little impact from the salmon die-off is from Terry Roberts, "'No Widespread Impact' to Coastline Following N.L. Salmon Die-off, Says DFO," CBC News, January 8, 2020. The article also described the difficulties encountered by DFO and MAMKA in assessing the damage.

The Fisheries and Marine Institute report is at https://www.gov.nl.ca/ffa/files /publications-pdf-2019-salmon-review-final-report.pdf.

Data provided by the provincial government in response to our Access for Information Act request showed that the Mowi die-off killed close to three million salmon.

The MAMKA report is at http://mamka.ca/wp-content/uploads/2020/04/04_24 _20-MAMKA-Northern-Harvest-Mortality-Event-2019-Final-Report.pdf.

Bill Montevecchi was interviewed in 2020.

Ian Jones was interviewed in 2020.

The mortality rates at Mowi's farms in Newfoundland and at farms operated by other companies are from data provided by the provincial government in response to an Access to Information Act request. Similar data came from Bill Bryden.

CHAPTER 21

Peter Stewart was interviewed aboard his boat in 2020. Others in the Liverpool community, led by Brian Muldoon, provided information for this chapter.

Cooke's expansion plans were from an article by Paul Withers, "Cooke Unveils Ambitious Fish Farm Expansion Plans in Nova Scotia," CBC News, March 29, 2019.

Cooke's $25 million loan was described in "N.S. Gov't to Loan Cooke Aquaculture $25M to Expand Farms," *Canadian Press*, June 22, 2012. Paul Withers described how Cooke used $4 million of the loan to finance Jon Grant's research in "How Funding University Research Could Mean Less Debt for Cooke Aquaculture," CBC News, April 4, 2018.

Milewski was interviewed. The paper on Port Mouton lobster catches that she wrote with Ruth E. Smith is "Sustainable Aquaculture in Canada: Lost in Translation," *Marine Policy* 107 (September 2019). The paper built on a previous work by Milewski and others, "Sea-Cage Aquaculture Impacts Market and Berried Lobster (*Homarus americanus*) Catches," *Marine Ecology Progress Series* 598 (June 28, 2018): 85–97.

The controversy between Milewski and Jon Grant was described by Aaron Beswick, "Dal Fish Farm Study Claims Data Lacking, but Another Researcher Calls Work 'Opinion Piece,'" Halifax *Chronicle Herald*, June 24, 2019.

The scholarly survey of industry-sponsored research was by Alice Fabbri et al., "The Influence of Industry Sponsorship on the Research Agenda: A Scoping Review," *American Journal of Public Health* (October 10, 2018): e9–e16.

Grant was interviewed in 2021. The study of a salmon farm in the Bay of Fundy is by Jon Grant, Michelle Simone, and Tara Daggett, "Long-term Studies of Lobster Abundance at a Salmon Aquaculture Site, Eastern Canada," *Canadian Journal of Fisheries and Aquatic Sciences* 76, no. 7 (March 8, 2019): 1–7, https://doi.org/10.1139/cjfas-2017-0547.

CHAPTER 22

Syd Dumaresq was interviewed in 2020. We attended Cermaq public meetings and spoke with other members of the Twin Bays Coalition.

Details of Keith Colwell's taxpayer-financed trips to Norway came from a spokesperson in his office. The letter about Colwell was by Wendy Watson Smith, "Letter: Minister Keith Colwell Is Wrong, Open Pen Fish Farming Is Not the Way to Prosperity for Rural Nova Scotia," *Nova Scotia Advocate*, September 5, 2019.

The Doelle-Lahey Report is at https://novascotia.ca/fish/documents/Aquaculture _Regulatory_Framework_Final_04Dec14.pdf. The response by the Ecology Action

Centre is at https://ecologyaction.ca/files/images-documents/Doelle-Lahey%20 Report%20Highlights.pdf.

The vote against Cermaq in Digby, along with Colwell's praise for the salmon-farming company, was in an article by Katy Parsons, "Amid Opposition to N.S. Salmon Farms, Minister Touts Benefits of Aquaculture Industry," CBC News, January 30, 2020.

David Kiemele's exchange with Julie Chiasson is from an article by Linda Pannozzo, "Cermaq's PR Fiasco," *Halifax Examiner*, March 13, 2020. The article was part of an excellent series on the topic by Pannozzo.

Cermaq's request to use lufenuron to combat sea lice was disclosed by Clayoquot Action, an NGO, and is at https://clayoquotaction.org/wp-content/uploads/2021/01 /A-2018-00720-lufenuron.pdf. The Cermaq documents can also be found at https:// www.halifaxexaminer.ca/wp-content/uploads/2020/03/Access-to-Information-2018 -lufenuron.pdf.

Cermaq's withdrawal of its application and Cooke's decision to continue the process attracted considerable press attention, including articles by Chris Chase, "Cermaq Withdraws Nova Scotia Expansion, Kelly Cove Reaffirms Growth Plans," Seafood-Source, April 9, 2020; and Paul Withers, "Salmon Farming Giant Cermaq Abandons Controversial Nova Scotia Expansion," CBC News, April 9, 2020. The company press release is at https://www.cermaq.ca/news/cermaq-canada-to-let-all-options-to-lease-in -nova-scotia-expire-1. Cermaq declined our request to interview Kiemele.

CHAPTER 23

The backbone of this chapter comes from our visit to the fish-monitoring station on the Magaguadavic River with Graham Chafe in 2020 and a day on the Miramichi River with Jason Curtis. Both visits were arranged with the help of Neville Crabbe of the Atlantic Salmon Federation.

Additional information about the monitoring station is at https://www.asf.ca /news-and-magazine/news-releases/salmon-escape-in-bay-of-fundy.

The impact of interbreeding is described by V. Bourret et al., "Temporal Change in Genetic Integrity Suggests Loss of Local Adaptation in a Wild Atlantic Salmon (*Salmo salar*) Population Following Introgression by Farmed Escapees," *Heredity* 106, no. 3 (January 12, 2011): 500–510. Also helpful was the FishBio report, *The Perils of Ferals: Hybridizing Wild and Farmed Salmon*, September 23, 2019, at https://fishbio.com/field -notes/the-fish-report/peril-ferals-hybridizing-wild-farmed-salmon.

The Atlantic Salmon Federation paper on interbreeding is at https://www.asf .ca/news-and-magazine/news-releases/statement-on-european-origin-aquaculture -atlantic-salmon-within-the-bay-of-fundy. The government study "Review of the Science Associated with the Inner Bay of Fundy Atlantic Salmon Live Gene Bank and

Supplementation Programs," Canadian Science Advisory Secretariat, August 2018, is at https://www.asf.ca/assets/files/2018_041-eng.pdf, and contains the warning about the threat to wild salmon.

Jason and Wayne Curtis were interviewed in 2020.

The history of DDT use is well documented. In 1959, the Department of Fisheries of Canada described the program until then in *The Canadian Fish Culturist*, published by the government at https://waves-vagues.dfo-mpo.gc.ca/Library/171231_1959.pdf. A U.S. EPA report, *DDT Regulatory History: A Brief Survey (to 1975)*, was published in July 1975, and is at https://archive.epa.gov/epa/aboutepa/ddt-regulatory-history-brief-survey-1975.html. On January 3, 2017, *The New Yorker* republished Rachel Carson's article on DDT from June 23, 1962. It is at https://www.newyorker.com/magazine/1962/06/23/silent-spring-part-2.

Robin Barefield's informed speculation is from "Why Do Salmon Jump and Other Questions," in her blog, *Kodiak Wildlife*, http://robinbarefield.com/salmon-jump-questions/.

CHAPTER 24

The restoration of the Penobscot River was well covered by the press and organizations and agencies involved in the project. Among the news articles are James McCarthy, "16-Year Penobscot River Restoration Project Teaches the Finish Line," Mainebiz.biz, August 22, 2016; Murray Carpenter, "Taking Down Dams and Letting the Fish Flow," *New York Times*, October 24, 2016; Matthew Chabe, "Penobscot River Restoration Project: Connecting 2,000 Miles of River to the Sea," *Bangor Daily News*, June 27, 2017.

The Penobscot River Restoration Trust produced a fact sheet at https://www.conservationgateway.org/Files/Pages/penobscot-river-restorati.aspx. A description of the project's results by the Nature Conservancy is at https://scholarworks.umass.edu/cgi/viewcontent.cgi?article=2271&context=fishpassage_conference.

Laura Rose Day's description of speaking with residents along the river and her encounter with Barbara Leonard and its aftermath are recounted by Peter Taylor in *From the Mountains to the Sea: The Historic Restoration of the Penobscot River* (Yarmouth, ME: Islandport Press, 2020).

The story of John Banks and the eagle feather is also told by Taylor, and by Philip Conkling, "A River Runs Through It," *Maine* magazine, October 2017.

Joshua Royte was interviewed in 2021.

The Greenland project was described in interviews by Bill Taylor and Neville Crabbe of the Atlantic Salmon Federation. The project's ups and downs were reported in news articles, including Monte Burke, "Endangered Atlantic Salmon Are Facing a New and Potentially Devastating Threat," *Forbes*, June 14, 2013; Patrick Whittle, "In Atlantic

Salmon Fight, Greenland Proves a Sticking Point," phys.org, March 13, 2016; and Hadeel Ibrahim, "Atlantic Salmon Group Strikes Deal to Stop Greenland Fishery for 12 Years," CBC News, May 28, 2018.

CHAPTER 25

Tracey Warmus Clarke and C. D. Clarke were interviewed in 2020 and 2021.

RAS technology is described in news articles and scholarly papers and by experts in interviews. A thorough description was provided by Jacob Bregnballe, "A Guide to Recirculation Aquaculture," Food and Agriculture Organization of the United Nations and Eurofish International Organisation, 2015, available at http://www.fao.org /3/i4626e/i4626e.pdf. Laura Bailey and Brian Vinci described the economy of scale in "Show Me the Money," *RASTECH Magazine*, February 4, 2020. The Research Council of Norway provided a lengthy comparison of closed-containment aquaculture systems in the 2019 annual report by CtrlAQUA.

Kirk Havercroft and David Roberts were interviewed in 2020 and 2021.

Many scholarly papers have identified insect larvae as a potential substitute for marine ingredients in salmon feed, including Ikran Belghit et al., "Potential of Insect-Based Diets for Atlantic Salmon (*Salmo salar*)," *Aquaculture* 491 (April 2018): 72–81. Brian Payton provided a summary of recent studies in "Taking the Fish Out of Fish Feed," *Hakai Magazine*, August 24, 2020.

The problem of "off flavor" was described in interviews and by Gary S. Burr et al., "Impact of Depuration of Earthy-Musty Off-Flavors on Fillet Quality of Atlantic Salmon, *Salmo salar*, Cultured in Recirculating Aquaculture System," *Aquacultural Engineering* 50 (September 2012): 28–36.

Kelly Conrad was interviewed in 2020 and 2021.

The pioneering work of the Freshwater Institute can be seen at https://www .conservationfund.org/our-work/freshwater-institute. In addition, Rick Barrows and Steve Summerfelt described the development of fish-free feed in interviews in 2020 and 2021.

Kerry Heffernan was interviewed in 2020. He appeared on an episode of *Top Chef Masters*, which can be seen at https://www.bravotv.com/people/kerry-heffernan.

Carrie Brownstein was interviewed in 2021. Whole Foods' description of its standards for farmed salmon is in an article by Brownstein from May 10, 2014, at https:// www.wholefoodsmarket.com/tips-and-ideas/archive/our-farmed-salmon-goes-beyond -industry-norms. The standards also were explained by Elizabeth Leader Smith from March 11, 2014, at https://www.wholefoodsmarket.com/tips-and-ideas/archive/truth -about-farmed-salmon-whole-foods-market; and at "Seafood Standards Like Nowhere Else," https://www.wholefoodsmarket.com/quality-standards/seafood-standards.

CHAPTER 26

Johan Andreassen was interviewed in 2021. Jose Prado, the chief financial officer of Atlantic Sapphire, was interviewed in 2020 shortly before he left the company.

Michael Grunwald wrote a marvelous article on Atlantic Sapphire, "Will Your Next Salmon Come from a Massive Land Tank in Florida?" Politico, July 14, 2020. Alan Gomez described the project, "The Future of Salmon in the U.S. Is . . . Florida?," *USA Today*, April 11, 2018. The article contains a useful graphic of the aquifer system beneath Florida that is key to the facility; it is at https://www.usatoday.com/story/news /2018/04/11/south-florida-salmon-farm/460570002/.

National Geographic described the aquifer system in an essay by Jon Heggie on July 29, 2020, and in its *Education Blog*, in "The Water Beneath Your Feet," by Jennifer Adler, a National Geographic Young Explorer; the blog is at https://blog.education .nationalgeographic.org/2017/03/09/where-does-your-water-come-from/.

Bill Taylor recounted his conversation with Glenn Cooke about a RAS pilot project in an interview.

Andreassen described his Google search in the interview.

Atlantic Sapphire described its losses of fish in a stock prospectus at https:// atlanticsapphire.com/wp-content/uploads/2021/03/Atlantic-Sapphire-AS-Prospectus -dated-30-April-2020.pdf. Andreassen also described the incidents in the interview.

Rachel Silverstein was interviewed in 2021.

Christian Nordby was interviewed in 2020 and 2021.

Nordic Aquafarms' troubles were described by Connell Smith, "Large Land-Based Salmon Farms Face Opposition in Maine," CBC News, December 19, 2019; and Chris Chase, "Opponents to Nordic Aquafarms' RAS File Objection to Pipeline Lease," SeafoodSource, May 8, 2019.

The Maine chapter of the Sierra Club detailed its opposition to Nordic Aquafarms in a March 4, 2020, submission to the U.S. Army Corps of Engineers, at https://www .sierraclub.org/sites/www.sierraclub.org/files/sce/maine-chapter/Testimony/NAF%20 testimony%20ACOE%20Mar.pdf.

Two members of the Sierra Club executive committee, Becky Bartovics and Jonathan Fulford, were interviewed in 2020 and 2021.

Erik Heim was interviewed in 2021.

The Whole Oceans project in Bucksport was described in numerous articles, including Nick Sambides Jr., "Bucksport Salmon Farm Receives the Last Permit It Needs to Start Building," *Bangor Daily News*, November 26, 2019; and Bill Trotter, "Whole Oceans Adds to Bucksport Holdings with 10-Acre Parcel Where Mill Once Stood," *Bangor Daily News*, December 11, 2020.

American Aquafarms' plan for a salmon farm in Frenchman Bay is at americanaquafarms.com. The opponents spell out their objections at http://friendsoffrenchmanbay.org/.

James Paterson's objections are part of a lengthy list of articles opposing the project at http://friendsoffrenchmanbay.org/industrial-fin-fish-farm/.

Crystal Canney was interviewed in 2021.

CHAPTER 27

The science and operations of Superior Fresh were described in interviews by Steven Summerfelt, Rick Barrows, and Brandon Gottsacker. The Conservation Fund and the Freshwater Institute describe the plant at https://www.conservationfund.org/projects/superior-fresh. Superior Fresh also provides information at https://www.superiorfresh.com/.

Elizabeth Dohms wrote about the innovative effort in "Jackson County Farm for Atlantic Salmon, Rainbow Trout Has Green Emphasis," *Leader Telegram*, August 31, 2017; see also Barry Adams, "Salmon in Tanks, Lettuce Under Glass Disrupt the Food Chain," *Wisconsin State Journal*, February 24, 2019.

A list of failed RAS projects is in SeaWestNews's article "RAS in Peace: The Quick and the Dead in Land-Based Fish Farming," November 28, 2019.

The controversy over changing the name "Marine Harvest" to "Mowi" was reported by Stian Olsen, "Thor Mowinckel's Family Protest at Name Change During Marine Harvest General Assembly Meeting," SalmonBusiness, December 5, 2018. The tweet is at https://twitter.com/fwmowinckel/status/1069955942807166976.

Havercroft and Summerfelt described the regular Zoom call among major RAS operators in interviews.

CHAPTER 28

UN FAO statistics on overfishing are at http://www.fao.org/state-of-fisheries-aquaculture.

Wolfram Heise's quote first appeared in a joint statement opposing salmon farming, "International Declaration Against Unsustainable Salmon Farming Sent to United Nations," November 7, 2008, at https://www.aquafeed.com/af-article/2602/International-Declaration-Against-Unsustainable-Salmon-Farming-sent-to-United-Nations/.

PETA's claim that salmon farm cages are so crowded that it is the equivalent of twenty-seven fish living in a bathtub is at https://www.peta.org/living/food/top-10-reasons-eat-salmon/.

Detailed results of the Environmental Defense Fund poll are at https://www.edf.org/sites/default/files/documents/BSG%20EDF%20Aquaculture%20Poll%20-%20National%20Report%20FIN.pdf.

BIBLIOGRAPHY

These books were integral to our research, and we thank their authors.

Anderson, John M. *The Salmon Connection: The Development of Atlantic Salmon Aquaculture in Canada*. Tantallon, Nova Scotia: Glen Margaret Publishing, 2007.

Carson, Rachel. *Silent Spring*. Boston, MA: Houghton Mifflin Harcourt, 1962.

Greenberg, Paul. *American Catch: The Fight for Our Local Seafood*. New York: Penguin Books, 2014.

———. *Four Fish: The Future of the Last Wild Food*. New York: Penguin Books, 2010.

———. *The Omega Principle: Seafood and the Quest for a Long Life and a Healthier Planet*. New York: Penguin Books, 2018.

Harpur, Mari Hill. *Sea Winter Salmon: Chronicles of the St. John River*. Westmont, Quebec: Linda Leith Publishing, 2015.

Isabella, Jude. *Salmon: A Scientific Memoir*. Calgary, Alberta: Rocky Mountain Books, 2014.

Johnson, Huey D. *Something of the Marvelous: Lessons Learned from Nature and My Sixty Years as an Environmentalist*. Wheat Ridge, CO: Fulcrum Group, 2020.

Kurlansky, Mark. *Salmon: A Fish, the Earth, and the History of Their Common Fate*. Ventura, CA: Patagonia Books, 2020.

Lien, Marianne Elisabeth. *Becoming Salmon: Aquaculture and the Domestication of a Fish*. Oakland: University of California Press, 2015.

Malarkey, Tucker. *Stronghold: One Man's Quest to Save the World's Wild Salmon*. New York: Spiegel and Grau, 2019.

Montgomery, David R. *King of Fish: The Thousand-Year Run of Salmon*. Boulder, CO: Westview Press, 2003.

Morton, Alexandra. *Not on My Watch: How a Renegade Whale Biologist Took on

Governments and Industry to Save Wild Salmon. Toronto, Ontario: Random House Canada, 2021.

Pollan, Michael. *The Omnivore's Dilemma: A Natural History of Four Meals.* New York: Penguin Press, 2006.

Taylor, Peter. *From the Mountains to the Sea: The Historic Restoration of the Penobscot River.* Yarmouth, ME: Islandport Press, 2020.

Trasande, Leonardo. *Sicker, Fatter, Poorer: The Urgent Threat of Hormone-Disrupting Chemicals to Our Health and Future . . . and What We Can Do About It.* Boston, MA: Houghton Mifflin Harcourt, 2019.

ACKNOWLEDGMENTS

We started this book with minimal understanding of salmon farming and its consequences. We were fortunate to learn from many people who were willing to share their expertise and experiences. Among them were academics, scientists, physicians, nutritionists and health experts, lobster fishers, workers at salmon farms, our neighbors, and people who have devoted their lives to protecting public health, the environment, and wild salmon.

Among the dozens of people who agreed to participate in interviews and follow-up interviews, we owe a special debt to the professionals at the Atlantic Salmon Federation, led by Bill Taylor and his communications chief, Neville Crabbe; and to Melvin and Laverne Jackman for their hospitality and the moose dinner.

Many excellent reporters and writers have chronicled the salmon-farming industry. We are grateful for their excellent work. We benefited particularly from the reporting of Lynda V. Mapes at the *Seattle Times*, Linda Pannozzo at the *Halifax Examiner*, and the crew at the Canadian Broadcasting Corporation. COVID-19 restrictions kept us from traveling to Norway. Fortunately, we were able to rely on Zoom and phone interviews with people there and on the work of Simen Saetre of Norway's national newspaper *Morgenbladet* and Kjetil Ostli of the online magazine *Harvest*. We also gained perspective from industry associations and websites like Undercurrent News, SeafoodSource, and SalmonBusiness. Please see the notes for fuller attributions.

The relationship between salmon and the environment was first brought to light by Rachel Carson in her seminal book *Silent Spring*, a work that remains an unsurpassed call to action. Many authors have since chronicled the fate of the environment and of the king of fish, including Alexandra Morton and her autobiography, *Not on My Watch*, and David R. Montgomery's *King of Fish*. While not about salmon, *The*

Omnivore's Dilemma, by Michael Pollan, opened new vistas on our relationship with food production. These books and others are listed in the bibliography.

We also learned from several documentaries, including the late Silver Donald Cameron's 2010 film *Salmon Wars*, the 2013 film *Salmon Confidential*, and the 2021 Netflix documentary *Seaspiracy*.

We were fortunate to have dedicated partners throughout this project. Conor Mintzer at Henry Holt and Company was the editor every writer wants—he made the book better through careful editing and penetrating questions. We thank Conor and Amy Einhorn, the publisher at Holt, for their unflagging support. We are deeply grateful to Jenna Dolan for the skill and care with which she edited our manuscript. Last but far from least, we thank David Halpern and Kathy Robbins, our agents at the Robbins Office, for their continued guidance and advocacy on our behalf. And our son, Nicholas, for setting up our website, www.salmonwarsbook.com.

After decades of working around the world, we now live in Nova Scotia, the ancestral and unceded territory of the Mi'kmaq First Nation.

INDEX

ABOUT THE AUTHORS

Douglas Frantz is a former managing editor of the *Los Angeles Times* and shared a Pulitzer Prize as a foreign correspondent at the *New York Times*. After his career in journalism, he was chief investigator for the Senate Foreign Relations Committee, an assistant secretary of state in the Obama administration, and deputy secretary-general at the Organisation for Economic Co-operation and Development in Paris. Before leaving journalism for a career as a private investigator specializing in international financial fraud, **Catherine Collins** was a reporter and foreign correspondent for the *Chicago Tribune* and a contributor to the *New York Times* and *Los Angeles Times*. Husband and wife, Frantz and Collins have written several nonfiction books together.